THE ENGLISHMAN FROM LEBEDIAN'—
A LIFE OF EVGENY ZAMIATIN
(1884–1937)

Ars Rossica
Series Editor: David Bethea
(University of Wisconsin–Madison)

THE ENGLISHMAN FROM LEBEDIAN'—
A LIFE OF EVGENY ZAMIATIN
(1884–1937)

J. A. E. CURTIS

Library of Congress Cataloging-in-Publication Data:
A catalog reference for this title is available from the Library of Congress.

ISBN 978-1-618112-80-4 (hardback)
ISBN 978-1-618112-81-1 (electronic)
ISBN 978-1-618114-85-3 (paperback)

Copyright © 2013 Academic Studies Press
All rights reserved

Cover design by Ivan Grave
On the cover: cartoon of Zamiatin by Nikolai Radlov (1920s).

Published by Academic Studies Press in 2013
28 Montfern Avenue
Brighton, MA 02135, USA
press@academicstudiespress.com
www.academicstudiespress.com

In proud and loving memory of my mother

Barbara Randall (1920-2012),

who made quite sure that her children had all the opportunities

that were not available to her own generation.

TABLE OF CONTENTS

LIST OF ILLUSTRATIONS VIII

INTRODUCTION 1

CHAPTER 1:   FROM LEBEDIAN' TO ST PETERSBURG (1884-1906) 6

CHAPTER 2:   FROM ASTRAKHAN TO ARKHANGEL'SK (1906-1916) 25

CHAPTER 3:   FROM PETROGRAD TO NEWCASTLE UPON TYNE (1916-1917) ... 51

CHAPTER 4:   PETROGRAD (1917-1921) 86

CHAPTER 5:   PETROGRAD/LENINGRAD (1922-1925) 117

CHAPTER 6:   LENINGRAD (1926-1929) 154

CHAPTER 7:   FROM KOKTEBEL' TO THE WARSAW STATION (1929-1931) ... 198

CHAPTER 8:   FROM RIGA TO CAGNES (1931-1932) 225

CHAPTER 9:   PARIS (1933-1937) 258

CONCLUSION 307

BIBLIOGRAPHY 357

ACKNOWLEDGMENTS 373

INDEX 375

List of Illustrations

1. Front cover: cartoon of Zamiatin by Nikolai Radlov (1920s).
2. Portrait of Zamiatin by Iury Annenkov (1921).

   SECTION 1 [BETWEEN CHAPTERS 3 AND 4]:
3. The river Don at Lebedian': the garden of Zamiatin's home ran down to the river-bank on the right.
4. Zamiatin's home on Pokrovskaia Street in Lebedian', rebuilt in 2009 to house the Zamiatin Museum.
5. Zamiatin as a toddler (mid-1880s).
6. Zamiatin and his sister Aleksandra (early 1890s).
7. Zamiatin as a graduate of the Voronezh *gimnaziia* (1902).
8. The student Zamiatin with his sister Aleksandra (early 1900s).
9. Zamiatin and his sister Aleksandra with their parents, Ivan Dmitrievich and Maria Aleksandrovna (early 1900s).
10. Zamiatin in St Petersburg (approx. 1910?).
11. Liudmila Nikolaevna Zamiatina (1920s?).
12. Zamiatin's design for a flexible dam (early 1910s?).
13. The icebreaker Sviatogor (later Krasin), constructed in Newcastle during 1916–17 under Zamiatin's supervision.
14. Zamiatin's 1916–17 home at 19, Sanderson Road, Newcastle upon Tyne: the memorial plaque to him by the front door was placed there with the support of Iosif Brodsky.
15. Zamiatin at the piano, examining a score of 'Préludes' by Scriabin (late 1910s?).
16. Self-portrait by Iury Annenkov, during the freezing winter of 1919–20 in Petrograd.
17. Illustration (1921) by Iury Annenkov for Zamiatin's story *The Fisher of Men*.
18. Portrait of Aleksei Remizov by Iury Annenkov (1920).
19. Portrait of Kornei Chukovsky by Iury Annenkov (1921).
20. Portrait of Aleksandr Blok on his death-bed, by Iury Annenkov (1921).

SECTION 2 [BETWEEN CHAPTERS 6 AND 7]:
21. Portrait of Zamiatin by Boris Kustodiev (1923, © René Guerra).
22. Cartoon by Boris Kustodiev of Zamiatin (1927), for the latter's *Biography of a Flea*.
23. Cartoon of Konstantin Fedin by Nikolai Radlov.
24. Cartoon of Aleksei Tolstoy by Nikolai Radlov.
25. Photograph of Zamiatin (1920s?).
26. Photograph of Zamiatin (Leningrad, 1929).
27. Photograph of Zamiatin in his study in Leningrad by A.A. Krolenko (1931).
28. Zamiatin wearing plus-fours, playing with the monkey Whisky at Boris Grigor'ev's house in Haut-de-Cagnes (1932).
29. Photograph of Zamiatin (1930s?).
30. The Zamiatins' home at 14, rue Raffet, Paris (XVI).
31. Irina Kunina-Aleksander (1957).
32. Konstantin Fedin and Maksim Gor'ky (1934).
33. The grave of Zamiatin and his wife Liudmila in the cemetery at Thiais (Paris).

SOURCES OF ILLUSTRATIONS:
— Annenkov Iury, *Portrety* (Petersburg [sic]: Petropolis, 1922): numbers 2, 16, 17, 18, 19, 20.
— Radlov Nikolai, *Voobrazhaemye portrety. Literaturnyi Leningrad* (Leningrad: Izdatel'stvo Pisatelei v Leningrade, 1933): numbers 1, 23, 24.
— the portrait of Zamiatin by Boris Kustodiev (number 21) is reproduced by kind permission of M. René Guerra.
— Zamiatin Evgeny, *Zhitie blokhi* (Leningrad: Knigoizdatel'stvo Pisatelei v Leningrade, 1929): number 22.
— BDIC (Bibliothèque de Documentation Internationale Contemporaine, Université de Paris X, Nanterre), Collection E. Zamiatine—F DELTA RES 614: numbers 10, 11, 12, 15, 25, 28.
— the photograph of Zamiatin by A.A. Krolenko (number 27) is reproduced here by kind permission of Sergei A. Krolenko.
— the picture of the icebreaker Krasin, originally Sviatogor (number 13) is © ITAR-TASS Photo Agency / Alamy.
— University of Tambov (Zamiatin Centre): numbers 5, 7; Zamiatin Museum, Lebedian': numbers 6, 8, 9 (family photographs by kind permission of Nina S. Zamiatina).
— author's photographs: numbers 3, 4, 14, 30, 33.
— all efforts have been made to trace the remaining unattributed images, and the author will be pleased to respond to any queries about these.

2. Portrait of Zamiatin by Iury Annenkov (1921).

Introduction

> Synthetism deploys an integrated dislocation of planes. In Synthetism, those fragments of the world which are placed within one spatial-temporal frame have never arrived there by chance; they are fused together through synthesis, and sooner or later the shafts projected from those separate parts inevitably meet in a single point, something entire always emerges from those fragments.
>
> *(From Zamiatin's essay "On Synthetism," published as the introduction to Iury Annenkov's 1922 album of pen and ink drawings,* Portraits.*)*

Reconciling the irreconcilable, paradox—these offer the key to Evgeny Zamiatin's art of Synthetism, as well as providing an insight into the personality of one of Russia's outstanding writers of the Revolutionary epoch. The neo-Cubist planes of Annenkov's well-known 1921 portrait of Zamiatin conjure the contradictory aspects of a man who lived different lives simultaneously, yet succeeded for the most part in integrating them and—against the odds—in retaining his integrity.

This highly intelligent and cultured man had to refashion himself throughout his life. He transformed himself from a provincial boy into an urban sophisticate; from the clever son of a priest into a conspiratorial Bolshevik; from an engineer into a writer; from a Russian in England into his deliberately-assumed guise as an "Englishman" in the new Soviet era; from a submissive lover into a confident husband; from the author of prose into a dramatist and writer for the cinema; from a revolutionary into a moderate socialist; from the teacher of a new generation of working-class writers into the champion of free speech against proletarian dogma; from a Soviet citizen into an émigré in France; from the nostalgic chronicler of the Russian backwoods into the prophet of the industrial age.

Throughout all this, he remained true to himself. He was not an opportunist, but relished confrontation. An intimate investigation of his life reveals the moral and political nuances which defined his position in two worlds—the USSR in the 1920s, and France in the 1930s—where he was constantly being challenged to come out with declarative statements about his deepest beliefs. He never seemed to belong to his own time, he was always in opposition to the prevailing ideology and culture; nor did he ever quite belong to his own place—he fitted in neither to provincial Lebedian', nor bourgeois England, nor Soviet Leningrad, nor émigré Paris.

On the other hand, Zamiatin's life encompasses a richer range of experiences than that of many Russian writers of his generation. Coming from a deeply religious family in the small town of Lebedian' on the river Don, he won a coveted place in 1903 at St Petersburg's prestigious new Polytechnic Institute to study maritime engineering. In the stagnant late years of Romanov rule he became caught up in the fervour of youthful revolutionary activism in St Petersburg, and was even imprisoned for a few months as a Bolshevik. This was when he got to know a fellow radical, the medical student Liudmila Usova, who would become his wife. But even as his technological studies were completed in 1908, he was writing his first story and, like Anton Chekhov and Mikhail Bulgakov, he would pursue a dual career for many years. For a decade he travelled the length and breadth of Russia inspecting the construction of dredgers, pumps and submarines, while simultaneously snatching time to compose acclaimed and controversial stories such as *A Provincial Tale* and *At the Back of Beyond*.

In 1916 his life entered a new phase, when he was sent to England for 18 months to supervise the construction of icebreakers on the river Tyne as part of the Allied war effort. His life in Newcastle inspired him to write entertaining satires of middle-class English society. He returned to Russia just in time for the October Revolution in 1917, but was denouncing the violence and authoritarian policies of Lenin and the Bolsheviks within weeks of the uprising. In 1919–20 he worked on *We*. The novel simultaneously warns against the dangers of social and sexual repression, and of the industrial mass production methods he had encountered in England, as well as prophetically anticipating the totalitarian nature of the Soviet state. For this reason it soon became obvious that the novel would not be publishable in the USSR.

Zamiatin returned in tweeds from his engineering work in England, to take up a central role in Soviet literary life during the 1920s as a highly efficient and professional editor, reviewer, and professor of creative writing, as well as the author of stories, articles, essays and plays. He suffered more arrests, this time "by the Bolsheviks," rather than "as a Bolshevik," and was nearly forced into exile abroad in 1922. Indefatigable as Maksim Gor'ky's lieutenant in his visionary projects, designed to keep literature alive while simultaneously educating the new generation of working-class writers, he carried on the task even after Gor'ky left for Italy. He engaged in a decade-long struggle to defend literature against the encroaching interventionism and regulatory powers of the state authorities. He was a superb and innovative stylist, creating the new school of Synthetism (or "neo-Realism"). He knew everyone, corresponded with everyone, participated in countless organisations and journals. He also played poker and drank into the small hours with the leading writers, poets, artists, and musicians of the day.

During this period the Soviet government and security organs took an extraordinarily close interest in cultural affairs. On several occasions, it became apparent that Zamiatin's fate was determined by the outcome of wrangling within the upper ranks of the Cheka (later GPU): in 1919 and in 1922 when he was arrested, and contradictory instructions kept arriving from Moscow; and again in 1929, when he seemed to have gained permission to leave the country after a campaign of persecution of him by the proletarian writers' organization (RAPP), but was forbidden to travel at the last moment. Gor'ky wielded an extraordinary influence over Stalin at this time (it wouldn't last much longer), as reflected in the intensely detailed letters they exchanged for several years between Sorrento and Moscow, weighing up every detail of literary affairs, and determining the fate of dozens of writers. When Gor'ky returned to Russia in 1931, both Zamiatin and his close friend Mikhail Bulgakov made desperate appeals for him to help them get out of the country. Gor'ky interceded personally on their behalf with Stalin, and Zamiatin was allowed to leave for the West that November. Why did Zamiatin succeed where Bulgakov failed? Because Gor'ky, who had long ago come to feel that he was alien to him as a writer, nevertheless owed Zamiatin loyalty and gratitude as one of his most faithful and energetic colleagues in the early years of Soviet power. Maybe Stalin, like Gor'ky, was also in some awe of his breadth of education: here was someone who combined a mastery of technology with writing, a true "engineer of human souls" before his time.

Zamiatin and Liudmila arrived in Paris in February 1932, and he spent his remaining years in France. His career as a writer went into decline, as financial exigencies forced him increasingly to rely on writing film-scripts for a living. On the one hand, Zamiatin remained a Soviet citizen and maintained links with the Embassy. His application to join the new Soviet Union of Writers in 1934 was—quite exceptionally—approved personally by Stalin himself in Moscow, and he attended the 1935 Anti-Fascist Congress in Paris, a blatantly pro-Soviet propaganda exercise. On the other hand, although he was explicitly tempted back to the USSR by several friends, including the ambiguous Konstantin Fedin, and met with many of those who were seduced into returning, he resisted their blandishments. Clearly, he would never align himself with the monarchist sympathies of the first-generation White émigrés; but he was also incapable of becoming a Soviet propagandist like many of his acquaintances. His frank correspondence with friends who were not living in the USSR traces his increasing dismay at developments back home, and his shrewd evaluation of their future direction. A wealth of documentary material in the form of correspondence and diaries, which has emerged from the archives in the post-Soviet age, has provided us with a deeply intimate portrait of a man who negotiated political pitfalls and uncertainties in France, as he had in Soviet Russia, with great surefootedness. His voice is sincere, witty and knowledgeable.

Zamiatin's renown abroad has largely been shaped by his anti-utopian novel *We*, completed in 1919–20. In a distant future, the collective has triumphed over the individual: the One State has imposed conformity on all its citizens, regulating their lives through scientific and mathematical precepts, and requiring absolute political allegiance. Although Aldous Huxley denied that he had come across *We* before he wrote *Brave New World* in 1931, George Orwell readily acknowledged that reading Zamiatin's novel had contributed to his own ideas for *1984*, published in 1949 (and he rated Zamiatin far higher than he did Huxley). After his death in 1937, Zamiatin seemed fated to disappear into obscurity in the West, at the same time as he was being airbrushed out of Soviet literary history at home. George Orwell turns out to be the vital figure who, together with Professor Gleb Struve, determined to secure Zamiatin's reputation after the Second World War. *We* had been available in English and French translations since the 1920s, but in 1952 the full text of the novel finally appeared for the first time in the original Russian, published by an émigré publisher in New York. Like Bulgakov's *Master and Margarita*, Zamiatin's *We* reached a Russian readership (albeit in his case only those in emigration) a quarter of a century after its composition. It would be sixty-five years and more before it finally became available to Russian readers at home, at the very end of the Soviet era. Only now has *We* been recognised in his own country as a defining text, warning of the political and technological dangers of the future century. In the 21st century his works have gained their true status, enthusiastically adopted as set texts in Russian schools and universities, and his reputation as a classic Russian author is assured. He has fulfilled his own prophecy to the effect that the future of Russian literature lies in its past ("I am Afraid," 1921).

Chapter 1:

From Lebedian' to St Petersburg (1884–1906)

And so—I am free. I have left far behind me the dreary, unspeaking walls, the iron clang of the bolt on the door, the scrap of blue sky pitilessly bisected by the stern bars, the grim and tormented faces of my comrades, and those silent days, grey and cold as stone. All that has vanished, into that gulf we call the past. I am free. And instead of the prison vaults the azure sky of springtime stretches away above me; and instead of the stone silence of walls the wind whispers warmly and tenderly. I can no longer see our Struggle, with its harsh and proud face twisted by suffering. They don't know how to struggle here. [...] Around me here there is cheap, trite contentment; people doze peacefully in their soft and cosy swamp... [...] I've already begun gradually to get down to work. For some reason music doesn't draw me as it usually does, nor singing. I sit alone with my books, and with my... fantasies. My fantasies? Do you think that they will pass? But how will they pass if I don't wish them to pass or rather, I cannot, do not have the strength to wish such a thing? How is a man who is ill to be cured, if he doesn't wish to be treated, to take any medicine? Is it necessary to be treated?[1]

The writer of these words was a young man of 22, just released in March 1906 after a three-month spell in solitary confinement in a St Petersburg prison on suspicion of revolutionary activity. Above all he was anxious here to impress the girl he had met only weeks before his arrest with the nobility of his feelings. Now confined by the authorities to his family home over 1,000 kilometres away in Lebedian', as far away again to the south-east of Moscow as the capital is distant from St Petersburg, he was chafing with frustration.

Lebedian' is a small provincial town in the very heart of European Russia. At the time of Evgeny Ivanovich Zamiatin's birth on 20 January 1884,[2] the place numbered around 800 houses with something like 6,000 inhabitants, a number which even in the present century has grown to not many more than 20,000. The little town spreads over the hilly slopes leading down to the upper reaches of the river Don which, still fairly narrow, has not yet acquired a formal embankment, and is still bushy, full of reed banks, little islets and ducks. Typically the homes of the local merchants and other townsfolk were extended with small verandas facing the road, where families would sit to drink their tea in hot weather. Zamiatin's father Ivan was good with his hands and did much to improve their modest one-story wooden house on dusty Pokrovskaia Street, creating an orchard out of the garden which tumbled down the steep slope right to the edge of the Don: the district, bordering on the black-earth region, is known for its abundant varieties of crunchy, juicy apples. There was a tennis court down by the river too, and bathing nearby. Later Ivan would build a second house next to their own for Evgeny's only sibling, his younger sister Aleksandra (1885–1957), when she married.[3]

Lebedian's situation on the Don, at the point of intersection between five different provinces (Tambov, Voronezh, Riazan', Orel and Tula), had established its significance as a thriving market town, and since the late seventeenth century a major horse fair would be held there three times a year, with exotic stalls, traders, card-sharps, and gypsies. Ivan Turgenev described the lively event in *Lebedian'*, one of the brief sketches in his 1852 *Hunter's Notebook*: "When they had concluded their deals, they hurried off to the inns or the taverns, depending on their rank… And all of them bustled about, swarming and shouting, quarrelling and making it up, cursing and laughing, up to their knees in mud." In a letter to "Katia" (possibly a cousin) written when he was eight, Evgeny says his mother has bought him a new ball for 75 kopeks at the January fair, held to mark the Feast of the Epiphany, and that they also purchased a new pony. The family must have been quite comfortably off by the standards of the day: in the same letter he tells her that his father has been made Chairman of the Famine Committee, and has bought some scales so as to be able to distribute the oats and rye provided by the authorities to the village priests, who would deliver it to the hungry. The railway reached the town that same year, in 1892.[4]

In his several short autobiographical accounts of his early life, Zamiatin portrayed himself as a bookish, solitary child who could proudly read the newspaper headlines to his parents by the age of four: reading and writing, like spelling, came to him "astonishingly easily, instinctively."[5] A couple of lengthy and very affectionate letters to his "Dear mama," written even before he had learned to separate his words properly, have been preserved. In one, written in the late 1880s or early 1890s, he reports that his sister Sanya or Sasha (Aleksandra) has been poorly with her glands, that the goat is pregnant, that the asters in the jar have begun to come up, and that he is eating eggs and drinking milk because he is fasting.[6] His mother, Maria Aleksandrovna, née Platonova, (1864–1925) was the daughter of the local priest; she had received a good education, had a gift for music, and liked to play Chopin, Brahms, Beethoven and Schumann. Zamiatin recalled lying on his stomach, reading under the piano, while hens and a piglet scratched around in the dust on the street outside the window framed with geraniums. His father, Ivan Dmitrievich Zamiatin, (1853–1916), was also from a clerical family, in nearby Lipetsk. In 1883, the year of his marriage, he was appointed priest for the church of the Pokrovskaia parish in Lebedian', taking the post over directly from his father-in-law, who died that same year. The young couple therefore established their married life in Maria's family home, where the household continued to include her widowed mother Anastasia (1836–1914), and her younger sister Varvara (Varia; 1872–1931). Ivan Dmitrievich is said to have been a kind man with a slight stammer, well-liked by his parishioners and steadily rewarded by the Church throughout his career for his exemplary service. The life of the household was dominated by religious observances, the reading of scriptures, a stream of visits from members of the congregation and local clerical figures, and family trips to nearby monasteries; or religious processions in the summer, "with the scent of wormwood, clouds of dust, and sweaty pilgrims, who scrambled on all fours beneath the icon of Our Lady of Kazan', itinerant monks and nuns, and the holy fool Vasia the Antichrist, alternately proclaiming the pious and the unprintable…"[7]

Zamiatin remembered a few traumatic moments from his early childhood: at the age of eighteen months being held up to the window and watching the red sun on a day when he was ill, and apparently close to death; the feeling of desolation he experienced after getting separated from his parents in the crowd at church in nearby Zadonsk a year or so later; and his mother and aunt Varia hurriedly closing up the house when cholera patients were being transported along the street. He could also remember his pride at setting off in long trousers for his first day at the local *gimnaziia*, or grammar school. His father, Ivan Dmitrievich, had taught Latin and calligraphy in a number of local schools, and was now in charge of religious instruction there. At the age of eleven Evgeny compiled a magazine, *Kaleidoscope*, while recovering from measles. After five years at school in sleepy Lebedian', and with a certificate signed by his teachers (including his father) for a book prize "for excellent behaviour, effort and achievement," the young Zamiatin transferred at the age of twelve to start boarding at the *gimnaziia* at Voronezh, the provincial capital a hundred kilometres or so to the south.[8] Like Lebedian', Voronezh stands on the bustling river Don, one of Russia's major waterways.

Describing his Voronezh school years from 1896 to 1902, Zamiatin mentioned one occasion at school when, aged about fourteen, he decided not to tell anyone he had been bitten on the leg by a rabid dog until the two weeks in which the infection might make itself apparent had passed. This was a boyish test of his own character, during which time he kept the only diary he ever wrote. He was then rushed to Moscow for a course of injections, but all was well. At the age of seventeen he wrote to his sister Aleksandra, herself away at school in a different town, a solemn if affectionate letter: he described playing the piano and visiting the theatre, enumerated the top marks he had received for all his exams, told her how much he had enjoyed Grigory Danilevsky's 1863 novel *Freedom* (which highlighted the inadequacies of the 1861 Emancipation of the Serfs), promised to send her some suggestions for the essay she was due to write (he had one to do himself on the lyrical digressions in Gogol's *Dead Souls*), and then embarked, as she had requested, on a lengthy (and somewhat pompous) disquisition on the true nature of love.[9] Despite the starred top marks he regularly received for Russian composition, "I didn't always find mathematics easy to get on with. Perhaps for that very reason (out of stubbornness) I chose the most mathematical course: the Shipbuilding Faculty of the Petersburg Polytechnic Institute." In actual fact, his reference from Voronezh noted his "excellent achievements […], especially in Russian and the classics, and in mathematics."[10]

Zamiatin acknowledged that the opportunities the shipbuilding course offered for students to travel the world had also provided a considerable incentive in his choice of higher education. And despite the fact that the nearest open sea was about 1,000 kilometres away both to the north and to the south, the river Don near Lebedian' and Voronezh had been a major centre for shipbuilding since the seventeenth century, so the subject was not an entirely remote one.[11] He completed his school studies in Voronezh in 1902 with a "gold medal," awarded for straight As in the final examinations—a medal he would soon have to pawn for 25 roubles in St Petersburg. He also received a certificate noting that there were no entries concerning him in the conduct record, and that "as for his moral conduct, Zamiatin (Evgeny) has been completely above reproach."[12] However, he was given a warning on his final day by one of the school officials about the behaviour of a former pupil, P. E. Shchegolev, who would later become an eminent literary scholar: "He also left here with a medal [...]. And now he has landed in prison. My advice to you is: 'don't write, don't follow that path.' This edifying advice didn't help me." Shchegolev was some seven years Zamiatin's senior, and would in fact become one of his close friends in St Petersburg.[13]

In applying to the Polytechnic Institute as part of its first ever intake in October 1902, Zamiatin was aiming for the very best: there were 500 applicants for the 25 places in the Shipbuilding Faculty, and those admitted had to come for interview with an outstanding academic record, a knowledge of foreign languages (he had studied Greek and Latin as well as French and German), and a reference confirming their "reliability." The Institute, created under the auspices of the Finance Minister, Count Witte, to promote industrial and economic development, was housed in magnificent new buildings. All the students lived in single rooms in comfortable hostels at Sosnovka, on the outskirts of the city, and the place was equipped with the facilities and teachers to train the élite of their generation. Like Pushkin joining the first intake of the Lycée at Tsarskoe Selo a century earlier, the future writer would be receiving the best education the country could offer. The Shipbuilding Faculty aimed to produce specialists "to whose native wits and talent higher education would open up new paths for discoveries and inventions."[14] He moved to the city in August 1902, to start life as a student there on 1 October. Within weeks of his arrival, however, he wrote to his sister Aleksandra to say he was anxious that he might have made the wrong choice in opting for shipbuilding rather than economics. It was not the difficulty that put him off, although he described his heavy routine of lectures from 9 until about 5, with a break for 90 minutes, on top of homework, but he did like the sound of the topics the economists were studying, which appealed to him more than mathematics. Anyway, he was going to sit in on a lecture for economists on medieval history before asking to change course.[15] But evidently he soon reconciled himself to his original choice.

A strength of purpose and an inclination to seek out the apparently paradoxical, less straightforward path are apparent in these glimpses of his early life, as they are in Zamiatin's reflections in that first letter to his girlfriend after emerging from prison in 1906 on the wisdom—or otherwise—of attempting to "cure" himself of his fantasies and creative impulses. The perverse pursuit of turbulent freedom rather than sedate happiness had been a key Dostoevskian theme, and would become an essential preoccupation in Zamiatin's writings as well. It perhaps comes as no surprise, therefore, that this child of a lower middle-class, pious provincial family, a modestly-ranked "hereditary honourable citizen" as the official designation put it, soon found himself caught up in the widespread revolutionary ferment of life in St Petersburg.[16] Tsar Nicholas II's reign had seen increased restrictions placed on such modestly democratic institutions as the *zemstvo* (local council) system, which had been introduced during the reform era of the 1860s; an aggressive policy of Russification had fostered regional discontent, and provided the fuel for anti-Semitic sentiments and the widespread pogroms of the turn of the century; and the emergence of a radicalised youth led to bonds being formed between oppressed workers and the well-educated but alienated left-wing political groups. This discontent was exacerbated when foreign adventure—an attempt to check Japanese ambitions with regard to China and Manchuria—ended in the Russian fleet's humiliations at Port Arthur in 1904 and Mukden and Tsushima in 1905.

Zamiatin was present on a white winter Sunday on Nevsky Prospect, the main street of St Petersburg, watching the clock with a large crowd: "And when the signal was given—one stroke, one o'clock—black shards of humanity flew in all directions along the Prospect, there were snatches of the Marseillaise, red banners, Cossack soldiers, yardsweepers, policemen… The first demonstration (for me) —was 1903. And the closer it came to 1905—the more feverish the turmoil, the noisier the gatherings." On 28 November 1904 he witnessed another demonstration on Nevsky Prospect calling for the creation of a Constituent Assembly (the first necessary step towards the introduction of democratic political structures); this was vigorously dispersed by the Tsar's loyal Cossacks, assisted by the police.[17] Shortly afterwards, the year of the first Russian Revolution opened with the notorious events of 9 January 1905, known as "Bloody Sunday." An unarmed procession of strikers from the Putilov Works was marching towards the Winter Palace to present a petition to the Tsar. The crowd, led by a priest, Father Gapon, included many women and children, and carried icons and portraits of the Tsar. Nonetheless, the troops panicked and began to cut them down, killing over a hundred demonstrators and wounding many more as they trudged through the snow. The outrage prompted by these events sparked a wave of unrest and sympathy strikes throughout the country. Some Polytechnic students had taken part in the march; one had been killed, and his funeral was followed by resignations and disturbances at the Institute. Zamiatin, who had as usual been granted leave to return home to Lebedian' for the Christmas holidays, sent a telegram to the Institute to ask what would happen about the start of classes; he was told that there would be no question of classes beginning before 15 February that year. In fact, classes at the Institute were suspended for over eighteen months because of the unrest, resuming only in the autumn of 1906.[18]

As a student Zamiatin had to live on the meagre income provided by his family; in December 1903 he was obliged to apply to the Institute authorities for a grant of a few roubles to travel to Moscow to receive medical treatment for some unspecified ailment; this he was accorded, along with relief from payment of some of his fees. In November 1905 he was granted permission to leave for Lebedian', even though he had not yet paid all the rent due for his hostel accommodation.[19] But he lived well enough, and his desire to travel was amply fulfilled by the course he had settled on: each summer was spent doing practical classes in shipyards, or afloat. Now he discovered "Russia, third-class railway carriages full of jokes and laughter, Sebastopol, Nizhny [Nizhny Novgorod, on the Volga], the factories on the Kama River, Odessa, the port, down-and-outs." In 1903 he was in Sebastopol (in the Crimea) from May until September; in 1904 he travelled to the river Kama, in the Urals north of Perm; and in the summer of 1905 he undertook as a 21-year-old the most exciting sea journey of his life, when he sailed on the steamship *Rossiia* from Odessa across the Black Sea, out into the Eastern Mediterranean, and round the coast as far as Alexandria. Everything he saw was exotic: "Constantinople, the mosques, the dervishes, the bazaars, the white marble quayside at Smyrna, the bedouins in Beirut, the white breaking surf at Jaffa, the green and black colours of Mount Athos, plague-ridden Port Said, the yellow and white colours of Africa, and Alexandria, with English policemen and traders selling stuffed crocodiles [...]. And Jerusalem, which was special, different from all the rest, astonishing—where I lived for a week or so with the family of an Arab I knew."[20]

His return from this summer trip in mid-June 1905 brought him directly into the epicentre of revolutionary turmoil, for his ship sailed back into Odessa just as mutiny broke out there on the battleship *Potemkin*. The crew of the battleship, one of the newest in the fleet, were already demoralised by the defeats during the Russo-Japanese War. After being threatened with harsh treatment for protesting at being served rotting meat, they rebelled against their officers. There was a stand-off outside the port of Odessa; and when a naval squadron was sent to quell the rebellion, their crews mutinied as well, and the *Potemkin* was allowed to escape to Romania. This episode gave the Tsar a stark warning that his armed forces could no longer be relied upon. Zamiatin wandered around Odessa for an entire day and a night with the engineer of the *Rossiia*, amidst gunshots, fires and pogroms. In his semi-documentary story *Three Days* (1913) he graphically described the events from the perspective of a ship passenger recently back from a trip to the Middle East, still overwhelmed with visual impressions of blinding heat and sand, and the silky sound of the waves. The story depicts the fascinated glimpses the passenger receives of the common people's spontaneous sympathy for the rebelling sailors, and the behaviour of the town's respectable citizens as they scurry nervously through the town, gather to gawp, or scatter in panic after a bomb is thrown. The narrator's principal concern is to rejoin his ship, which, after an alarming time spent in close proximity to the *Potemkin* and the new squadron sent from Sebastopol to quash the uprising, slips away from Odessa and along the coast to Ochakov.

When Zamiatin returned north to St Petersburg, it was to find the city in disarray with strikes and meetings, but vivid, exciting and fun. "The summer of 1905 was gaudy, a particularly bright blue, taut, packed to the brim with people and events. […] In those years to be a Bolshevik was to take the line of maximum resistance; and so I was then a Bolshevik."[21] He actually joined the Bolshevik section of the Russian Social-Democratic Workers' Party [RSDWP (b)] that September. While studying at the Polytechnic Zamiatin had become involved in student affairs, and was a member (and by the end of 1907 the Chairman) of the students' Senior Council. As he commented twenty years later, "All that seems like a whirlwind now: demonstrations on Nevsky [Prospect], Cossacks, student and worker groups, love, enormous meetings at the University and in the Institutes. Then I was a Bolshevik (I'm not a Bolshevik now), and I worked in the Vyborg District: at one point I kept a printing-press in my room.

I battled against the Kadets [moderate Constitutional Democrats] in the Senior Council."²² By the second week of October 1905 Soviets [Workers' Committees] had been set up, and the country was almost brought to a standstill by a nationwide general strike. The Tsar was forced to issue a Manifesto on 17 October representing a significant step towards constitutional reform: it provided for a parliamentary Duma, which was to be elected on a very limited suffrage, but would have the right of veto over legislation; and it also promised civil rights, including freedom of speech and assembly. On the Left, however, people were still not satisfied with these concessions.

By this time Zamiatin had become a Party activist: in mid-November 1905 he had hastily to change his address, so as to be able to carry out more discreetly tasks such as distributing leaflets and hiding weapons or explosives. There were still no classes at the Institute. He worked at the Vyborg District headquarters of the RSDWP (b) and attended numerous meetings, including one on 22 November to discuss a referendum about Party factions. It was on this occasion that he first met an attractive young medical student, Liudmila Nikolaevna Usova (1884–1965), who was working with the Bolsheviks alongside Zamiatin's fellow-students from the Polytechnic, Boris Krylov and the bibliophile Iakov Grebenshchikov.²³ He recalled later that he had spotted a pretty girl as they sat in the crowded library before the meeting began, and was then both dismayed and pleased to discover that he was to carry out his revolutionary tasks under her command. He bridled at her authority over him, while being charmed by her liveliness and directness, and soon found himself infuriated and resentful of her closeness to Boris Krylov. "Oh, how pleased I am! How cross I made her today! I want to hurt her, be unpleasant. She is threatening not to talk to me. So does that mean she really is indifferent?"²⁴

However, within days he went to the Iavorskaia Theatre together with Liudmila, to see the première of Evgeny Chirikov's *The Jews*. With its appeals from the stage for an end to the exploitation of the workers, and its graphic depiction of a pogrom, the play caused a sensation. Written in 1903 in response to a notorious pogrom in Kishinev that spring, the play had initially been banned in Russia, but was staged in 1904–05 in Berlin, London, New York, Chicago and Boston. What Zamiatin remembered of the evening, though, were the childlike simplicity with which Liudmila kissed her mother goodbye as they left for the theatre, and his delight when she watched the play from the row behind him with her head resting on his shoulder.²⁵

At the end of November 1905 he applied as usual for formal permission to return to Lebedian' for the holidays, but on this occasion he did not in fact leave the capital. On 3 December, the entire executive of the St Petersburg Soviet, which was dominated by the young Trotsky, was arrested. On 11 December, Zamiatin himself was arrested, along with 30 fellow-members of an armed unit at the RSDWP (b) Headquarters of the Vyborg District, in the flat of a certain Konstantin von Shul'man.[26] The police burst in and discovered the group with plans and firearms. Zamiatin was obliged to do some quick thinking: on the previous evening a "wing-eared" worker he knew called Nikolai V. had visited him and asked to leave a bag of explosive gun-cotton with him, because he was being followed. The discovery of the gun-cotton in his room, sitting in a paper bag on the windowsill next to some sugar and some salami, as well as the Socialist Revolutionary leaflets under his bed, could have meant the death-penalty. After he had been searched and roughed up during the arrest, he managed to scribble a quick note and drop it out of the window to acquaintances in the street, asking them to remove "anything unsuitable" from his accommodation. When he and the others were taken off for questioning, and during all the time he endured in solitary confinement, he had no idea whether his request had been carried out or not.[27] This gnawing anxiety as to whether compromising material has been discovered is something D-503, the engineer hero of his futuristic novel *We*, would suffer; and it is perhaps not insignificant that in the novel Zamiatin uses the same unusual term, "wing-eared," to characterise the figure of S-4711, whose role in the revolutionary conspiracy led by the "Mephis" remains deliberately ambiguous.

After the brief preliminary enquiry into his case, he was placed in solitary confinement in the prison on Shpalernaia Street. He wrote from there to his father. In a restrained attempt to console him—all letters from the prison were of course scrutinised by the censor—he made a remark which scarcely carried much conviction, to the effect that: "Your faith, my dear father, will help you to bear your grief. Perhaps your grief will teach me to have better faith." One observer reports that the grief did indeed take its toll on Ivan Dmitrievich, whose health deteriorated through subsequent years. In the same letter Zamiatin advised his father that when his mother—who at his request became the main person who campaigned for his release—came to St Petersburg, she would be able to find out where he was by going to visit the Usova family, whom he described as "very nice, straightforward people."[28] The rest of Liudmila's family consisted of her mother Elizaveta Ivanovna, and her sister Maria Nikolaevna. A medical student like her sister, Maria Nikolaevna also belonged to the RSDWP (b), and she was arrested along with Boris Krylov and some 70 others the day after Zamiatin; Krylov had a printing press and 500 proclamations confiscated. Liudmila herself only narrowly escaped being arrested early in April 1906, and Zamiatin begged her not to take unnecessary risks, since her imprisonment would cause him such pain. On 17 April 1906 she submitted an appeal to the police for her sister Maria to be released, which was eventually successful.

Zamiatin was officially charged on the last day of December 1905. As it turned out, his friends had succeeded in emptying his room of the compromising materials, and on 19 January 1906 the police reported that: "During the search of Zamiatin nothing criminal was found, but in view of his presence in the flat, where according to his words he had come as a correspondent of the *New Life* newspaper in order to obtain material for a newspaper feature from the 'Office of Fibre Products,' there is no basis for drawing a definitive conclusion about his non-participation in planning an offence against the state before the enquiry has established all the circumstances of the case." Meanwhile, his mother had arrived in the city. Having appealed to the Director of the Polytechnic Institute, Prince A.G. Gagarin, for support, she submitted a request to the Police Department in late February for her son to be released to live under supervision at home, describing his "chance" association with the political radicals as "a youthful indiscretion."[29]

During his three months of solitary confinement he made notes on his reading of philosophical tracts and of studies such as the popular German psychologist Max Nordau's book *In Search of the Truth (Paradoxes)*;[30] he read fiction (Zola, Sienkiewicz), worked to improve his English (which he had started to learn at the Institute), and apparently wrote a few poems. The experience of prison, despite the physical discomforts, was not altogether disagreeable. He felt that it had hardened him, and there was also a sense of being caught up in an elemental experience:

> Have you ever bathed in the surf? I can recall now the last time I bathed in Jaffa. A huge breaker of a turbid green colour, topped with shaggy white foam, slowly rolls closer and closer — and suddenly with a roar it seizes you in its embrace, hurls you

and crushes you and bears you along... You feel like a tiny piece of wood in its great power, you are without strength or will, and you discover some sort of strange pleasure in your insignificance and your powerlessness, a pleasure in giving yourself up entirely to the power of this warm, strong monster... A few more surges, and you are thrown out on to the hot sand, under the hot sun... So it was in the heat of Jaffa. And it was something like that in the cold of St Petersburg. It was irksome, and yet I was glad, terribly glad about that wave.[31]

Liudmila wrote to him and brought parcels, but none of his replies to her from prison survive. He did, however, preserve some notes he made for himself there, which he quoted in one of his letters to her after his release. On 12 February 1906 he was reflecting on the importance of living life to the full, in the present, regardless of the consequences: "Should I take care not to waste my life? Look after it? So as to extend it for longer? But that would be the same as giving someone a wonderful piece of music, full of Chopin's tenderness, the fire of Mozart, the bacchanalia of Wagner, the grandeur of Beethoven or the melancholy of Tchaikovsky—and then advising them not to play it all at once, but... just a line each day. [...] And the only people who can respond to that wonderful music, full of joy and suffering, are those who throw back their heads and drink life down, swallowing greedily, without glancing down to see whether there is much left at the bottom, who don't concern themselves to find out whether they are drinking poison or a healing draught..."[32]

Thanks to his mother's efforts, Zamiatin was released from prison by 13 March, conditional upon his living outside the capital cities, and under police supervision. Liudmila and he were able to spend 15 hours together during the three days before he had to leave St Petersburg for Lebedian', and his letters that spring are full of an anxiety that that time had somehow not been spent well. It was scarcely surprising that they should have been awkward together in the circumstances: "we were both somehow strange, somehow different, as though somehow we didn't recognise one another."[33] He had been reluctant to talk about things, since he was overwhelmed by his emotions—not least of frustration and pain at the immediate prospect of parting. But he was overjoyed when, having said goodbye near the Post Office in the city, she then reappeared at the station to see him off properly.

The ten surviving letters Zamiatin wrote to Liudmila from Lebedian' in the spring of 1906 are particularly revealing.[34] Written by a 22-year-old to the object of his first serious love, they had to perform a number of functions simultaneously. After all, their brief relationship to date was based almost exclusively on three weeks of getting to know each other as they pursued their covert revolutionary activities, during which time issues of authority and submission tangled with bursts of jealousy on Zamiatin's part. The relationship developed over the following three months on the basis only of their prison correspondence, sustained by occasional visits. The few hours they had spent together after his release had been cut short by his internal exile to a town 1,000 kilometres away. This was therefore a love affair which had barely had the time or opportunity to establish itself, and he was determined to keep the small flame alive, even from a great geographical distance. These first letters therefore contain reflections on their shared past and prospects for the future, and declarations of his feelings, in order to anchor their love in reality; and his loneliness in Lebedian' prompted him to important affirmations about himself, an account of his feelings and even his personality, so that she should understand who it was she had become involved with. They also include a conscientious—perhaps even slightly overemphatic—reiteration of the revolutionary convictions which had provided the basis for their meeting in the first place.

In that first letter of 26 March, in which he had commented on being free at last, Zamiatin described his longing for work, danger and struggle after nearly four months of forced inactivity. He clearly expected that some of his letters might go astray, and for this reason he used a fairly simple code based on the transposition of letters of the alphabet when referring to certain political events, such as the forthcoming Fourth RSDWP (b) Congress, which was held in Stockholm that April.[35] In his next letter he was defensive about suggestions apparently made by the enigmatic Nikolai V. that his commitment to the revolutionary cause was superficial or insincere. He countered that although those who are most fanatical about their ideas are likely to prove the most active in a revolutionary movement, it is often the case, "as that subtle psychologist Nietzsche correctly observes," that those with a more active nature may lack creative powers (6 April). He assured Liudmila that prison had only strengthened his resolve to serve the Party, and told her that he was proposing to use his period of exile to extend his understanding of issues such as the agrarian question and the role of the Kadets [Constitutional Democrats], as well as the limitations placed on the powers of the proposed Duma by new decrees published that spring. He'd been reading Trotsky's recently published book *One or Two Chambers?*, and commented with dismay on the ill-treatment, reported in the press, of Party comrades. He'd drawn up a list of some fifteen publications he wanted her to send him on top of the socialist newspapers he was already receiving. These included Bebel, Kautsky and others, variously writing on anarchism and socialism, Marx and Nietzsche, marriage and free love, the intelligentsia and the proletariat, social democracy and scientific socialism, and the agrarian question. He acknowledged that these were not all for his own use, since he hoped to contribute to the cause by lending such publications to those who wanted to borrow them locally.[36]

By April he had some reason to hope for an amnesty; this was a proposal which had been mooted in connection with the opening sessions of the First Duma (which was dominated by the liberal democratic parties, the Socialist Revolutionaries having decided to boycott the elections). He was scornful about the "treachery" of those on the Left who were pressing for collaboration with the Duma. This spirit of compromise, he observed, could mark the final defeat of the 1905 Revolution. On 9 May, he was still hoping that his own so-called "waywardness" would be "generously forgiven." However, he admitted that he was mostly finding it hard to concentrate on his political studies, since he was too easily distracted by thoughts of her. He addressed her fondly as his "dear" or "sweet" "Lyusi," using a non-standard diminutive presumably formed as a calque from the English "Lucy"; yet at the same time he continued to use the Russian polite form *Vy* rather than the more intimate *Ty*. At this period in the history of Russian manners, this could just have been a conventional courtesy, and it is notable that he continued to use it to Liudmila even after their marriage, and throughout their entire correspondence. Looking back again on the difficult hours they'd spent together when he was released from prison, he apologised for his awkwardness and for his "correctness," which presumably inhibited him from displaying his true feelings. In his first letter to her certain passages have been cut out, and in what has survived he confined himself to requesting a photo of her as a schoolgirl and to "pressing her little hand" in parting. He was rarely frank at this stage, preferring to offer her glimpses of transferred eroticism in his evocation, for example, of supple young spring leaves on the trees in the garden, quivering under the tender kisses of the rain. But then he immediately became self-conscious, self-mocking: "And now, when I've written this and read it through, I laugh, I'm almost ashamed! So tell me, it is comical isn't it, it's stupid? Or not? I'm always like this. I'm a divided person, I'm split in two. One 'I' longs to believe, and the other will not allow him to; one longs to feel, and desires beauty, while the other mocks him and points a finger at him. One is soft and warm, the other is cold, sharp, and merciless as steel. And the cold triumphs, it always has triumphed—ever since I began to be a sentient being. And life has been equally cold. And that's why I've always sought novelty, variety, dangers—otherwise it would all have seemed too cold, too empty" (9 April).

He urged her to become a true friend, such as he had never had previously, asked her to trust him like a brother, and to tell him more about how she felt towards him. He was rather appalled to learn that Maria, now presumably released from prison and living with her sister again, had been reading his private letters to Liudmila. He evidently sensed that she had not been entirely encouraging about their relationship, and acknowledged that she was perhaps right to describe him as an egoist, a predator constrained only by his code of behaviour as a member of the intelligentsia. He also asked Liudmila to be indulgent towards his fantasies, pleading that anyone who found themselves stuck in Lebedian' would go mad and start behaving and speaking foolishly. He even developed his own "theory of foolishness," arguing that deliberate, conscious foolishnesses are productive, just as in higher mathematics, where no hypotheses can be made which do not *a priori* contain elements of inaccuracy, approximation and error. In other words, reason itself always necessarily contains elements of foolishness.

By now he was becoming desperate to get out of Lebedian', complaining to Liudmila of "the musty streets of this musty little town, where you can meet members of the [anti-Semitic] Black Hundreds organisation, along with empty-headed maidens who think of nothing but clothes and flirting" (6 April). He was shocked at the sight of the local police officers going through intensive training, "all in black, on black horses… They gallop back and forth, hurl themselves with drawn sabres on invisible (because internal) enemies, and learn how to cut people down according to all the rules of the art… They have rifles dangling on their backs, and whips hanging from their saddles…" (22 April). He was finding life at home difficult too, with a stream of visitors who disturbed him when he tried to settle down to some reading. His sister Aleksandra was about to get married to a literature teacher from the Lebedian' *gimnaziia*, a stern man some 12 years her senior, named Vladimir Volkov. As far as Zamiatin was concerned, this was one of the pressures which was bringing about the disintegration of his family's life:

> There is a drama unfolding in my family, a wordless, quiet drama. A drama like Chekhov's *Cherry Orchard*, like *Uncle Vania*. The family is collapsing, the beautiful décor is falling apart, and all that are left are old, bare, empty walls.
>
> My mother has lived her whole life through her children—through my sister and me. Now the children have gone—my sister to get married, and I have moved away, towards a different and alien life. And she is left standing there, and can see nothing in front of her but empty space: she has no purpose in life, and she has no air to breathe. To experience such a thing is unbearably hard. But it's also hard to watch.
>
> My sister is someone with high-principled, spiritual needs. I had thought to draw her into the circle of the interests which I myself live by. She was planning to go to University in the autumn… but has got married instead. And it seems to me that her husband is made of entirely different stuff, and that she will soon become disillusioned with him. I fear that she feels that too. And it's hard to watch that as well.
>
> And I myself am weary. I'm weary because there is no life here to provoke or arouse me, thrill me and prevent me from becoming too absorbed in my thoughts. And sometimes, like today, it gets to the point where it seems you can't believe in anything, not even in yourself, and there is nothing left in your heart, no energy and no ideas—it's as empty there as in a deserted house… (9 May)

His silence about his father in this description is striking, and would seem to betoken a distance between them which did nothing to bridge the gulf opening up within the family between mother and children, brother and sister.

He was also not feeling well: he developed flu, and complained of headaches, insomnia, and jumpy nerves. But above all, he was determined to get back to St Petersburg: "After all, the spring months of the 23rd year of your life don't come around twice…" (5 May). He was trapped in Lebedian' partly by his financial circumstances: "All

I have is just 25 roubles of my own, but to ask my father for money to live in St Petersburg for a cause which he considers to be harmful in general, and harmful for me in particular—I don't want to do that. [...] That's the reason why I would like to get myself fixed up with practicals in Piter [St Petersburg] if possible, or if not, then with a job on the St Petersburg-London route." He was therefore trying to establish contact with the Dean of the Shipbuilding Faculty, Konstantin Boklevsky, known for his generous interest in his students' affairs. "The one thing I do know is that I won't last here much longer. I will get away and go somewhere. And indeed my inclination to travel draws me as well" (22 April). On 30 May his documents were at last stamped by a police inspector in Lebedian', to record his departure, while a further police stamp relating to his temporary registration at an address in St Petersburg is dated 4 June. However, he was apparently still not entitled to be fully registered in St Petersburg.[37] While his exact legal status at the time is not entirely clear, it seems that the terms of his internal exile were no longer being enforced very rigidly in the atmosphere of political relaxation associated with the First Duma.

It is notable that the authorities at the Polytechnic were by no means unsympathetic to the plight of one of their more brilliant, if politically troublesome students, and were to prove very supportive of him over a number of years, and even decades. Presumably in response to his request to Dean Boklevsky for work, Zamiatin was sent off within a couple of weeks of his return to St Petersburg to do practicals (with a paid stipend) in Finland, at the Sandvik Docks in Helsingfors [Helsinki].[38] In this way he would avoid the unwelcome attentions of the St Petersburg police. He arrived there shortly after 20 June, as he told Liudmila in his letters, for once again the couple found themselves parted, again after a mere 2–3 weeks, following the pattern of their frustratingly intermittent relationship. He described to her entertainingly how he and his fellow-student, who looked and felt like savages amongst the neat and elegant Scandinavians, visited the sauna there and admired the unselfconscious locals as they swam, jumped, dived and drank coffee more or less in the nude. He was also impressed by the freedom of the pairs of lovers who embraced in the parks in the evenings: he longed to share all this with her, even though she had apparently resolved to spend her holiday with friends on the Volga for the sake of her health (she was to develop tuberculosis). "When I saw those couples I thought of you. I wanted to wander around, go out in a boat, sit on the rocks and listen to music—with you." Evidently this particular letter had its intended effect, because Liudmila soon changed her plans and joined him. Zamiatin would remember that Helsinki summer fondly: "A room with the sea and the rocks beneath the window. In the evenings, when you could scarcely make out people's faces—they held meetings on the grey granite. At night the faces became invisible, and the warm black stone seemed soft—because SHE was next to me, and the rays from the floodlights at Sveaborg seemed light and tender."[39]

His comment here about meetings is a reminder that Finland at this time was still very much a part of the Russian Empire, and had indeed been subject to increasingly repressive policies of Russification since the turn of the century. The freedoms then won for Russia in the 1905 Revolution were awarded to the Finns as well; but the radicalised workers in the Red Guard led by Johan Kock were pressing at this point for more fundamental democratic concessions. Zamiatin was once introduced to Kock—in the nude—at the bathing pool. Then news arrived of ominous developments back in Russia: Tsar Nicholas II, infuriated by the Duma's confrontational attitude, had sent in troops to occupy the Taurid Palace, and decreed on 9 July that the First Duma should be dissolved. For nearly three weeks there was political turmoil in Russia as the revolutionaries strove to incite a mass uprising in protest. Nearly half the members of the dissolved First Duma crossed into Finland.[40] Zamiatin described one of the meetings he attended in Helsinki, which was addressed by the modernist writer Leonid Andreev: "It was in 1906. The Revolution had not yet become a lawful wife, jealously guarding its lawful monopoly on love. The Revolution was a youthful, fiery-eyed mistress,—and I was in love with the Revolution..."[41] Andreev's readers knew him as a short story writer, and turned out in large numbers to hear what he would have to say about the political issues of the day. A solemn and articulate speech by the author, in which he foretold the imminent execution of the crowned head of the Russian nation, was greeted with an excited ovation. Soon there was a serious mutiny at the naval base of Sveaborg in the Gulf of Finland, and the Tsar sent a naval squadron from Kronstadt to quell the subversion of the Finnish Red Guard. At some point during these upheavals Zamiatin decided to make his way back to St Petersburg in disguise, "wearing different clothes, cleanshaven, and in a sort of pince-nez."[42]

The Tsarist authorities were all too aware of the extent to which the students of the Polytechnic—and indeed many of the staff—were implicated in revolutionary activities, and they sent spies to monitor meetings held there. The universities had been granted their autonomy by the Tsar in August 1905, and the revolutionary parties had become very active on their premises as a consequence.[43] On 29 September 1906 the Institute received a complaint that a meeting of 42 workers, 56 female students and 15 male students had taken place in the buildings of the Institute the previous week. On 28 October there was a report that a crucial meeting of the Socialist-Revolutionary Party had been scheduled to take place in the Institute the following day: Dean Boklevsky was instructed to prevent the meeting from taking place, if he wished to avoid the police becoming involved. During November and December there were further complaints about meetings involving up to 1,500 people, many of them workers, at which professors called upon students to support the transfer of land to the people, inflammatory leaflets were distributed, and calls were made for a Constituent Assembly, or for the violent overthrow of the existing order; subversive poetry was declaimed and revolutionary songs were sung. On one occasion the police authorities protested that, despite an explicit request, the Institute's senior officials, Director Prince A.G. Gagarin and Professor A.S. Posnikov, had moved far too slowly to break up a meeting at one of the Institute hostels, thus allowing five workers and ten female students to escape.[44]

While all this was happening in the autumn of 1906 Zamiatin was finally back at his classes at the Polytechnic, having established his left-wing credentials and come relatively unscathed through the ordeals of imprisonment and internal exile. At last he and Liudmila could be together, with only such interruptions as were dictated by their normal working routines and commitments. He had broken away from his home and upbringing, and established himself as an independent adult. And it was at this point, even as he was completing his qualifications as a shipping engineer, that he embarked on an entirely new path, and wrote his first piece of fiction, the story *Alone*, inspired by his experiences in prison in December 1905-March 1906.

CHAPTER 2:

FROM ASTRAKHAN TO ARKHANGEL'SK (1906–1916)

Shortly after he had returned to his shipbuilding studies at the Polytechnic in the autumn of 1906, a photograph of 1907 shows Zamiatin amongst a group of senior student representatives (*starosty*) alongside the founding Director of the Institute, Prince A.G. Gagarin. This was a defiant gesture, where the students arranged to have themselves photographed in solidarity with the Prince, who was being forced into retirement on the express order of Nicholas II for failing to exercise due authority. During the summer of 1907, the student hostels at the Institute were all closed down to discourage further political activity, and Zamiatin had to seek lodgings at a succession of addresses nearby.[1] He graduated from the Institute on 21 May 1908 (only 11 of the original intake of 25 students succeeded in graduating that year), having submitted a dissertation "On selecting the principal dimensions of cargo vessels," which included an appendix of sketches and diagrams. One other surviving example of his technical drawing, an ingenious design for a flexible dam, where a rubbery sheet could be curved back to block the flow of water, demonstrates his precise and elegant draughtsmanship.[2] Now a qualified maritime engineer, he promptly submitted an application to the Ministry of Trade to get work. However, the Ministry made enquiries about his political reliability, and when they were sent a reply from the police authorities detailing his December 1905 arrest, he was refused employment. During the later part of 1908, the Polytechnic authorities evidently interceded on his behalf, and by the end of October the police informed the Ministry that the threat of criminal proceedings had been lifted. He was immediately granted an Institute bursary to enable him to take a postgraduate course to study the construction of shoreside installations. On 19 November he not only received his diploma, signed by Dean Boklevsky, but he was also appointed at the same time to the position of Instructor at the Institute. And again thanks to Boklevsky's help he was taken on a week later as an engineer in the Department of Commercial Ports, his official post for the next ten years, until 1918.

Over the course of 1909 we get a variety of glimpses of Zamiatin at work: during August and September he was checking over technical drawings for the White Sea dockyards at Arkhangel'sk, visiting the massive Putilov and Metallichesky factories, where parts were made for battleships, translating parts of a French engineer's article on cranes, and attending the delivery of a new hoist. The following summer, he was appointed to a technician's post at the Black Sea port of Poti. Between 1909 and 1915 he would publish a dozen or more articles on developments in the design of ships, dredgers, submarines and icebreakers, becoming a vigorous advocate of the replacing of steam by the internal combustion engine. From 1911 onwards, and despite his shaky political status, Dean Boklevsky regularly reconfirmed him as a "Lecturer in Maritime Architecture" at the Institute.[3] For years to come Zamiatin would count engineers and colleagues from the Polytechnic amongst his close friends.

During these years he had to keep constantly on the move, lest the police authorities catch up with him, since he was still not officially permitted to reside in St Petersburg under the terms of his internal exile. He came in and out of the city and to the Polytechnic, but he had to find living accommodation on the outskirts, particularly in Sestroretsk, a seaside resort on the Baltic to the north-west of the city, and on the coast at Lakhta, which was a bit closer. He was fortunate that there had been an administrative mix-up about exactly which educational institution he belonged to, which prevented the authorities from dealing with him as they intended: "A summons to appear at the police station. At the police station they showed me a green document concerning the search for a 'University student, Evgeny Ivanovich Zamiatin,' with a view to expelling him from St Petersburg. I declare quite truthfully that I have never been a student at the University, and that there must be some mistake in this document. I remember the police-officer's nose, which was hooked like a question mark: 'Hmmm... I'll have to make some enquiries.' Meanwhile I move to a different district: there I receive another summons six months later, there's another green document, another 'student at the University,' another question mark and further enquiries. And so it went on for five years, until 1911, when they finally corrected the mistake in the green document and I was booted out of St Petersburg."[4]

When they did finally catch up with him in June 1911, Zamiatin told Liudmila that he had been given 3–4 days to leave St Petersburg for good; once again his only hope was for Dean Boklevsky to try to sort things out. In the meantime he would have to take leave from his job, since if the police caught him in the city he could risk three months in jail. Boklevsky wrote to the City Governor asking that Zamiatin should be granted permission to reside in St Petersburg, but this request was turned down "in view of the unfavourable information about engineer [...] Zamiatin which is held by the Okhrana [secret police]."[5] One interim solution Boklevsky came up with was to start sending him away on trips, for example to the Kolomensky factory near Moscow during July 1911. Later that month Zamiatin attended the City Governor's office, where he was presented with a summons to go straight round to the Okhrana; he went over to call on them very apprehensively, destroying some of Liudmila's letters and other documents on the way. In the event they were perfectly courteous, but they did still insist that he should leave St Petersburg, and this was confirmed in an official letter from the City Governor to Boklevsky on 5 August. In September he went down for a visit to Lebedian', and worked there on a paper for submission to a Congress he was hoping to travel to in 1912 in Philadelphia. He didn't get to America for the Congress, but the piece was published in two parts in the monthly *Russkoe sudokhodstvo* (*Russian Shipping*) during 1912 under the title: "The future of maritime shipbuilding and of dredging projects in sea canals and ports."[6]

The documentary records we have for Zamiatin's life during his late 20s are mostly fragmentary, apart from the letters he wrote to Liudmila when they were separated, as happened fairly frequently. She was occupied in various towns in the St Petersburg region with her medical work in midwifery and gynaecology, and he was travelling the length and breadth of the country for his shipbuilding work. They were both tremendously busy, moving around because of work, or anxieties about the police, and later on due to health problems. One theme which, perhaps surprisingly, does not reappear in his letters during these years is that of revolutionary fervour. There is no documentary trace of further active participation in the radical socialist cause by either of them, perhaps because the scrutiny had become too oppressive, or because they were too involved now in their own working and personal lives.

November 1908 had been a turning-point for Zamiatin professionally, but also in his literary career. "I completed my studies in shipbuilding at the Polytechnic Institute. [...] Together with the pages of my design for a turret-deck vessel there lay on my desk the pages of my first story. I sent it off to the journal *Obrazovanie (Education)*." Completed in 1907, *Alone* describes a young student, Belov, who has already spent three months in solitary confinement. Cut off from his revolutionary comrades, he dreams of Lel'ka, with whom he has shared evenings of exhilarating political debate. He exchanges letters with her from his prison cell, and his days become filled with erotic fantasies and dreams of love. She responds with kindness and packages, but eventually reveals that she is about to go away with her husband-to-be. Utterly devastated, Belov throws himself down from the prison gallery to his death. Here Zamiatin's recent experience of imprisonment is developed into a tragic tale, rendered all the more vivid for the author by the fact that in his own case fortune smiled upon him, and the woman he had dreamed of turned out to reciprocate his feelings.

In another story from these years, *A Girl* (1910), the theme of ardour and longing experienced by someone imprisoned by circumstances is transferred to a young girl, Vera. Trapped by her obligations to her invalid mother, she is so overwhelmed by erotic longings that she overcomes her social inhibitions and entices a somewhat embarrassed young man to her home—but as they start to kiss her mother appears and the young man flees, leaving Vera seething with desire. What is striking in the context of the early relationship between Zamiatin and Liudmila, and indeed in the way sexuality unfolds as a key theme in his work, is the nexus of images associating sexual desire with female authority, and even violence. Belov's dreams about Lel'ka involve him serving as a slave to a goddess, longing to be "forgiven," and to be "taken." When Vera attempts to seduce the young librarian, she "seizes his face and neck with her hot, slender fingers and fastens upon him with a kiss—so as to press her teeth against his, and to make their teeth grind against one another. She needs to drink life from him, quickly. Maybe only a few minutes remained." Feeling that they were rather too hysterical in tone, Zamiatin chose not to include either *Alone* or *A Girl* in later volumes of his collected work. In 1928 he wrote: "When I now meet people who've read that story [*Alone*], I feel as awkward as when I used to meet one of my aunties, whose dress I once peed on in public at the age of two."[7] Towards the end of 1908 he also wrote his first published literary criticism, in which he denounced the complacency of a recently-launched St Petersburg journal, *Novye mysli* (*New Thoughts*), whose editors had promised to 'soothe the digestion' by excluding anything polemical—in other words, by ignoring the political and social evils of modern Russia.[8]

Experimenting with fiction had become Zamiatin's new pastime. However, few of the other short stories and novellas written between 1906 and 1912, while he was finishing his studies and then launching his career as a teacher and practitioner of maritime engineering, were even completed.[9] In November 1908, around the time when he submitted *Alone*, he wrote to his sister Aleksandra telling her he had been working on his French and on his engineering (he was about to draw his first salary), but most of all now on literature. He'd started going to literary evenings, where young writers gave readings of their works. His novella *The Tea Rose*, one of a planned cycle of four, had gone down well and provoked a lot of discussion. He was planning to return to Lebedian' that December, since he found it easier to write there.[10] Indeed, whenever he came to visit, his adoring mother would make sure his room and papers were still arranged exactly as he had left them. By the summer of 1910 he was torn as to how to plan his holidays—should he go and spend his free time with Liudmila, or should he spend it writing? "My poor literature! That's also jealous of you, and is also trying to tempt me." A couple of weeks later, echoing Chekhov's famous dictum, he talked of betraying his real wife—literature—in order to spend August with her.[11]

During the years from 1906 to 1912, Zamiatin's intimate life went through great happiness, and then despair. His letters in the early years of his settled relationship to his "dear little mouse" (May 1908) or "lily of the valley" (June 1909) are suffused with the erotic tenderness of the young lover—"I kiss your little creases—like the calyx of the lilies." These "creases" (*ugolki*) will reappear as a distinctive feature of the erotic temptress I-330 in *We*. In 1908 he composed a poem for Liudmila (not something he did often), entitled *Desire*: "I will fall on the fire,/ Into the flame of your embraces."[12] Incidentally, social pressures—not least from his own very religious family—will presumably have ensured that they were in fact officially married, but there is no documentary evidence to tell us the date of any such ceremony. By the summer of 1909 Zamiatin addressed his "darling Lyusin'ka" in one and the same letter as his child, his love, his wife and his tender mother. They may already have begun to realise that it was possible they would never have children by that time: "The instinct of child-bearing, of motherhood... It may even be that <u>that</u> won't happen, and maybe our love will become even stronger as a result? Maybe you'll give to me what you would have given to a child? And maybe it will be sweet for you if <u>I</u> place my head on your breast and take it with my lips like a child, and call you mother? Maybe you as a mother will forgive me—your child—everything? And maybe it will be sweet for me to give you, who are weak and tiny, all my strength, to hold you like a child on my knees and to carry my child in my arms?"[13] In these letters he writes tenderly of her lips, her small teeth, her intimate smells, her menstrual flow, the tender sharpness of her breasts through her blouse, the dear curve of her wrists with their light hairs, and his longing to embrace her legs and lay his head on her knees, or of kissing her breasts through her dress—all images which would be revisited in his fictional writing.

By the end of June 1911, he was reflecting on the dimension authority played in their relationship. The tentative suitor of his early letters still makes an appearance here, and their bond is clearly strong, but the balance of power has clearly altered as well:

> My little mistress. How delightful it is to subordinate myself to you in my thoughts, and to kiss your hands as I kneel before you. But oh, I don't love myself or you for that—for the fact that my love for you, and yours for me, obliges me to subordinate myself to someone, to something—even though that someone is you; for the fact that in some respects I'm inhibited with myself, that in some ways I rein myself in—even if it is done for the sake of the greater purity and fullness of our caresses, of your caresses. I don't know: is it my youth (still), or the habit of too free a morality, or depravity, or simply a physiological phenomenon—but all these women I see every day have an effect, alas, on my curiosity. It would give me pleasure to see how this one, or another, or even a tenth one—some unapproachable goddess—would become shameless and obedient. Most probably I would precisely "see" this from somewhere up above, smiling, forgetting about my own participation. With you, when I'm with you, I'm never like this—apart from you I think no-one knows or has seen the real, unfeigned me.[14]

In keeping with his reading on free love, their relationship was broad enough to acknowledge at least the possibility of infidelity. In August 1910 he confessed to having felt a little wistful at the thought of how full of life and desire she was, and how close she came to giving herself to someone else; he hoped that she would wait just another 10 days or so for him. On the other hand, he admitted in June 1911 that he had spent much of the previous 2–3 weeks with a certain "Maria Andreevna," and that he had kissed her—"though not right to the end"—maliciously enjoying the flirtation, until Maria Andreevna had fallen in love with him; but that she was now gone from their lives, for he had been reluctant to risk any kind of shadow falling between himself and Liudmila.[15]

After five years of a happy erotic relationship with Liudmila, however, a new factor emerged in their lives, which came to affect the vigour and nature of their sexual relations. By the summer of 1911, when he was away working in the Moscow region, he began to suffer the recurrence of an unpleasant condition which had first manifested itself the previous summer:

> Alas, doctor—I am suffering: *cholera chronica*. Do you remember? it's like last year. [...] Over the entire week from last Monday until this one, I've only once attempted to eat a meal, [...] (I was under the impression that I'd recovered) —and alas, it got even worse. All this time I've been feeding myself bouillon and tea. And I'm terribly hungry. I've already taken salol and Hunyadi János mineral water, and then again salol with benzonaphtol—and all to no effect. Yesterday I finally went to the doctor here (very kind, like almost all doctors), and from him I received bismuth with opium. At mealtimes I watch enviously as others consume all sorts of salamis and hors d'oeuvres, while I eat a modest bouillon and semolina, like a little kiddy. Yesterday I felt really terrible, my head was hurting and I was very weak—perhaps because I'd not slept properly on the journey. Today I'm all right.[16]

Zamiatin's misery over his digestive problems, which were to plague him in the form of crippling colitis for years to come, became a central theme of his letters to his medically-trained wife. This particular episode lasted another ten days or so, and he reported diarrhea, a furred tongue and dramatic weight loss, together with discomfort, headaches and weakness; and infuriatingly, the various doctors he turned to all gave him conflicting advice about what to eat. All of this was happening—and perhaps the two were not unconnected—while he was constantly travelling from place to place, both because of his work commitments, and because of the problems he was still experiencing with securing a residence permit.

By August 1911 he had become so ill that he retreated to Lebedian', where he could be looked after by his mother. His need for care therefore turned out to be one means of reconciling himself to the family environment he had shaken off rather defiantly as a young student, and over the next few years he would turn to home quite often for help when he needed to recuperate. Clearly he had succeeded in alarming the family with his letters about how poorly he was, since both parents as well as his brother-in-law came to meet him at the nearby town of Elets: "partly, it seems, because… they believed they were going to have to lift me out of the railway carriage." His first letters to Liudmila that summer from Lebedian' are presented in the form of medical bulletins, displaying what was to become a characteristic preoccupation with every detail of his condition:

> I slept for 7½ hours. Last night I used an enema with bismuth—with no result: nothing, except the enema itself and some mucus.* Slight cramps. The doctor was visiting my father this morning. So they hauled me out too—although I was sure I could tell him more about colitis than he could tell me. And so I told him. The doctor concluded [...] that my diet was excessively strict: I ought to be eating chicken etc. It would be better for me to drink Vichy than Borzhomi water. And so on this first morning I am having cocoa with rusks. At 12—purée of rice and bouillon. At 2.30–3 a 3-course meal: bouillon, purée of chicken (v. tasty), and bilberry blancmange. At 5.30, tea and a half-glass of powdered "Nestlé" for children (a sort of jelly or blancmange—it's rather nice). At 8–8.30 meat bouillon and chicken purée. [...] After I'd taken some food I experienced some quite sharp pains in my stomach, but I determined that these were largely nervous—so without being put off I continued to eat. I had some appetite. My tongue was all right. I didn't use enemas. I went to bed at about 11. Temperature—35.9 degrees. Pulse 48–50. Weakness.
> *No stools during the entire journey.[17]

This was of course a dismal kind of letter for a man of twenty-seven to be writing to his young wife, who would cease to be his wife "in the full sense of that word" for the next six months or more.[18] He spent the best part of a month in Lebedian' that summer, but also travelled to Moscow with his mother at the end of August to consult a specialist, who concluded that it was a case of colitis, together with neurasthenia. He tried further medication, including arsenic injections, and began to feel rather better, eating meat and cauliflower, and even drinking decaffeinated coffee. But by mid-September he had suffered a relapse and was back on the puréed rice, although he returned to work in St Petersburg shortly thereafter.[19]

He spent a miserable Christmas at the end of 1911. His health had deteriorated again, and he found himself writing to Liudmila from a sanatorium to the north-west of Moscow at Podsolnechnaia, attended by Dr Shchurovsky, the specialist he had visited in the summer. He stayed there for six weeks, and his letters were filled with complaints about poor sleep (he was hypersensitive to light, and to noise), the bedbugs in his room, and about the incompetence of the cooks who seemed unable to meet his dietary requirements. Relief was provided by chatting with the other patients, reading books and newspapers, playing the piano and billiards, and a little skating when he was feeling stronger. However, somewhat remarkably, he was also managing to write; this happened towards the end of his stay, when his condition had stabilised and he had managed to gain nearly ten pounds in weight. He finally returned to work in St Petersburg in the third week of February 1912, this time accompanied by his mother so that she could continue to look after him. But six months later he was back in the sanatorium. By now he had devised a grading system to describe his excretions in his letters to Liudmila, using a points system ranging from 4+ to 2=. He was again passing the time with billiards, piano, chess, some fishing, and a little writing. His weight before his admission had fallen to just over nine and a half stones (60 kilograms), but when he realised that he had lost even more weight since arriving, he abandoned the sanatorium in favour of Lebedian'. From there he sent her a melancholy letter: "Things are now such that no woman excites me, and none is dear to me. I'm indifferent to them all. If there is anything in me at all, it is for you. I dare not even give that something a name, because of course it's just a flash of pale summer lightning from a distant thunderstorm. But in any case I feel nothing more for anyone else. That's the truth, perhaps a very sad one, and shaped by the fact that I'm entirely dead and empty, that I treat life with a deliberate shallowness, and that I often hate myself."[20]

The years from 1910 to 1913 seem to have included several utterly depressing moments of this kind, judging by these occasional glimpses we gain into his state of mind. However, this also represented a period when he developed increasing self-confidence, born perhaps out of the habit of a stable relationship, less shaken now by the eddies of self-doubt, and feeling more sure about Liudmila's loyalty and devotion to him. The years from 1905, when they first met, up to the eve of the First World War are also marked by two other manifestations of his "settling down." Firstly, he was developing his professional career as a maritime engineer. And secondly, he was starting to write more substantial and successful stories, which soon began to attract public notice.

1911 was the year in which, by his own account, Zamiatin "first seriously started writing." He recalled travelling back one day by train from Lebedian', with its rich black earth, towards colourless, quotidian St Petersburg: "At some small station, not far from Moscow, I woke up and raised the blind. Right in front of the window, as though mounted in a frame, the physiognomy of a station policeman floated slowly past, with his low forehead crammed down over his face, small eyes like a bear's, and terrible square jaws. I just had time to read the name of the station: Barybino. And that's how Anfim Baryba was born, and the story *A Provincial Tale*."[21] The narrow forehead and angular face, with its iron jaws and square mouth, reappear directly in the opening lines of the story, to introduce the stupid but cunning lad Baryba. The boy is thrown out of his home for failing his school exams, and becomes a feckless opportunist who is first humiliated, then seduced by the grotesquely obese and predatory merchant Chebotarikha; after escaping from her clutches, he goes on to steal money from a monk and betray all his friends. Written in an elliptical style, drawing extensively on the ill-educated vernacular of the Tambov region, the text has a dreamy, lyrical quality. At the same time, it offers a scathing indictment of the moral vacuum in Russian provincial life. Zamiatin mostly wrote the story "in the snow, solitude and quiet. […] If I have any significance in Russian literature, then I am entirely obliged for this to the Petersburg Police Department: in 1911 they sent me out of Petersburg, and for a couple of years I led a very solitary life in Lakhta. There, thanks to the white winter's quiet, and that of green summer, I wrote *A Provincial Tale*."[22]

His first period of incarceration at Podsolnechnaia in 1911–12 had also seen him embarking on another story: "Last week I went mad and started writing a new tale (about life in Vladivostok!) under the impact of some stories told by one chap here in the sanatorium. I wrote two chapters and the entire outline—and then I set it aside. I tire easily."[23] This was the starting point for what would eventually become *At the Back of Beyond*. In fact he was writing these first two major stories in parallel during 1912. Both of them define themselves in their titles by their locations, specifically by their remoteness from the "civilised" metropolis. Like Gogol' with his Ukrainian tales, Zamiatin started his writing career by drawing on what he knew best, the hapless eccentrics and sexual peccadilloes of sleepy provincial life. And like Gogol', he saturated these stories with dialecticisms, and with a mingling of Christian and pagan local lore.

These were also years which involved an enormous number of trips for Zamiatin in connection with his work. Altogether, he would send letters to Liudmila from no fewer than 39 different towns between 1906 and 1917. All of this makes him one of the best-travelled authors of his generation, someone who truly knew the working life of the Russian provinces at first-hand, and who had journeyed from the very top to the bottom of European Russia, frequently along its mighty rivers as well as by rail. It is not unreasonable to speculate that this was one of the many characteristics which would draw him closer to his future literary patron, Maksim Gor'ky—who himself had travelled the length and breadth of Russia twenty years earlier, during the poverty-stricken, brutal childhood on the Volga and vagrant teenage years so vividly described in his autobiographical trilogy, published between 1913 and 1922. One further boost to Zamiatin's literary career came with the lifting at last of the ban on his living in St Petersburg—he benefited from an amnesty for internal and external exiles announced by the Duma early in 1913, as part of the tercentenary celebrations of the Romanov dynasty.[24] Gor'ky returned to Russia in December 1913 after eight years spent in America and Italy as a Bolshevik in exile, thanks to the same amnesty.

As the editor Sergei Postnikov remembered it, the young man he'd never heard of before turned up in St Petersburg in February 1913 and offered him the story *A Provincial Tale* for his moderate left-wing journal *Zavety* (*Precepts*), which had been launched the previous year. He and his fellow-editors R. Ivanov-Razumnik and Viktor Miroliubov immediately recognized its outstanding qualities.[25] They agreed to publish the story, with only one slight alteration, that May. *A Provincial Tale* had an enormous impact: Postnikov collected as many as 300 references to it in reviews, many of which singled out its author as one of a rising generation of talented writers. This link with *Zavety* would soon bring him into contact with a range of established writers, such as Aleksei Remizov and Mikhail Prishvin. Zamiatin presented Ivan Dmitrievich with a printed copy of *A Provincial Tale*, simply inscribed "To father."[26] One wonders what the latter's reaction was to this narrative, recognisably set in Lebedian', in which having been thrown out by his father, Baryba is then crass enough to return home to show off what he has so scurrilously achieved in life—only for his unforgiving and censorious parent to throw him out again. It was scarcely a portrayal of happy filial relations.

It must have been frustrating, at the very moment of his triumphant emergence on to the literary stage, for Zamiatin to find himself then sent far away from St Petersburg, consigned by his work commitments to the other end of Russia, and parted once again from Liudmila. In June 1913 he was assigned for six months to the important southern commercial port of Nikolaev, situated just inland from the Black Sea coast, on the river Bug. He had a tedious journey there, nursing a very sore thumb which he had caught in the door of the train. Although he was based in Nikolaev he had to undertake frequent trips on the port's behalf, carrying out quality control before approving the formal acceptance of vessels or machinery built for Nikolaev in factories at Lugansk, Nikopol'-Mariupol' and Donetsk-Yur'evsk, or the Russian-Belgian factory at Enakievo. From there he reported: "I've had to work about 6 hours a day here. And on some days the work is in the forge itself. The heat is hellish, the maws of the ovens gape all around you, there's hammering and smoke—it's desperately tiring. In the evenings all I've been capable of is lying down and staying there, with a book to glance at."[27]

As the summer of 1913 wore on, the poor food, inconvenient travelling hours and sleeplessness caused his colitis to flare up badly and this, presumably combined with his recent excitement over his literary début, drove him to rebel. He received an instruction to visit yet another factory at Tsaritsyn, but decided to head back to Nikolaev instead, declaring that if he was to be subjected to many more such journeys he would give up working for Nikolaev altogether.[28] He had nevertheless enjoyed one trip which took him along the Volga, and he had "met some curious types" in his wanderings from factory to factory, collecting useful material for his notebooks. These early notebook entries consist of dialect vocabulary lists and descriptions of people and places, together with anecdotes and popular sayings.[29] In Nikolaev he expected a dressing-down because of his premature return and his resolve not to undertake such trips again. But in fact the works manager was very courteous, "either because I was wearing my tunic and badge, or because I dropped into the conversation that I was, by the way, a Lecturer at the Institute. In a word, the whole business ended with that fool Kutkin setting off tomorrow for the factories, while I'm going to stay sitting here." Thereafter his bosses allowed him to work reduced hours, in order to protect his fragile health. While his colleagues did the travelling, he was expected to visit factories nearby, but not every day. This was an important victory. He used the time thereby gained to establish a writing routine (wrily described as "scribbling on paper"), which shifted the balance in his life conclusively away from his technical career to that of a man of letters.[30]

By mid-July he told Liudmila: "I will only go over twice a week to the squadron of dredgers, which is about 8 versts [kilometres] up the river Bug. But otherwise I'm going to sit at home [...], and I'm going to play the piano and maybe write a couple of things." Although he was still suffering from bouts of colitis, he started to sound happier. He described with some enthusiasm a sea journey along the coast to Kherson, where he was testing a pump—and he suggested that Liudmila should come south and join him for an excursion to Kherson, or even across the Black Sea to Constantinople, with the help of a friendly port technician who might be able to contrive for them to travel there without passports.[31] In August he described with amusement his first experience of being handed a bribe, which he promptly returned to the discomfited master of the vessel.

On the strength of his new literary success, he received a number of invitations during the summer of 1913 to contribute to journals, including one from Viktor Miroliubov, who was breaking away from *Zavety* to set up a new journal of his own.[32] He responded with a brief story written towards the end of July called *An Impractical Chap*, about a charming and dreamy Moscow student who ends up getting shot when he fails to run away from Tsarist soldiers. He then spent some time "planing the story down to remove the bits that stuck out," as he put it, and was looking forward to showing it to Liudmila on her forthcoming visit.[33] Apparently, the prototype for his hero was Zamiatin's book-loving friend, Iakov P. Grebenshchikov: "The eternal student

Senia, who perishes on the barricades in the story *An Impractical Chap*, is in fact alive to this day—he's my former comrade from student days Ia. P. G-v. There is nothing in the story of his actual appearance, nor of the real events of his life—and nevertheless it was precisely from this man that the essential tonality of the story was derived. Later on he became the founder of a sect of book worshippers. In the first, hungry years of the revolution he often dropped by to see me, and he always had with him a bulging bundle of books—he bought them with his last resources, with money he'd obtained by selling his trousers to a Tatar. And, made up so as to become unrecognisable, he also appeared on stage in the role of 'the Mamai of 1917' in the story *Mamai*."[34]

Zamiatin also asked his experienced editor Miroliubov for advice, as he was now being pressed to put together a collection of stories. Miroliubov was firmly of the view that he should wait until he had a substantial volume to offer his public: "That which is yours will not escape you."[35] The implicit challenge was one to which Zamiatin responded immediately. True, he described to Liudmila the way he felt he was still sometimes struggling with his fiction: "On Thursday I placed a piece of clean paper in front of me, and a pencil, and said: 'Now come on, you fool, write.' You see, Mila Nikolaevna—sometimes you're simply seized with horror when you sit before a clean white sheet of paper: what to write? How can one write anything? And then that fear of the *primae noctis*, so to speak, passes, and you work, if not with a kind of lustfulness, then at least as though your pencil had been dipped in Vaseline, and it slips easily over the paper. And so in four days 25 pages have been created out of nothing—6 chapters. It's true I'm not pleased with all of it, but there are parts I like. And for the most part those are the unexpected ones, parts that I hadn't planned in advance." He apologised for his vanity in going on about his writing: "But what am I to do, Mila Nikolaevna, when it's the only thing I can cram into the rather empty and tattered sack of my present-day existence."[36] The idiosyncratic form of address he uses to her here was partly a diminutive of Liudmila, partly a variant form of the word for "my dear" (*milaia*), and it would become established as his most typical usage to her in later letters. On 22 September he finished this next new piece he'd been working on, his semi-autobiographical account of the 1905 mutiny on the battleship *Potemkin*, and sent it straight off to Miroliubov under the title *Three Days (From the Past)*.

Liudmila seems to have made a brief visit to Nikolaev during September, and was succeeded there by his mother. Zamiatin was dismayed that Maria Aleksandrovna was only going to stay 2–3 weeks, since he was apprehensive about how he would cope on his own after that. However, his mother had been promising for some time to provide him with a specially trained servant, and this was the moment when Agra (Agrafena Pavlovna Grozdova) arrived to start looking after him. Thereafter she would become the mainstay of the Zamiatins' household, keeping house for them right up until their departure from Soviet Russia in 1931. Still, from the second week of October, after his mother's departure, he was tormented by erotic longing for Liudmila and he wrote plaintive letters imploring her to visit him again. His only consolation was that the new servant was doing a good job of looking after him. He was also looking forward to the planned launch of some new destroyers, an event at which the Tsar himself was supposedly going to be present (he didn't come), and for which he would have to hire a frockcoat, as well as a top-hat. The occasion was, however, attended by Dean Boklevsky. On the invitation card for 18 October Zamiatin underlined the phrase "with your spouse" and added a (presumably regretful) exclamation mark.[37]

Sergei Postnikov and Ivanov-Razumnik had been a little put out that *An Impractical Chap* had not come to them, and they now pressed him to write something new for *Zavety*, promising that this time they would pay him more.[38] So he decided to push himself to complete the Vladivostok story which he'd been toying with since January 1912. By mid-October he had written 40 pages of *At the Back of Beyond*, and once Liudmila had promised that she would come back, he set himself the target of completing it before she arrived.[39] But he soon grew weary: "I just can't do it. Like yesterday—I sat myself down, wrote, and then couldn't sleep until about 3. So, once you're here, I will plunge myself into you, and renew myself, and I'll read you what I've written—and perhaps only then will I start writing again, slowly and gradually. [...] Still—the draft work has been done, and it's turned out 80 pages or more. I'm not too pleased with it for the time being. Or to say more: for the time being I'm just fed up with it, and somehow I can't make myself think about it, but instead, only about... yes, you know of course about what, and about whom."[40]

But while he was waiting for her to arrive he was seized by a fresh burst of inspiration: "I felt the need for something different, so I got to work on a new and entirely unexpected story, which I've almost completed." This was probably *The Womb*, which tells of a peasant woman who murders her husband after his violence causes her to lose her lover's baby. What is most striking in this story is not the issue of justice and retribution, but the sensuality of her pregnancy and of her anticipation of how she will feed her baby. "After all, Afim'ia was a young, well-fed, strong lass, how could she not wish for a child? After all, her womb, like dry land, was waiting for rain in order to give birth. After all, her breasts, like buds in the springtime, had filled out and swelled, and were just waiting to blossom, were waiting to flow with sweet milk. And is there anything sweeter in a woman's life than this: to pour out your whole self, to lose blood and milk, to bear and nurse your firstborn? [...] Oh Lord, how the babe will suck, just here, and here..." Further glimpses of the brutality which shapes a peasant woman's life would occasionally appear in other stories, but the fascinated preoccupation with fertility, so painfully relevant to the childless young Zamiatins, would recur throughout his fiction, right up until the late 1920s.

Liudmila came back to visit him in Nikolaev during the second week of November, and by the end of December he was able to tell her that he was on his way home at last to St Petersburg. He could feel real confidence that a new phase in his life had begun to open up. He was still dependent on working as an engineer and lecturer for his regular income, but the numerous complimentary responses to his *Provincial Tale*, and the surge of inspiration which had led to the creation of such varied stories during 1913, suggested that literature would provide the way forward. His health was still poor, but (notwithstanding his grumbling) he had the support and affection of his wife, as well as the care of his servant, to make his home circumstances more comfortable. The lifting of the official ban on his living in St Petersburg removed a source of petty harassment. He was in a position to hope that 1914 would be a year full of interesting prospects.

Preserved in Zamiatin's Paris archive is an elegant scrapbook covered in black and gold fabric, an immaculately compiled album containing over 150 cuttings about him, dating from 1913 to 1923. Beginning with some of the reviews of *A Provincial Tale*, they convey the immediate and powerful impression he made as a new writer. Several critics felt sure they could identify the influence on his style of the neo-Realism of Aleksei Remizov, with its eccentric blend of Slavonic archaisms and modernist narrative techniques, although Zamiatin himself would subsequently deny that he had read much of Remizov at the time he started writing. One Moscow reviewer would fall into a trap where many would follow, declaring that with all his colloquialisms the unknown Zamiatin must be "a self-taught man. There is no doubt that this is not a bookish man, not a man who has absorbed the cleverness of the printed sheet, but rather all the quivering, powerful breath of real life. He writes as he speaks." Boris Eikhenbaum, writing in July 1913, was much shrewder about the supposed autodidact. Welcoming a new and very original talent from whom much could be expected in the future, he argued that the link with Remizov was not through imitation, but rather an organic similarity in their approaches to narration. Remizov had made a close study of Russian folktales to achieve an epic narrative effect, and in Zamiatin's work too the author is simply absent: "You have no idea what Zamiatin himself is thinking, or what language he himself speaks in."[41]

The year 1914 began well, with the publication of *An Impractical Chap* and of *Three Days (From the Past)* in the first and second issues respectively of Miroliubov's *Ezhemesiachnyi zhurnal dlia vsekh* (*Monthly Journal for All*). Zamiatin published some book reviews there as well, and maintained his connection with this journal for the next couple of years. In mid-February, prompted by another new acquaintance, the writer Aleksei Tolstoy, he wrote to Nikolai Angarsky to offer his Moscow publishing house the volume of stories he had now assembled, consisting of *A Provincial Tale, At the Back of Beyond, An Impractical Chap, Three Days* and *A Girl*.[42] He evidently received an encouraging reply. But on 12 April a further brief note to Angarsky requested the immediate return of all the stories.[43] The project had been scuppered by the scandal which erupted that March over the publication of *At the Back of Beyond* in the third number of *Zavety*, the first specifically literary scandal in Zamiatin's troubled relations with the political authorities of the day. For as soon as it came out the entire edition of *Zavety* was withdrawn by the censors and "placed under arrest," due to the story's supposed immorality. In the work, set in Russia's Far Eastern naval base at Vladivostok, a naïve young narrator from Tambov is appalled and intrigued to hear of the sexual practices of the stern officer Shmit and his beautiful little wife Marusia. He cannot understand her remark that she loves even Shmit's cruelties, especially when she is blackmailed into sleeping with the General and then forced to endure coldness, beatings and marital rape by Shmit. She cannot escape, and yet she does not quite want to, because she understands that his cruelties are a dreadful manifestation of a deep passion and love, and that the suffering is something which they both share. In the final lines of the story the narrator drinks his own sorrow away with strained gaiety, "that same desperate merriment with which ancient Rus' [traditional Russia], driven to the back of beyond, makes merry nowadays." The "Resolution" passed by the St Petersburg Committee for Print Matters on 11 March 1914 concluded:

> The tale is divided into 24 chapters and is devoted to a description of the inner daily life of a small military unit in the Far East. This life is depicted in the most repellent fashion. Zamiatin does not stint on vulgar colours, in order to give the reader a deeply offensive impression of Russian officers. With this purpose Zamiatin scrapes together in his tale a whole series of trivial facts, and doesn't hesitate before the most indecent scenes. [...] According to his description Russian officers do nothing but swear and beat their soldiers, indulge in depravity, get drunk, and stir up brawls in the Assembly in the presence of foreign officers invited for a celebration. [...] At the same time Zamiatin, determined still further to humiliate the officers depicted in the tale, describes the most intimate aspects of married life, those unsuitable for public dissemination, and uses pornographic expressions, thereby offending against decency.[44]

This decision was reconfirmed on 22 April: the editor, N.M. Kuz'min, attempted to have the ban lifted by offering to remove the incriminating passages, but the court decreed that "it was not possible to remove from this story the individual passages which are utterly indecent, because these are so numerous, and equally because the entire story in its content and its plot is blatantly immoral." So in the end the journal was hastily reprinted, with Viacheslav Shishkov's story *A Rapid Trial* in place of Zamiatin's, even though that meant that the page numbering was not consecutive. A fairly light-hearted response to all this fuss came in the first week of April from his sister Aleksandra, in the form of a postcard of his school in Lebedian': "V[ladimir] V[asil'evich] Volkov — her husband] and I were planning to go abroad this summer, and I was on fire with dreams of Venice and Switzerland, but alas he was not granted leave, since Kosykh [Director of the School] is going away himself, and so I had to cool down again. I don't know whether we shall get away anywhere. And so, have they sent the author of *At the Back of Beyond* to the back of beyond yet? Daddy is going to the Crimea. I have no other news. I kiss you. Your sister A.V."[45] *At the Back of Beyond* would not in fact be published until 1923.[46]

After Nikolaev, Zamiatin was not allowed to escape his work commitments entirely, even though his stomach continued to torment him throughout these years. In the second week of April 1914 he was obliged to leave all the literary brouhaha in St Petersburg behind, and set off travelling for his shipbuilding work again—this time, though, it was abroad, to Germany. He began his second ever trip outside Russia with a few days in Berlin. Like all Russian travellers, he had to get used to the fact that the calendar in Western Europe was thirteen days out of step with the one at home, so as with many of his later letters from abroad he used the dual dating system (here inaccurately), giving the date in his first letter to Liudmila as 14/23 April. What is more unusual is that he even clung to Russian clock time as well, giving the time as 9pm, Petersburg time. He described his day spent shopping for clothes for the two of them, in the overwhelming heat; he also visited the Tiergarten, which he found delightful with its lime trees and its tulips. The next day he went to the Zoo, where he was enchanted by some African baby antelopes who could lick their own eyes, and a curlew with a sky-blue tongue. He was now joined by another engineer from the Commercial Ports Authority, E. A. Romanov. They visited the Palais de Danse, where he was amazed by the tango, and the following evening they left Berlin for the port of Stettin. It seems likely that he was going there in connection with the Tsarist navy's contract for the enormous icebreaker, *Tsar Mikhail Fedorovich*, which was built there by Vulkan-Werke A. G. and delivered to Tallinn in Estonia later that year.[47] We do not know exactly how long he stayed in Germany in that last spring before the War.

A second journey for work that summer took Zamiatin away for about 10 days through central Russia (to Moscow, then Nizhny Novgorod, along the river Oka to Murom, and along the Volga to Rybinsk and Arzamas, before returning to St Petersburg on 9 June). While he was in Moscow he attempted to track down an address for their friend from revolutionary days, Boris Krylov. His letter to Liudmila of 4–5 June was written sitting in the bow of a steamer going up the Oka river, enjoying the breeze and the scent of the forests. He has been relishing the sing-song pronunciation of an "elegant" young lady from Murom, and on the boat he stayed up late with another local character, jotting down the words of some songs with great interest. The prospect of acquiring more such materials if he travelled further by boat cheered him up when his visit to the factory at Kulebaky turned out to be ghastly—a steamer 12 hours late, unimaginably aggressive mosquitoes, a room which was damp, smelly, and situated directly across from the billiards room, and carpenters who started work at crack of dawn.[48]

In July he retreated to Lebedian' for a couple of weeks of rest and quiet. He travelled there by train with an agreeable general, with whom he discussed politics, the recent near-fatal knife attack by a woman on the monk Rasputin, and the strike in St Petersburg which had brought thousands of workers on to the streets to demonstrate in support of the oil-field workers of Baku, who had suffered police oppression. Perhaps the subject of "politics" also included the assassination in Sarajevo on 28 June of Archduke Franz Ferdinand. At his family home he spent the time in a tennis shirt, playing croquet, reading Chekhov in the shade since it was so hot, and picking and eating the ripening pears and apples—with predictable consequences for his stomach. Despite this material comfort, his letters to Liudmila were critical: "Ah, my darling, I despise Lebedian' just as you do." […] "It's dreadful, darling, dreadful: how contemptible Lebedian' is."[49] On this occasion his ire seems to have been aroused specifically by the gigantic fleas which had prevented him from sleeping properly. Meanwhile, Liudmila was over in the Urals with her family, in Zlatoust, typically having a holiday without him. By 25 July, the main topic of his letters of course shifted to the looming war, which had already caused the trains to run less regularly and threatened the closure of the daily newspaper *Rech'* (*Speech*), which he tried to read faithfully whenever he was travelling, and which now seemed to be adopting a more "petriotic" line, as he put it. From 1906–17, this newspaper was the organ of the Kadet [Constitutional-Democratic] Party; Zamiatin's loyalty to it seems to reflect a clear shift in his politics, away from his youthful Socialist-Revolutionary ideals to a more moderate socialism. In the summer of 1914 patriotism seemed to be the general sentiment: "Yesterday in Lebedian' everyone except me went up and down with portraits and flags, and cried hip-hip. Whereas I sat at home and wrote."[50]

The weather then cooled down, and this helped him get down to work on his latest story, *The Town of Alatyr'*: "it's almost written, there's just one part of a chapter to go. There are 9 brief chapters in all, making about 20 pages of typescript. For the moment all this is of course just in draft, but I think it really won't be bad: it's quite amusing."[51] This was another gentle satire of the sleepy provinces, involving the police chief's daughter Glafira, desperate to be kissed and jealous of her own cat suckling its kittens, the ludicrous aspiring poet Kostya

Edytkin, and a postmaster of princely rank who proselytises the use of Esperanto. On 28 July (the date of the formal declaration of war) he wrote another very short story in the space of a single day, possibly *The Sergeant-Major*. On that day he could hear the bells ringing in all the churches, on the occasion of the opening of the relics and canonisation of the 17th-century Bishop Pitirim of nearby Tambov, which made him feel that all the people should be out dancing.

He believed he was very likely to be summoned back to work before long, because of the War; presumably the state of his health rendered him unfit at the age of 30 for active service, and in any case his specialism would have been of strategic importance. The State Duma had recently voted to divert funds for shipbuilding and port construction away from commercial purposes in favour of defence and the strengthening of the Black Sea Fleet. He assumed this would mean that only he, and one other engineer employed on the icebreaker projects, might be retained; many of the rest of his acquaintances were likely to be called up, or reassigned to military tasks. In the meantime, he was missing Liudmila badly, and offered to come and join her in Zlatoust, where he had already written to her six times.[52] We do not know whether he carried out this plan, but soon he was indeed back on duty, and parted from her for the fourth time that year. He left Petrograd (it had been renamed in a patriotic gesture since the outbreak of war in August) on 7 November 1914, on his way back south. This time the wartime disruptions to the train timetable meant it took him over 48 hours to reach Nikolaev. The very next day he had to set off for Kherson, where as before he was involved in the testing of pumps. The temperature had dropped to 10 degrees below zero. He found both the work and the company dull, and complained that he did not even have *Rech'* to read; instead, he was reading about submarines, and stories from the *Mir prikliuchenii (World of Adventures)* magazine:

> I've just got back from a walk. The samovar is wheezing on the table. Outside the window it's frosty, the sky's like crystal, and there are Christmas stars. The air and the sky are the only two decent things in Kherson—the rest is rubbish, especially the bread rolls. Fortunately, I find I have to take the air quite a lot of the time. I get up just after nine. Towards eleven it's our duty, mine and the old man's (we decided to take turns) to go to the pump. Lunch at the factory there is at one: ham, salmon, butter, cheeses (excellent), a ten-pound jar of caviar, tea. We're on duty

> at the pump from 11 until four, and on deck all the time. At five or thereafter it's time for dinner. After dinner I read and—*horreur*—I sleep for an hour, or an hour and a half. Then I go for a walk. Then it's time to start over again.[53]

To his dismay, it appeared that he would have to stay in Kherson for some time, and he had to ask Liudmila to warn the Institute that he would be unable to teach his classes in the Shipbuilding and Engineering Faculties. By 16 November, he had discovered a bedbug in his room, which reduced him to further *horreur*, so he was obliged to move. But then to his delight the river began to freeze over, and since that meant that his work would have to be suspended, he was now counting on leaving by 22 November.

In December, Miroliubov pressed Zamiatin for a new contribution, which led to the appearance in the first volume of *Ezhemesiachnyi zhurnal* for 1915 of the story *The Sergeant-Major*, about an illiterate but forceful peasant in the 1860s, at the time of the Emancipation of the Serfs. Evgeny Lundberg from *Sovremennik* (*The Contemporary*) also approached him, and he gave them his sentimental sketch *April*. And on 12 March 1915 he received a note from Arkady Gornfel'd at *Russkie Zapiski* (*Russian Notes*), informing him that his story *Salted Beef* had been accepted for publication.[54] A further mark of his new standing as an established writer had come at the end of January 1915, in the form of a request from the distinguished literary and social historian Semen Vengerov for him to provide information for the second edition of his *Critical and Biographical Dictionary of Russian Writers and Scientists*. In February he was elected a member of the "Society for Assistance to Needy Writers and Scientists," with the support of Vengerov and Ivanov-Razumnik.[55]

However, by 30–31 March Zamiatin found himself once again on his way to Nikolaev, complaining as ever about the overcrowding, the heat, the smoke-filled compartment and the porter's failure to obtain a first-class ticket for him—only the aspirin Liudmila had provided gave any relief. Then he discovered that there were no fast trains any more, and he wouldn't even get to Nikolaev until the evening of 1 April—"*horreur*, curses, the devil!" Regretfully, he was just finishing his Jack London book, although when he did get to Nikolaev he started reading more Chekhov—probably the recently-published volumes of his correspondence—as well as his constant companion, the *Rech'* newspaper. This trip lasted about a week.

His second trip of 1915 took him literally the length and breadth of European Russia in order to visit factories: starting from Petrograd on the Baltic in the first week of May, he travelled via Saratov down to Astrakhan, situated on the mouth of the Volga where it flows into the northern end of the Caspian Sea. Again the train caused him distress, first of all because of the heat, and then when he found bedbugs even in the "international" carriage. Next he travelled all the way back to Iaroslavl', 200 kilometres north-east of Moscow, where the glories of the Volga did much to offset his insomnia. He then went southeast back along the Volga, and turned north-east up the Kama river to Sarapul, which is not far from Perm in the western Urals. Three weeks later, on 8 June, he was back in hateful Astrakhan, which stank of hydrogen sulphide, and where the assaults by the flies were "worse than those of the Germans." He then travelled to the Caspian port of Baku in Azerbaidzhan, at the south-eastern tip of the Caucasus mountains; but he enjoyed the three-day sea journey there, and by 17 June he was in the Georgian capital Tiflis [Tbilisi], which he found very attractive, before driving north along the Georgian Military Highway, a beautiful route over the high mountains, to Vladikavkaz. Thence he went on to Lebedian', where he spent the rest of June and early July. However, instead of going back to Petrograd after that, as he had expected, he received a telegram instructing him to travel via Moscow to Nizhny Novgorod on the Volga. He therefore wrote to Liudmila inviting her to travel with him from Nizhny for a day's journey along the Volga to Kazan', after which he would accompany her back up the river all the way to Rybinsk, a trip together of some 600 kilometres, all of which he reckoned would take her 5–6 days. We do not know whether she accepted his sudden invitation.

At the end of July he was on the move yet again, but this time heading north. First he travelled more or less due east from Petrograd to Vologda, then another 500 kilometres due north the next day, to arrive at his destination, the White Sea port of Arkhangel'sk. There he found that the temperature was more like St Petersburg in October, and he felt cold even in a thick woollen coat. When he discovered that there were no rooms to be had in the town's hotels, he was obliged to travel onwards to one of the icebreakers, the *Canada*, which he was there to inspect, and beg for a cabin on board. He found the onboard routine a bit strict for his liking, especially the early and noisy start to the day at 7am. But then the sun came out, and he began to enjoy things more, especially when, after inspecting two submarines, he was invited to eat with an engineer, and relished the salmon and the pies baked with local cloudberries and whortleberries. On 8 August he travelled on to Soroka, on the steamer *Murman* — as chairman of the expedition he had claimed for himself a large single cabin, about which he felt slightly shamefaced — but was then glad to be turning for home. The trip was to inspire in him two powerful stories about the fishing folk of the Arctic region, *Africa* and *The North*. After three drafts, he had completed the first of these by 16 October. The writer B.A. Lazarevsky noted: "The young, as yet not very well-known author Zamiatin read out his story *Africa*… The story is like music, against the background of maritime industrial life. You would think, what with the ferocious cold, how could there be a place with those harpooner-whalers for elegant dreams of love? And yet… it all came out tenderly and touchingly in his work. […] Later we talked about it at length. Remizov and Kliuev were in ecstasies about it, and so were the others…" Zamiatin had been acquainted with the eccentric and erudite Aleksei Remizov since at least 1914, and had developed by now a confident, bantering familiarity with him.[56]

That October there was then a technical problem over the first publication of his stories in book form, under the title *Provincial Life*. This was so full of misprints that he insisted the entire print-run should be recalled and destroyed, and he got his friend, the historian and literary scholar Pavel Shchegolev (the man who had graduated from Zamiatin's school in Voronezh a few years before him), to support him.[57] On 8 February 1916, he was finally able to present Liudmila with a copy of *Provincial Life*, which (now reprinted properly) ran to just under 200 pages.[58] Other texts Zamiatin wrote during 1915 include a first draft of his folksy tale of peasant love *Stubborn Folk (Ivan and Maria)*, and his miniatures *The Little Deacon* and *Pet'ka (A Bad Lad)*. *The Little Deacon* tells the story of a naïve provincial priest who resolves to clamber up to the very clouds on the mountain where Moses stood — only to discover when he reaches his destination that inside the clouds there's nothing but darkness, cold and damp. *Pet'ka*, about a child who wrecks a new toy by investigating how it works, was probably commissioned by Remizov as a contribution to a volume to raise funds for a children's home, although when the volume did appear in 1916 under the title of *Gingerbread for Orphaned Children*, Zamiatin's contributions were two other sketches, *The Little Pictures* and the "fairy-tale" *Stupid Angel Dormidon*. Most of these early stories of Zamiatin's continue to draw upon his profound knowledge and fondness for the Russia of old, with its traditional rural settings and its sing-song peasant diction. What is absent here entirely is any sense of the urban present, or of radical politics. This nostalgic focus is reflected in a glimpse of his reading during March-July 1915, provided by a list of the books Zamiatin borrowed from Iakov Grebenshchikov, as he had been doing regularly since at least the end of 1912: a glossary of prison and other vernacular terms for "having a drink"; a volume of fairytales from the Perm region; a translation of a German book on the sciences of physiognomy and chiromancy; an 18th-century children's book about the Orthodox faith; and a book by the folklorist S.V. Maksimov on "dark powers."[59]

He was now being assailed with invitations from all sides: next it was Aleksandr Izmailov from the journal *Birzhevye vedomosti* (*Stock-Exchange Gazette*), inviting him to submit a couple of brief stories, and promising that the editorial board would not constrain him with regard to the mood of his works, or restrict any references to the War.[60] During February he worked on a draft of *God—A Story*, continuing his mocking depiction of religion, where a lachrymose postman seems like a god to the cockroach living in his room. On 25 February, he must have been pleased by a review in his favourite newspaper, *Rech'*, where Iuly Aikhenval'd welcomed the *Provincial Life* collection enthusiastically: "There is no doubt that with this book he enters our literature as a master, with a very individual physiognomy and a lively, glittering talent."[61] That day too the distinguished artist and illustrator Dmitry Mitrokhin offered him tickets for the private view of one of the 'World of Art' exhibitions, "and also to say to you once again what a delight your stories are, and how much I like them. As for *Alatyr'*, well I would like to get straight on and create some illustrations for it—it's such a charming and dreadful grotesque."[62] On the last day of February the poet Sergei Esenin presented him with a copy of his *Radunitsa* (*All Souls' Day*), which had appeared at the end of January, with an inscription to Zamiatin as a storyteller "with a bow, and with ardent faith."[63]

However, just as he was celebrating all these welcome marks of recognition, Zamiatin found himself obliged to leave Russia and go abroad again. On 16 January Remizov had inscribed a copy of his recent stories in comical English to: "Sir Eugene John Zamiatin."[64] He and his friends had known for some time that he was about to be seconded and sent on a protracted trip to England, as a contribution to the war effort. But all the excitement was clouded by a further, sad event.

On 5 March 1916, Zamiatin's father Ivan Dmitrievich died of pneumonia, and his son reached Lebedian' just too late to see him for one last time. He observed that he found this occasion even more dreadful than that of his mother's death nine years later, even though he loved his father less than his mother.[65] By 12 March he had been issued with a passport for foreign travel, and he set off for England a couple of weeks later. It would be eighteen months before he returned to his native country.

Chapter 3:

From Petrograd to Newcastle upon Tyne (1916–1917)

No longer regarded now as quite such a subversive young man, Zamiatin was sent to England in March 1916 on an official mission by the Russian Minister of Trade and Industry, Prince Shakhovskoi. The Prince had applied to His Imperial Majesty to permit Zamiatin, in his capacity as a civilian maritime engineer, to travel abroad in order to supervise the construction of icebreakers in Britain. As Zamiatin later explained: "During the years of the Great War the Baltic Sea—that 'window into Europe' which Peter the Great had cut 200 years before—was closed off by the German Fleet. In order to maintain communications with her Allies, Russia was obliged to cut a new 'window into Europe'—far in the icy North, through the White Sea and the Arctic Ocean. A whole squadron of icebreakers was urgently needed for the purpose. Every inch of the Russian shipyards was taken up at that time by new battleships and transport ships, and for that reason the icebreakers had to be ordered in Britain—three at Messrs Swan Hunter & Wigham Richardson's at Wallsend, one at Armstrong's in Newcastle, two at South Shields and one in Glasgow. I spent nearly two years in Britain working as chief surveyor of three icebreakers."[1] As a civilian, Zamiatin would not normally have been entitled to be paid expenses for such a trip, but the circumstances of war altered that. By 22 February 1916, he was granted permission to travel and given an allowance of 20 roubles per day, plus 350 roubles of travelling expenses.[2] His passport for foreign travel contains an exit stamp delivered in Petrograd on 24 March.[3]

The links between Newcastle shipbuilding and the Russian government had been established several decades earlier. In 1852–53, Charles Mitchell had founded his Yard at Low Walker on the Tyne, and after building a number of ships for the Russians he was invited by the Tsarist government in 1862 to set up a yard in St Petersburg, to spearhead the shift from wooden ships to iron vessels. In 1868, in recognition of his services, Tsar Alexander II awarded Mitchell the Order of St Stanislas, 2nd Class. In 1871 the Grand Duke Constantine came up to Newcastle to visit the Low Walker Yard, and was entertained at "Mr Mitchell's magnificent residence at Jesmond Towers." A newspaper account of the visit reported that "altogether, the firm have been more intimately concerned in the material and social progress of Russia than any other British firm." Charles Mitchell, together with his partner Henry Swan, built over 90 vessels for Russia. In 1882 the firm merged to become Armstrong Mitchell, and after Mitchell's death in 1895, it merged again in 1897 to become Armstrong Whitworth, employing 25,000 men by the turn of the century. In 1895–96, in a massive project which took four years to complete, the icebreaking train ferry *Baikal* was assembled in Newcastle, then dismantled again and transported in nearly 7,000 packages to Siberia, where it was reassembled under the supervision of engineers from the Tyne and launched on Lake Baikal in 1899. This provided the vital link between the two halves of the Trans-Siberian railway before the construction of a rail link round the southern shores of the lake. 1895 marked the beginning of the firm's contracts for purpose-built icebreakers, and they gained a reputation for being at the forefront of their design by the early 1900s. Amongst other notable icebreakers produced at Low Walker was the enormous *Ermak*, completed in 1899; this was the first such vessel to be designed for polar use.[4] Zamiatin's trip thus represented just one further link in a very long-established Anglo-Russian commercial relationship.

    He set off from Petrograd on 24 March, and parted from Liudmila at Beloostrov Station, near the Finnish border. His first messages home were sent three or four days later from the Finnish-Swedish border, and then from Christiania [Oslo], which he had finally reached after having had to share his train compartment with "…a real German. *Affreux*!" In Christiania he noted that there was already a time difference of one hour between Russia and Norway, "but I am stubbornly not going to alter my watch. Nor will I alter it in England, where the difference will be 1 hour and 40 minutes. And that way, it will feel as though my régime hasn't altered: I'll be going to bed late, and getting up late." Soon after his arrival in England, on 21 May, Britain adopted for the very first time the practice of putting clocks forward an hour to create British Summer Time. A week later he was still managing not to get up until 10:30 or 11, much to the astonishment of the rather slovenly English maid, and on 12 June he was still resisting the new-fangled notion: "Some days I get up at 10, which is really 9, because they have so-called summer-time here."[5]

Another disorienting factor was again the discrepancy between the Russian Julian calendar and the Gregorian calendar used in Western Europe, which meant that he had jumped forward 13 days, well into April, as soon as he set foot outside Russia. His passport was therefore stamped on departure from Norway on 11 April, confirming that he was travelling in order to inspect icebreakers being built for the Russian government in Newcastle and Glasgow.[6] Every letter Zamiatin sent Liudmila while he was away carried the two dates, so his very first English missive, sent from the magnificent Hotel Cecil on the Strand in London, is dated 3/16 April. He soon started to date his letters the other way round, with the local date taking priority and placed first. He signed these letters to his wife of ten years surprisingly formally, as E Zamiat, EvgZ or Evg Zamiat, E. Zamiatin or Evg. Zamiatin.

He travelled to England from Bergen on a rather scruffy ship, instead of the smart *Haakon* as intended: "There were strong winds all the way over, and the ship was rolling terribly. I spent half the journey lying down, and missed one main meal and a breakfast. I was thinking that you, poor Milusha, would have simply died from such a pitching and tossing. The suitcases slid across the floor, the bottles flew off the table on to the floor, and you banged your head against the walls as you walked. We travelled for about 40 hours." On arrival he was dismayed by his first impressions of his destination: "What a horrible town Newcastle is. All the streets and all the houses are identical, do you understand, absolutely identical, like those grain stores in Petersburg near the Aleksandr Nevsky Monastery." Zamiatin was met at the Norway Wharf in Newcastle by a Russian engineer who saw him through the formalities and accompanied him the next day down to London: "it's a journey of about 6 hours. And just the same sort of grain store towns flashed past the window, all the same, all neatly clipped. It's terrible, what a lack of imagination!"[7] His passport was stamped by the Aliens' Registration Offices in Newcastle, and then Bow Street in London, on 13 and 14 April. He spent a rather lonely first week in London: he met a couple of Russians, including the distinguished journalist and literary scholar Zinaida Vengerova, but mostly did shopping, visited the tailor, and then over the Easter weekend travelled around the city on the top deck of an omnibus and sat in a park. He also discovered that drinking with your spoon still standing in your teacup was considered a grave social faux-pas (a detail he would re-use in *The Islanders*). "Up until then I had only once been in the West, in Germany, where Berlin turned out to be an 80% condensed version of St Petersburg. Whereas in England it was different: in England everything was new and strange, rather as in Alexandria or in Jerusalem that time."[8]

He was only expecting to stay for a month in Newcastle after his return from London on 23 April, before travelling on to establish himself for the rest of his stay in Glasgow. However, within a week of his return north it emerged that he would have to stay put in Newcastle, much to his disappointment: "It's a big city, but utterly dull. The Russians here are not my sort of people, the theatres are completely stupid, [...] and the English are terribly virtuous..." His first few weeks were spent lodging at 10 Cavendish Place. He was invited to a party by the Russian consul and out of misery drank more than he had for six years, arriving home to his landlady after 3 in the morning.[9] He complained to Remizov about the food: "I'm not living too well in England, where they feed me with nothing but ginger and pepper, which are only good as a preparation for fiery Gehenna."[10] By 24 May, he had moved into permanent lodgings in the house of a shipbroker at 19 Sanderson Road, in the very respectable district of Jesmond, close to an attractive park with a ravine and waterfall called Jesmond Dene, which had been created for the city by the shipbuilding magnate Lord Armstrong in the 1880s. "My lodgings are in the English fashion: a dining-room, sitting-room and kitchen downstairs, a small study, bedroom and bathroom on the first floor, and on the second floor a room for the maid and an attic—and that's the entire house. But it's cold in the rooms, empty and dull." One thing the house did have was a roulette board, and by late June he decided to try and relieve his loneliness by inviting some guests round to play: "The Russian consul and his wife, the Italian consul, the French consul and his wife, a Portuguese captain and a Spaniard, secretary to the Russian consul. An amusing little group, wouldn't you say? But all the same I'd prefer Iashka Grebenshchikov to the whole lot of them."[11] Another stamp in his passport suggests that he went down to visit London again early in July.

Zamiatin's first six months in war-time England are documented in the thirty or more missives he sent home to Liudmila, and by very little else. They constitute a sustained wail of misery, boredom, loneliness, frustration and reproachfulness. At first, his reproaches are directed against himself. He grieves: "that I have so ruined your life. And this is what I thought: perhaps I met you a little too early. It should have been later, when I had had time to 'come off the boil' as they say in Tambov about cabbage soup; you should have been my last love. And as it is, perhaps it will happen that you will be my first and my last love (that's really your decision), but it is all painful."[12] Her first letter took about three weeks to reach him, and then there was nothing more for a further week. This must have been particularly infuriating in a city where there were still 4–5 postal collections and 3–4 deliveries every day.[13] By late May he began to suggest that she might consider joining him in England, and when he received no reply for a further two weeks, he told her that his longing for her had simply made him ill: "It is a much stronger attack than in Nikolaev in 1913, because at least I'm not a physical larva any more."[14] This did not mean that he was not still suffering with his stomach, and he also repeatedly asked her to send him the medicine on which he relied. On 18 June he sent her a telegram, in an English which had clearly not yet become fluent (he'd been taking lessons from an Italian): "If you wish and could come New-Castle our quarter transmit with furniture till January or leave furniture conservation telegraph answer Zamiatin. [sic]"[15] When she did finally reply to this suggestion that she should rent out their flat or put the furniture into store, it was to refuse—twice—to come. He wrote very bitterly on 27 July:

> It was important that your decision should be an entirely free one (you know what a fan of freedom I am). […] I will not tempt you any more, or myself, with the thought of your coming to England. […] And in fact, it was quite entertaining, as all new things are, because hitherto it has rarely happened that women refuse me. […] And truly, *chère* Usova, you are a *femme fatale*: you are destined, it seems, to arouse every passion in me, […] one after another. This is becoming dangerous… […] Only to think—here's a man of well over 20, who's travelled far away, and by night he occupies himself with dreams predominantly coloured in pale blue, pink and bright red, instead of peacefully sleeping. […] What better solution than to summon up that most correct and merciless police constable, reason, as you were the first to do and as I have done now. […] And as for what you wrote: "I have grown plumper, which seems wrong and shameful when you are away," well that's nonsense. Youth and health are the things you should be least ashamed of; you can feel ashamed of being not youthful and not healthy, such as I am.

Rather meanly, he mentioned having received a letter from Maria Mogilianskaia, whom Liudmila had "poisonously" described in a letter as one of the "adornments" in his life, but told her the content of the letter was "too intimate" for him to tell her about it. If she thinks of him at all, he asks her to send more books and medicine: "And if you don't send them, well, thank you for your former kindnesses." In an angry postscript he added: "I just happened to remember: ten years ago you weren't afraid to come and join me in Helsingfors [Helsinki]. How much water has flowed under the bridge since then; has it all flowed away? That was just a platonic remark: the question of your travelling now has been decided, amen. You have decided, and I have decided too."[16] Five days later there was more of the same:

> No one has ever filled me with such bitterness as you. [...] All the same, I still unfortunately haven't managed to rid myself of these obsessive thoughts about you. I can't write, or work, or sleep. I'm not living, but writhing. [...] How could it happen that you don't understand how much I need you now, and how much I want to see you? If you had been your former self, the person I left half a year ago, as I remember you in Beloostrov, it wouldn't have occurred to you to hide behind this excuse about the difficulties of the journey. [...] I don't know what has changed. Perhaps you place too much value on the charms of a peaceful "life with no grief," of life without me. Perhaps you've found for yourself something more suitable and comfortable than I am, I who am always, like my "little deacon," reaching for a heaven which doesn't exist. Well, all right then, I won't stand in your way. [...] And yet now more than ever before I've understood what you mean to me. And to know that I've discovered this too late... Perhaps I won't write for a while, until I've driven this all out of myself.[17]

Soon after this, he received several letters from her, as usual in erratic order. The first surviving, rather resentful letter from her in Petrograd is dated 15 July (the 28th in England):

> And so you want me to change my decision if you are going to stay until January? If you want that, if you need me to come, and if it's not a passing whim, then I will come. Only you'll really need to bear in mind that I've not yet entirely liberated myself from those "dark forces" which you so dislike in me.

And altogether I'm far from being the person I would like to be. So—there's one of the main reasons why I refused previously. Are you not afraid? Think about it. It was mainly for you that I didn't want to come, just you remember that. As for external reasons, bear in mind that I probably wouldn't be able to go back to the infirmary afterwards, since my relations with the senior doctor are very tense. [...] We'd have to keep the flat on. Do I need to tell you how much I want to be with you, about how miserable I'll be if you stay a long time in England, and I'm left here? I don't think I need to. [...] And don't forget that in the autumn the climate will be even worse, as will therefore your health. And that here your "Beautiful Lady" [Blok's name for his muse], Literature, awaits you. [...] And I am scared of the journey![18]

This went a little way towards appeasing him: "Well, it seems I wasn't right about everything. But I am right about the fact that your not coming here is a mistake. Your refusals and your failure to reply to my last telegram poured so much cold water over me that my longings have begun to fade. But this will cost me dearly. I'm living with an erratic heartbeat and a permanent lump in my throat. Everything leaves me indifferent." The next day he was a little more conciliatory: "I tried to write, but I can't. So again I'm trying every way of wearing myself down: on Saturday I didn't get home until 8am—we played cards, made merry and drank. But it's not much help." On 9 August he'd spent half the previous night in the front garden, enjoying the beautiful weather: "And I so despised you for not being here—it would have been such an extraordinarily sharp and special night. It's bitter and painful for me to lose you, and with every day I sense you going farther and farther away. And soon you will be completely gone. And out of sheer stubbornness I will simply help you to leave."[19]

This flood of needy complaints finally proved more than Liudmila could bear; on that same day he received the news he'd been longing for, and replied with a telegram: "Lettre reçu arrivez vite telegraphiez Zamiatin [sic]."[20] On 10 August, she wrote to say that she had just received his letter of "the 14th of July" (presumably the long and bitter one of 27 July cited above):

Evgeny Iv[anovich], ever since your departure I've not ceased wishing I could be with you, in other words, to travel to England. And if our relationship had been a "civilised" one, then believe me, I would immediately have replied to your first telegram with a full acceptance. But I could still recall all too well how you sought refuge from me in the journey to England. I haven't yet forgiven you all the horrors of last winter... You haven't once given me to understand that I am no longer for you that "monster" whom you had to flee. [...] What makes you think that I'm living without sadness? [...] After all, I'm no less lonely than you. [...] How distant and unkind your letter is— I could never have written you one like that. Maybe in the end it would be better for us not to see each other any sooner than the New Year.[21]

But she stuck to her decision to go to England after all: "I can't believe that I'm coming to join you, and I'm fearful, unbelievably fearful about it all: I fear your disappointment, your 'inconstancy,' and I'm fearful about the journey itself... After all, we can't keep undertaking experiments, and I'm so scared that this one might prove to be the last one. Until your telegram I hadn't taken any steps to acquire a foreign passport. In a day or so I should hear from the police-station that there are no objections to my travelling abroad." One of his colleagues had told her that Zamiatin could have chosen to return to Russia that October, and she asked him rather pointedly why he'd not chosen to do so. "And I want to say one more thing. After all isn't it true that if you'd been living in a cultural centre with lots of acquaintances, [...] whether in Russia or anywhere else, then you wouldn't have wanted to see me and wouldn't have summoned me?" But a few days later she too was more conciliatory: "How could it happen that I didn't understand how much you need me precisely at the moment? [...] I didn't understand, kept over-interpreting everything, how I despise myself now." She could scarcely believe that it was she who needed to assure him of her love: "And maybe my arrival won't be so joyous for you after all, for there's so much bitterness in everything. But dear Evgeny Iv[anovich], be a little fair towards me. [...] Will you definitely come to meet me at the quayside? Perhaps this letter will arrive after I do, for I think there won't be any particular delay at the Consulate and I should be able to leave on about the 8th or 10th. Well, farewell, and au revoir."[22] The final telegram he sent her, on 1 September, simply responded: "Health pretty well glad at last see you Zamiatin."[23]

This exchange of letters provides an echo of what was perhaps the deepest crisis in their relationship, dating back to the previous winter—in one autobiography Zamiatin even talked of having received a summons to a duel in the stormy, snowy January of 1915–16, and perhaps this was related to his complicated love life.[24] By this stage, Liudmila has become much the less assertive partner in their relationship, and as we will see, she remains a slightly shadowy figure and stays in the background for much of the rest of their lives together. Yet through the recriminations their passionate bond remains apparent, and they both succeed in moving beyond their rancour to make some sort of dignified rapprochement possible. In the absence of other evidence, our impressions of Zamiatin's time in England are very much shaped by this initial unhappiness; and yet these letters cover only the first six months of his stay, and once Liudmila had joined him they spent an entire year living there together. There are almost no documentary traces of how they spent their time, and for all we know they may have been very happy, exploring the country and sharing their amusement at the quaintness of English life. We simply cannot say how things were; but never again would their correspondence reflect anything like this degree of mutual unhappiness and resentment, and when they did return to Russia it seems to have been as a secure and settled couple.

In any case, Zamiatin's life was perhaps not always quite as gloomy as he painted things to Liudmila. In a letter to Iakov Grebenshchikov on 28 August (admittedly after he had received the news of Liudmila's decision to join him), he was far more jaunty. The letter was mostly written in a pseudo-folksy style, using dialect terms from his home region near Tambov, and presented a joky, "laddish" account of his time in England, with late nights and drinking: "And as for the local girls, well there's not a word to be said against them, except good ones. Their hair is fair all over, which is, I know, something you're very fond of. Their personalities are pleasant, and they're plump where it matters, and altogether all is as it should be." He was asking Grebenshchikov's help in preparing a second edition of his collection *Provincial Life* (which did not materialise), and in return he promised to bring him back from England "a travelling wife": "they're very handy, you can carry them in your pocket or your briefcase, you inflate them for use like a pillow, and they cost a mere fourteen shillings."[25]

He seems to have attended a variety of events locally, including some public spiritualist séances—out of boredom.[26] After she joined him, they presumably found various ways of entertaining themselves as well as spending time with his acquaintances in Newcastle. He had told Liudmila to bring her medical diploma with her, but there is no evidence of her having worked while she was in England.[27] As an inhabitant of Jesmond, Zamiatin was living in one of the most salubrious and respectable parts of town. There was a long-established tennis club just down the road from their house, which they may have used. He described "returning home in the evenings from the factory in my little Renault."[28] At a time when most of the shipyard workers in Newcastle travelled to work using the very extensive and efficient tramway service which had been in place since 1901, and horse-drawn transport was only just being phased out, driving a car was quite glamorous. It was probably the case that very few, if any, of his Russian writer friends drove cars either—Maiakovsky did not purchase his own Renault in Paris until 1928.

The Zamiatins certainly used the car to spend some time exploring the North-East as well. There are many spectacular places to visit in the region, including perhaps the sprawling ruined castle of Dunstanburgh on the Northumberland coast. In his 1923 autobiography he described "having travelled a lot in England and Scotland."[29] At some point he made a visit to Edinburgh, where he was impressed by the sight of the castle in black outline against the sunset, "something of a recollection or a dream." He wrote that in England he had: "built ships, seen the ruins of castles, listened to the crashing of the bombs dropped by the German Zeppelins, and written the story *The Islanders*."[30] He also appears to have visited London in November 1916—presumably with Liudmila—since his notebooks include details about the Lord Mayor's Show. On one of his London trips he was scathing about a British production of *The Cherry Orchard* with its ludicrous costumes, although he was intrigued by the liberalism of the theatre censorship regulations which had made it possible to stage the plays of Oscar Wilde (the very mention of whose name outrages Lady Campbell in *The Islanders*).[31]

Zamiatin and Liudmila's participation in the cultural life of Newcastle may have been limited by their command of the language. For example, there is no trace of their having joined the elegant lending library of "The Literary and Philosophical Society of Newcastle upon Tyne," always referred to as the "Lit & Phil." The Lit & Phil is situated right next door to the Central Station with its Hotel, where Zamiatin stayed on first arriving in Newcastle. With several thousand members, a book collection of well over 60,000 volumes, and a rich collection of music, including 700 scores of modern British, French and Russian music purchased in 1914, as well as a distinguished programme of lectures and recitals which was kept going throughout the War, it might have seemed a natural place for them to spend some time.[32] The musical life of the city was rich, and the Laing Art Gallery, opened in 1904, reflected the wealth of this "Metropolis of the North" with its population of a quarter of a million people.

Altogether, very few letters have survived to reflect the period from September 1916 to September 1917, the twelve months which they spent together in Newcastle. This is scarcely surprising, given the wartime interruptions in postal and other communications with Russia as a result of the suspension of ferry services across the North Sea to Norway. One letter which appears to date from the later part of 1916 was addressed (in draft) to Vul'f and to Varia, who seem to be family relations. He told Vul'f half-sternly that it was painful for him to have to include a reproach with his New Year greetings, but asked Vul'f how he, "as the eldest," could have omitted to explain to Varia that babies do not come from storks — and now it was too late. On the back of this same sheet he wrote kindly to Varia, hoping that "a light touch of maternity" had only enhanced her beauty. He joked that while she had been increasing the population, he had been at the other end of the world, threatening to diminish it by running over young Britons in his car, which he delighted in driving at 15 miles per hour.[33] On 18 December he and Liudmila sent Remizov a letter from Sanderson Road, to say that they were suffering from the cold due to the lack of Russian stoves, and they'd had to resort to drinking whiskey to keep warm.[34] Two days later, he also wrote to his former editor Miroliubov:

> It's already nearly a year since I left Russia. I've got completely fed up with foreign parts in the course of this year, I can tell you. I'm hoping to tear myself away from here in January-February and come home, and even if I have to live a life of fasting, at least it would be in Russia. I've grown hungry here in England: there's as much meat as you want, but not many real people. It's all machines, coal, soot and din. [...] I'm on my treadmill from morning to night, I've been spinning round all year. And writing has been out of the question: I haven't written anything, although my hands have itched to sometimes. It's turned out absurdly somehow: a stormy wind has transported me over to England, and I'm living here for some reason, doing goodness

knows what—just not what I want to be doing. Is it possible that things will continue in this way? Surely the New Year won't turn out the same?³⁵

Zamiatin was anxious during his time abroad not to lose touch with literary developments in Russia, but Russian books were hard to obtain; he had begged Liudmila to post some to him—Esenin's new story *The Ravine*, a new book of Russian occult tales, and the Russian translations of Jack London's *The Iron Heel*, and of William J. Locke's *Derelicts*—he evidently still preferred to read in Russian rather than English, which was after all not a language he had studied at school. He had been reading Chekhov's correspondence again too.³⁶

While he was away his own stories continued to be published back in Russia in a steady flow: *Stubborn Folk* was reprinted from the *Provincial Life* volume, and *In Writing* was published in *Birzhevye vedomosti* on 21 March 1916, although he vowed never to give them anything else since they paid so poorly.³⁷ *Africa* was published in *Severnye zapiski* (*Northern Notes*) that spring, and Zamiatin continued agitating to get his scandalous *At the Back of Beyond* published in Moscow, despite the 1914 ban on it.³⁸ It seems likely that Maksim Gor'ky had first noticed Zamiatin at the time of the 1913 publication of *A Provincial Tale* in *Zavety*, although they didn't meet at this stage. Early in 1916 Gor'ky's new journal, *Letopis'* (*The Chronicle*), published a review by Viacheslav Polonsky praising the story and commenting that Zamiatin "writes succinctly and harshly, as though he were carving contours out of stone."³⁹ In the next number of *Letopis'* (no.4), Gor'ky published *God*, *The Little Deacon* and *Pet'ka* (under the title *A Bad Lad*), the story originally intended for Remizov's charitable project.⁴⁰ Zamiatin was intensely frustrated to be cut off from all this excitement, having left the country just at the moment when he was becoming so much better-known, and he badgered Liudmila to cut out and send him all his reviews, especially of the *Provincial Life* volume.

In September 1916, another letter from Semen Vengerov arrived, requesting further information for his *Critical and Biographical Dictionary of Russian Writers and Scientists*. Vengerov now asked him to comment on the intellectual and social influences which had shaped his development, and how he had attained "such a brilliant command of popular speech." wondering, as reviewers so often did, whether Remizov had influenced him.⁴¹ In his reply three months later, Zamiatin answered that his language was shaped by his upbringing in Lebedian', and especially by his maternal grandmother Anastasia Vasil'evna, who knew masses of folk sayings, spells and omens. He had also picked up some of the pithy speech of the Kostroma region from friends, including Grebenshchikov. "I got to know Remizov in person not very long ago, and indeed started to read his books comparatively late. Remizov and I have different storehouses of language: his vocabulary derives from manuscripts and rare books, whereas I have scarcely drawn upon books so far. The fundamental dissimilarity between me and Remizov will probably become more and more apparent as time passes." In the rough draft of this letter he added that Remizov and Ivanov-Razumnik had played a part in raising his awareness of the importance of the instrumentation [phonic organization] of prose. He also mentioned his particular fondness since childhood for Gogol': "I love Gogol' to this day, and I think that it is not least because of his influence that I have a tendency towards caricature and the grotesque, towards a synthesis of the fantastic with reality." This is perhaps the first written mention of his concept of synthesis, which would become an essential component of his definition of Synthetism, or "neo-Realism." He affirmed to Vengerov that *Africa, God, The Little Deacon* and *Pet'ka* had the most to say about his inner philosophical convictions. Perhaps this was because of the pessimistic strain the stories share, with hopes and dreams inexorably destroyed and religion offering no consolation. Intellectually, he felt that he had developed independently for the most part, although Marx and Nietzsche had a considerable impact on him at one point, if in a somewhat "heretical" fashion. "For the last 7–8 years I've been reading and admiring the poems of the Symbolists, both ours and the French. One of my favourite books is Baudelaire's *Les Fleurs du Mal*."[42]

However, he was intensely depressed by his failure to write anything new since arriving in England. During his miserable first months he complained constantly that he was finding it impossible to do any of his own writing, or even to bring himself to play on the piano at Sanderson Road. The first trace we have of any creative work in England is a draft of *The Honest Truth*, dated "27/14 July 1916, Newcastle" — in other words, a piece written on the same day that he wrote his bitterest and lengthiest letter to Liudmila. Appropriately, the story consists of a letter written home by a servant-girl, whose initially upbeat account of her new life gradually reveals her deep unhappiness.[43] A month later he told Grebenshchikov: "during these entire five months I haven't written one sensible line, being extremely occupied with drunkenness and debauchery."[44] However, the prospect of Liudmila's arrival seemed to release his creative energy, and drafts of a couple of new miniatures date from 9 September 1916 onwards.[45] It is surprising, however, that he should also have embarked at this point on *The Sign*, another of his Russian "monastery" tales steeped in provincialisms, when he was so far from home.

By far the most significant piece of writing he accomplished during his stay in England was his satire on life in Jesmond, *The Islanders*. The main drafts of *The Islanders* are dated "June/July1917, Newcastle," although there are some versions of the beginning under the title *Campbell—A Tale* which date back to late January.[46] Zamiatin took a sardonic view of the more genteel aspects of Newcastle society in the reign of George V, the British monarch who bore such a close physical resemblance to his cousin Tsar Nicholas II. In the story, Vicar Dewley epitomises all the sanctimonious and repressive values of British middle-class society.[47] Along with his parish council, the local society of bell-ringers, and the Salvation Army, he attempts to live his life according to his "Ordinances for Compulsory Salvation," which timetable all his activities, including copulation on every third Saturday. Jesmond consists of rows of identical houses with scrubbed front steps, inhabited by thousands of identical "Sunday gentlemen," turned out as if by a factory. The Vicar insists to his wife that if life can be made to run smoothly, like a machine, then society will move mechanically towards achieving its goals. But erotic attraction supervenes: the Vicar's wife falls for the naïve Campbell, a slow-moving man with square features. Campbell is in turn knocked from his cautious certainties by falling for a disreputable dancer, Didi Lloyd, who herself has been led astray by an immoral and subversive Irishman, O'Kelly—and all ends tragically. Some of the same themes of sexual repression and hypocrisy would later be taken up in Zamiatin's second English story, *The Fisher of Men*, which is set in London during the Zeppelin raids.

The Islanders is entirely shaped by Zamiatin's experience of England, from the topography of Newcastle and its suburbs down to the "worm-like" lips of Campbell's mother Lady Campbell, so clearly modelled on those of Lady Noble, the widow of Lord Armstrong's old friend and early business partner, Sir Andrew Noble.[48] Zamiatin's ear for idiom unerringly captures the diction of English for a Russian readership as well. And just as the Petersburg stories had represented a fundamental shift in Gogol's writing career after his Ukrainian tales, so *The Islanders* represents a really significant break with Zamiatin's previous writings, in terms of shifting away from the Russian provinces, and away from the earlier "folksiness" of his style: what emerges now is an urban tale, more spare in its language, and more modernist in its narrative organisation. And in a remarkable number of ways, both stylistic and thematic, his satire of bourgeois England in *The Islanders* also closely prefigures his anti-Utopian novel *We*, set in a distant future which bears the unmistakable features of post-Revolutionary Russia.

Zamiatin did not have much spare time for writing, since his official work commitments kept him very busy. His visit to England had placed him at the heart of the engineering boom which secured victory for the Allies. During the First World War the region made a key contribution to the war effort, with the construction in the Tyne shipyards alone of a total of 1,130 new vessels, and with 1917 as the peak year of this astonishing productivity. At a celebratory meeting held in Newcastle in July 1919, where a telegram from the King was read out congratulating the engineers and shipbuilders of the North-East on their splendid record, it was noted that bombings by Zeppelins had only succeeded in interrupting the night shifts fifteen times, the longest break of over six hours having been on 2 April 1916, less than a fortnight before Zamiatin's arrival. "Why we were not more often and more effectively raided and bombed is one of the mysteries of the war," said one contributor. There was a report of Sir Joseph Maclay's speech on the occasion: "In the latter part of 1916 the conditions of this country were alarming indeed, and he did not think it had been recognized how much we depended not only upon our navy, but upon our merchant shipping. [...] It was not the ships of the navy which the submarine looked for; [...] the enemy realized that it was upon the Mercantile Marine that this country so much depended, and that if it could be removed, then our country would be starved, and not only our country, but our Allies, with whom we were so closely associated."[49]

Newcastle's huge significance in international terms was reflected by the fact that in 1920 there were still Consuls and Vice-Consuls based there to represent 23 different nations from Europe, the Americas and the Middle East.[50] With so many foreigners working on the ships and at the munitions factories, there was strict supervision in case of any subversion or spying: the *Register of Aliens* for the Wallsend Slipway and Engineering Company listed details of all foreign nationals employed, and even a single day's absence was reported that same day to the local Superintendent of Police.[51]

Zamiatin had described to Liudmila how he was obliged to travel regularly to four different factories, with further occasional visits to two others, each taking 40–50 minutes to reach. This was a typical day: "After morning tea I settle down to my calculations for an hour or two, then I eat and set off for the factory, returning for supper at about 7; after supper my assistant the mechanic often comes round, and we have to talk about the jobs for another couple of hours. And this, by the way, is the hardest time, when the designs have to be approved." Sometimes the evenings were taken up with correspondence with the factories, "…and all in English. I have no time even to read books, and the newspapers lie untouched." On 13 June 1916 he travelled up to spend three days in Glasgow: "it's a good city, there's no comparison with Newcastle, and it's a shame that I wasn't destined to live there." However, he returned with a "right English" stinking cold.[52]

The two largest vessels completed for the Russian state under Zamiatin's supervision during 1917 were the icebreakers *Saint Alexander Nevsky* and the *Sviatogor*.[53] He later described the *Alexander Nevsky* as his "brainchild": he had drawn up the preliminary designs for her, "and not one drawing for this vessel went on to the workshops unless it had been checked over and signed 'Chief Surveyor of Russian Icebreakers Building E. Zamiatin' [sic]."[54] But she was not finally completed until after he had left Newcastle; in other words, until after the October Revolution. The political upheavals of 1917 then led to the suspension of all the Tsarist orders for icebreakers, and indeed Armstrong Whitworth was eventually obliged to claim compensation for the work from the British Admiralty (although by 1920–21, undeterred, they were already busy negotiating lucrative new contracts with the Bolsheviks for the repair of railway locomotives).[55]

Zamiatin must have followed the immediate destinies of these two vessels after their launch with some dismay. Because of the broken contract, the *Alexander Nevsky* was initially seized by the Royal Navy after completion and renamed *HMS Alexander*; but she was eventually handed back to Russia in the early 1920s, when she was renamed the *Lenin*. Between the Wars she performed regular duty clearing a way through the ice for ships in the southern part of the Kara Sea heading for the mouths of the Enisei and the Ob rivers in Siberia. The *Sviatogor*, a near sister of the *Ermak* and of the *Tsar' Mikhail Fedorovich*, whose construction at the Vulcan yard Zamiatin had inspected in Stettin in

1913, was the largest icebreaker in the world when it entered service, and it was used in the Arctic seas off Murmansk and Arkhangel'sk to enable shipping lanes to be kept open for the Allies. But within less than two years of its construction, in 1918, the *Sviatogor* was scuttled by the Bolsheviks near Arkhangel'sk in an attempt to block the river Dvina against British forces during their intervention against the Revolution. However, the British then succeeded in raising her, and incorporated her into the Royal Navy, until she too was finally restored to the Russians in late 1921, after the United Kingdom granted the Soviet government diplomatic recognition. In 1927 she was renamed the *Krasin*, and took part in famous Arctic rescues in 1928 and 1934.

Zamiatin was involved to a varying extent in the construction of several other icebreakers at the Walker, Wallsend and South Shields yards on the Tyne, and at Sunderland on the Wear. These included the *Dobrynia Nikitich* ("one of five or so smaller icebreakers"), the *Ilia Muromets*, and the *Koz'ma Minin* and *Kniaz' Pozharsky*, which Zamiatin described as "twins," and which were completed in November and December 1916.[56] His visits to Glasgow in 1916 and 1917 may have been associated with the construction of the icebreakers *Ledokol VI* and *Ledokol VII* at the Ferguson Bros. Shipyard at Port Glasgow.[57]

In 1932, already in emigration in France, Zamiatin looked back with enormous affection to the designing of these apparently clumsy vessels: "I'm not even sure that you can call an icebreaker a ship. As everyone knows, a ship is a maritime creature, it can only travel on the water, whereas an icebreaker is an amphibian, and undertakes half its journey on dry land. On dry land?! Yes, on dry land, because ice is, of course, dry land." It is a paradoxical craft, with a propeller at the wrong end, the capacity to rock from side to side to heave itself off the ice, and to use anchors to propel itself backwards if necessary. "And if you haul it out of the water and take a look at it in a dry dock, then you can see that the contours of its steel body are rounded and more feminine than in many other vessels. In cross-section an icebreaker is like an egg—and it's just as difficult to crush as it is to crush an egg with your hand."[58] In his report on "Shipbuilding in Russia" in December 1934, he noted the inauguration of a vast new Soviet building programme of ice-breakers: "The construction of this ice-breaking flotilla will be commenced in 1935. Mention might be made that this will be the first case of the construction of icebreakers at home. All former Russian craft of this kind have been built abroad, and mainly in Great Britain."[59]

Liudmila's apprehensions about her journey over to England in September 1916 had been well-founded. Apart from the disagreeable nature of the rough 40-hour journey across the North Sea, such as Zamiatin had already described to her, there were also of course the increasing risks of wartime travel. She planned to travel on the *Jupiter*,[60] which boasted the "finest and fastest" passage from Scandinavia, with only 22 hours of open sea. For the first two years of the conflict none of the ships on the routes between Norway and the Tyne were sunk; but only two months after Liudmila made her safe passage, on 16 November, a German U-boat sank the *Vega* with its cargo of food for Britain. Fortunately no lives were lost, but the services were suspended. They were tentatively re-opened in March 1917, although almost immediately 18 lives were lost in the sinking of the *Pollux*, and after that summer's Battle of Jutland, in which the British lost 14 ships and the Germans 11, the Germans declared unrestricted submarine warfare against merchant shipping. In the course of 1917 the *Haakon VII* was damaged, the cargo ship *Algol* vanished, probably sunk by a torpedo, and on 12 December a devastating attack was launched by four German destroyers against a convoy of eleven ships. Two days after that disaster, Lloyd George proclaimed the need to counter the submarine offensive: "Victory is now a question of tonnage, and tonnage is victory. Nothing else can now defeat us but a shortage of tonnage."[61] In his notebooks Zamiatin observed: "It felt as though we were on an island, like Robinson Crusoes. And around us was the grey North Sea, full of steel sharks." And, he added: "We are surrounded by alien, peculiar Man Fridays. [...] We can share their language. But will we ever come to any mutual understanding?"[62]

Zamiatin had been keeping in touch with political developments at home: he devoured the copies of his favourite newspaper *Rech'* which he managed to obtain in London, taking out a 3-month subscription for it as soon as he arrived there, which he then got Liudmila to renew.[63] From early in 1917 news of the dramatic events at home made the couple become desperate to go home, despite the dangers: "When the newspapers began to be splashed with fat headlines about the 'Revolution in Russia' and 'Abdication of the Russian Tsar,' it became unbearable to stay in England."[64] However, it was to be several months before they finally got permission to leave. Zamiatin's passport was stamped in London by the Norwegian and Swedish Consuls on 6 September 1917, and at the Russian Embassy there on the 10th, and again on the 17th, when it was noted—in the French of diplomacy, naturally—that: *"il retourne en Russie pour reprendre son service et que ses signes distinctifs sont: cheveux chatain [sic], moustache blonde coupeé, yeux gris, taille 5f. 10 inches anglaises."*[65] Since April all passenger ships had been travelling to Bergen in convoys for safety, and setting out from Aberdeen (in Scotland) instead of Newcastle; so his passport was stamped again in Aberdeen on 23 September. Their journey back to Russia in late September 1917 was by now an extremely hazardous undertaking.[66] In his 1922 and 1928–29 autobiographies, Zamiatin noted: "I very much regret that I didn't see the February Revolution and only knew the October one. [...] It's rather as if you'd never been in love, and one fine morning you wake up and find you have been married for a decade or so. [...] I returned to St Petersburg just in time for October, [...] on a scruffy and elderly little English steamship (which they wouldn't mind losing if it were sunk by the Germans). [...] It took a long time to sail to Bergen, fifty hours or so, with dimmed lights, wearing life-jackets all the way, and with lifeboats at the ready."[67] His passport was seen in Bergen on the 25th, in Stockholm on the 29th—and he and Liudmila arrived back home together in Petrograd on 30 September 1917.

3. The river Don at Lebedian': the garden of Zamiatin's home ran down to the river-bank on the right.

4. Zamiatin's home on Pokrovskaia Street in Lebedian', rebuilt in 2009 to house the Zamiatin Museum.

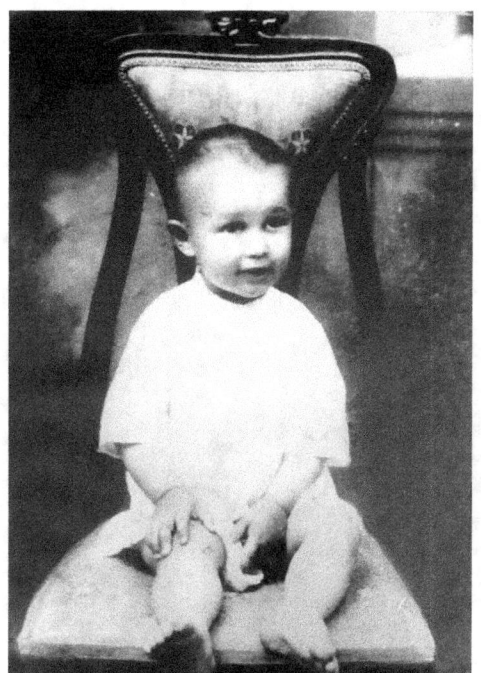

5. Zamiatin as a toddler (mid-1880s).

6. Zamiatin and his sister Aleksandra (early 1890s).

7. Zamiatin as a graduate of the Voronezh *gimnaziia* (1902).

8. The student Zamiatin with his sister Aleksandra (early 1900s).

9. Zamiatin and his sister Aleksandra with their parents, Ivan Dmitrievich and Maria Aleksandrovna (early 1900s).

10. Zamiatin in St Petersburg (approx. 1910?).

11. Liudmila Nikolaevna Zamiatina (1920s?).

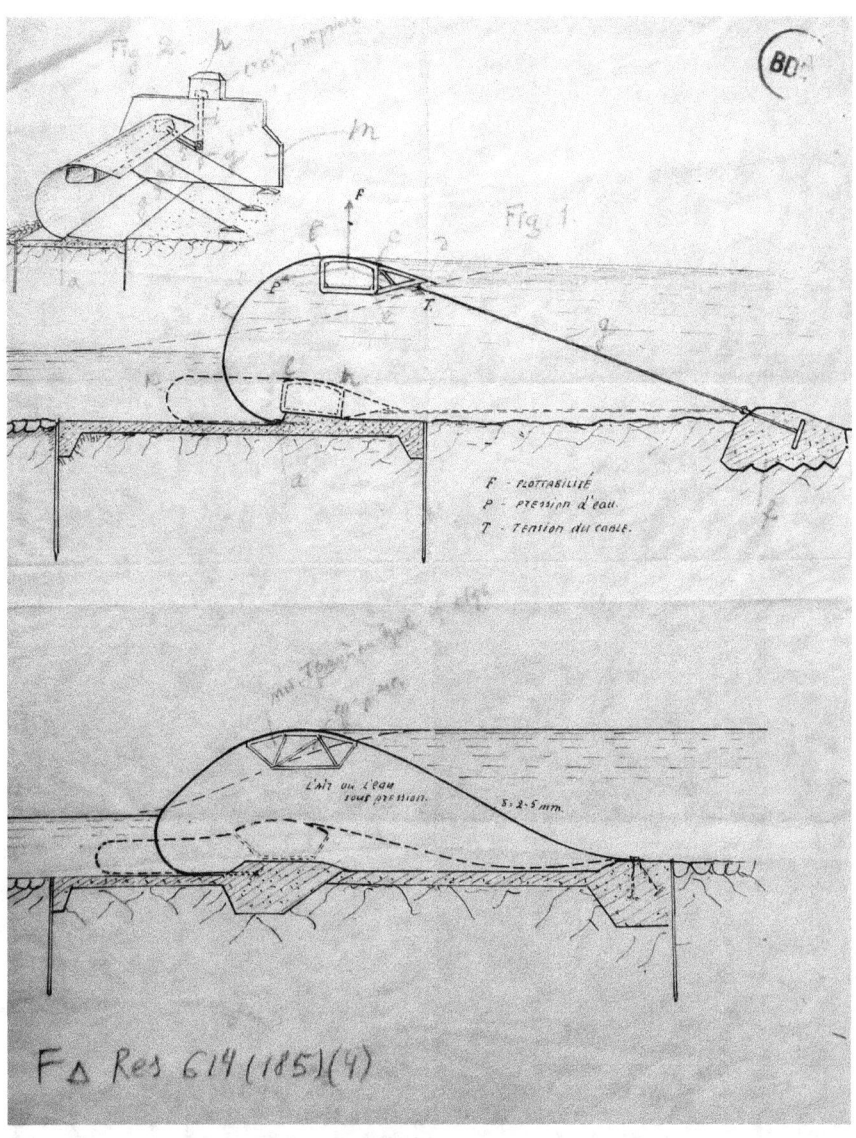

12. Zamiatin's design for a flexible dam (early 1910s?).

13. The icebreaker Sviatogor (later Krasin), constructed in Newcastle during 1916–17 under Zamiatin's supervision.

14. Zamiatin's 1916–17 home at 19, Sanderson Road, Newcastle upon Tyne: the memorial plaque to him by the front door was placed there with the support of Iosif Brodsky.

15. Zamiatin at the piano, examining a score of 'Préludes' by Scriabin (late 1910s?).

16. Self-portrait by Iury Annenkov, during the freezing winter of 1919–20 in Petrograd.

17. Illustration (1921) by Iury Annenkov for Zamiatin's story *The Fisher of Men*.

Алексей Ремизов   Alexis Remizoff

18. Portrait of Aleksei Remizov by Iury Annenkov (1920).

19. Portrait of Kornei Chukovsky by Iury Annenkov (1921).

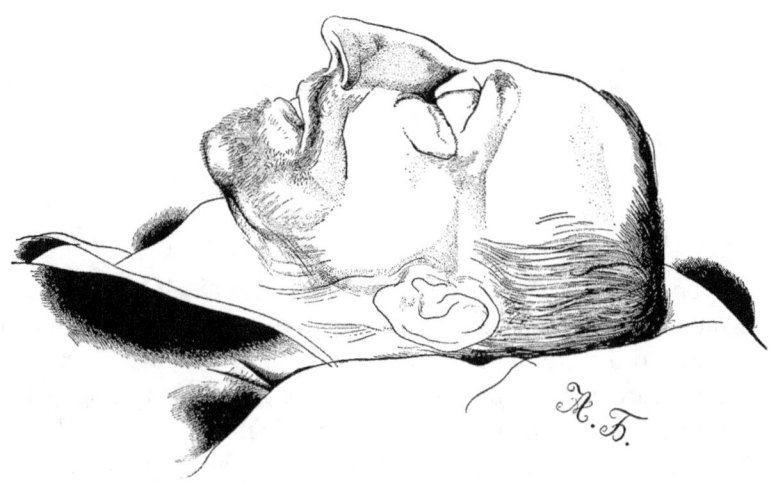

20. Portrait of Aleksandr Blok on his death-bed, by Iury Annenkov (1921).

Chapter 4:
Petrograd (1917–1921)

Upon his return to Russia, and finding himself caught up just weeks later in the tremendous upheavals of the October Revolution taking place in the city all around him, Zamiatin promptly jettisoned his primary career in the shipyards as an engineer, retaining only his part-time teaching post at the Polytechnic. With a new world apparently opening up, he decided that now was the moment to throw himself fully into pursuing his vocation as a writer. His role during the 1920s would be not only that of an author, but also that of a literary specialist—as a critic, reviewer, editor and administrator—and equally as a teacher of the new generation of writers. He brought to these tasks an uncommon degree of professionalism, the legacy of his previous experiences of employment. Now in his early 30s, he was someone accustomed to working independently and to taking responsible decisions, and he possessed considerable personal authority. In the documents that have survived to illustrate the next decade or so, the personal largely recedes from view, and the public figure steps forward.

The Zamiatins created a striking impression when they arrived back home: "I recall a greyish autumn day in 1917. At that point Petersburg was no longer Petersburg, nor yet Leningrad—but Petrograd. […] There was a ring at the door. […] In came a young couple, fresh and cheerful and smartly dressed, not in a Petersburg style, but precisely in an English style. The Zamiatins had only just returned then from England. […] The English way of life had suited them, they had quickly adapted to it and taken on some aspects of English ways, and to the end of their days they preserved English manners in their look, their style of dressing and of welcoming guests. […] He was living at that time with his wife, who was a graceful, extremely attractive small woman with frail health." His neighbour Avgusta Damanskaia goes on to describe him chopping wood in the bitter winter months with a short English pipe clenched in his teeth, then sitting down afterwards to relax at the piano by playing studies or nocturnes by Scriabin, not as a virtuoso, but with a genuine lyricism which belied the apparent cold restraint of his outward manner.[1] Even though his first impressions of England had been rather hostile, he had brought back with him to Russia the outward trappings of an English gentleman. His somewhat formal guise as an "Englishman" in dress and manner in post-Revolutionary Russia was an image which he would foster, since this conservative mask seemed to embolden him to assume a certain independence of spirit amongst his peers, something which he cherished above all things.

One crucial new friendship he made at this time was with Maksim Gor'ky. He was the notorious author of socialist classics such as his play set in a doss-house, *The Lower Depths* (1902), and the novel about rebellious factory workers which was later to provide the design model for Soviet Socialist Realism, *Mother* (1906). After his return from political exile in 1913, Gor'ky had thrown himself into the literary and cultural life of St Petersburg, establishing himself as the leader of progressive literature through his publishing ventures and his encouragement of young writers, especially those of humble social origins.[2] He had already published some of Zamiatin's stories in *Letopis'* during 1916, and immediately after the latter's return in 1917 he accepted a new story, *Eyes*. This was Zamiatin's allegorical sketch about a yard-dog with beautiful, painfully human eyes, who runs away briefly from his brutal master, but returns abjectly for a bowl of rotting meat. However, his first conversation with Gor'ky in the editorial office was not about this text, but all about technology and the construction of icebreakers. Gor'ky himself was patchily educated as far as mathematics (and indeed foreign languages) were concerned, and he was fascinated by Zamiatin's range of expertise. Much later, Zamiatin recalled: "I returned to Petersburg only in the autumn of 1917, and met Gor'ky then for the first time. And so it happened that I encountered him and the Revolution simultaneously. For this reason the image of Gor'ky is unfailingly linked in my memory with the new, post-revolutionary Russia." Soon he would be caught up in helping to run the ambitious projects Gor'ky, in his role as unofficial Bolshevik Minister of Culture, undertook in order to preserve literature and keep writers alive during the grim years of the Civil War (1918–21): the "World Literature" scheme to publish foreign classics in translation, a series of the "100 Best Books of Russian Literature," the Committee for "Historical Drama," teaching at the Literature Studio, and at the House of Arts.³ Meanwhile, however, one essential reason for their closeness lay in their very similar reactions to the October 1917 seizure of power by the Bolsheviks, and its aftermath.

Zamiatin's fictional and non-fictional writings of 1917–19 convey his instant hostility to the Leninist leadership, and to Bolshevik policies and methods. The excitement he had felt in England about the overthrow of the Tsar in February 1917 soon turned to dismay when the liberal constitutional aspirations of the Provisional Government were swept aside in the Bolsheviks' October coup, consolidated in January 1918 when they forcibly closed down the democratically-elected Constituent Assembly. He accused the Bolsheviks of "stealing the honourable title of socialists and democrats, until it became entirely indecent for them to bear these names."[4] Within weeks of the October Revolution, he started publishing blatant personal attacks on Lenin in his four *Fairytales about Fita*, where Fita is a strange "predominantly male" being, balding and pot-bellied, who is born spontaneously from a pile of dusty papers in a police basement. In one tale, Fita attempts to quash starvation and cholera by decree; in another, he tears down a cathedral to build a pointless road; in the third, he compels the "free" citizens to march and sing songs of praise to him; and in the final tale, anticipating the One State in *We*, Fita obliges all citizens to live in a barracks and wear identical grey uniforms, with shaved heads and numbered metallic badges. Ultimately, Fita decrees that everyone—including himself—should become equally moronic in the name of happiness and egalitarian democracy, and utter nothing but grunts. In June 1918, using the pseudonym "Mikh[ail] Platonov" (based on his mother's surname), which he adopted for many of his publications during these months, Zamiatin published *The Great Sewage Disposal Man*, about a man who takes power in Russia, "poetically" obsessed with sewage schemes, and who simply comes to stink more and more of excrement.

His absolute abhorrence of violence finds expression in a sketch he wrote in the final weeks of 1917, *Thursday*, in which the ignorant older brother (called *"bol'shen'kiy"* to associate him with the Bolsheviks) mindlessly slaughters anyone and anything which disagrees with him.[5] Opposition to violence is also the theme of the very first article he wrote after the Revolution, which was published in Gor'ky's short-lived anti-Leninist journal *Novaia zhizn'* (*New Life*) on 11 January 1918. It was prompted by the lynching on 6–7 January of two

Constitutional Democrat politicians, who were under arrest, by sailors who burst into the hospital where they were being treated. Zamiatin indicted the recent articles in *Pravda* (*The Truth*) which had fomented the violence by calling for a campaign of mass terror, in the wake of an assassination attempt on Lenin at the beginning of the year.[6] Gor'ky echoed his outrage about the lynching in articles of his own in *Novaia zhizn'* during these weeks.[7]

In articles written during that spring of 1918 ("About Lackeys" and "The Rebellion of the Capitalists"), Zamiatin tried to show how violence breeds violence. Furthermore, he condemned the left wing of the Socialist-Revolutionary Party for joining forces with the Bolsheviks at the very moment when Soviet militias were arresting and executing the workers in whose name they had carried out the Revolution, after those self-same workers demonstrated against them.[8] In December 1917 he wrote *The Cherubim*, in which Russia is depicted as a land of bayonets, torture and executions, where angels simply dare not settle.[9] One of his most powerful miniatures of this period, *The Dragon*, published in March 1918 in the Socialist-Revolutionary newspaper *Delo naroda* (*The People's Cause*), portrayed a "dragon" man who boasts of having mercilessly despatched a member of the intelligentsia, and whose eyes, the only "two slits through from the world of delirium into the world of men" remain for the most part concealed under his heavy cap. Only very briefly does he emerge as a human being when he puts his bayonet down on the floor of the tram, and warms a frozen sparrow back to life in his cupped hands. Zamiatin was appalled when the death sentence, triumphantly abolished the very day after the October Revolution, was reintroduced the following summer to deal with opponents to Soviet power.[10] In the spring of 1919, he issued a heartfelt plea for the phase of Revolutionary destruction, however necessary it had been, to cease, and for peace and reconstruction to take place: "You cannot plough with a machine-gun. And it has long since been time to get down to some ploughing."[11]

He was also dismayed by developments on the cultural scene. From 1918 to 1920, during the tumultuous years of the Civil War, the Bolsheviks allowed the radical Proletkul't [Proletarian Culture] movement to assume a virtual monopoly over cultural policies. These writers had proclaimed their scorn for traditional art with a programmatic poem by Vladimir Kirillov entitled *We*, in which they promised to burn Raphael's paintings and demolish museums in the name of a future in which exclusively proletarian artists would glorify the achievements of factory workers. Zamiatin warned that they would end by creating a culture of slaves, and destroy art altogether.[12] He drew a distinction between those whom such authoritarian policies would "domesticate," and those free spirits who would remain "untamed." The true artist was identified in his mind as a typical Scythian [from the fierce ancient warrior tribes who ranged over the steppe regions north of the Black Sea], a restless nomad on horseback who never settles down:

> This is the tragedy and also the tormenting happiness of a genuine Scythian: he will never rest on his laurels, he will never stand alongside the confirmed victors, with those who rejoice and sing songs of praise. The destiny of the true Scythian is to bear the thorns of the defeated: his faith is heresy; his destiny is the destiny of the Wandering Jew; his labour is not for those around him, but for those who are far distant. And in all eras this labour, according to the laws of all monarchies and all republics, even including the Soviet one, has been simply rewarded, with official lodgings—in jail. [...] A hatred of freedom is the most reliable symptom of that fatal disease, bourgeois philistinism. Trimming all thoughts right back to the same level, dressing everyone in the established style of uniform, turning all heretical lands towards your faith by artillery fire [...]—this is how in Russia they used to cure sectarians and socialists of their delusions.[13]

During the spring of 1919 he formulated a variation of this argument in favour of his key article of faith at this time—heresy—in his article "Tomorrow": "Anyone who has found his ideal in the present is like Lot's wife, already turned into a column of salt, rooted to the ground and incapable of moving any further. The world lives only through its heretics—Christ the heretic, Copernicus the heretic, Tolstoy the heretic. [...] Today negates yesterday, but will become the negation of the negation tomorrow, always following the same dialectical path, which carries the world on to infinity in a grandiose parabola. Yesterday was the thesis, today is the antithesis, and tomorrow is the synthesis. [...] And the only weapon worthy of a man, of the man of tomorrow, is the word. For decades the Russian intelligentsia and Russian literature have battled, using the word, for the great tomorrow of humankind. And the time has come to brandish this weapon once more."[14] This, then, is the intellectual and political background from which would emerge Zamiatin's most finely-honed weapon against repressive policies, the novel *We*, which he began to draft during the rest of 1919.

Throughout his first years back in Petrograd, before he embarked on *We*, he was writing, publishing, and constantly being approached for articles and stories. He had been catapulted from complete literary isolation in England to chaotic excitement at the heart of the new cultural scene in Russia, and clearly revelled in finding himself courted, respected and needed. During the first half of 1918 he established an acquaintance with a number of well-known writers, including the leading Symbolist poet Aleksandr Blok. While he was struck by the combination in Blok's appearance of the ethereally chivalric and the down-to-earth man living in the present, Blok in turn expressed amusement at how his own preconception of Zamiatin — based on reading his stories set in the Russian provinces — had been that he would look like a country doctor with a beard. Instead, his appearance was that of "a Muscovite... Englishman." For three years they worked regularly together in an editorial capacity for organizations such as "World Literature," where Blok commanded the affection of Gor'ky as well as the warm admiration of Zamiatin, who sensed in him not only an intensely committed and perspicacious writer, but also a lonely figure with a unique sense of the crisis in the humanities threatening to engulf Russian culture. By the summer of 1919, he detected in Blok a transformation from the man who, at the beginning of 1918, had apparently welcomed the Bolshevik coup in his brilliant and controversial poem *The Twelve*. Blok was suffering both spiritual anguish and physical ill-health during the years before his death in August 1921, and shared in 1920 with Zamiatin a moment of bleak honesty about his feelings for Russia, which he characterised as "a love filled with hatred."[15]

Zamiatin also continued his friendship with Aleksei Remizov, whom he had got to know before the War, through the journal *Zavety*. During 1918 they exchanged several letters about practical matters such as royalties; but Zamiatin also began to gain status within Remizov's extraordinary literary group "Obezvelvolpal" ("The Great and Free Monkey Chamber"), rising from the rank of "candidate" to "prince" and "cavalier." This whimsically constituted, comically-run group was dedicated at its heart to the cause of freedom of speech, based on Remizov's admiration for E.T.A. Hoffmann, whose works would shortly provide the Soviet-era Serapion Brotherhood with their *raison d'être*. Soon after Zamiatin returned to Russia in 1917, he was invited to append his signature to a document elevating P. E. Shchegolev to a high rank in the group: his name appears on the manuscript, which is illustrated and written in Remizov's beautiful and elaborate calligraphy, alongside those of well-established writers such as Blok, Prishvin, Ivanov-Razumnik, Boris Bugaev [Andrei Bely], Aleksei Tolstoy, Vasily Rozanov and Remizov himself. It was a further confirmation of his present standing among the literary élite of the capital.[16]

During his first winter back in Russia, Zamiatin became involved in countless projects. Between October 1917 and the summer of 1918 he published half-a-dozen or more stories and articles in the moderate Socialist-Revolutionary journal *Delo naroda*, which had clearly come to suit his own political stance. His main connection with the journal was through the man who had "discovered" him for *Zavety*, his friend Sergei Postnikov, a committed Socialist-Revolutionary who had been an elected member of that ill-fated Constituent Assembly which was disbanded by the Bolsheviks. The government banned *Delo naroda* briefly in October 1918, and then finally closed it down in the spring of 1919.[17] During the first half of 1918, Zamiatin was particularly busy, appearing at literary events or in print alongside Gor'ky, Blok, and other stars of the literary scene such as Anna Akhmatova, Fedor Sologub and Konstantin Bal'mont;[18] he wrote letters on behalf of *Delo naroda* to commission new writing;[19] he looked over the first stories of the young writer Nikolai Tikhonov;[20] and he published a brief piece at the end of April denouncing the Government decree calling for all public monuments to the tsars and their loyal servants to be pulled down.[21] Early that summer he also reverted briefly to his "engineer" mode, and published an article casting doubt on the feasibility of the Government's plans to harness the waters of the northern rivers for energy supplies.[22]

In the summer of 1918 he paused for breath from his febrile public engagement with the political and cultural issues of the day, and returned for a while to fiction. In the middle of June he wrote the early drafts of his second "English" story, *The Fisher of Men*.[23] He again anticipates here some of the themes and images in *We*, such as the overwhelming erotic impact of the music played by the organist Bayley. Like the engineer D-503, who is self-conscious about them, the amorous Bayley has atavistically "ape-like" hairy arms. Meanwhile, Laurie Craggs, like Mrs Dewley in *The Islanders*, conforms to the stereotype of the "unaroused" Englishwoman. She is described as having a pink curtain over her lips, to which the cord has been lost. As so often in Zamiatin's works, lips may stand for labia. The story culminates during a Zeppelin raid over London, when Bayley seizes the opportunity to part the curtain (or intact hymen) which has concealed her essential nature hitherto. The recklessness of sexual passion achieves beauty in defiance of the repressive social hypocrisies of suburbia: to her dull and hypocritical blackmailer husband's anxious enquiry as to whether she has been wounded during the raid, Laurie can only reply a smiling "Yes... That is, no. Oh, no!"

During June and July he also worked intensively on his story originally entitled *The Pie* (*The Protectress of Sinners*), a delightful tale in which the peasants creeping up at night to expropriate the convent's assets are completely disarmed by the Mother Superior, who feeds them pie.[24] A first draft of another story, involving the nearby monastery town of Zadonsk, was written on 23 July in Lebedian', confirming that Zamiatin had by then travelled back to his childhood home for a summer break.[25] It had not been easy to get there: "We keep being ready to leave Piter [St Petersburg], our bags are packed, but we haven't moved a step: in Zlatoust, where Liudmila Nikolaevna plans to go, shots are being fired and bullets are whistling—all to celebrate the boundless love the Russian Communards have for mankind. In Tambov Province, where I was planning to go, there is carnage between those peasants who are solidly in favour of Soviet power, and those who stand even more solidly in defence of their grain. […] If these little disasters cease and no greater disaster ensues, then I'm planning all the same to set off in a week or two." In this letter to the critic Polonsky he added: "I'm suffering from gripy stomach pains today, from all my Communist reading"—perhaps another, more prosaic reason for his decision to retreat to the home comforts of Lebedian'.[26] He returned briefly to Petrograd in August, where he was scheduled to appear alongside Gor'ky at a charity occasion on behalf of poverty-stricken intellectuals. By the 24th, he was leaving again for his home town, promising that his next long tale, *The North*, would be ready within the month.[27]

He would be parted for the next two months from Liudmila, as was by now their habit when it came to their summer holiday plans. His first letter to her was written on 29–30 August, when he had reached Moscow, after a sleepless journey where an acquaintance had prattled ceaselessly to him in his deafer left ear. Then in the street he suffered the same fate that she had recently endured; his wallet was stolen. Fortunately he did not lose too much money, but several documents went, including his internal passport, and he was not sure whether he would be allowed to travel further without it: "You see what it means, to let me out on my own." The other important news he had to impart, given the acute food shortages that year, was that it was now permitted to bring up to 1.5 poods (about 25 kilogrammes) of bread into Moscow. The price of bread had consequently already dropped there, and he was hoping this benefit would be extended to Petrograd in due course. It took him two days of queuing (behind "three thousand or so other people") to obtain a ticket for Tambov in order to get to Lebedian', and he then purchased a newspaper in which he read "the extraordinary adventures of Uritsky and Lenin (poor thing, you'll be in despair, I am sure). All around people were saying there would be searches at the station today, and that they would be checking the documents of all passengers. I, as a man who has no passport, was thrilled..."[28] On 30 August 1918 the police chief Moisei Uritsky had been assassinated in Petrograd, and there had also been a new attempt on Lenin's life by a disgruntled Socialist-Revolutionary, Fanny Kaplan. Within days the Bolsheviks unleashed the official campaign of Red Terror, in which thousands of alleged enemies of the Revolution suffered atrocities and execution.

One rather striking feature of Zamiatin's letters and memoirs of the years from 1918 to 1921 is how little the dangers and violence of the Revolution and Civil War seem to impinge with any truly threatening immediacy on his day-to-day life. After all, he was living in Petrograd during the very months when the Bolsheviks took power there, with fighting going on in the streets around him. By way of contrast, we could think of Mikhail Bulgakov's Civil War novel, *The White Guard*, which depicts the terrifying uncertainties and risks the Turbin family dread, looming outside the very door of their comfortable apartment in Kiev. Like Bulgakov, Zamiatin came from a family of priests, so both writers could have been arraigned purely as class enemies according to the crude justice of the day. However, Zamiatin also had Bolshevik credentials dating from the time of the 1905 Revolution, and his closeness to Gor'ky seems to have gained him admittance to a sort of inner sanctum, where (at least to begin with) he could focus with confidence on the literary concerns of the day without too much fear of arbitrary repressive actions against him. He remains an incisive, courageous and uncompromising commentator on events and on political developments, but he conveys no real sense of alarm about any personal risk to himself or to his wife.

When Zamiatin did finally clamber into his train back to Lebedian' in the late summer of 1918, it was terribly overcrowded, and an extra locomotive had to be summoned to get it up the hills; one person actually died in his carriage, and the corpse was transferred to a pig truck. In 24 hours he consumed one glass of tea and some bread, as well as all the pills he had with him. "I've probably never been so exhausted in my life. If I'd known, I wouldn't have risked the journey. Despite all the decrees, the Red Army troops in Lebedian' are not allowing anyone leaving the town to take any flour away. And so you can even get white flour here. The Soviet deputies [...] have forbidden bathing here on pain of death by shooting (after all, the water in the river hasn't been boiled!)" (3 September).[29] He continued to make sardonic comments about the Bolshevik authorities: "The nights are of iron, black with countless stars. In the house there is a smell of apples (there's a basket of them under my writing desk, and a rack full of Chinese apples [oranges] on the piano). In front of the open verandah there are lime-trees, and the street is green. But all the same the Soviet deputies are galloping along the street. There are arrests under way of hostages. A decree has been issued on the registration and compulsory training of all males between the ages of 18 and 40" (9 September). This latter remark reflects the measure of 29 July 1918 making all men in this age group liable to military service, so it was perhaps fortunate that one of the documents he did not lose to the pickpocket in Moscow was the one concerning his medical exemption from military service. He complained that there had been compulsory billeting of the homeless in people's houses, including his mother's, and it had become difficult to concentrate on any writing.

"The Communist comrades in Lebedian' have made themselves very busy. The other day (about a week ago) they closed every single shop, of every kind, not just the foodstores; it turns out that they're nationalising all trade, far outstripping Moscow in their spirit of enterprise. And so for the time being—since last week—it's been impossible to buy anything, meat, matches or salt. They say the shops will open soon: at the moment they're doing stocktaking. We'll see. You can manage to get meat and other things here through your friends" (9 September). In fact he had been eating rather well, with 3 eggs for breakfast, and doughnuts with sour cream (which Liudmila would have adored), and he promised to try to send some supplies to Petrograd before the rules tightened up again. So a fortnight later he despatched his housekeeper Agra with 25 kilograms of grain and a box of apples and pears, while he tried to decide where it would be best to spend the winter: "It'll be bad there, and bad here. Here it's cramped in the house, and this life isn't really for me. But in Piter there may be no food and it may be cold" (24 September). He tried to persuade Liudmila to join him in Lebedian' from October, assuring her that Agra would be there to look after him, so she could go and get work in the local hospital. He was smoking too much, failing to put on weight despite the excellent food, and not getting on too well with his writing, although *The Protectress of Sinners* was more or less ready to be sent off. But Liudmila decided not to come, and a fortnight later he told her what a wonderful, warm autumn she had missed, and how she would have enjoyed the crisp apples and become even more beautiful. He was setting off towards the end of October for Petrograd, but now did not expect to be able to bring back more than half a pood (8 kilograms) of grain or bread with him, because of the recent confiscations.

He managed to complete the story *The North* in Lebedian' by working outside before it got too hot, and then going off to read on a garden bench in the afternoons, "and all this without a coat, wearing just my light blue golf jacket—in October!" (19 October). He had rewritten the story twice, but expected, as usual, to have to do it at least once more when he got back. A lyrical, sensuous evocation of the love affair between the simple, slow-moving Marei and the wild redhead Pel'ka, *The North* is set in the Arctic regions he had visited three years previously. If Marei is reminiscent of Campbell in *The Islanders*, Pel'ka is a small, slim, sexy woman like Didi (and like I-330 in *We* and Placidia in *The Scourge of God*). These women, often more or less boyish in appearance, are defined by sharpness and angularity: they do not fall pregnant or seek motherhood, and instead they enjoy, and seem to promise, sheer pleasure. In their sexual encounters it is the submissive man who is penetrated by the woman, burned by a knee or by nipples, stung by an elbow or lips or green eyes, pierced by a voice, halted by the lances of eyelashes. With this inversion of conventional active/passive, masculine/feminine traits, it is the women in Zamiatin's fiction who often initiate and control sexual relations.

He also told Liudmila about a lecture he had given at the new People's University in Lebedian', which the authorities had insisted should not be on modern-day England as originally planned, but on

"Contemporary Russian Literature." He gave his audience an account of the evolution of Russian literature since the realist period, represented by writers like Chekhov and Gor'ky, through their antithesis in the shape of the Symbolists, including Bely and Blok, (he dismisses the Futurists—apart from Maiakovsky—as somewhat infantile), and the emergence of a new synthesis in neo-Realists like himself. He characterised the latter as writers who engage with the real world, often that of the provinces, using dialect, sometimes through the improbable or with strong humour; their method is that of economy, and of vivid impressionism, deploying a language which is orchestrated like music.[30]

When Zamiatin returned that autumn to Petrograd, he threw himself into the projects which Gor'ky had devised. The first of these, which Gor'ky launched on 4 September 1918, was the "World Literature" project designed to introduce progressive foreign writers to Russian readers—but it was also importantly a means of providing some sort of income for writers on the brink of starvation in the prevailing conditions of economic and social collapse.[31] Over the next few years Zamiatin would edit and introduce for "World Literature" translations of Dickens, H.G. Wells, Jack London, G.B. Shaw, Upton Sinclair, Romain Rolland, O. Henry and others. One of our sources of information about this hectic period are the distinctly catty diaries of the popular children's writer Kornei Chukovsky, who can be relied on to produce a sour account of most of his acquaintances, and specifically of Zamiatin, since he evidently found him pretty insufferable. On 5 March 1919 he described him wearing "a little green English suit"; in May he noted his huge and "unexpected" success when he read *The Town of Alatyr'* at a literary evening, where the audience listened "reverentially."[32] But as the most fluent English speakers, the two of them were jointly in charge of the English section of "World Literature." At the same time, Zamiatin, Chukovsky, Blok and Nikolai Tikhonov made enthusiastic plans for a new almanac, *Tomorrow*, to be edited by Gor'ky. Zamiatin seems to have written his article of the same name, "Tomorrow," for publication in the journal.[33] It was to be a non-Party publication dedicated to defending culture, unifying intellectuals, and restoring spiritual links with the West; the first volume was also to include his story *The North*, which he had revised that May.[34]

The House of Arts was another major project, and under the leadership of Gor'ky and Tikhonov there was a grand opening on 19 November 1919 in the former Eliseev Palace on Nevsky Prospect, whose owner had run the most luxurious food store—a St Petersburg Fortnum & Mason's—before the Revolution. In Blok's account of the occasion, the poet Nikolai Gumilev and the artist Iury Annenkov were notable for their greedy consumption (in the two rooms which it had proved possible to heat) of the sweets, buns and hot tea which came from Eliseev's store. As an extension of the "World Literature" scheme, Gor'ky had organised Translation and Literary Studios to train young writers at the House of Arts, and invited Zamiatin to lecture on the techniques of fiction. His lectures covered topics such as "The Psychology of Creativity," "On Language," and "On *siuzhet* and *fabula*" (the terms adopted by the Russian Formalists as tools to analyse plot structure).[35] The Studio provided lectures on literature for over 300 students, mostly from modest backgrounds, and included a poetry studio run by Gumilev alongside the prose sessions run by Zamiatin, as well as courses given by Bely, Viktor Zhirmunsky, and the Formalists Viktor Shklovsky, Iury Tynianov and Boris Eikhenbaum. As Zamiatin put it, "there was an epidemic of cultural education in shivering, starving, typhus-ridden St Petersburg. Literature is not education in itself, and for that reason the poets and writers became lecturers. And there was a strange monetary currency: rations, acquired through substituting lectures for poetry and novels."[36] The House of Arts also provided residential accommodation for over 60 writers, including Gumilev,[37] Tikhonov, Ol'ga Forsh,[38] Mikhail Slonimsky, Mikhail Zoshchenko and Osip Mandel'shtam. The Eliseev household servants were still in place, and looked after the new inmates. When all else in the city was in darkness, it was a place full of light and warmth and music, with a mirrored hall and an extravagant décor, including several Rodin sculptures, and even some food available, especially their famous cakes. There was endless chatter: Slonimsky's smoke-filled room was always full of people, and became the birthplace of the Serapion Brotherhood.

Another scheme developed by Gor'ky and the publisher Zinovy Grzhebin in association with "World Literature" was to produce a 100-volume series of the great texts of Russian literature, from Fonvizin in the eighteenth century right up to the present day, based on a list drawn up with great care by Blok. The series editors included the usual key names: Blok, Gor'ky, Zamiatin, Gumilev, and Chukovsky. Chukovsky described how, on the same day as the grand opening of the House of Arts (19 November), most of these writers had already attended three separate meetings in another aristocratic house on Mokhovaia Street, which had been allocated to Gor'ky for his "World Literature" projects. These meetings involved the sections planning "Historical Drama," "World Literature," and the "100 Best Russian Books"; and were a splendid mixture of serious discussions and gossip. As they sat, the artist Iury Annenkov was drawing a brilliant portrait of Tikhonov in return for a pood (17 kilogrammes) of white flour, due to the universal scarcity of food and firewood.[39]

Throughout 1919 Zamiatin had sporadic skirmishes with the Bolshevik police; clearly his oppositional publications had not gone unnoticed. Each time, Gor'ky rescued him. Early in the year, his mother was entirely evicted from the family home in Lebedian'; in Petrograd Zamiatin appealed to Gor'ky for help. The latter sent a telegram and a letter to intercede with the local Soviet, and Maria Aleksandrovna was allowed to move back in.[40] On 15 February, the Cheka, (recently re-named as the Committee for Suppressing Counter-revolution and Speculation), undertook a search of Zamiatin's flat, removed some of his correspondence, and detained him. Under interrogation, he explained that he currently belonged to no Party, even though he had belonged to the Bolshevik wing of the RSDWP as a student. He denied affiliation with the Socialist-Revolutionaries, although he acknowledged that his literary activities had brought him into contact with some of them. We can assume that he did not mention a conversation he had around this time with his former editor Miroliubov, during which he denounced the Bolsheviks and revealed that he was increasingly drawn towards the Socialist-Revolutionaries, who were encouraging him to write more for *Delo naroda*.[41] He simply explained to the Cheka that he held two posts, one as an editor for "World Literature" and the other as a teacher at the Petrograd Polytechnic Institute. He drew attention to his professional and personal links with Gor'ky: "At the present time, since—at the instigation of this same Gor'ky and a whole number of critics—I have come to the conclusion that my vocation is literature, I have no connection with politics or political parties, and am therefore extremely surprised by this search and this arrest." He was released that same day and the case abandoned.[42] This seems to have been the same arrest which he described in his 1923 autobiography, mistakenly dating it to the following month: "In March 1919, together with A.A. Blok, A.M. Remizov, R.V. Ivanov-Razumnik and [the painter] K.S. Petrov-Vodkin, I was arrested and spent a night on Gorokhovaia Street [home of the Cheka]."[43] These detentions had been prompted by the discovery of a "Socialist-Revolutionary" plot in Moscow; most of the writers and artists involved were released almost immediately, while others such as Blok were kept for a couple of nights longer.[44] Zamiatin was briefly detained once again in May, and on the 20th, Gor'ky had to intercede again on his behalf with the Petrograd authorities: "I request that you should release E.I. Zamiatin, who is someone of vital importance to the work of "World Literature," and as a Lecturer at the Polytechnic. You would greatly oblige me by acceding to my request."[45]

Apart from these occasional details, we have scant evidence about Zamiatin's movements during 1919—we don't know, for example, where he spent that summer. But there's little trace of any other creative writing that year, which lends strong credibility to Alex Shane's argument that this must have been the period when he completed most of his work on a first draft of the novel *We*.[46] This is supported by some autobiographical notes Zamiatin wrote during 1920: "In 1919 I wrote a long tale, which in the prevailing censorship conditions is scarcely likely to get printed in the foreseeable future."[47] He took as his inspiration his recent experiences of England, driven by the exigencies of wartime towards the intensive mechanisation of labour, as well as his distaste for the sexually-inhibited social conformism he had found in the West. He then blended these together with what he anticipated might emerge from the rhetoric of Bolshevik power about the Communist state of the future, spelling out the nightmare implications of the Proletkul't poet Kirillov's poem *We*, whose title he borrowed. In Zamiatin's novel, the One State is a totalitarian régime set in the distant future, which vaunts the egalitarian rationalism of the collective over the creative and sexual freedom of the individual. All the citizens ("numbers") of the One State live according to norms laid down by the authorities, which govern their work, their leisure, their sexual activity and their freedom to procreate. A rebellion is attempted by a group of subversives (the "Mephis") led by I-330, a *femme fatale* who has seduced the chief engineer D-503 into doubting the mathematical certainties that have governed his hitherto conformist existence. D-503's value to the rebels lies in the fact that he is the designer of the "Integral" rocket, which is destined to achieve the conquest of other planets. The text of *We* is made up of the diary kept by D-503, and his language reflects his increasing turmoil as he succumbs first to erotic temptation, then to the arguments which challenge the "rational" foundations of the One State. The attack on Communist Utopianism is quite obvious.

The novel stands as an indictment of the West as much as it prophesies the dangers ahead for the Soviet state, and thereby establishes unexpected equivalences between bourgeois England and post-Revolutionary Russian society. George Orwell certainly read the text in this way a quarter of a century later: "It may well be [...] that Zamyatin did not intend the Soviet régime to be the special target of his satire. Writing at about the time of Lenin's death, he cannot have had the Stalin dictatorship in mind, and conditions in Russia in 1923 were not such that anyone would revolt against them on the ground that life was becoming too safe and comfortable. What Zamyatin seems to be aiming at is not any particular country but the implied aims of industrial civilisation. [...] It is in effect a study of the Machine, the genie that man has thoughtlessly let out of its bottle and cannot put back again."[48] Orwell's error in attributing the writing of *We* to 1923 rather than 1919–20 only further underlines his point that it was far too soon after 1917 for Zamiatin to be offering a critique of Soviet socialism in its fully realised, totalitarian form. Orwell's own satirical targets in *Nineteen Eighty-Four*, which was shaped to some extent by his reading of *We*, were similarly universal rather than specific: "My recent novel [*1984*] is NOT intended as an attack on Socialism or on the British Labour Party (of which I am a supporter), but as a show-up of the perversions to which a centralised economy is liable, and which have already been partly realized in Communism and Fascism. [...] The scene of the book is laid in Britain in order to emphasise that the English-speaking races are not innately better than anyone else, and that totalitarianism, if not fought against, could triumph anywhere."[49] The broad political reach of Zamiatin's satire in *We*, however, was not understood by its earliest readers.

He apparently also wrote his two brief satirical "Fairy-tales" in 1919, *The Church of God* (about the man who cannot eradicate the stink of the corpse from the church he has built, using money stolen from the merchant he has just murdered) and *The Natives* (about two cannibal tribes, who each accuse the other of immorality). These were not published until 1922, when they probably contributed to his further arrest.[50] In October he wrote his brief memoir of meeting the recently deceased Leonid Andreev in Finland in 1906, which he read with great success at an Andreev commemorative evening that November, attended by a very young Vladimir Pozner.[51] If it is true that 1919 was largely taken up with the writing of *We*, then perhaps that was largely completed by 1 December, when he wrote his lengthy biographical article about Julius Robert Mayer, the "heretical" founding father of the study of thermodynamics.[52]

The Zamiatins had been living in Petrograd since their return from England at 19, Shirokaia Street, but the end of 1919 saw them moving to a flat on Karpovka Embankment in a building situated on one of the larger islands in the Neva, a few blocks to the north of the Peter and Paul Fortress.[53] One of their neighbours and close friends at Shirokaia Street had been the painter Boris Grigor'ev (they shared a mutual friend in Iury Annenkov).[54] Seeing how difficult things were becoming, in October 1919 Boris Grigor'ev escaped in a small boat from Russia to Finland with his wife and young son.[55] A year later another of the Zamiatins' neighbours from Shirokaia Street, Avgusta Damanskaia, would also flee the country to settle in France.

The "Historical Drama" project which Gor'ky had initiated in the spring of 1919 was gathering pace, and by March 1920 there had been 45 meetings of its Editorial Board. The plan was to illustrate key moments in history through drama, with particular emphasis on religious and scientific issues, and topics were assigned accordingly.[56] Zamiatin's own contribution, *The Fires of Santo Domingo*, was completed in 1920: it is clearly of a piece with the issues of brutally-enforced orthodoxy and heresy which are central to *We*, and must have been written shortly after the novel.[57] Like the young writer Lev Lunts, who set his play *Outside the Law* in Spain, but with no attempt to disguise its topical relevance, Zamiatin's play about the cruel tyranny of the Inquisition in Seville had plenty of contemporary resonances. After he had moved to France in the 1930s, he drafted the following account of the play: "In the XVIth century we may find a parallel with the present day, when fanatics of political dogmatism consider themselves entitled to 'save' people by means of violence and terror. Just as in the Middle Ages, in the modern world entire peoples live in constant fear, under the surveillance of countless spies."[58] The play was fated never to reach the stage, despite Gor'ky's comment that it was "interesting and meaty." Remizov too wrote admiringly of Zamiatin's handling of language in this first play of his, adding that actors and theatres should be vying to stage the somewhat "operatic" text: "He has perfect command of the language, he loves words and values them, and he deploys them with great art. [...] Its success is guaranteed." Chukovsky, however, found the play too intellectual, too filled with obscure language and allusions: "it seems to me that Zamiatin has a strangely weak sense of the audience he is supposed to be addressing."[59] When it was eventually printed in 1923, it was met with enormous hostility by Marxist critics such as the notorious V.I. Blium, who argued that Zamiatin had simply "transposed into the play the trivial chatter of our intelligentsia, who are so weary of the Revolution."[60]

Drama, and Shakespeare in particular, became a significant preoccupation for Zamiatin during the winter of 1919–20. On 22 January a production of *Othello* premiered at the newly-founded Bol'shoi Dramatichesky Theatre (BDT) in Petrograd. Zamiatin had revised the translation, and contributed helpfully to discussions of the play with the cast.[61] He also worked with Blok over the summer of 1920 on a revision of the Russian translation of *King Lear* for the BDT, where Blok was Chairman of the Board. "During one of the final evening rehearsals it suddenly became unbearable, and it was decided that the scene where Gloucester's eyes are put out should be omitted. I remember that Blok was in favour of keeping in the scene of the plucking out of the eyes: 'Our times are just the same as the sixteenth century... We are perfectly capable of watching the cruellest of things.'"[62] This production of *Lear*, designed by Mstislav Dobuzhinsky, received its première on 21 September. Simultaneously, he worked on a revision of the translation of *The Merchant of Venice*, and "Shylock," as he referred to it, in a production directed and designed by Aleksandr N. Benois, opened at the BDT on 27 November and ran for three seasons.[63]

All of these tasks were of course entrusted to him as someone whose English was considered fluent. One person who was not so impressed with his English was the children's writer Samuil Marshak, who had been a student in London before the War: "I was walking along Mokhovaia Street and heard Zamiatin talking to some young lady in English. At the top of his voice! for all the street to hear! and badly, like an English caretaker."[64] Perhaps Marshak was observing the extent to which Zamiatin's spoken English had been coloured by his time in Newcastle, where his days at the shipyards were partly spent with Geordies and working men with northern accents, rather than the received southern English accent Marshak and other Russians of his generation may have learned; so that this remark may be an example of a British class snobbery transposed to Russia.

Altogether, 1920 became quite an "English" year for Zamiatin, since alongside his work on Shakespeare he did a great deal for "World Literature" on H.G. Wells, writing prefaces to translations of his *War of the Worlds*,[65] and *The Time Machine*.[66] The latter's science-fiction, while differing in many respects from Zamiatin's political anti-utopia, had undoubtedly provided a significant inspiration for *We*. That autumn, H.G. Wells came on a visit to Petrograd, and Zamiatin was of course the natural choice to help welcome him at the reception held on 18 October at the House of Arts. Wells thanked the assembled writers, led by Gor'ky, for the opportunity to observe the "curious historical experiment" constituted by their Socialist Revolution. Stung by this condescension, the novelist Aleksandr Amfiteatrov retorted that the writers had actually come there that day largely because of the lavish food being served, rather than to meet Wells, and Viktor Shklovsky, author of a fascinating Formalist analysis of *Tristram Shandy*, shrieked furiously about the despicable post-Revolutionary British blockade of the country, which was reducing the Russian people to hunger and misery. It was left to Zamiatin in his fluent English to smooth things over and declare the occasion closed.[67] Early in January 1922 he would complete a lengthy essay called "Notes on the Works of H.G. Wells" ["Herbert Wells"]. Recalling his own first experience of seeing an aeroplane twelve years earlier, he observed that Wells's stories, with their blend of precise science and fairytale, seemed like fantasies for the present day: "but tomorrow they could become part of everyday life."[68]

On 4 July 1920, Zamiatin became a founding member of the writers' organisation which was to provide the main focus for his administrative activities during the 1920s. This was the Petrograd branch of the VSP [All-Russian Writers' Union], chaired by Akim Volynsky. The VSP campaigned vigorously for freedom of speech as well as concerning itself with the legal rights and material welfare of its members, in close association with the House of Writers. Zamiatin was an energetic and efficient member of the VSP, involved in drafting many of its proposals over the next few years.[69]

Only one letter from Zamiatin to Liudmila has been preserved from that year, written in the summer of 1920. It is addressed to her as Milusa, and also to the teddy-bear Misha, who, along with a boy doll they named Rostislav, had come to occupy a permanent place in their household. These toy figures were well known to the Zamiatins' friends: Akhmatova would later dedicate one of her signed photo portraits to Rostislav, while Annenkov depicted him in the corner of his famous 1921 portrait of Zamiatin.[70] The whole question of childlessness as a domestic grief had by now become a recurrent theme of his writing—for example, in the unconquerable urge of the curvaceous O-90 in *We* to break the law and have a child to suckle, even at the risk of her own life. For him, it was a lack which would find an outlet in a variety of surrogates, such as his "parental" feelings for his icebreakers, for the Serapion Brothers, and for the youth of Soviet literature in general.

This particular letter to Liudmila was written while she was staying at a holiday dacha outside Petrograd, towards Sestroretsk. A whole colony of dachas had been made available that summer to the people who worked at "World Literature" and the House of Arts, although they were very primitive and consisted just of bare walls and a roof. The Chaliapins were there, along with the Chukovskys, the Annenkovs, the Grzhebins, the Remizovs and many others.[71] In other words, Zamiatin was now both working and relaxing alongside the most eminent cultural figures of the day. During his time at the dacha colony of Ermilovka that August, he drafted early versions of what would become the joyously blasphemous and improper story *How the Monk Erasmus was Healed*.[72] The story parodies a miracle tale, with the innocent monk Erasmus inadvertently provoking scenes of frantic masturbation in the monastery, and visions of clouds dripping breast milk and sperm, all thanks to his paintings and his reading of the Song of Songs. Eventually the Father Superior realises that only by allowing him to achieve a full sexual experience with the visionary figure of Mary of Egypt will his extraordinary erotic suggestiveness be "healed." This story is perhaps the most blatantly transgressive of his impious tales, which reflect the deep gulf which had long ago opened up between him and his devout father.

In October 1920, by contrast, Zamiatin wrote his haunting story *The Cave*, describing the impoverished life of an ordinary couple in the freezing conditions of Civil War Petrograd, likened to a new Ice Age, and the dehumanising effect that this has on human behaviour. It strips them of all hope as their civilised values fall away, until they are reduced to suicide.[73] In that same month he completed his story *Mamai* (originally entitled *Mamai in 1917*), referring to the Tatar leader who was defeated by the Russian prince Dmitry Donskoi at the 14th-century Battle of Kulikovo; but his modern-day Mamai (modelled, as we know, on Iakov Grebenshchikov) is an avid book-collector, whose ferocity is directed only at the mouse who has eaten the money for his next cherished purchase. However, beyond the humour, the story also provided an opportunity to describe the frightened atmosphere in Petrograd homes, with night-time raids and confiscations a constant threat.[74] *Mamai* appeared in the first number of the new House of Arts journal, *Dom iskusstv* (*House of Arts*), which came out at the end of February 1921,[75] and his combative article "I am Afraid" was printed in the same number. This was a strongly-worded attack on the authorities' ongoing attempts to regulate literary work, and on the opportunism of many pro-régime writers, concluding: "I am afraid that we will have no true literature until people stop considering the Russian *demos* to be a child whose innocence needs to be protected. I am afraid that we will have no true literature until we cure ourselves of this new kind of Catholicism, which no less than the old one fears every heretical word. And if this illness turns out to be incurable, then I am afraid that Russian literature will have only one future—its past."[76] This piece created a considerable stir, provoking forceful ripostes from the young writer Konstantin Fedin in the February-March number of *Kniga i revoliutsiia* (*Books and the Revolution*), and also from the influential Bolshevik critic Aleksandr Voronsky.[77]

A sense of the extent to which Zamiatin was now a central figure in the literary world of Petrograd is reinforced by the number of books in his library which bear dedications to him from their authors, including Shklovsky (his book "*Siuzhet*" *as an Aspect of Style*) and Anna Akhmatova (her collection *Anno Domini*).[78] It was during this period that he also became friendly with Boris Pil'niak, another young writer who had published with Miroliubov, probably when Pil'niak was staying with Gor'ky.[79] In his article "Paradise" Zamiatin bemoaned the tedious euphony of most writers' praise of the régime, with Pil'niak a rare exception amongst them because he truly is an artist: "He is a man who would suffocate in the distilled air of heaven; he needs earthy air, sinful air, the kind which is full of smoke and mist and the perfume of women's hair, the scented breath of cherry blossom and the strong exhalations of the soil in spring."[80] In another piece (tentatively entitled "Notes of a Dreamer") he reflected that many writers like himself who started out as socialists, and suffered for that cause in their time, find it hard to resist the temptations of officially-condoned success—as, for example, Maiakovsky with his 1918/1921 propaganda play *Mystery-Bouffe*. However, the true writer should remain an impractical and stubborn dreamer.[81]

After the devastation of seven years of war, revolution and civil war, and as a consequence of Allied blockades and of War Communism, which attempted to achieve the complete nationalisation of all property and all trade, living conditions had become exceptionally difficult. In January 1921, Zamiatin wrote a comical poem about the cost of a packet of Chinese tea (30 000 roubles) and blamed the White General Wrangel' and the Allied intervention for creating the financial crisis.[82] A week or two later, Chukovsky reported in his diary, as a major excitement, Akhmatova's gift of a bottle of milk to him for his daughter.[83] Akhmatova herself was in need of money, and was taken on by "World Literature" as a translator the following day.[84] Meanwhile, Zamiatin was complaining about the lack of trams in Petrograd, which meant that he was tiring himself out walking back and forth through the snow to his classes at the Polytechnic.[85]

By the middle of February, Chukovsky found himself obliged to leave Petrograd with his family for the country in order to escape the threat of starvation; his diaries for the next few months are full of concerns about rations and bread. Asking to be dispensed from his duties at the VSP, he explained: "The cause of my illness is hunger. Never have the writers of Russia led such a hard life as they do at present. On 7 June my whole enormous family and I simply didn't sit down to eat. On 8 June we had soup and a piece of bread each. On 9 June we all had herring, but without bread. It's an age since we have seen butter or eggs. My daughter, who has just had an operation, is getting thinner by the day. My sons weep from hunger."[86] The Bolshevik authorities themselves finally acknowledged that the country was on its knees, and towards the end of March 1921 Lenin announced at the 10th Party Congress a New Economic Policy (NEP). This, by allowing small-scale private enterprise, was designed to kick-start the economy and help to rebuild Russia. The successes of NEP during the 1920s would gradually relieve the day-to-day hardships suffered by individuals, as well as building the foundations for the rapid industrialisation of the 1930s.

It seems rather remarkable that, in the midst of all these privations and struggles to secure a hand-to-mouth existence, some of the younger writers who had been nurtured by Gor'ky's visionary cultural institutions should have chosen this moment to set up their own independent literary organisation. The Serapion Brotherhood was founded on 1 February 1921; its initiators were Mikhail Slonimsky, Lev Lunts, Nikolai Nikitin and Vladimir Pozner, whose ages ranged from 26 down to 16. Over the next year or so they were joined by others, including Zoshchenko, Fedin, Tikhonov and Elizaveta Polonskaia. Taking inspiration from E. T. A. Hoffmann's collection of tales, *The Serapion Brothers* (1819–21), the guiding principles of this group included a commitment to individual literary experimentation rather than any collective ideological platform. The first Serapion Brotherhood publication came out in the summer of 1921, and they flourished until 1923–24, when political pressures, emigrations and the deeply-mourned death at the age of 23 of Lev Lunts in Germany brought about the gradual dissolution of the group.[87] Various senior figures, including Gor'ky as well as Zamiatin, came to serve as their mentors. Zamiatin would later observe: "As far as technique is concerned, the majority of the Serapions were my pupils. In 1919–22 there was a literary studio at the House of Arts in St Petersburg, where I used to give lectures on 'The Techniques of Prose Fiction.' The Serapion Brothers were born in this studio, and I was their midwife."[88] In the autumn of 1920 he had received a flattering letter from Nikolai Nikitin, then his student at the House of Arts: "I'm waiting impatiently for the start of my studies with you. I can sense the enormous use they have been to me, and I don't know how I can thank you for that. You've turned me from someone who was blind into someone who can see. Literally!"[89]

Later on, Nikitin would wonder whether Zamiatin's influence had not been harmful to them, especially as regards his preoccupation with stylisation and his enthusiasm for "provincialisms." However, Nikitin acknowledged: "He taught those young people the purest love for the Russian language and for its poeticisation, and selfless love for the language, [...] a deep understanding of what the Russian language was, how weighty it was, and how much it meant for literature."[90] A fellow lecturer at the House of Arts, Andrei Levinson, recalled Zamiatin's real talent for working with students: "He restrained them with a steely hand and with his mocking, sideways glance. He subjected these unruly youths to discipline. He had a gift for demonstrating to a pupil a device which would be subtly calculated and economical, one which would conserve energy and hit its target at the same time." Polonskaia would recall that "Zamiatin could be very harsh. But he was a clever man, a remarkable man."[91]

In the spring of 1921, Zamiatin was still to be found everywhere, giving lectures and attending editorial or organisational meetings. Andrei Levinson, who fled abroad in March, later wrote recollections of him at this time which once again singled him out for his supposed "Englishness":

> His influence is exceptionally powerful: for those who know only the small stack of his books, it is at times rather mysterious. His power is personal, it is the direct emanation of a hardened will. The whole of Zamiatin is of a harmonious cut; everything

in him is precisely fitted; he is strong and supple; he is unhurried, and never puts a foot wrong; he is unforthcoming, and doesn't waste words. His hair is parted, there's a mocking smile on his lips, and at the corner of his smile there's a pipe: it contains a strong tobacco, consistently aromatic: Navy Cut. He is an Englishman out of Leskov; a coloniser in a white helmet; Mister Zamiatin; Zamiatin Effendi; a gentleman.[92]

In May, plans to publish a new fortnightly newspaper, *Literaturnaia gazeta* (*The Literary Gazette*), edited by Volynsky, Zamiatin, Tikhonov, and Chukovsky, bore fruit in the shape of a first edition which included another article by Zamiatin on the freedom of the press, "It's time." However, the largely anti-Bolshevik sentiments of the majority of contributors were deemed unacceptable, and the publication was banned.[93] Chukovsky and Volynsky were left to oversee the printing in Petrograd while this dispute was unfolding. Zamiatin had set off with the artist Mstislav Dobuzhinsky for a holiday in the country, at a retreat for writers and artists that had been made available to members of the House of Arts at Kholomki, in the Pskov District. This was where Chukovsky had gone when he left Petrograd with his family in February. By coincidence, Kholomki had been the family estate of that same Prince Gagarin who had been the first Director of the Polytechnic Institute; it was his widow, Princess Maria, who allowed Chukovsky and Dobuzhinsky to organise the holiday home on her estate, and on her sister's neighbouring estate at Bel'skoe Ust'e. One day, she showed Chukovsky the messages of support Prince Gagarin had received while defending his students against police persecution under Nicholas II—including a grateful note signed by the student Zamiatin.[94] That spring, Zamiatin spent about a week there, enjoying the good weather and filling his notebooks, even failing to return to Petrograd by 23 May as originally intended.[95] His conversations with Princess Maria and her daughter Sof'ia stimulated him to compose preliminary sketches for a novel, *The Oaks*, clearly set in Kholomki, and reflecting the Gagarin family's life there before the Revolution.[96]

It is important to note what a busy summer he had that year. After Kholomki he went to Moscow, in part at the instigation of Boris Pil'niak. He read *The Fisher of Men* on 13 June to an audience of writers, including Boris Pasternak, who was complimentary; he read the same story to a potentially more hostile, pro-Soviet audience on 24 June, provocatively adding *The Cave*. To his surprise, this reading also went well.⁹⁷ He saw Gor'ky, and the publisher Grzhebin (hoping in vain to collect royalties); he also proposed to lobby the Commissar for Enlightenment [Minister of Culture], Anatoly Lunacharsky, to lift the ban on *Literaturnaia gazeta*. At the same time, he was trying to interest one of the Moscow theatres in his play *The Fires of Santo Domingo*.⁹⁸ He had been intending to spend some time in Lebedian', where his mother was ill, but he discovered that the trains to nearby Elets had not been running since early May—the track had been damaged, probably in an act of sabotage by the anti-Bolshevik peasant insurgency led in the Tambov region at this period by Aleksandr Antonov, a former Socialist-Revolutionary. Instead, Zamiatin accepted Pil'niak's invitation to go and spend a few days with him in Kolomna, an ancient town just over 100 kilometres to the south-east of the capital. Finding a long queue for tickets at the railway station, he managed to obtain one by bartering four rolls baked by Liudmila. He was delighted by the churches, monasteries and fortress of this town on the Moskva river, although he found Pil'niak's untidy household and late nights a bit hard to stand.⁹⁹ Equally, Pil'niak was not quite sure at this stage how much he liked his new friend, and evidently found him a little irritating on that visit: "I think it is his misfortune that as a man he is almost entirely an engineer, and scarcely a writer at all (things which are fairly irreconcilable), and as a man he is not very successful, although he is talented and clever." Pil'niak went on to suggest that Zamiatin's writing was cold and unfeeling, although he did at least acknowledge that his essays were very accomplished.¹⁰⁰

So Zamiatin did not manage to reach Lebedian' on this occasion, and was soon back in Petrograd. He did, however, write to Chukovsky, who was still in charge at Kholomki, that in Moscow he had been pursued by two different women, to one of whom he would not give any more than "the appropriate 4–5 inches of his body," while to the other he might have given a portion of his soul. During the first half of July he was busy editing the second number of the *Dom iskusstv* journal, looking after all the other publishing ventures he was involved in, and finishing off articles his friends had failed to complete—and thinking enviously of Chukovsky enjoying the scented lime-trees and cuckoo song. Evidently because of the frustration of his Lebedian' plans, he was considering returning to Kholomki, more specifically to Bel'skoe Ust'e, perhaps even together with Liudmila. He had been trying to raise some money to enable her to have a holiday (and also to get some dental treatment for himself—his fillings had been falling out) by penning another of his prefaces to the works of H.G. Wells. It is intriguing that he was thinking of bringing Liudmila, since it appears that at this time he had got involved in a rather painful romantic entanglement with the Gagarins' daughter, Princess Sof'ia, who now helped to manage her father's former estate; perhaps she was the woman to whom he had considered offering part of his soul?[101] His married life with Liudmila appears to have been punctuated by occasional, casual liaisons of this kind, but on the whole they do not seem to have done any lasting damage. If going to Kholomki should prove impossible, he told Chukovsky, it would not matter: "I will just sit here and finish polishing my most malicious novel" (*We*), which he was currently "ill" with.[102]

In early August he was still in Petrograd, working for a Committee set up with Gor'ky, Remizov, Bely, Akhmatova, and Blok to provide assistance to the people starving in the Volga region. Gor'ky would in fact leave Russia that October, partly in order to work on this Committee's behalf as well as for health reasons, and would not return for several years.[103] Zamiatin had continued to take part in Remizov's "Great and Free Monkey Chamber," in which he had now risen to the rank of "Zamuty the Meek, Archbishop of the Monkeys and Prince of Monkeys in the World."[104] But on 28 July he found himself bidding farewell to the Remizovs, who had also decided to get out of Russia. He inscribed Remizov's wife's album with an apt parting quotation from the unpublished *We*, a paraphrase of the ironic passage in which the state poet R-13, like Dostoevsky's Grand Inquisitor, seems to argue that happiness is more important than freedom: "That ancient legend about Paradise is actually about us, about today, and it contains a profound meaning. Just think: those two in the Garden of Eden were offered a choice—either happiness without freedom, or freedom without happiness. There was no third option. They chose freedom, and ever after yearned for fetters. And it's only now that 'We' have once again succeeded in fettering people—and so we have made them happy."[105]

And indeed, August 1921 was going to prove a traumatic month: on the 7th, the same day that the Remizovs actually crossed the frontier, Aleksandr Blok died.[106] Four months earlier, Zamiatin had noted that Blok looked weary at the BDT as he read his poems about Russia: "There was a certain mournful, melancholy and tender solemnity about that last evening of Blok's. I remember a voice from behind me in the audience: 'This is like a wake!' And indeed, this was Petersburg's wake for Blok. As far as Petersburg was concerned, Blok left the stage of the Drama Theatre and went directly beyond that wall, along whose dark blue crenellations death walks like a watchman; on that white April night Petersburg saw Blok for the last time."[107] The sad announcement of his demise was promptly communicated by Zamiatin to Chukovsky, together with some further, very alarming news: "Yesterday Blok died at 10:30 in the morning. Or, to be more precise: he was killed by this life we live, in caves, like cattle. Because it was, it was still possible to have saved him, if people had managed to get him abroad in time. The 7th of August 1921 is as unbelievable a day as that one in 1830 [1837] when people heard that Pushkin had been killed. I am a man made of steel, and there are few people I care for, it's rare for me to love. But I did love Blok, and to know that he is dead—well, what is there to say. [...] On Tuesday of last week Gum [Nikolai Gumilev, Akhmatova's former husband] was arrested, and no-one knows why."[108]

Annenkov claims that the long-sought permission for the very frail Blok to travel abroad for treatment, which Gor'ky had done his best to arrange, arrived just one hour after his death. He himself went to Blok's apartment while he still lay there, and made a sketch of the poet on his death-bed. Zamiatin and Akhmatova both attended the funeral on the 10th. The official response in *Pravda* to Blok's death was so perfunctory that it caused outrage, and Zamiatin was one of many writers who rushed to pay the poet his due in print. His brief and impressionistic obituary, published later that month in *Zapiski mechtatelei* (*Notes by Dreamers*), recorded his grief at the loss of a noble, gentle idealist. Describing the funeral, he observed that it was attended by all that was left of literature in Russia—and how little of that there turned out to be.[109]

The poet Gumilev, his colleague and partner in so many of Gor'ky's schemes, had been arrested by the Cheka in connection with a supposed monarchist conspiracy, and to the horror of the literary community he was sentenced and promptly shot in the last week of August, along with 60 others. Zamiatin recalled a conversation he had some time afterwards with Gor'ky, where the latter recounted in a fury how he had actually persuaded the authorities in Moscow to spare Gumilev's life, but that the Petrograd Cheka had merely hastened to carry out the sentence when they heard of the possibility of a reprieve.[110] According to Chukovsky, Zamiatin was deeply shocked and troubled by Gumilev's execution.[111]

By late August, Zamiatin was back in Kholomki, having been pressed to return by Chukovsky, who was feeling disappointed that his fellow writers weren't taking up the opportunities he had worked so hard to contrive there, for them to relax and enjoy the bountiful provision of bread, milk, eggs, grain, flour, and apples. Chukovsky was also concerned about Sof'ia Gagarina, who was exhausting herself with running the estate's affairs and pining for Zamiatin, despite herself being pursued by Dobuzhinsky: "All you need is to take pity on her. Of course she's completely different from us, she's moulded from a different clay, and she loves horses, dancing, and birthday parties; she prays for hours and detests the Jews, she's never heard of Blok, nor will she ever know anything about him—but don't push her away. After all, she wants, nothing, <u>nothing</u>. Just a kind word."[112] That summer, the writers who enjoyed the abundance of food at Kholomki included the poet Vladislav Khodasevich, Mandel'shtam, Zoshchenko, Slonimsky, and Lunts.[113] It was a far from luxurious establishment, as Khodasevich recalled: "We lived there like modern-day Robinson Crusoes. There were about twelve rooms in the house, but the windows were intact in only three of them. There were only three beds, so people slept on the floor or on straw. [...] The village folk refused to accept Soviet money. Having been warned about this in advance, the visitors brought things with them for barter. [...] You could get a 2-month supply of milk in return for a tablecloth, a chicken and ten eggs for a piece of soap, or a sack of flour for a bottle of eau de cologne."[114] Letters from Khodasevich, vaunting the orchard with its 1,500 apple trees, establish that Zamiatin was staying at Bel'skoe Ust'e by 27 August, and that he was planning to return to the city with the Dobuzhinskys on 8 September.[115] There were some happy moments, recorded in drawings by Sof'ia Gagarina and others, including one of Zamiatin driving his friends in a cart, pulled by a scruffy-looking horse.[116] All the evidence suggests that he was there without Liudmila.[117]

After Kholomki, Zamiatin spent a couple of weeks at home, and then set off in the last week of September to try again to get down to Lebedian'. After a difficult three-day journey, during which he distracted himself by reading Alexandre Dumas' novel *Ange-Pitou*, he finally arrived, and was dismayed at the poverty he now found there: the sugar he had brought was greeted with inordinate excitement, and he discovered that his family had had to sell their cow for bread, and were subsisting largely on potatoes.[118]

All these details take on a certain importance simply because a much-quoted memoir by Annenkov states that the summer of 1921 was when Zamiatin really finished writing *We*. True, Zamiatin himself had mentioned a final "polishing" of the novel at the end of July. But the upheavals and traumas of that August, together with the brief holiday fortnight he spent in the crowded writers' colony, probably without Liudmila, scarcely accord with Annenkov's description:

> I spent a happy month's summer holiday with him in 1921 in a remote village on the banks of the Sheksna. We had a tumbledown *izba*, let out to us by the local Council. Each morning until midday we lay on the warm, sandy bank of the beautiful river. After eating, we went for long walks among the wild sunflowers, the forest strawberries, and the slender-stemmed mushrooms, and then we came back to the sandy bank of the Sheksna, home to the tastiest sterlet fish. [...] All the same, we did a great deal of work, sitting amongst the bushes or lying in the grass, Zamiatin with his school exercise books, and I with my sketch-pad. Zamiatin was "cleaning up," as he put it, his novel *We*, and was working on translations of H.G. Wells or Thackeray. [...] Towards six in the evening Zamiatin's wife Liudmila Nikolaevna expected us for our extremely modest supper, although sometimes a little sterlet we'd discreetly fished out would appear on the menu. And then later, as the white night drew on, there'd be lime-tree tea with saccharine.[119]

It has been suggested that Annenkov's reference here to the river "Sheksna" (which is over 300 miles away from Pskov, in Vologda province), instead of the river "Sheloni" which runs near Kholomki, was simply a slip of the pen. It seems more likely that, when writing this memoir much later on, he was in fact confusing the year rather than the river, and that he was most probably thinking of 1920: as in 1919, we know very little about Zamiatin's summer travels that year. Certainly Zamiatin himself mentioned that he had spent time in Vologda province at some point, although we don't know when that actually was.[120] We may therefore with some confidence date the principal work on *We* to the years 1919–20, rather than 1919–21, as Annenkov's memoir implies.

Be that as it may, the two men would subsequently discuss Zamiatin's science-fiction dystopia at some length, with Annenkov professing his admiration—as a non-scientist—for the power and beauty of technology. Zamiatin responded ironically, drawing on many of the points he had tried to make about the utopian One State in *We*: "I give in: you're right. Technology is all-powerful, and entirely a blessing. The time will come when there'll only be systems and purposefulness in everything, when man and nature will be turned into a formula, into a keyboard." He pointed out that in the simplified world of the future there would be no need for flowers or trees, let alone music; only the railway timetable would be preserved from the past: "Any deviation from the norm will be called madness. And so those Shakespeares and Dostoevskys and Scriabins who deviate from the norm will be tied up in strait-jackets and placed in padded cells. Children will be manufactured in factories, hundreds at a time. [...] My dear friend! in such a purposeful, organised and exact universe you would start to feel nauseous within half-an hour... There are two valuable impulses in man: the brain and sex. All science derives from the former, all art from the latter. [...] You have become infected with idolatry of the machine. [...] And what lies beyond, Annenkov, beyond your endless technological progress? [...] In point of fact, your very own drawings and paintings argue against you much more effectively than I can myself."[121]

The fact of the completion of the novel, "a lengthy, fantastical story," had been mentioned in the Western press as early as spring 1921,[122] and now the time had come to think about trying to get it published. On 23 August came an announcement in *Zhizn' iskusstva* (*Life of Art*) of a projected Russian publication of *We* in volume 4 of *Zapiski mechtatelei*.[123] That autumn he sent the novel to Grzhebin in Berlin, for inclusion in a planned Russian-language edition of his *Collected Works*—a further mark of his considerable standing now as an established writer. Grzhebin had been allowed to leave Russia on 3 October to set up a publishing house in Germany, whose editorial board still included Zamiatin, and which would work in collaboration with the Soviet authorities.[124] Around this time, Zamiatin also sent some of his short stories for translation to the USA, at the request of a large New York publishing company.[125] That winter he gave the first public reading of the entire novel, in two sittings, to a packed audience at the Institute of the History of the Arts.[126]

November 1921 saw the first draft of Zamiatin's article "On Synthetism," destined as the introduction to a superb volume of portraits by Annenkov which was published by "Petropolis" in August 1922. In the volume, Zamiatin's essay is printed alongside the famous 1921 portrait of him against the background of a fragment of a literary article torn from a New York paper, with the boy doll Rostislav peeping over his shoulder. His essay outlines the evolution of art in recent years in dialectical terms, shaped by the constant movement from affirmation (represented by Rubens, Repin, Zola, Tolstoy, Gor'ky, Realism, and Naturalism) to negation (Schopenhauer, Botticelli, Vrubel', Verlaine, Blok, idealism and Symbolism), and on through the negation of the negation to synthesis (Nietzsche, Whitman, Gauguin, Seurat, Picasso, neo-Realism, Synthetism and Expressionism). The volume included portraits of many of Zamiatin's circle of acquaintances, thinned now, at the close of the traumatic years of Revolution and Civil War, by death or emigration: Blok, Benois, Akhmatova, Gor'ky, Volynsky, Kuz'min, Shchegolev, Chukovsky, Pasternak, Grzhebin, Remizov, Sologub, Khodasevich, Shklovsky, and even H.G. Wells. As Annenkov put it in his Preface, all his subjects were marked by the Revolution, "and all of them serve as a vivid reminder to me of those tragedies and hopes, those low moments and hopeful times which we were fated to live through together, side by side."[127]

Chapter 5:
Petrograd/Leningrad (1922–1925)

Those intellectuals who had survived the Civil War in Russia were about to discover what life was going to be like as domestic stability was finally restored in the new state, which would be formally constituted as the USSR in December 1922. For Zamiatin, now a key figure on the literary scene, and with a recently completed novel ready for publication, the NEP era would seem to offer a whole range of hopeful opportunities, even if these eventually ended in frustration. He and Liudmila saw in the year 1922, the first year of peace after seven years of strife, with a party in the company of Chukovsky, the Fedins, and the Khodaseviches, later joined by Annenkov, Eikhenbaum and Tynianov. However, the occasion was powerfully overshadowed by their mournful recollections of Blok and Gumilev. Further seasonal celebrations included a masked ball in the "World Literature" offices, organised by Zamiatin and Tikhonov.[1] In early May that year he and Liudmila would move from Karpovka Embankment where they had been living since 1919, into an apartment in the same building as "World Literature," at 36 Mokhovaia Street.[2]

He was writing less now, "probably because I have become more demanding towards myself."[3] In February, his two 1919 miniatures deploring revolutionary violence, *The Natives* and *The Church of God*, finally appeared in print. One of the most influential Bolsheviks in the literary politics of the day, Aleksandr Voronsky, who had been endorsed a year previously by Lenin and Gor'ky to set up the journal *Krasnaia nov'* (*Red Virgin Soil*), had this to say about them: "Zamiatin is a considerable artist and an intelligent man. This can be seen in his *Provincial Tale*, his *Islanders*, and in his wonderful article about H.G. Wells. But the October Revolution struck Zamiatin a painful blow. Pieces such as *The Natives* and *The Church of God* are reprinted by the émigré press abroad with gleeful cackling and hissing—and truly, their place is over there, rather than in the beleaguered Soviet camp. This is low-grade propaganda." In April, Voronsky would write a letter to Lenin in which he described Zamiatin as "standing aside" from the new literature of the Soviet Union.[4] The controversial publication of these miniatures, which indeed garnered acclaim abroad—Marc Slonim in the Prague journal *Volia Rossii* (*Freedom of Russia*) talked of his "marvellous, intelligent and relevant tales"—certainly helped to thicken the dark clouds which were starting to gather over Zamiatin's head in official circles that year. Further controversial publications in the Berlin journal *Golos Rossii* (*Voice of Russia*) that spring and summer—of "Paradise," *The Dragon*, and *The Cave*—did not help matters.[5] Another provocation was the publication by "Petropolis" in Berlin of the hilariously improper story *How the Monk Erasmus was Healed*, for which Boris Kustodiev completed his 40 equally risqué illustrations in early June.[6]

Zamiatin's major preoccupation at this point was to get *We* published, either in Russia or abroad. In a letter of 22 February to Pil'niak (who was visiting Berlin), he mentioned, alongside his accounts of all-night Shrovetide revels and drinking, that he had sold the novel to the "Alkonost" publishing house, and that the first part was supposed to appear the following month in St Petersburg in their journal *Zapiski mechtatelei*.[7] "Alkonost" had been the main publisher of the Symbolists and other poets since the Revolution, and their books had included the first separate edition of Blok's *The Twelve*, with illustrations by Annenkov. Meanwhile, the first three volumes of his *Collected Works* (under the titles *At the Back of Beyond*, *The Islanders*, and *Fairy-tales*) were just beginning to be published by Grzhebin in Berlin. And he was hopeful that that would not be all: "The fourth will be the novel *We*—my most light-hearted, and at the same time my most serious piece."[8] Apart from Grzhebin, there were others in emigration who also had their eye on the novel. The editors of the Paris-based *Sovremennye zapiski* (*Contemporary Notes*) wrote that spring to Sergei Postnikov, who had slipped out of Russia to Finland in the autumn of 1921 and was also then in Berlin, pressing him to negotiate a contract for the publication of the novel on their behalf: "we've been dreaming of getting Zamiatin for ages."[9]

There was interest in the novel further afield as well, from the large American publishing firm which had approached Zamiatin for his stories the previous year.[10] Paul Kennaday, Managing Director of the Foreign Press Service, wrote on 21 July from New York to tell him: "We have received your *Islanders* and turned it over to Mr Zilboorg, who will, I believe, very soon undertake its translation. But Mr Zilboorg is particularly anxious to get your *We* and I hope that will be in our hands before long." Shortly afterwards, Zilboorg himself explained: "For an entire year I have been occupied with trying to find a means of establishing contact with you and getting hold of your novel *We*." This comment is interesting in suggesting that news of the novel's completion had even reached the USA by the middle of 1921. Gregory Zilboorg [Grigory Zilburg] went on to try to reassure him about his credentials as a translator: he was himself Russian, and had been the editor of the Kiev journal *Teatral'naia zhizn'* (*Theatrical Life*) before moving to the States three years earlier.[11] The novel thus seemed poised for wide publication abroad, in Russian and in translation, since on 22 July there was a report in *Golos Rossii* that the publisher "Alkonost," itself now transferred to Berlin, would be publishing the novel there.[12]

In March, Chukovsky was again making snide remarks in his diary: "Zamiatin came to visit me, bringing lots of news, had a smoke, and left—he's such a smooth, confident, cleanly-washed, robust... Englishman from Tambov." He also derided his enthusiasm for stories about the ludicrous actions of the censors:

> Zamiatin is very fond of such anecdotes, and he tells them slowly, as he smokes, and all the while his expression is that of a cat being stroked. Altogether he's an extremely pleasant, polished chap, very clean and comfortable, who knows what's what; he's able to maintain excellent relations with everyone, everyone likes him, and he's cautious; but all the same he's nice. And I for one am sincerely glad to see his well-fed face. [...] He's very skilful when it comes to sulking cautiously against the authorities—just enough to please the émigrés. He makes out that he's an "Englishman," but he doesn't really speak English, and really knows strikingly little about English literature and life. But even this is endearing in him, because essentially he's a kind person, he doesn't interfere, he's pleasant to talk to and share a drink with.

Despite this sneering, Chukovsky knew that Zamiatin was also a very reliable and efficient person to work with, and so he joined him and Tikhonov in setting up yet another new journal, *Sovremennyi zapad* (*The West Today*), to acquaint readers with contemporary western literature. At the same time Chukovsky and he were working together on editions of Dickens, including *Hard Times*, for "World Literature."¹³ However, that summer an unfortunate incident ensured that Chukovsky's private opinion of Zamiatin emerged into public view, causing a very unpleasant scandal. Chukovsky had written a letter to Aleksei Tolstoy in Paris, urging him to consider returning to Russia from emigration. Right alongside a remark about people who were "unworthy scum" he added a comment about Zamiatin, describing him again as "a very nice man, very, very nice—but he's fastidious and cautious, he's someone who has never felt anything." Tolstoy took the extraordinary decision to publish this private letter on 4 June in the newly-founded Berlin newspaper *Nakanune* (*On the Eve*), the one émigré newspaper which was permitted in the Soviet Union because of its policy of building bridges between writers who had fled abroad and the homeland. This publication aroused considerable indignation.

A fortnight afterwards Chukovsky wrote to Zamiatin to ask him to put the whole episode behind him, and to continue to trust him as "a loyal and reliable comrade." The awkwardness of the situation was exacerbated by the fact that the first edition of *Sovremennyi zapad* had to be signed off by the two of them before the end of the month.¹⁴ On 30 June, Zamiatin wrote to him rather stiffly, addressing him now formally by his name and patronymic, mentioning that he had tried to ignore earlier rumours about Chukovsky's maliciousness, but could now no longer quite trust him: "I know that if tomorrow or in a month's time I'm put into prison (because there isn't a more incautious writer than me in the Soviet Union at present), if that should happen, then Chukovsky would be one of the first to go and intercede on my behalf. But in less serious situations—for the sake of an eloquent phrase, or for the devil knows what—Chukovsky would fling me to [Aleksei] Tolstoy, or to anyone else, without thinking twice about it." In a first draft of this letter Zamiatin also pointed out that the remarks had been so wounding precisely because he had felt that Chukovsky was one of the five or ten people who would appreciate what he wrote. They would continue to collaborate for the next couple of years, but their correspondence shows that they never recovered their previous, easier friendship.¹⁵ Zamiatin received consolation from one of the young Serapions, Nikolai Nikitin, who wrote to him: "So you are 'cautious,' are you? And I am entirely open only with you, so I am counting on that caution of yours."¹⁶

Earlier that year the ardent Bolshevik Sergei Gorodetsky had suggested in *Izvestiia* (*The News*) that, as a leader of the Serapions, Zamiatin was passing on to his pupils reactionary views, along with those lessons on technique.[17] He certainly remained affectionately attached to them all, publishing a review that May praising a recent volume of stories by Zoshchenko, Lunts (whom he considered the most promising of the Serapion writers, although the young man would leave for Germany 2 months later),[18] Vsevolod Ivanov, Slonimsky, Nikitin, and Konstantin Fedin. He described Fedin as the most confident of them all, firmly set in the stylistically unadventurous Gor'ky mould of realism, while the rest pursued something closer to his own neo-Realism.[19] In December, Nikitin and Zoshchenko wrote to Voronsky to challenge Zamiatin's claim that he had been a mentor for them: "That's not correct in reality, nor is it formally." They suggested that anyone with his knowledge of technique could have taught them: "We didn't learn from Zamiatin's prose, but from the classics, and from our own student stories when we read them out." However, Nikitin would acknowledge his role more generously in a piece published in 1926: "Zamiatin was the person who taught me my craft, true mastery. My whole start came with the Serapions."[20]

This was a rather exceptional phase in the relations between cultural figures in the Soviet Union and in the Russian emigration. Zamiatin had numerous friends who had contrived to leave Russia— Khodasevich only that June, Lunts imminently, Pozner, Grigor'ev, Remizov, Grzhebin, Levinson, Postnikov, Damanskaia—and others who seemed to get official permission to travel abroad without too much difficulty, like Gor'ky and Pil'niak. There were tensions and suspicions between the two sides, of course. But the *Nakanune* newspaper project was part of the Bolshevik policy at that point of presenting a more welcoming and forgiving appearance to the outside world, to tempt some its citizens back home; and this seemingly conciliatory mood of the Soviet government during the early years of NEP meant that it was still possible for writers in Russia to contemplate publication abroad, and to maintain a fairly regular correspondence with their friends in emigration. The end of May 1922 brought the Zamiatins a letter—not the first since he had left for Finland in 1919—from Paris, from the painter Boris Grigor'ev. He encouraged Zamiatin to publish *We* in Paris rather than Berlin, but added a note of warning: "All the same, whether it is advisable to undertake such a business with people in Europe is something you should consider carefully first of all."[21]

Zamiatin was certainly inclined to be circumspect for the moment about his intentions: his next letter to Postnikov in Berlin was discreetly signed "Karpov," a pseudonym obviously alluding to his own recent address. Without explicitly naming any people or any works, he alluded to his volume *The Islanders*, which was about to be published by Grzhebin in Russian, suggesting that Postnikov should try to arrange for translations of it into French or Czech. "I've only just completed my long work [*We*], the beginning of which I read you last summer. I'll send it to you when it's appeared here. What about printing it simultaneously in your Paris journal [*Sovremennye zapiski*]? Have a word with them. […] Things are getting difficult here with books and publishers. Printing costs are unbelievable, books are perishing and the publishers are going bust. I wonder whether it will prove necessary because of this for me to travel to where you are. You've settled there now — write and tell me, in your opinion, whether I could live tolerably over there." Pil'niak, however, who was staying with Remizov in Berlin, wrote to him discouragingly about life for Russians in Germany: "Tell everybody not to come over here, unless they want to feel like fools."[22]

Despite the Soviet government's conciliatory signals, the political situation within Russia was in reality far from getting easier. Just how deeply suspicious the authorities were of Zamiatin became apparent when they finally took decisive action and arrested him, along with many others, on the night of 16 August 1922. This time he would spend nearly a month in prison. The background to this episode, which would culminate in the mass expulsion that autumn of intellectuals from Soviet Russia on the "Philosophers' Steamships," is well explained by Aleksandr Galushkin:

> Almost the first mention of expulsions belongs, as we know, to V.I. Lenin: judging by his letter to F.E. Dzerzhinsky of 19 May 1922, the plan for expulsions had already taken shape by that time. [May was the month of Lenin's first stroke, one of several that would increasingly incapacitate him and lead to his death in 1924.] This action […] formed part of the widely unfurling attack "on the ideological front" which took place at the end of 1921 and on into 1922, and it should be considered alongside other comparable "undertakings," such as the trial of the right-wing Socialist-Revolutionaries in the summer of 1922; the arrests of Mensheviks and members of the clergy; the increasing harshness of state control of book-publishing, which led, in

part, to a whole range of journals and almanacs being closed down, and to the closing of several cultural, educational, and literary organisations, such as the Petrograd House of Writers and House of Arts, as well as campaigns against the Proletkul't movement in *Pravda*.[23]

This new hostility toward the Proletkul't movement was an indication that the authorities were becoming aware of the need to bring left-wing groups under stricter Party control, as well as making sure that right-wing forces did not attempt to rally under the apparent liberalisation offered by NEP. On 16 July, Lenin specifically urged Stalin to press ahead urgently with the expulsion of writers from Petrograd.[24] In Zamiatin's case, Iangirov speculates that the telegrams from Paris and Berlin that summer inviting him to allow the publication there of *We* may have given particular prominence to him as a subversive figure. It is obvious, in any case, that his arrest completely dashed those hopes.[25] He was interrogated on 17 August. He insisted again that he no longer had any party affiliation, and had simply been working six days a week as a writer and at "World Literature," while travelling out to the Polytechnic once a week to give lectures. He also made it clear that he was aware of the difficulties of émigré life for writers, who would, as he saw it, inevitably need to return to their native land in the end. He was convinced that it was the role of an intellectual to speak out, and that Soviet interests would best be served not by political repression, but rather by winning over minds.[26] His interrogators remained unimpressed, and charged him formally with anti-Soviet activity, which he was accused of engaging in ever since the Revolution. Zamiatin protested, pointing out that instead of leaving, like other opponents of the régime, he had stayed in Soviet Russia and continued to work. Somewhat bizarrely, he was then presented by the GPU with the immediate option of leaving the country, "to travel to Germany for two weeks at his own expense," to which he agreed. This was an option offered to many of the detainees, to expel them from the country without it becoming too costly for the government.

N. Volkovysky recalled him remaining calm and sucking on his cigarette holder in the cell, and returning delighted from his interrogation with the news of his sentence of deportation to Berlin.[27] In the meantime, various people had begun to take an interest in his case, as part of that astonishingly close monitoring of the individual profiles of cultural figures by the security organs, and by the Politbiuro of the Communist Party, which characterises these early years of Soviet power.[28] One of the rising stars in the GPU in Moscow, Genrikh Iagoda, attempted to intervene on his behalf with a telegram sent on the day of the interrogation: "If you have arrested Zamiatin E.I., then release him, explaining that there has been a misunderstanding." However, he was promptly overruled, that same day, in a telegram from the Deputy Chairman of the GPU in Moscow, Iosif Unshlikht. So Zamiatin stayed in prison. His file contains three letters vouching for him, one from "World Literature," another crucial one from the Polytechnic, emphasising how vital Zamiatin was to their work (he was standing in for Dean Boklevsky at the time), and a third from the VSP, signed by Volynsky and Akhmatova.[29] By then, Akhmatova had become a close friend: in April she had presented him with a second inscribed volume of her poetry, *The White Flock*, and it appears that her enduring bond with Liudmila dates precisely from these tense August and September weeks in 1922. Evidently Annenkov, Shchegolev, Pil'niak and, most importantly, the hitherto hostile critic Voronsky, had all been campaigning for his release. The final result was that Zamiatin's sentence to expulsion abroad was suspended on 31 August until further instructions, on the personal orders of Feliks Dzerzhinsky, Chairman of the GPU.[30] But his Petrograd interrogators remained convinced of his guilt, and appealed directly to Stalin, calling him a covert and confirmed member of the White Guard—a somewhat strange accusation, given his record of anti-Tsarist activity and 1905–06 conviction for being associated with Bolshevism.

Events continued to be confusing. On 7 September, Iagoda signed a certificate, to be shown at the border, confirming that the GPU had no objection to Zamiatin leaving the country for Germany on 11 October "for an indefinite period." He was released from detention shortly afterwards,[31] and drafted a letter to Voronsky, thanking him for his efforts on his behalf in Moscow, which had done much to relieve the anguish of his mother and of Liudmila: "I didn't have too bad a time in prison—it was rather more cheerful than in that same Shpalernaia prison in Tsarist times, when I thoroughly damaged my health in true, strict solitary confinement. It's amusing, isn't it? that I was imprisoned then as a Bolshevik, and now I'm imprisoned by the Bolsheviks. And the most important thing is that before going abroad and truly beginning to digest everything, and then pouring out all that is happening now on to paper (this will clearly happen), it would have been irksome for me as a writer not to have seen who's in prison these days, and what for, and how it is. I say this in all seriousness." Zamiatin went on defiantly to suggest that Voronsky and the others who criticised him should learn to understand that "those who see the defects in life today, and the mistakes in everything going on around them, are not necessarily Whites, any more than those who shout 'Hurrah' about everything are Reds." He explained the circumstances in which he had written *The Natives* in 1919, which had been provoked by the fact that Soviet executions were taking place simultaneously with official denunciations of the West's use of the death penalty, to which he remained adamantly opposed; it was an issue he found deeply troubling. At that moment he believed he really was about to be sent abroad, and wrote this letter to Voronsky as a farewell: "It's for the best: [...] given the persecution of me, which will continue and makes it difficult for me to stay here, you'll understand this. It won't be easy for me abroad either—precisely because I'm not a White, but it will be different there and less hard, I think. If they send me away somewhere within Russia, or if they just leave me in St Petersburg, [...] then I'll ask you to help me get away abroad—for a while."[32]

Zamiatin eventually received the certificate from Iagoda allowing him to leave, but the situation remained completely unclear.[33] He did not know that, thanks precisely to Pil'niak and Voronsky's appeals to the Politbiuro Chairman Lev Kamenev in Moscow, his "sentence" of exile had already been rescinded. As Annenkov recalled: "Zamiatin was exceedingly pleased about the resolution sending him into emigration: at last, a life of freedom! But Zamiatin's friends, not knowing his opinions, began to intercede energetically on his behalf to the authorities, and in the end they achieved their goal: the sentence was lifted. Zamiatin was released from prison and [...], to his deep disappointment, he learned from Boris Pil'niak that his exile abroad was not to take place."[34] His disciplined, "English" capacity for being very discreet about his own views in front of his acquaintances seems to have backfired here, since it cost him an opportunity to escape.

On 19 September, Lev Trotsky published an article in *Pravda* in which he decried Zamiatin's influence on the "sterile" Serapions, and commented on the *Islanders* volume: "Ultimately the author is himself an islander, and indeed belongs to a small island, to which he has emigrated from contemporary Russia. And whether Zamiatin is writing about Russians in London, or Englishmen in Petrograd, there is no doubt that he remains an internal émigré."[35] This suspicion about his political trustworthiness was once again a price Zamiatin would pay for having adopted the guise of an "Englishman" in Russia. The writer and memoirist Mikhail Osorgin, who was one of those deported on 24 September on the first "Philosophers' Steamship" (as it became known), believed that it was Trotsky who had singled Zamiatin and the other writers out for arrest and exile.[36] Zamiatin and Annenkov were amongst the few people bold enough to go and witness the departure of the dozens of Moscow intellectuals and their families as they departed from Petrograd for their sea journey to Stettin. "Soon after his release from prison Zamiatin was present with me on the Nikolaevskaia Embankment, to see off a number of writers who were being deported. [...] Immediately afterwards Zamiatin put in a request to be sent abroad, into exile, but received a categorical refusal."[37] On the whole he seemed not too cast down by his experiences, returning promptly to his teaching and to his literary activities. Chukovsky, always quick to carp, commented on his behaviour at a meeting of the Serapions with a visiting Danish writer at The House of Arts on 30 September, a week after the first ship had departed: "Zamiatin was playing the liberal. When the conversation turned to writers, he said: yes, we love our writers so much that we even export them abroad. [...] All Zamiatin's 'struggle' is just for show, it's bogus."[38] The House of Arts itself was doomed to closure by the end of the year.

Voronsky replied to Zamiatin's "farewell" letter on the very same day that October when he was completing a lengthy article about his work for *Krasnaia nov'*, in which, as he told him, he had praised him for many of his stories, but criticised him for *The Dragon*, his "fairytales"—and *We*: "Lying in front of me is your novel *We*, which Pil'niak sent me. It makes a very painful impression. Truly. Is this all that October has inspired you to, and all that has ensued since then, up to the present day? How is this your 'most serious and yet most light-hearted piece'? It's your most gloomy and misanthropic. It's early days to be firing such satires at us. Somehow you don't seem to be looking in the right direction." Nevertheless, Voronsky suggested that it might still be possible to print the novel with some cuts; and indeed took the opportunity to ask for permission for his publishing house, "Krug," to publish *A Provincial Tale*. But when Voronsky's article appeared in print that December it was predominantly hostile, describing his personal influence on the Serapions as one of the reasons for their fascination with the craft of words, rather than the social import of their writing: "Zamiatin has taken a very dangerous and inglorious path. This needs to be said frankly and firmly."[39]

By 17 October the publisher of "Alkonost" and *Zapiski mechtatelei*, Samuil Aliansky, writing from Germany before returning to Russia, felt obliged to adopt a semi-humorous code in a letter to Zamiatin—presumably for fear of exacerbating his current difficulties. Addressing him as though he were a woman ("Dear Evgeniia Ivanovna..."), he ticks "her" off for her frivolous behaviour which has led to her spending several weeks in a "public house" (normally the Russian euphemism for a brothel), and risks leading "her" to a worse place. As for *We*, he observes (without naming the text): "your most recent romance [the word in Russian is the same as for 'a novel'] is so indecent, that despite the fact that the whole world knows about it I have decided against [...] recounting it to everyone." This provided confirmation, in other words, that he would not now risk publishing the novel abroad in Russian.[40]

The second "steamship" of exiled intellectuals—this time Petrograders, for the most part—departed on 15 November, and was seen off by a larger crowd of academics, writers, and artists, with Akhmatova amongst their number.[41] Volkorysky, recalling how Zamiatin had somehow fallen out of the whole picture, described how "he saw us off with a sad face from the jetty at which stood the German steamer which was to take us all away into exile abroad. He was envious of us, and quietly told us that he was hoping soon to meet up with us in Berlin."[42] He now appealed to the well-connected Pil'niak in Moscow for help, but Pil'niak pointed out that it was really rather awkward for him to request permission for Zamiatin to leave, so soon after asking for him not to have to go. In December, Zamiatin went to Moscow to lobby on his own behalf.[43] On the 14th, reflecting the astonishing importance apparently attached to his case, the Secretary of the Central Committee arranged for every single member of the Politbiuro to be sent a copy of his recently-published play, *The Fires of Santo Domingo*. If no objections were raised after they had considered the text, Zamiatin was to be permitted to leave. In actual fact, due to Lenin's rapidly worsening health, these were the very same days and weeks when Stalin was engaged in a vital struggle with Trotsky for the political succession. Nobody in the Politbiuro had the time to focus on Zamiatin's play, and for another year or so he would remain in a state of uncertainty about whether he would be allowed out.[44]

In late autumn of 1922 an approach from the publishing house "Akvilon" prompted a new burst of creative writing in Zamiatin. There is some uncertainty as to whether he had previously met the painter

Boris Kustodiev, who had so wickedly illustrated his bawdy story about the monk Erasmus that summer; probably they had met. Zamiatin had been very impressed some years previously by a Kustodiev painting he had seen at a "World of Art" exhibition, at the time when he was writing *A Provincial Tale*: "True, Kustodiev saw ancient Rus' [traditional Russia] with different eyes from mine; his eyes were a great deal more affectionate and softer than mine, but it was the same Rus', it united us—and it was inevitable that we should meet sooner or later." "Akvilon" was hoping that Zamiatin would write an article to introduce a volume of water-colours Kustodiev had painted in 1919–20. "However, I ended up not writing an article, but did something different: I spread out in front of me all those Kustodiev beauties, cabmen, merchants, innkeepers, and nuns—[...] and the story *Rus'*, which went into the collection of the same name, simply wrote itself."[45] In the story, set in the imaginary town of "Kustodiev," Zamiatin conjured up a gorgeous beauty, Marfa, the plump "Russian Venus" of one of Kustodiev's most famous nude paintings, and recounted her life with her merchant husband, and then with her gypsy lover after the husband's death from eating poisonous mushrooms. The timeless world he described was that of old Tsarist Russia, of towns just like Elets and Lebedian', a world "which some of us five years ago—or was it a hundred years ago?—have seen with our own eyes." The story was a striking reversion to the atmosphere of *A Provincial Tale* a decade earlier, since when so much had changed—and particularly in the five years since 1917; but it lacked even that story's satirical edge, savouring instead the physical and sensual delights of the sleepy Russian provinces. After his arrest, and amidst the anguished discussions about whether to emigrate, this story reads like an escapist dream.

Zamiatin marked the end of 1922 by composing the second episode of his entertaining *Brief History of "World Literature" from its Foundation to the Present Day* for the Christmas celebrations. The piece is full of in-jokes, and he portrayed himself as the virtuous "Evgenes," who simply writes "pious and instructive tales, thereby serving as an example to many." At one point, however, he is "thrust into a dungeon" by "warriors" who reproach him: "Where is your piety? You don't write a single word in praise of our true pagan gods and their statues."

Toward the end of the year there were several more encouraging developments concerning *We*. He received a postcard in December from Zilboorg in New York, to say that the English translation of *We* was virtually complete, and that he was now hoping to receive Zamiatin's play (presumably *The Fires of Santo Domingo*).[46] Late December 1922 also saw him returning one final time to the novel, in the sense that he drafted a piece intended as a preface to the text. This time his hopes of the work's publication within Russia had been raised by Ivanov-Razumnik and Sergei Mstislavsky, who had started a new journal that year, *Osnovy* (*Foundations*), in the spirit of the earlier *Zavety*. Anticipating his article "On Literature, Revolution, Entropy and Other Matters" Zamiatin responded in this preface to critics like Voronsky, by arguing the necessity of further storms and revolutions: "Fortunately, we live in stormy times. [...] There are some good folk who dream of travelling towards a stateless régime in the sleeping car of evolution. These good folk have forgotten about the dialectic, and about the inexorable law of social inertia: the state will outlive itself and its tasks, but of course will not willingly wither away—and once again there will be lightning, storms and fires. That is the law, which forever adorns with a stormy 'r' the softness of 'evolution.' The distant breath of that storm, which perhaps none can yet hear, is to be found on the following pages."[47]

That December, Zamiatin also became involved in attempts to obtain official approval of the constitution of the VSP. In a defiant gesture, the writers' organisation had submitted a list of members which included several of the people who had recently been expelled from the country, as well as Zamiatin himself. On 28 December, the GPU insisted they should be excluded, in an unprecedented—and ominous—act of intervention in the running of a literary group. Just a few weeks after the eventual legalisation of the VSP and confirmation of its Constitution by the GPU, Zamiatin was re-elected to its Board by a large majority (48 votes out of 54). Late in May 1923, the GPU in Moscow again expressed concern about his being on the Board; in June a special meeting of the Petrograd VSP—with Zamiatin present—was held, to agree upon a response. They firmly defended their right to independence, arguing that the elections had been held according to the rules, and that the VSP presented an "encyclopaedic mosaic" of views, which was in itself a guarantee against ideological subversion: "Even Dostoevsky and L.N. Tolstoy could not aspire to more than one vote in a consultative organ whose purpose is collectively to defend the interests and protect the lives of writers." The issue was apparently left there.[48]

The issue of whether he should be exiled abroad resurfaced on 2 January 1923, when new instructions were sent from Moscow urgently requiring his expulsion. At the same time, the Petrograd GPU reiterated its view of the previous August, that Zamiatin "had never ceased for a moment his anti-Soviet activity." He was summoned to their Counter-intelligence department on 17 January, where he signed for two foreign passports for him and Liudmila to leave the country. The trouble was that they were required to set off almost instantly, within one week. A couple of days later he travelled down to Moscow to try to negotiate some delay before they had to leave. Pil'niak tried to set up a meeting for him with Trotsky. Whether that took place or not, Zamiatin was evidently successful in his request, and Moscow eventually confirmed permission for him to delay his departure by two months. News of all this soon reached the West, with reports in the Estonian and German press of his unexpected new opportunity to emigrate. On 14 March he applied to the GPU for a further delay in his departure, adding a letter to a certain Comrade Agranov:

> When I, with you as an intermediary, approached the GPU at the end of January this year with a request to defer my departure abroad, I asked for a delay until the start of navigation, so as to be able to travel by steamer and avoid all the hardships of international rail travel. I indicated the first half of April as the likely time for navigation to open up; that's how it's been in past years, but this year the quite exceptionally extended frosty weather means that navigation will only become possible at the beginning of May, maybe even 10–15 May. In view of this, I would earnestly request you to assist me in extending the delay I was accorded, until the time when the first steamers leave on the Petrograd-Stettin line, that is, until about 10 May. The fact that I spent the winter not abroad, but in Russia, hasn't brought any harm to Russia, and maybe it has even been of some use—through my work for "World Literature" and at the Polytechnic. No harm, naturally, would come of my staying here for another short period. But for me this delay is very important, since apart from everything else I have to take with me abroad my wife, who is ill (with tuberculosis), and for whom I will have to ensure more or less tolerable conditions on the journey.

This remarkable letter reveals that Zamiatin was not by now in any great hurry to leave, and also displays his airy confidence in bargaining with the authorities over the date of his departure, citing scarcely compelling reasons for his request (he also mentioned how much more it would cost to travel by train). It was quite a gamble. His case was reviewed at two different levels by the Moscow GPU on 23 March, but his arguments were deemed inadequate, and so his request was initially turned down. Once again, however, a higher instance within the GPU hierarchy intervened, and on 4 April it was decided that the Petrograd GPU should be instructed to allow him to stay until the steamers could sail.[49]

Zamiatin's friends still believed his departure to be imminent. On 21 March, Voronsky wrote what he evidently considered a farewell missive to him: "I sincerely regret your departure. Please, don't work for ephemeral Russian publications abroad. Honestly, it's not worth it. I firmly hope that in three months or so you will be able to return to Russia and establish yourself here more solidly. Keep in touch with us. If you have any problems to do with money, please let me know. Send us whatever you write. And let us know your address."[50] Pil'niak also urged him not to break with Russia for good, and assured him that they would soon be working and drinking vodka together again. Meanwhile he and Voronsky had been trying to work out how they could support him abroad, and were proposing to send him a sum every month from the publisher "Krug" and the journal *Krasnaia nov'*, in return for exclusive rights over his works. In a detail which illustrates the confusing paradoxes about writers' freedom to travel abroad at this period, Pil'niak also mentioned a trip to London he himself was taking with Nikolai Nikitin that summer, arranged through Leonid Krasin, the Ambassador in London.[51] Chukovsky was scathing: "I was walking along Nevsky Prospect with Anna Akhmatova, who [...] was telling me that on Saturday they had once again had a farewell party for Zamiatin. I find this astonishing: the man has been leaving for about a year, and every Saturday they lay on a farewell party for him. And actually nobody is sending him into emigration: he's knocked at every door, bowed to every Communist—and now he's making himself out to be a political victim."[52]

However, it gradually became clear over the following weeks that the plan to emigrate had somehow fallen through. This emerges in a letter of 7 June from Zamiatin to Iakov Blokh, founder of the "Petropolis" publishing house in Berlin: "I spent the entire winter living in preparation for the railway station, with packed suitcases; and soon, it seems, I shall begin to unpack them for a while. In February [sic] they handed me a passport with the request that I should leave within the week. I couldn't do that, and obtained a delay until the steamships started sailing. And now, apparently, they've lost enthusiasm for parting with me (although I've received no official notification of this—but it does seem so). Maybe they won't want to part with me later either—God knows; but if their love for me turns out not to be that great, then maybe I will take a passport and come over for a while."[53] On 8 June, Nikitin wrote to him from London, "regretting your misunderstandings with our Moscow friends. Perhaps that's a word that isn't quite appropriate, but I am afraid to think otherwise." Presumably, this is a reference to his difficulties with the GPU. Nikitin commented that Zamiatin would probably have felt more at ease in England than he did, since "you have a strong London heart." He also reported that "Mr John Galsworthy asked me to send you his greetings. Recently we dined together at the monthly meeting of our PEN Club."[54] Galsworthy, who had recently completed *The Forsyte Saga*, was the first President of the International PEN Club, founded in 1921. Nikitin was over there with Pil'niak on an official mission to write about the British economic situation, and a few days later they wrote Zamiatin a humorous joint letter, partly with the intention of consoling him for not being there himself, by telling him how dull it was. They had also seen H. G. Wells and Rebecca West, who sent their greetings too.[55]

During all this uncertainty, Zamiatin continued to promote *We*. In January 1923 he gave a reading to a small gathering at "World Literature,"[56] which provoked another of Chukovsky's nasty comments: "Oh, how dull and pretentious and petty. [...] Not a single animated passage, even by accident. [...] He cautiously and frequently talks about the need for anarchism, praises the wild condition of freedom, denies any ferrule, any norm, any order—and yet he's a petit-bourgeois from his head to his toes. [...] They call him *maître*—what kind of *maître* is he, he's just a *centi-maître*. Everyone listened without enthusiasm."[57] On the other hand, Viktor Kliucharev, an actor at MKhAT [the Moscow Arts Theatre], wrote to thank him for letting him read *We*, which had given him "enormous pleasure." He also initiated a new departure in his writing by urging him to make a stage version of *The Islanders* "before his departure."[58] That spring Zamiatin was still waiting to hear news from Mstislavsky at *Osnovy* of how *We* was faring with the censors.[59] Meanwhile he was continuing to negotiate other publications, such as the reprint by "Krug" of his collection *Provincial Life*, with a print run of 3,000 copies.[60] That month, the Kustodiev and Zamiatin volume *Rus'* was published in an edition of 1,000 copies, which sold out almost at once, prompting the publisher "Akvilon" to plan an immediate reprint.[61]

All the while there was the usual hectic round of social contacts, with Akhmatova amongst others. She revealed that she was fully caught up in the playful use of dolls in the Zamiatin household (the boy doll, poignantly assigned the patronymic of his "father" Zamiatin, was Rostislav Evgen'evich Rastopyrin, and the teddy was "Misha in his pelt"): "I will come round to you tomorrow with Rostislav. I implore Liudmila Nikolaevna and 'Misha in his pelt' to forgive me for abducting R.E. Rastopyrin for tonight." The following month Akhmatova would inscribe a portrait of herself to her "dear friend Liudmila Nikolaevna Zamiatina, with love and gratitude" for her support (which may have included medical advice) at the time. On 1 April 1925, a mutual friend, P. Luknitsky, noted how fond Akhmatova had become of Liudmila: "She talks about her with great warmth, is glad to see her and grateful to her for her care and attentions." The same diarist also recorded Akhmatova's liking of Zamiatin for his uprightness and boldness, even though he took little or no interest in her poetry."[62] As he himself put it, "I'm a dilettante as far as verse is concerned."[63]

In April 1923 Zamiatin wrote "The New Russian Prose," which was published that August. It was a review of current writers, a task to which he was driven, as he claimed, by the current absence of professional critics. He affirmed that by that point the Serapion Brothers were no longer brothers at all; "they all have different fathers; and it's not by any means a school, or even a tendency. […] It's just a chance meeting of travellers in a single railway carriage." As for the Moscow writers, Pil'niak was described as the most striking of all, along with Pasternak, "who belongs to no family or tribe. He is not a 'new such-and-such,' but immediately became—'Pasternak.'" For many Russian writers abroad, he observed, emigration seemed not to have proved fruitful. An exception was Aleksei Tolstoy, although Zamiatin was rather condescending about his *Aelita*, (a science-fiction novel which is sometimes mentioned alongside *We*). He described the "European" Il'ia Erenburg as "perhaps the most modern of all Russian writers at home and abroad," and spoke admiringly of his irony and innovative compositions. For the future, Zamiatin noted a number of authors who had turned, like Erenburg, Tolstoy and himself, towards the fantastic, and predicted a maturing "away from the depiction of the everyday towards that of essential being, away from physics towards philosophy, and away from analysis towards synthesis."[64] The young

Erenburg, who similarly admired Zamiatin as "a true European," was delighted by this opinion of his *Julio Jurenito*, and wrote to him from Berlin to say how much he appreciated these comments from "a great master," hoping that it would be possible for them to meet one day.[65]

With thoughts of leaving Russia abandoned for the time being, Zamiatin turned back to fiction during June, embarking on *A Story about the Most Important Thing*. In this text, fulfilling his neo-Realist goal of a synthesis of the real with the fantastic, the futile hostilities of the Civil War are conjured in the capturing during a skirmish of one man by his own former cell-mate, and in the poignancy of his discovery of exalted love on the very eve of his execution. Intersecting this narrative plane are two others, one of them a sketchy story of the last survivors on a star, which is steered to crash into the Earth as they seek a planet with plenty of air where there will be no more killings. Out of all this destruction, it is suggested, it is not impossible that some new life will grow, just as the agonised contortions of the caterpillar as it turns into a chrysalis, in the story's third plane of reality, will eventually lead to rebirth in a miraculous new form. The story is very elliptical, with highly condensed patterns of imagery, evidently reflecting his renewed, intense focus on literary creation at this point, rather than on the distractions of his dealings with the GPU.

In June, Zamiatin read extracts from *We* at an evening of the Petrograd VSP.[66] In July, one of the first announcements appeared of its forthcoming English-language publication by Dutton & Co. in New York.[67] That summer, belying the accusation that he knew little about English literature, he wrote to Chukovsky about several books that were being considered for translation by "World Literature," including Hardy's *Far from the Madding Crowd*, Lawrence's *Sons and Lovers*, and Arnold Bennett's *The Card*, as well as works by Sinclair Lewis and Conrad. He observed that they still lacked a novel for the latest new journal they were launching, *Russky sovremennik* (*The Russian Contemporary*), and suggested facetiously: "Should we not publish *We*—in the guise of a translation from the Portuguese? Its success would be guaranteed. In my old age I've started working on short stories again: I'm writing *A Story about the Most Important Thing*. If I don't go off the rails I should finish that soon, and then for relaxation I'll start something frivolous, *The Immaculate Conception*."[68] During the second week of July, he drafted the first version of this new story, which would become *The Miracle of Ash Wednesday*. In this impish tale, a demonic Czech doctor amuses himself by convincing a naïve young priest that he has given birth to a boy-child as the result of his physical relations with his archbishop. As so often in his fiction, members of the clergy are depicted as being either highly-sexed, or sexually confused, or effeminate, reflecting a disrespect which would again have shocked his pious father.

Zamiatin and Liudmila spent that summer apart as usual, from the end of July through until about the middle of October. The question of his emigrating was apparently still under discussion in Moscow by Voronsky, Kamenev, Lunacharsky, and Unshlikht at the GPU, as he told her: "For the time being everything seems to suggest that I will have to go [abroad]. I don't care. I'm fed up with everything here, I feel cramped, and I need something new. [...] I'm doing nothing, just reading Conan Doyle and *World of Adventures*, and I feel lazy, peaceful and bored. [...] If I did have to travel, by God I would set off willingly" (26 July).[69] He had stayed behind in Petrograd while Liudmila travelled to Nizhny Novgorod in order to start up her medical work again, with the Red Cross. The couple had evidently been through another rocky patch, and after she complained that he had driven her away he replied:

> I needed to spend some time on my own. I simply no longer had the strength to bear your tormented look, and to recall at every moment that I was to blame, and then all those conversations. And now I've moved on a little, and regained my equilibrium. It appears that my earlier state of "stony lack of feeling" is returning (for the relief of which there is a prayer in the Orthodox Church) —that condition of my recent years, when life functions only on the surface, just down to a depth of one inch. And yet all the same my "ill will" —if that's what it was, was not perhaps that malicious or egotistical. I was so upset that your life had become confined to the kitchen, to trifles, to Agrafena and to clean tablecloths. And I wanted to make an attempt to fill you with something else (because I'm not capable myself of filling you with anything except grief). And I'm not yet convinced that that attempt has failed. As for me, don't worry in the slightest. I've suffered no new griefs. I've long ago got used to the business about going abroad. (31 July)

In these letters he makes passing mention of a woman called "Mary," whom Annenkov refers to as a local beauty he and Zamiatin had both been pursuing at the time—or was it still the same "Maria" he had flirted with in the past? Perhaps this was one of the reasons for the strain in his relations with Liudmila that summer. He then asked how she was getting on at the surgery: "Of course it's turned out to be nothing like as fearful as you imagined, and I'm sure that you are on top form, and people have already started to adore you" (5 August). When Liudmila left Nizhny for her holiday in Zlatoust he hoped she would feel pleased at having earned money of her own, and more confident in herself, "and that you have had a good break from the kitchen, from Agra, from me and all the nastiness of life in St Petersburg" (12 August). In the meantime, he had been getting on fine with Agra, who had been regularly putting the dolls Rostislav and Mikhail [Misha] to bed; having sewn a new jacket for Rostislav, she was about to finish making one for Zamiatin too. "I'm glad that you have seemingly begun to sleep better and generally to recover. [...] Have you stopped coughing in the evenings? Of course you can push me away, as has often happened: 'That must be a matter of indifference to you,' but there you go—it isn't a matter of indifference to me" (14 August).

Meanwhile, he had heard from Kennaday in New York that the translation of *We* had been delayed while Zilboorg prepared for his medical exams (he went on to become a distinguished psychoanalyst and historian of psychiatry). Kennaday also let him know that *The Islanders* would not be acceptable for publication in the USA (presumably because of its mocking of Anglo-Saxon social *mores*?). Ivanov-Razumnik, whose colleague Mstislavsky had been trying to get *We* published in *Osnovy*, had come by and read the novel for himself. He liked it so much that he invited him to read it at the literary organisation he ran, "Vol'fil" [The Free Philosophical Association]. Zamiatin read the first 12 chapters there on 10 August,[70] but then handed the task over to someone else because he wanted to get away for a holiday.

On 15 August he sent a note to Akhmatova (whom he addressed teasingly as his "dear great contemporary"), promising to drop by that evening before leaving Petrograd for Koktebel', in the Crimea. Over that summer of 1923 the poet Maksimilian Voloshin had taken the decision to provide free holiday accommodation for writers, scientists and artists at his extensive villa there, and some 200 people benefited from his generosity.[71] Twenty other people were staying while Zamiatin was there, and he was put up in a very modest whitewashed room. He developed a simple routine of swimming, resting, walking and sunbathing. Cheap food was available (i. e. at prices of 30 to 40 million roubles, according to the inflated prices of the day), but the abundance of lovely fruit took its toll on his digestion, and he complained of insomnia—even though in his definition that seemed to include nights where he slept for as much as seven hours. He mostly kept to himself, only visiting Voloshin in the evenings to hear his stories about the Crimea during the Civil War, and to use his excellent library. He had brought his own Civil War piece, his *Story about the Most Important Thing*, to work on. At Voloshin's request, he gave readings over the ensuing weeks of *We*, *The Cave*, and *The Town of Alatyr'*.[72]

Chukovsky arrived just in time to hear the reading of *We*; he and Zamiatin shared an impatience with their affable host's endless chatter, and Chukovsky described how Zamiatin learned to slip past the porch of Voloshin's house without being noticed. They spent hours lying together naked on the beach or collecting stones, and Chukovsky observed that he had "a good strong body, as shiny as a black man's, although he's hollow-chested. [...] Zamiatin brought a whole pile of outfits, and wore a different one each day; he parts his hair in the English fashion (when his comb broke he started parting it with a fork), and the women fell in love with him in droves." While they lay on the beach, Zamiatin read Pavel Florensky's *Concepts of the Imaginary in Geometry* (1922), which explored the relationship between Einsteinian relativity, geometry, and literary aesthetics, and found in the work similarities with concepts he had developed in *We*. This same book, with its affirmation that several versions of a single reality can fruitfully co-exist, would have an influence subsequently on Mikhail Bulgakov's approach to the issue of the truth of the Gospels in his masterpiece, *The Master and Margarita*.[73] When Chukovsky returned to Petrograd he noted in his diary: "I find Zamiatin's novel *We* hateful. You have to be a castrate not to be able to see what the roots are of today's socialism. [...] ... in one line of Dostoevsky there is more intelligence and anger than in the whole of Zamiatin's novel."[74]

On 10 September, Zamiatin composed a rather mournful letter to Liudmila, drawing once again upon the painful imagery of emptiness which so often reflects his sense of failure towards her, offset in his fiction by the imagery of fullness he associates with female fertility: "Your last letter left me with a bitter taste, both because you don't feel like writing to me any more, and because of the thought that perhaps it's better like this. What right do I have to say to you 'Don't go there', or 'Come here'? [...] ... and what can I offer you, I, who am a broken reed, utterly unwell and empty—and God knows what I'm to do to fill this emptiness with something."[75] After four weeks the other Koktebel' guests were turning for home, and he was wondering whether he should leave too. "But I have to go from here to Lebedian', and I don't feel like it." He hadn't managed to write anything of his own, but he had edited the translation of another Wells novel. "Sometimes I wonder: what people are around you there, and what are your relations with them? Don't drink too much wine, it's better not to" (10 September). But he was still in the south over two weeks later, when the weather finally turned autumnal. "I've more or less decided to ignore the Institute and all my other affairs in Piter. I'm very reluctant to be jolted all the way down to Lebedian' from Moscow, so I don't know whether I'll go" (28 September). He had managed to gain four pounds over the summer. "The other day I received a letter from Voronsky. He writes that he went to see the GPU Prosecutor and spoke to him about me. According to Voronsky I need to make an application to the GPU for my case to be reviewed, and for me to be left in peace. So that means that all this irksome business is still dragging on. Since your last letter from Nizhny I haven't received anything. After that letter I began to miss you for several days, and then it all settled to the bottom again. I'm living, but somehow there's nothing I want: neither to walk, nor to eat, nor to love, nor to write, just to lie in the sun and not think about anything. Tomorrow it's your name-day and I've no gift for you—I don't have anything" (28 September). On 3 October he finally set off north, sharing a first-class compartment with Chukovsky, and both of them bringing back mounds of grapes and pears. It is striking that in these letters, and after nearly 20 years together, Zamiatin still addressed his wife consistently using the polite form of address—even when he was recounting how he was woken one night by a mouse perched on his hand, and how she would have died of fright.

In Moscow he caught up with Pil'niak; he called on Voronsky and submitted the application to the GPU; and he also saw the people from the MKhAT First Studio who were urging him to write a play based on *The Islanders*. "Altogether it seems to me that in Petersburg I shall need to sit down at my desk and put an end—at least temporarily—to my dissolute, wandering life-style." He admitted somewhat disingenuously that he was not going to Lebedian', partly because of the difficult overnight travel in the train there and back, and the fact that he would only be able to stay three or four days: "It would be awkward to turn up at the Institute at the end of October instead of the middle of September."[76]

One of the first things he wrote after his return home in mid-October (perhaps inspired by his recent reading of Florensky, with its bold application of the most modern mathematical notions to Dante's vision of the underworld) was the article that would become "On Literature, Revolution, Entropy and Other Matters." He prefaced this with an epigraph taken from his own unpublished *We*, about the logical impossibility of determining a "final" number, or indeed a "final" revolution. Reflecting on the way entropy or dogmatism always undermines the eventual course of any revolution, whether it be social, artistic, or scientific, he proclaimed that "heretics are the only (bitter) remedy for the entropy of human thought," and that the writer has to be like a child, who always asks the simplest and most profound questions—"why?" and "what next?" Like the new mathematics, the newest art is neither realistic nor objective, but created from shifts and distortions; the Euclidean world had been entirely left behind now, after Einstein.[77] He sent the article off to Voronsky, but was well aware that it would be a struggle to get it past the censors.[78]

On 11 November, an inscription to Liudmila on a copy of the volume of stories *At the Back of Beyond* (from which the censors had cut both *The Protectress of Sinners* and *The Dragon*) suggests perhaps that their separation over the summer, and her return to her medical work, had indeed enabled them to revive their relationship: "To Mila Nikolaevna, who is marvellous, and new. Evg. Zamiatin."[79] A couple of days later they wrote an affectionate joint letter to Lunts in Hamburg, who was now in very frail health after suffering a stroke. Zamiatin filled him in on all the literary gossip about the Serapions, and reported on his own recent writing, including *Ash Wednesday*, which he described as being as indecent as *Erasmus*, "since in summer the lecherous demon is strong." He also complained that his own "innocence" was being protected by the authorities, who were now systematically preventing letters from abroad from reaching him. In February 1924 he joined in the writing of a loving collective missive to the now desperately ill young man, in response to a joky piece Lunts had sent to mark the third anniversary of the founding of the Serapions. Three weeks later, when he wrote again, Liudmila added an affectionate note wishing him better health and sending love from herself, "Misha" and "Rastopyrka." On 7 May, he wrote about the prospects for Lunts's plays (the most recent one had been dedicated to

Zamiatin). Since Lunts died just a couple of days later, at the age of 23, it is likely that the letter did not reach its addressee.[80]

Earlier, in the summer of 1923, a young Moscow-based critic, Iakov Braun, had visited with the intention of writing a study about Zamiatin. One of the very few pieces of critical writing in Russia sympathetic to Zamiatin after 1917, his article came out under the title "An Exacting Man" in the edition of *Sibirskie ogni* (*Siberian Lights*) for September-December 1923. Braun noted his scepticism and the merciless focus on bourgeois philistinism (*meshchanstvo*) in his pre-revolutionary writings. He traced the "intellectual biography" of the novel *We* from Dostoevsky's Grand Inquisitor through *The Islanders* and the stories about Fita, coming to maturity in the play *The Fires of Santo Domingo*. Although Braun felt that Zamiatin's scientific outlook placed some limits on his artistic achievement, he nevertheless described him as "the most cunning writer in Russian literature," with the capacity constantly to outgrow himself: "Zamiatin is a considerable and joyous manifestation of modern literature."[81]

At the beginning of winter 1923, Zamiatin visited the wheelchair-bound painter Boris Kustodiev nearly every morning for two weeks, at the latter's request, in order to sit for his portrait. Later he fondly recalled those conversations, "about people, books, the theatre, Russia and the Bolsheviks," with Kustodiev leaning forward to ease the pain as he laughed. Kustodiev was particularly unwell at the time, and after an unfortunate occasion when an involuntary spasm of his legs sent his paints flying, he had to have his legs tied to his chair. Soon afterwards he endured a lengthy operation on his spine under local anaesthetic, to remove a tumour that was threatening the precious movement in his right hand. Confined as he was to his four walls, Kustodiev particularly enjoyed sharing travellers' tales with his visitor; and Zamiatin noted how avidly he watched from the window, gathering the visual impressions for his colourful and elaborately detailed paintings of Russian life.[82] However, just as he was gaining the friendship of one painter, Zamiatin was to lose the companionship of another. During the summer of 1924, Iury Annenkov was allowed to travel to the Venice Biennale, where some of his portraits appeared in the Soviet Pavilion alongside his principal contribution, a huge full-length depiction of Trotsky as military leader. When the exhibition ended he simply stayed on, and went to visit Gor'ky in Sorrento before travelling to Germany and finally settling in Paris, where he had lived from 1911–13. He never returned to the USSR. His ballerina wife Elena had also managed to get out, and she sought work with Diaghilev's company in Paris, where Annenkov's first wife, Valentina, was already employed.[83]

On 17 February 1924, Zamiatin was invited to read extracts from *We* to critics and writers at the Institute for the History of the Arts in Leningrad (five days after Lenin's death on 21 January the city had been renamed again). Pil'niak had arrived that day to stay with the Zamiatins, and presumably attended the occasion.[84] A few weeks later, a well-informed émigré publication in Prague carried a report that the censors in Moscow had given their final, negative verdict on the question of whether *We* could be published in Russian in the USSR.[85] This may have been the last reading of the text in public before it was banned.[86] The ban was confirmed when the novel was discussed by Gublit [the Leningrad Literary Department] in late April and early May, as the literary scholar Abram Efros described it: "Yesterday Zamiatin's 'Integral' breathed its last. [...] I was solemnly invited to hear their resolution: [...] 'We are not used to such things even being submitted to us for consideration: had it been anyone else, we would simply have closed the publishing house down, but to you we will simply give this warning, that henceforth we will not tolerate such things here.' [...] The conversation became very outspoken. [...] And the end result was that each side stuck to its position. [...] So, you see, a utopian novel constitutes a threat to the state!"[87]

Even after it was officially banned, Zamiatin continued to allow private individuals to read *We*. Vsevolod Rozhdestvensky wrote to him the following year: "What you gave me is wonderful. I am indebted to you for one sleepless night and a day which was completely derailed. I have no regrets, of course, and I would heartily beg you to leave the manuscript with me for another 3–4 days. We're reading it aloud at home (it won't go anywhere further than that). I believe that it is a long time since a book of our own times has disturbed me so much."[88]

Il'ia Erenburg, who would play a significant part in Zamiatin's life subsequently, was visiting from Berlin. He enjoyed almost unique freedom to travel in those years as a figure sympathetic to Moscow who had acquired many contacts among the left-wing intellectuals of Europe during his political exile prior to 1917. Their first meeting took place that March. By December, Erenburg had moved from Berlin back to Paris, where he had lived from 1908 until the Revolution, and he wrote enticingly about the lively evenings in his favourite haunt, the Café de la Rotonde in Montparnasse. He had been trying to place

Zamiatin's works in Czechoslovakia and France. However, the fact that the USSR had not signed the International Copyright Convention meant that French writers were receiving nothing when their works were translated into Russian, and in retaliation French publishers were disinclined to take on Russian works for translation into French.[89]

Notwithstanding the Soviet authorities' banning of *We* for domestic consumption, Zamiatin went on negotiating for further translations of the novel abroad during 1924. In January the first German translator who considered it, Wolfgang Groeger, concluded that the novel was talented, but had "too little that was Russian" for German tastes.[90] During August, and again that December, Zamiatin received letters from Roman Walter, asking for permission to obtain the text of *We* from Dmitry Umansky, whom he had appointed as his representative after meeting him that April in Leningrad.[91] But Umansky was not to prove a very satisfactory agent, and eventually Zamiatin had to apologise to Walter for his failure to respond.[92] Umansky's translation of *The Cave* appeared in Germany in January 1925,[93] and Zamiatin then wrote to Fedin, whose German was fluent, to ask him for his opinion of it, because he had received letters from Berlin criticising the version and urging him to offer the novel to Walter instead.[94] On the far side of the Atlantic things were going rather better. In July 1924, Zilboorg wrote from New York that he had at last received the proofs of the English translation of *We*. By 1 November the advance copies had already been sent out to reviewers, but the launch of the book was held back until the US Presidential Elections had taken place on the 3rd. A film company had expressed interest in the work, and Zilboorg undertook to send copies to H.G. Wells and to the Russian scholar D.S. Mirsky in London.[95]

The project that really dominated 1924 for Zamiatin was the new journal, *Russky sovremennik*, which one critic would describe as the last free journal to be published in Soviet Russia. Zamiatin was a key member of the editorial board, along with Gor'ky (from abroad), Tikhonov, Chukovsky and Abram Efros.[96] Due to the easing of commercial restrictions under NEP they had received permission to publish the journal, which was to appear every two months, as a private enterprise.[97] In mid-April the editorial board travelled in comfort down to Moscow at the expense of Nikolai Magaram, their sponsor. Tikhonov asked them to declare in Magaram's presence that they had no intention of using the journal, however indirectly, to attack Soviet power: "We all replied 'no,' and Zamiatin also answered 'no,' but not as energetically as, for example, Efros."[98] The launch was followed by a feast at Magaram's which went on until seven in the morning, with a groaning table, liqueurs and 30-year-old port.⁹⁹ On 23 April, Zamiatin sent Liudmila an affectionate note, addressing her as ever in the polite form, but uncharacteristically signing it simply with his initial, and promising to return home within a couple of days: "Let the boys [i.e. the dolls] look after you all the better until Friday. E. Thank you for the letter. It was so nice that I am simply ashamed."¹⁰⁰

By the middle of May, when the first number of *Russky sovremennik* appeared, work was already in full swing on the second number. The first, remarkable number included writings by Akhmatova and Sologub, Eikhenbaum and Tynianov, Gor'ky, Leonov, Andreev, Pil'niak, and Babel', as well as Zamiatin's *Story about the Most Important Thing*. As for that story, Pil'niak also contributed a note for the journal's humorous pages, in which he pointed out that Zamiatin had got his caterpillars entirely muddled in it.¹⁰¹ In general the story was not well received: Khodasevich wrote from Paris to Gor'ky, commenting that it was "very bad" and "forced"; Gor'ky agreed with him, commenting that "an excess of intelligence" was something which hindered Zamiatin as a writer, and that despite his efforts to write in a more "European" fashion, he had still written nothing better than *A Provincial Tale*. Fedin also wrote to Gor'ky in July, commenting sourly on how dry and academic the entire journal was.¹⁰²

Meanwhile, Zamiatin described to Chukovsky his utter exhaustion as he rushed to complete an article reviewing current journals for the second number of *Russky sovremennik*, with the help of at least 50 cigarettes a day. This was "On the Contemporary and the Modern," completed on 8 July. In this piece Zamiatin complained that few authors had had the courage to describe the events of the previous decade in a truthful way; he had, however, spotted the potential of one emerging new author, Mikhail Bulgakov, whose story *Diaboliada* he described as reflecting a true instinct for cinematic composition, fulfilling his criteria for neo-Realism with its "fantastical aspects, rooted in the everyday." He also singled out the Jewish writer Isaak Babel' for his particularly successful use of the Gogolian device of *skaz*, where the author's *persona* is masked by a naïve first-person narrative voice.¹⁰³ While Zamiatin was in Moscow in November that year, he would go with Pil'niak to attend a public meeting at which Babel' was obliged to defend his cycle *The Red Army Cavalry* from the indignation of the Red Army Commander Budenny, who had accused him of defaming the Army in his stories.¹⁰⁴

Boris Grigor'ev wrote to them several times in the course of the year, with rather contradictory messages about life in emigration. He had been in America, where he had at last achieved real success, and was entranced by the American people, the abundant food, and the skyscrapers with their neon advertisements. On a recent holiday in Brittany they had danced the foxtrot in the American style. However, a couple of months later he claimed to be seriously tempted by the suggestion that he should come home and design the sets for Zamiatin's plays, since he was now fed up with America, and longing to visit Russia again. In December a postcard from New York raved again about his triumphs there, and the fact that he was about to travel to Florida to paint some portraits in the fashionable resort of Palm Beach. Soon, he wrote again from New York to tell them he now had no desire to return to Russia, and felt love only for France and Paris. Grigor'ev pressed them to let him know when they were going to leave, and offered to put them up. In point of fact the "threat" of compulsory exile—and therefore the option for Zamiatin of travelling abroad—had finally been withdrawn that year: on 8 August 1924, the criminal case which had been hanging over him since his 1922 arrest was finally abandoned by the Leningrad OGPU [formerly GPU]. In the autumn of 1925, Grigor'ev observed ruefully that "all sorts of real bastards keep turning up in Paris, but we still can't see our dear friends the Zamiatins."[105]

By the time this official news came through, Zamiatin had escaped from all the bustle of Leningrad, and had been recovering in Lebedian' for the better part of two weeks. He had been quite tempted by the friendly invitation Voloshin had issued for him to go back to Koktebel' in the summer, but he was enjoying lazing in the sun in Lebedian' and reading, surrounded by the scent of apples (he mentions ten different varieties in his letters).[106] Liudmila was apparently there with him on this visit, as a humorous document awarding her possession of one of the apple-trees there is dated 25 August, but she left soon afterwards for Zlatoust.[107] Within a couple of weeks Zamiatin wrote to her there (fondly calling her his "*druzhechka* [sweet friend]—to use a Lebedian' word"), rather regretting not having gone south. He was in Moscow by 15 September.

The second number of *Russky sovremennik* had appeared in mid-August, and Zamiatin was now working on the third. With Tikhonov away in the Caucasus, and Chukovsky ill ("as usual"), he had a sense that the future of the journal was insecure—especially since even Voronsky's *Krasnaia nov'* now seemed to be coming under much more intrusive political pressure. In late September, Chukovsky confessed his own rash foolishness in slipping a line referring to an icon back into *Russky sovremennik* after the censors had finally approved the text, which caused a further delay before the third number went on sale that October.[108] Zamiatin offended Gor'ky in this volume with his 1921 memoir of Blok, in which he hinted that Gor'ky was rather fickle in his literary affections, and had failed to do as much as he could to help Blok leave the country for treatment in his final weeks. Gor'ky also disapproved of the contributions by Pil'niak and Shklovsky, and announced to Tikhonov that he wished to remove his name from the editorial board.[109] In letters to Fedin and Slonimsky over the following months, Gor'ky began to distance himself more and more explicitly from Zamiatin, whom he again reproached for having adopted an "Einsteinian" dry and theoretical approach to literature.[110] In May 1925 Gor'ky described *The Story about the Most Important Thing* as "no longer art, but just an attempt to illustrate some philosophical theory or hypothesis."[111] He even discouraged some Czech writers he knew from translating Zamiatin, and recommended Babel', Leonov, Fedin, and Tikhonov instead.[112]

By 1 November, the fourth number of *Russky sovremennik* was already typeset, and due to be published within a fortnight.[113] However, on the 5th *Pravda* published an attack on the journal, and the publisher Magaram decided to withdraw further funding. This seriously jeopardised the journal's future, and Zamiatin turned to Pil'niak for help in seeking a new sponsor.[114] He was also the main author of their riposte to the *Pravda* article.[115] Entitled "To the Pereguds from the editorial board of *Russky sovremennik*," it evokes Nikolai Leskov's absurdly-named character Onopry Opanasovich Peregud, who spends his life denouncing any potentially subversive behaviour to the authorities. Zamiatin declared: "There are no people hostile to the Revolution at *Russky sovremennik*, but there are people there who are hostile to those survivals from the past such as fear of the truth, obsequiousness and smugness, whatever colours they disguise themselves in." And he affirmed that the journal's concern with great literature remained a legitimate purpose.[116] This did not go down well. On 12 December, Chukovsky went in to see the censors about some last-minute details concerning the fourth number, which was now due to appear before the New Year holidays, only to be told that the journal was to be closed down entirely. Eventually they obtained permission for the volume to be published, despite the opposition of one particular censor, Bystrova, who claimed that the journal could do terrible harm to workers and Red Army soldiers. Then they discovered that the promissory note they had used to pay the printers would not be honoured, and that the printers had confiscated the print-run. Meanwhile, by contrast, an émigré publication in Berlin was proclaiming *Russky sovremennik* to be "the most interesting and cultured of Russian journals."[117]

In December there were further indications of a general clampdown in the cultural sphere. Il'ia Ionov, head of the Petrograd branch of "Gosizdat" ("State Publishing"), finally succeeded in closing down "World Literature" as an independent publisher.[118] On 16 December, Zamiatin therefore wrote one final episode of his *Brief History of "World Literature" from its Foundation to the Present*, to add to those he had composed in 1921 and 1922. Laconically, he wrote a "Third and Final Part": "They've swallowed it up! because they're illiterate." And he signed and dated this, and marked it with a sign of the cross. The events of these days are reflected in Chukovsky's humorous collective scrapbook *Chukokkala* in a number of verses and drawings by other members of "World Literature," alongside Zamiatin's "epitaph."[119]

The fourth and final volume of *Russky sovremennik* appeared in January 1925, but the editorial board had now been officially disbanded. They held their last meeting on 14 January, and on the following day they had a group portrait taken by the photographer Nappel'baum. In some subsequent Soviet publications, Zamiatin, who was standing at one side of the group, was airbrushed out of the picture. He and Chukovsky both left the ensuing party early, impatient with their colleagues' sentimentality: "Blok and Gumilev died at the right moment!" remarked Zamiatin, and Chukovsky agreed with him.[120] Nine months later news of some attempts to resurrect *Russky sovremennik* reached Gor'ky, who wrote to Fedin from Sorrento complaining: "that would mean Zamiatin's dry, cerebral creations and Chukovsky's prattling all over again."[121] The prospect of resurrecting the journal soon faded, and on 24 December Il'ia Gruzdev (the only critic amongst the Serapions) told Gor'ky: "I never really believed seriously that *Russky sovremennik* would be revived, and now it seems the question has been finally taken off the agenda." Although he did not entirely like the journal, he acknowledged that it had been the only place where writers could say what they wanted about literature, and so he regretted its demise.[122]

The other major preoccupation for Zamiatin during 1924 had been his shift towards drama. On 18 January, a letter from the MKhAT actor Viktor Kliucharev, who was also responsible for repertory, reiterated his suggestion of the previous year that Zamiatin should write a play for their Studio based on *The Islanders*. At the same time, he communicated a formal invitation, based on a conversation Zamiatin had previously had with the director Aleksei Diky, for him to write a play for MKhAT based on Nikolai Leskov's 1881 story *Leftie* (this would become *The Flea*). Zamiatin chose to complete the stage adaptation of *The Islanders* first.[123] Now renamed *The Society of Honourable Bellringers* (a reference to the parish organisation which upholds Vicar Dewley's moral stance in the story), the full draft of his 4-act tragicomedy was ready that June.[124] It received the censors' stamp of approval on 29 September, but the MKhAT Studio eventually turned it down. Instead, on 9 January 1925 he signed a contract for a production of the play in Leningrad.[125] On 3 July, the director of Moscow's Korsh Theatre wrote to say that they wanted to take *The Bellringers* for their 1925–26 season.[126] They commissioned an excellent design for the play from Boris Erdman, brother of the playwright Nikolai Erdman, but in the end proved reluctant to pay the costs.[127] The first performance in Russian of *The Bellringers* in fact took place not in Russia, but on 24 September in the Latvian capital, Riga.[128] This was just a matter of weeks before the Leningrad production, where it was put on at the Malyi Opernyi (formerly Mikhailovsky) Theatre, but was not a success.[129] There was some consolation when he signed a contract for *The Bellringers* and *The Flea* to be published (he inscribed a copy of the latter in February 1926: "To Mila Nicolaiwna for the memory of 19 Sanderson Road" [sic]).[130]

The Leskov project, which like *The Islanders* had an "English" dimension that Zamiatin particularly relished, really seized his imagination. Leskov's whimsical story *Leftie* revolves around a left-handed craftsman from Tula, who manages to uphold Russia's international prestige by deftly adding horseshoes to an ingenious life-sized silver flea created by some English silversmiths. With his own recent experience of working alongside English engineers at the cutting-edge of modern technology, Zamiatin was the ideal person for the task. By 3 February he told Kliucharev: "Leskov's flea has bitten me so hard that already last week I made a preliminary sketch of the play."[131] Perhaps it was in connection with this project that he borrowed a volume that week from Grebenshchikov entitled *Folk Drama of the North*.[132] In his version, Leskov's plot is framed by elements of Russian folk comedy and *commedia dell'arte* buffoonery. Where Diky was mostly interested in "the destiny of a Russian genius," Zamiatin was primarily interested in the story's fairytale and folk dimensions, i. e. its improbabilities, contradictions and anachronisms. "Making a decent stage version of *The Flea* is one thing; but to create a new play using Leskov's material is something else again." And once he had completed a draft of the first act in April, Diky became very enthusiastic about his interpretation.[133] Even the hardline establishment critic Sadko (V. Blium) congratulated MKhAT on their choice of Zamiatin's free adaptation of the Leskov original, as a means of resolving what was commonly called the "repertory crisis" for theatres in the new Soviet era.[134]

However, when Zamiatin visited MKhAT in Moscow in late November, he concluded that the beautiful but entirely naturalistic designs for the production by the landscape artist N.P. Krymov just would not do. He wrote to Kustodiev the same day, imploring him to take on the commission instead, and despite the considerable pain he was suffering, Kustodiev promptly agreed.[135] Zamiatin returned to Leningrad, and their work together proceeded at a furious rate: it was evidently a very happy and successful collaboration. He was delighted with the new designs for the sets, costumes and props, which were "merry, bright, amusing and mischievous," precisely capturing the fairy-tale and fairground atmosphere he had been seeking. As Zamiatin said in his 1927 memoir of Kustodiev, "He worked on *The Flea* with great enthusiasm. And that was understandable: here the colours of his beloved Rus' could come to life at full strength. And I think I'm not mistaken if I say that it was one of his most successful — perhaps the most successful — of his designs for the theatre. [...] This was almost the first of his major works in which he departed entirely from his usual realist manner and showed himself a master in what was apparently a completely different sphere for him — in the grotesque."[136] The première was now fixed for 11 February 1925. On 31 December Zamiatin added a "confidential" section to one of his letters to Diky, admitting that he wanted to get down to Moscow for 10 days before the première not just so that he could help out with the production, "but also because of certain affairs of the heart. As you know yourself — that is also no laughing matter." Zamiatin then suggested a sudden new idea to Diky for the cover of the programme: how about simply printing on it the well-known crest of the Moscow Arts Theatre, only with a flea instead of the famous Chekhovian seagull?[137]

The Aleksandrinsky Theatre in Leningrad also expressed interest in *The Flea* — they lacked good actresses, and this play with its predominantly male roles suited them very well — and rehearsals began there in February 1925.[138] By this time, Zamiatin was already in Moscow.[139] On 6 February he wrote apologising for his silence to Liudmila, and reporting (perhaps not quite in full?) on his busy days, including a reading of *The Bellringers* the previous evening at a writers' club, and of course the intensive final rehearsals of *The Flea*.[140] He then sent her a telegram summoning her to Moscow for the gala dress rehearsal on the 9th. Arrangements were made so that Kustodiev could come down too, and be lodged in the theatre itself. When it came to the dress rehearsals every new set was greeted with applause, and Zamiatin believed that the success of the show was in no small part due to Kustodiev's designs.[141] Diky inscribed a poster to Liudmila, recording "their shared excitement, anxieties and joys at the birth of the flea."[142] After the première on 11 February 1925, the play would run successfully until the autumn of 1930, and then again after a short interval for several more years.

Chukovsky described a visit to the Zamiatins at this time: "Both he and she are intoxicated with the triumph at the Arts Theatre. The triumph was indeed considerable, and fully deserved. He told me that for 6 nights in a row he had gone out and got drunk with the actors afterwards. His mother came to one of the performances." On 26 February he again noted Zamiatin's great happiness at the almost simultaneous publication of *We* in America, and the success of *The Flea* in Moscow. A month later, however, he noted in his diary that his son Nikolai, a budding writer in his early twenties, had been to see *The Flea* in Moscow and described it with scorn as "terribly vulgar."[143]

On 11 March 1925, Zamiatin sent a long letter to Avraam Iarmolinsky (Head of the Slavic Department at the New York Public Library), whom he had met the previous year when he was visiting the Soviet Union with his wife, the poet Babette Deutsch.[144] He was kept indoors by a belated snowstorm, so he had time to write properly. He told Iarmolinsky that the Leningrad production of *The Flea* was scheduled for the end of April. The two plays, together with the crisis over *Russky sovremennik*, had consumed him over the past five months; but he was now intending to return to a new project, a novel which he had started the previous autumn about Attila the Hun (*The Scourge of God*), in which he would be drawing "parallels" with the present day, although he was toying with the idea of turning that into a play as well. He had finally received a copy of the English translation of *We*, although the reviews Zilboorg sent had not reached him. Babette Deutsch published her own review of *We* in *The New Republic* later that March, and she was one of several reviewers to criticise the work's very stilted translation (perhaps not surprising, since English was not Zilboorg's native tongue).[145] However, on 23 March she sent Zamiatin a letter to tell him, "your novel enjoyed a very favourable reception here. Both of us have the kindest remembrances of you and your wife." Iarmolinsky added a postscript, shrewdly asking to be sent a full set of *Russky sovremennik*, which with its unique publications was destined to become a bibliographical rarity, for the New York Public Library.[146]

In 1925 Erenburg wrote several times from Paris, wanting to obtain this American translation of *We*, and pressing Zamiatin to arrange for Umansky to send him the Russian text as well, since he was proposing to approach publishers such as "Kra" and "La Nouvelle Revue Française" about the novel. He had already succeeded in placing two of the stories from *The Islanders* volume with French journals.[147] That year Zamiatin also wrote to Semen Liberman of "Ladyzhnikov" publishers in Berlin, offering him a whole range of works for translation into German in his new journal *Russische Rundschau*, including *We*, and telling him that he too could obtain the original from Umansky in Vienna. Letters came back from Liberman, again criticising Umansky's translations, so on 18 October, Zamiatin wrote back to authorise him to place his works with different German translators, as well as some Polish ones. In December, Liberman wrote to say that a new translator, Charol, had just delivered his version of *The Islanders*; and that Zamiatin's *Mamai* would appear in *Russische Rundschau* in January 1926.[148]

During March and April of 1925, Zamiatin drafted a new story, X, a light-hearted account of the pathetic experiences of a priest in May 1919, who has abandoned his faith to some extent because of "Mar-x-ism"—but really because of "Mar-f-ism," i. e. the charms of Marfa, a Russian beauty worthy of Kustodiev he first encounters as she bathes in the nude. He gets himself into a terrible tangle, makes the sign of the cross in public, and ends up in the hands of the Cheka. With that story out of the way, Zamiatin settled down to the idea he had mentioned previously, of making a play out of his Attila project. By the middle of May he was reading some scenes from his "just completed *Tragedy about Attila*" to members of the VSP. He would continue working on further drafts of the work, returning to it several times between 1925 and the spring of 1927.[149]

Zamiatin was still in a whirl of professional commitments. With such a well-established reputation, he was now often approached by writers for advice and help. It is notable that throughout these years he provided that help unstintingly, and his archives contain dozens of touching letters of thanks, testifying to his scrupulous attention to new writers. A typical example were the letters he received in the first half of 1925 from a certain Viktor Dobrovol'sky, a former Professor at a Naval Institute who had lost his leg in an accident, and who now asked for help in finding a publisher for his stories; later he wrote with warm gratitude for all Zamiatin's helpful suggestions.[150] Other instances of his concern for others were apparent that spring, when some of his friends and colleagues got into difficulties with the authorities. In February he went to talk to Gor'ky's first wife Ekaterina Peshkova, to see if she could intercede on behalf of the unpopular Tikhonov, who had just been arrested. When Tikhonov was released from prison in June, it was Zamiatin who arranged for him to go and recover with Voloshin in Koktebel'.[151] In April, Zamiatin came to share with Chukovsky his horrified impressions from the "trial" of Shchegolev, apparently involving accusations that he had removed materials from the archive he ran.[152] In May he was in Moscow, where he expected to meet Diky at the trial of the actor Kliucharev, who was sentenced to a month's detention for assaulting a journalist.[153]

In the meantime, Zamiatin also wrote again to Iarmolinsky, thanking him for the various reviews he had sent, which suggested *We* had indeed been well received, although so far he had not seen any of the money Zilboorg had promised for it. In September 1925 Zilboorg reported that the sales of the novel had been disappointing despite the largely positive reviews, and expressed regret that Zamiatin's stories and plays had still not reached him, since he believed that the plays might be a better commercial proposition.[154] Zamiatin added to Iarmolinsky: "I've been sitting and writing for a month now. But instead of a story, it's a play again, a Romantic tragedy this time. A very distant, and very close epoch: Attila." The first three acts—which he had unexpectedly ventured to compose in verse—had already been completed, and he was hoping to finish it by the middle of July and then go down to the Caucasus, since he was feeling unwell.[155] He left Leningrad for a rest cure on 25 July.

A week later, he arrived in the spa town of Kislovodsk in the northern Caucasus, where a doctor examined him and concluded that his spleen was enlarged, and that his colitis was nervous in origin, so he was embarking on a programme of baths and a strict diet. On 5 August he replied to a letter from Liudmila in which for some reason she asked his forgiveness: "Milusha, my dear—how painful your letter was to me, how painful! How can there be any talk of 'forgiveness' when it is I who feel guilty?"[156] He commented that it was understandable that she should occasionally hurt him, when he had been tormenting her. He even wondered whether the literary process—thinking on behalf of fictional characters—had diminished his sensitivity to real people. And in a passage where he quite exceptionally used the familiar "*ty*" form to her, he added: "Well, to hell with all that psychology. Anyway, there is one thing which you have to believe, and that's that if there's one person whose pain I feel as my own, then it is yours" (5 August). He had already changed rooms five times in nine days in his hotel, in his quest for peace and quiet, and was wondering whether Lebedian' was really the only resort that suited him. But he was soon eating better and enjoying the baths and being wrapped in damp towels, although he felt his brain had turned to jelly. At one point he spoke to a journalist acquaintance about his Attila play, "and I felt as though this was all to no good purpose, that nothing good would come of it in the theatre, and that I had somehow written a 'Soviet' play. Me! I even snapped my pencil in two" (2 September). A week later he decided to abandon Kislovodsk, finally returning to Moscow on 20 August. Here he found that the production of *The Flea* was still a sell-out, and that MKhAT were keen for him to read the Attila play to them. That reading did not go particularly well, and he had begun to realise that the play needed some fundamental reworking. While he was in the theatre, he was invited to hear the first reading of a new play by Bulgakov, which would be staged the following year as the hugely successful *Days of the Turbins* (based on his novel *The White Guard*).

At the very end of that year he found himself on 19 December unexpectedly rushing down to Lebedian', having received news that his mother had fallen gravely ill. To his great sadness, he was too late. As he told Liudmila, Maria Aleksandrovna had been hoping she would come as well, since she might have been able to help treat her. He himself had lapsed into his habitual "stony lack of feeling." When his father died in 1916 it had been more frightening, although he had loved his mother more.

And so the three of us are sitting in the sitting-room by the lamp, auntie Varia, Zhenia [his nephew Evgeny] and I. And mother is lying on her own in the unheated room. And I will never see her again; and what's worse, she will never see me again. It's worse because of course she loved me ten times more than I loved her. And I feel bitter now that I took relatively little care of her. So many trifles, mere nothings, which could have brought her joy. And now it's too late. It's strange that it all turned out exactly as with my father: she fell ill in the same way, on the same day, on the Saturday; the end came on the same day, the Friday; and in the same way I arrived on the Sunday, just hours later than was necessary.

He was expecting to leave two days later, after the funeral, but could not decide whether to stay in Moscow or come on home: "What would you advise, you, who are the only mother I have left? [...] For the sake of—I don't know what—look after yourself." And he signed the letter simply "E."[157] It was a bleak end to a year which had begun so well.

Chapter 6:
Leningrad (1926–1929)

After his successes in New York and Moscow in 1924 and 1925, the second half of the 1920s saw Zamiatin fighting an increasingly hopeless battle against the Soviet authorities in his attempts to get published or staged in his own country. And all the time tantalising letters kept coming from abroad, hinting at richer prospects and enticing freedoms—he seemed to be appreciated outside Russia so much more than he was at home.

In January 1926, Erenburg wrote from Paris to let him know he had at last received the Russian typescript of *We* from Umansky in Vienna: "I have now read *We*. In my opinion the project is grandiose. It's a real shame that the book was not published as soon as it was written. [...] The business with the 'soul' is powerful and convincing. And altogether the tonality of the book is very close to me at present (its Romanticism, its protest against mechanisation, and so on). The only thing which took me aback was the rhythm; its chaotic nature and dynamism have more of Russia in 1920 than of the glass city." The American translation of *We* also reached Erenburg by the end of March, so he was going to show that to some French publishers, before coming to Leningrad some 3 weeks later.[1] Meanwhile, Zamiatin was grumbling to Iarmolinsky that Zilboorg had stopped replying to his letters, and hadn't sent him any royalties (these reached him eventually in June). He had started giving Iarmolinsky advice about current literature, on this occasion for a poetry anthology, for which he recommended Akhmatova, Pasternak, Khodasevich and Marina Tsvetaeva.[2] A new sphere of translation opportunities seemed to open up for his own work when he was approached that February by the writer and journalist Otokichi Kuroda, an acquaintance of Pil'niak's, offering to translate *The Cave* into Japanese, and letting him know about his efforts to place both *We* and *The Flea* in Japan.[3] Soon after that, Liberman sent him the German version of his story *The Eyes*, together with 20 Deutschmarks from the translator Charol.[4]

Boris Grigor'ev was still leading a glamorous life as a sought-after painter abroad. In Milan he was just setting off in evening dress to a *palazzo* where his works had been so well hung that they "shone like diamonds," and only a single wall separated his paintings from those of Botticelli and Bellini. He was planning to spend most of the year in Italy, visiting Venice, Naples, and Tuscany, though he was alarmed by the "terrible power" of Mussolini. "And by the way, Evgeny Ivanovich, I thought you were intending to come to Paris and New York?! But where are you, dear friend? Why have you not come to Europe? How we would embrace you!" Gor'ky, who continued to serve as the focal point for a wide range of Russian intellectuals in emigration, had sat for Grigor'ev for three weeks, and the new portrait was ready to be exhibited in Venice that March: "We became real friends. He is a true genius and a saintly man. [...] He's exceptionally gentle, sincere and sensitive. As for the portrait, he said: 'It's the first time that I feel it's me on the canvas.'" There were exhibitions coming up in Prague, Dresden, Philadelphia, Pittsburgh, and Munich, and plans for the Grigor'evs to travel from France to America that autumn. But he had not forgotten Liudmila and Zamiatin, asked after his writing, and reiterated his longing to see them.[5]

A rather touching letter also arrived in January 1926 from a cousin in Tambov province, the archpriest Mitrofan Andreevich Zamiatin, who asked to read all his works and promised that he would pay for the books. Mitrofan, four years younger than Zamiatin, was one of the thirteen children of his father's brother Andrei Dmitrievich, and as a child had spent some time living in the Zamiatin household and attending the local school in Lebedian'. Zamiatin's uncle Andrei, himself a priest as well, suffered arrests and exile from 1926 onwards, and died in 1933; cousin Mitrofan suffered arrests and exile from 1929 onwards, and was eventually shot in 1937.[6]

Zamiatin continued to be a conscientious member of the VSP; in 1928 he would describe it as Soviet Russia's "oldest literary organisation, which unites a great number of the best-qualified masters of the pen in the USSR."[7] He took on new roles in the organisation in February 1926, and over the next three years he would organise many of their literary celebrations and commemorations, as well as helping to arbitrate in disputes.[8] He also contributed to VSP discussions about the role of literary criticism. On the literary scene a resurgence of proletarian ideology was coming to dominate critical attitudes, especially through the increasing influence of VAPP (the All-Union Association of Proletarian Writers, renamed RAPP in 1928). In a draft essay (not published at the time) Zamiatin dismissed critics as being like body-lice, which one can get used to but never tolerate, and which can spread diseases. Just as in 1919–21, he argued, the proletarian arbiters of culture were again making absurd attempts to standardise all literature, and their ignorant and damaging attacks were sometimes more like political denunciations—one such example being the recent diatribes against writers such as Mikhail Bulgakov.[9] That April a cartoon by the VAPP militant Leopol'd Averbakh in their new journal, *Na literaturnom postu* (*On Literary Guard*), assigned Bulgakov and Zamiatin to the despised category of bourgeois writers, alongside Erenburg and Aleksei Tolstoy. Pil'niak, on the other hand, was placed slightly more favourably in a group of "right-wing fellow-travellers," a term denoting tolerated opponents which had gained currency with Trotsky and Voronsky in recent years.[10] Towards the end of June, Georgy Gorbachev also warned against the right-wing threat represented by the bourgeois writings of Bulgakov, Zamiatin, and Erenburg.[11]

On 20 June (he marked his letter "Trinity Sunday") Zamiatin wrote to the poet Ivan Eroshin, whose letter of two years earlier he had just turned up again, envying him his statement that he was a happy man: "I'm envious, because I certainly can't call myself a happy man: nothing is ever enough for me, and I always want more. And I often encounter difficulties, because I'm an unbending and self-willed man. And that's how I shall remain. I was glad to find and re-read your letter just now as well, because it reminded me of 1918, the House of Arts and the Studio. It's agreeable for me that you have good memories of that time. To all appearances, life then was incomparably harder than it is now—and yet how much better it was!"[12]

While Zamiatin was coming under attack in the official press, he may have been comforted by the regular messages of support he received in private. The young poet Iury Kazarnovsky (who would soon find himself in a prison camp at Solovki, on the White Sea) wrote from Rostov-on-Don to his "beloved heretical *maître*," to say how much *Russky sovremennik* had meant to the younger generation: "You were the first to say boldly what everyone feared to say—and this will never be forgotten."[13] That summer, the 39-year-old Iasha Grebenshchikov also took the opportunity to reiterate his deep affection for Zamiatin: "I love you very much. I've especially come to love you over the last few years. And I'm proud and happy about your relationship with me. […] If the Good Lord were to give me some opportunity to prove my love in action, I would be truly happy."[14]

After his theatrical triumph at MKhAT in Moscow, Zamiatin now signed contracts with the BDT in Leningrad for productions of both *The Flea* and *Attila*. He had read extracts from *Attila* at a literary evening at the Philharmonic on 12 May 1926, and read the entire piece to the Artistic Council of the BDT the following day. The finalised text was to be delivered by 15 August, and in return the BDT guaranteed to put *Attila* on during 1926–27, retaining exclusive performance rights to the play for three years.[15] These were the introductory words he provided for the play: "The author assumes that throughout the history of mankind there have been parallel epochs. [...] Just such a parallel to our own epoch with its 'displacement of peoples' is offered by that epoch of great world wars, of an ageing culture fighting against a fresh wave of barbarian peoples—the Goths and the Slavs. There is historical evidence for assuming that Attila was by no means the savage and unthinking destroyer that Roman historians have made him out to be. He was undoubtedly an enormously wilful and temperamental man, but one who was well educated by the standards of his time (in his youth he had been kept as a hostage in Rome, and had studied there). And he was a subtle politician."[16] For eighteen months, Zamiatin had been exploring the historical sources, starting with the Roman historian Priscus who had met Attila in person. The project had been initially conceived as a novel which would explore Attila's family background and time spent as an adolescent in Rome, but it was now focused more narrowly as a drama on his public and domestic life in his final years. In a questionnaire Zamiatin once filled in about his personal library, he reckoned that he had accumulated 1,000–1,200 books in fifteen years, three-quarters of which were fiction and poetry, while the rest were books about philosophy, technology, mathematics, sociology, and the history and theory of literature. Having stated that he didn't usually need books to stimulate his writing, he nevertheless acknowledged that for his historical plays (*The Fires of Santo Domingo* and *Attila*) he had naturally consulted a wide range of sources, usually in Leningrad's Public Library.[17]

Meanwhile, the BDT was moving ahead with preparations for *The Flea*, and on 15 June he held a party in his flat, attended by Akhmatova and Shchegolev, to celebrate the completion of the fresh designs Kustodiev had created for this production in the northern capital.[18] That summer, the BDT director Nikolai Monakhov let him know that he would be starting work properly on *The Flea* at the beginning of October, and asked him to send some new *chastushki* (humorous ditties) for the text, which was being considerably reworked to distinguish it from the MKhAT production.[19]

He hesitated about where to go for his holiday that year—he'd been invited back to Koktebel', or Kazarnovsky had offered to find him a place to stay in Sochi,[20] while Chukovsky was recommending a dacha in Luga, amongst pines and hills.[21] But he opted in the end for the familiar surroundings of Lebedian'. As he set off on 24 June he inscribed a photo of himself sitting in a carved armchair to Liudmila: "In light rain, and before departing—to our spouse Mila Nikolaevna, offering her my lips—Evg. Zamiatin."[22] In July he confessed to Chukovsky that he had been overwhelmed by laziness since his arrival.[23] But the highlight of that summer in Lebedian' for him and for Liudmila, who had evidently joined him, was the visit he arranged there for Kustodiev:

> It wasn't easy to get there: two nights in the train, and one of those spent in a second-class carriage. But when I started to tell him about the fields of rye, the hill encircled with churches, and the orchards hung with juicy apples, Boris Mikhailovich suddenly got fired up and decided that he absolutely had to see all this. I left for Lebedian' earlier. Boris Mikhailovich arrived there with his family only about six weeks later, at the beginning of August. […] This was "authentic," this was ancient Rus'. I lived a street away, five minutes' walk from the Kustodievs' apartment. Each day either my wife and I would go round to see Boris Mikhailovich, or they would bring him to our garden in his wheelchair, or else we would all set off for the banks of the river Don, out to the pastures and the open fields. And then I saw how Boris Mikhailovich devoured everything with greedy eyes, how he rejoiced in the huge distances, a rainbow, summer rain or a crimson apple. That summer the apples were particularly good in our orchard. We would often keep back a branch for Boris Mikhailovich, then wheel him over to it in his chair, so that he could pick the apples himself.[24]

Unfortunately it turned suddenly cold and wet at the end of August, and Kustodiev retreated to Leningrad. His son later recalled: "He liked Lebedian'. He liked the quietness of the remote provinces. Jokingly, he used to say that not even the Revolution could wake up this little town. […] He showed me a whole series of remarkable studies of Lebedian', all executed in watercolours."[25]

Even before Kustodiev's arrival, Zamiatin had been trying to plan the later part of his summer. As he told Shchegolev: "I need, if only for a month, to go and rinse out my stomach with Borzhomi or Essentuki mineral water—otherwise, like you, I'll only be drinking milk this winter. And as well I need to send Liudmila Nikolaevna somewhere away from here: it's been a very chilly summer."[26] By the beginning of September he had got as far as Moscow, where he developed a heavy cold. He spoke to several theatres, including MKhAT, about *Attila*, but didn't meet with much enthusiasm. He dined at the Writers' Union with Diky, Pasternak, Nikitin, and Pil'niak (who had just returned from a long trip to Korea, Japan, and China). On the 17th he told Liudmila he was finally leaving for the south, to Gagry (near Sochi, on the Georgian Black Sea coast), and expecting to return in mid-October: "I'm going without any appetite, without rejoicing. If you were going with me, then I would be glad at least because you were glad, as you were glad in Lebedian'. Well, maybe the sunshine will help a little."[27]

He was still feeling dismal when he wrote to her the next day from the train: "Where am I dragging myself to, and what for? After all, you can't run away from emptiness, from misery, from loneliness, or from the life you have lived. I'm just running for the sake of it, out of stubbornness. I am weary of all the problems in Moscow, but I also don't want to come back to Petersburg. Home? I don't have a home of my own—or so it seems to me at present… And—full stop. I'd do better to smoke a cigarette and write about something else" (18 September). He endured a freezing ride from Sochi to Gagry for 6 hours in an open bus. However, he met up with some friends—Nikitin was there—and they enjoyed a couple of beautiful walks: "I'm sorry that you're at Mokhovaia Street instead of seeing all this. Ultimately it's all wasted on me, because I'm somehow lifeless, but you would have been glad of it all" (23 September). His weight rose to nearly 11 stones. To his dismay, he then saw a newspaper in which the BDT failed to mention *Attila* in its programme for the new season (7 October). And on 15 October the Vakhtangov Theatre in Moscow wrote to him about *Attila*, to turn it down: "Above all your play is beyond our strength. And apart from that it's slightly hazy in its dramatic action."[28]

Once again, there seemed to be far more enthusiasm for his works abroad. That summer Liberman wrote from Berlin urging him to send three of his plays—*The Fires of Santo Domingo, The Bellringers,* and *Attila*—for translation into German. A translation of *The Islanders* was in hand, and he claimed to have interested someone in *We* as well.[29] A letter arrived from London too, assuring him that people there were following his literary career with interest, and offering to translate his recent works in consultation with Sir Bernard Pares, Director of the School of Slavonic and East European Studies in London.[30] In 1926, Bernard Pares's colleague at London University, D.S. Mirsky, who had already translated *The Cave* into English, devoted a book chapter and part of an article on contemporary Russian literature to Zamiatin, describing him as one of a handful of "living classics" in the USSR.[31] In August, Roman Jakobson in Prague wrote to let him know details of the planned publication of *We* that autumn in Czech; first it would be serialised in V. Koenig's translation in the newspaper *Lidové noviny* (October-December), and then it would appear in book form the following spring with "Aventinum," which also published Erenburg. Jakobson remarked that the Russian typescript he was working with was rather untidy, and lacked any of the characters written in the Latin rather than the Cyrillic alphabet, and so he too was anxious to obtain a copy of the English-language edition.[32] It is notable that these entirely straightforward publications of the novel in Czech were not often referred to subsequently by Zamiatin.

On 15 November he spoke on behalf of the VSP at a fifth-anniversary memorial evening for Blok held at the BDT. As he was reluctant to discuss his work as a poet, he chose to speak about him as a much-loved man: "Blok was a man of unusual enthusiasm, nobility, unusual sincerity, honour and uprightness. And what mattered was that he wrote his poems not in ink, but in his own blood. […] In Blok we love what is best within us. […] And the poet Blok will live on for as long as there are dreamers and eternal wanderers—and that is an immortal tribe here in Russia."[33]

Zamiatin had borrowed a book of *chastushki* from Grebenshchikov to help with the task of creating new materials for the BDT *Flea*.[34] The director, Nikolai Monakhov, whom he had admired since his performance there as Shylock in 1920,[35] consulted with Kustodiev closely, in order to create a production which would move even further away from Leskov's literary text towards a stylisation based on folk humour and the traditional *lubok* (popular print). The text of the play had been published during 1926,[36] and generated a great deal of public debate. On 29 November, four days after the BDT première, there was even a formal academic discussion of the work by some of the leading critics of the day, including Eikhenbaum,

Zhirmunsky, Mokul'sky, Vinogradov and Vaginov. The proceedings were published in January 1927 along with contributions by Zamiatin, Kustodiev, and Monakhov.[37] Zamiatin's article noted that the themes of Russian folk theatre had occasionally penetrated to the stage, but that its forms rarely had. He had relished creating an entirely unrealistic, stylised comic drama, in which merry playfulness would predominate.[38]

In December 1926, he also wrote a satirical account of *The Biography of the Flea* for a meeting of the joky "Figa" association, (named after the rude gesture where a thumb is thrust between the first two fingers), which laid on occasional evenings of literary parodies during 1926–27. Kustodiev drew a frontispiece for this text, a portrait of Zamiatin dressed as a monk, smiling sardonically and making the rude gesture with his hairy hand, as well as a number of other comical and suggestive illustrations. The narrative recalls Zamiatin's scurrilous tale of the monk who supposedly gives birth to a child; this time, it is the monk Zamuty who gives birth to the flea, which in no time grows into a demonic temptress who first seduces MKhAT, then languishes for a whole year at the Aleksandrinsky Theatre before she is rescued from death by Monakhov of the BDT; but a proletarian critic demanding that she contribute something towards Soviet industrialisation brings about her early demise. The volume was eventually published in 1929, in a print-run of 500 copies.[39] In January 1927, he was busy drafting a further comic text for "Figa," together with Zoshchenko and Marshak. This piece, in honour of the director Vsevolod Meierkhol'd's imminent visit to Leningrad, teased him about his sensational production of Gogol's *Government Inspector*, which had opened in Moscow the previous December. They proposed that Meierkhol'd should go ahead and desecrate some other classics of the Russian stage, whose titles they offered to modernise for him: Lev Tolstoy's *Power of Darkness* would become *The Electrification of the Countryside*, while Turgenev's *Month in the Country* would be renamed *Four Saturdays of Volunteering on the Land*.[40]

On 4 January 1927, the Riga Theatre of Russian Drama (whose director had worked with Zamiatin at the BDT, and which had been performing *The Bellringers* since the previous September) held their own première of *The Flea*.[41] At the same time Zamiatin received a letter from London from Zinaida Vengerova recalling their former acquaintance, which dated back to his stay in England a decade earlier. She had heard about *The Flea*, and believed she could get it staged in

Britain or the USA because of its Anglo-Russian themes. By the following summer, she had made a preliminary translation of the play into English and given it to an American playwright, J. Balderston, to show to some theatre managers. However, by January 1928 she had to admit that nothing had come of her hopes for placing *The Flea* in America, where it was considered too "high-brow."[42]

In January 1927, Liudmila was in Moscow. Zamiatin told her he had received a letter from his aunt Varia in Lebedian', complaining of the bitter cold and asking for help, so he was going to send some money. Varia, a few years younger than Maria Aleksandrovna, lived all her life in or near the family home which had been their parents' house—she never married. He had always felt particularly close to her, and kept in touch with her after his mother's death.[43]

On 2 February, Grebenshchikov wrote again to Zamiatin to declare his affection for him: "I truly love you very much. I value you and respect you deeply. […] I consider you a very decent man, and I honour that decency." But he went on to strike a note of caution: "My dear friend, reflect on my request, and listen to it: be more careful. Throw bravado to the devil. […] Maybe this will sound bookish, but: take pity upon others, and upon yourself. These are dark and troubled times. […] Be more restrained, hold yourself more aloof."[44] One new example of Zamiatin's "lack of caution" that same month was his article "The Purpose," a contribution to a literary debate about the aims of modern literature between Marietta Shaginian, who had been close to the Serapion Brotherhood, and Leopol'd Averbakh from VAPP. Zamiatin argued that it was time to move beyond class hatred, and that it should not be the purpose of art to serve the class that was in power, which could lead only to servility. Writers have a duty to look beyond the everyday into the future. "The purpose of art, including literature, is not to reflect life but to construct it, to organise it (lesser arts such as photography and journalism exist to reflect life). But what does 'organising life' mean for fiction?" The artist, he replies, has to look towards the greater goals that humanity is pursuing, and use his skills of pathos or irony to stir and inspire the reader. Bold satires are therefore ten times more useful than novels about dairy cooperatives. This article was not published in his lifetime.[45]

That February he also completed *Comrade Churygin Takes the Floor*, a story he had begun the previous year.[46] Here, an ill-educated orator recounts the events of the February 1917 Revolution as they were perceived in a village in the provinces. Like the *skaz* narrators of some of Zoshchenko's stories, the speaker has absorbed a garbled version of Bolshevik slogans, and although he claims his political consciousness has been raised, he also still instinctively uses religious phrases. He describes the villagers' ignorant enthusiasm for Rasputin, and their assault on the estate of the local landowner, who manages to fob them off for a while by persuading them that his statue of Mar-s is in fact a figure of Mar-x. On 1 August Gor'ky commented to Tikhonov that *Comrade Churygin* was just "a clumsy imitation of Zoshchenko."[47] In reality, though, Zoshchenko's stories would never have ended in the pointless bloodbath which Churygin describes. Another review of it that month in *Pravda* accused it (quite inaccurately) of being a satire on the October Revolution of 1917.[48]

Early in March 1927 Zamiatin went down to Moscow, where he was as usual initially preoccupied with his sleeping arrangements: "For the moment they've given me a large room (horrors! three windows—it's true that they're narrow ones, but all the same...), and I'll only be able to move into a small one tomorrow."[49] He had gone to look over the proofs for a new volume of stories, *Impious Tales*, which was published soon thereafter by "Krug."[50] At Easter (24 April) he inscribed a copy: "To my honourable wife from her impious husband."[51] While he was in Moscow he read his Churygin story at the Writers' Union, and it went down well. He went to Bulgakov's *Days of the Turbins* at MKhAT—"a good show." He also saw Meierkhol'd's *Government Inspector*, visited him at home and met there Nikolai Erdman, author of the very successful satirical comedy *The Mandate* (1925). Meierkhol'd invited him to give a reading of *Attila*, but told him afterwards that although it was well constructed, he feared it was inconceivable to stage it with period costumes and weapons without it turning into a kind of spoof. The Malyi Theatre was also dragging its feet over *Attila*, and he had an unpleasant surprise at the State Publishing Authority ("Giz"), where they told him that they would have reservations about publishing it. "So that's clear: as I expected, I'll be bringing *Attila* home with me."[52]

While he was there, MKhAT evidently suggested a new project to Zamiatin, because they were seeking one-act plays for the celebrations that year of the tenth anniversary of the October Revolution. Bulgakov, Pil'niak, and Babel' were amongst those they also approached. In the last week of March, Zamiatin went back to his 1920 story *The Cave* and wrote two scenes for a possible adaptation, which was never staged. Patently, the story's bleak view of life during War Communism would scarcely have fitted a triumphal occasion, and it was somewhat quixotic of him ever to imagine that the theatre would take it on. A film version of the same story was made by F. Ermler in 1928 under the title *The House in the Snowdrifts*, but the text was such a loose adaptation of the original by B. Leonidov that it even contrived to acquire a happy ending. Zamiatin insisted that his name should be removed from the credits.[53] Another project he embarked upon in the spring of 1927 was an adaptation for the stage of Saltykov-Shchedrin's grotesquely satirical novel *History of a Town* (1870), under the title *The Town of Glupov*.[54] Both the Vakhtangov theatre and the Riga theatre, which had been staging his earlier plays, would express interest in this project.[55]

Early in 1927, Zamiatin had received a message from Zilboorg reporting that although the critics had liked *We*, overall sales had been very disappointing: after the initial $100, only about $10 more royalties had accumulated by the previous July. Zilboorg had also failed to find a publisher for his other works.[56] In Prague, meanwhile, a chain of events began to unfold which would have major repercussions for Zamiatin in the future. On 23 December 1926, Marc Slonim, editor of *Volia Rossii* in Prague, wrote to Postnikov asking for the text of *We* in Russian. This was just after the publication of extracts from the novel in Czech in *Lidové noviny*, and before the publication of the full text, also in Czech, by "Aventinum." In 1927 Slonim went on to publish significant portions of *We* in *Volia Rossii* in a distorted Russian-language version, claiming that it was not the original Russian text—even though we know he may have had a copy in his possession—but a back translation from the Czech. By now, a straightforward publication of the novel abroad in Russian would have been a highly provocative undertaking. A significant piece of evidence to support the view that Zamiatin was in fact aware of the controversial plan to publish *We* in Russian in Prague, even in the mangled and incomplete version that appeared in *Volia Rossii*, has survived in the form of a dedication he wrote in Leningrad on a photo of himself. The addressee was Nadezhda F. Mel'nikova-Papoushkova, a resident of Prague and regular contributor to *Volia Rossii*, who was also closely connected to Postnikov and Erenburg, and to the novel's Czech translator, V. Koenig: "To Nadezhda Filaretovna—to commemorate our Russo-Czech action. Evg. Zamiatin. 10-XI-1927."[57] What other "action" could he have had in mind by this cryptic reference, if not the devious plan somehow to get his novel into print? In this regard we may also recall his earlier joky suggestion to Chukovsky that *We* should appear in *Russky sovremennik*, disguised as a translation from the Portuguese, which was itself a light-hearted reflection of the burning desire he had to see it published. After her return to Prague from that visit to Leningrad, Mel'nikova-Papoushkova let him know that she was trying to place his plays (*The Flea* and *The Bellringers*; she was less hopeful about *Attila*). She was also negotiating a translation of *The Islanders*, and asked him to send her an authorisation to represent him. Finally, she added: "What about your trip to Europe? We're expecting you. Just tip us the wink, and you'll have a visa. All your friends send their greetings. And if you have any other stories or novels, send them to me, and I'll make every effort to place them."[58]

In April or early May 1927, Erenburg supposedly wrote to inform Zamiatin of the "shocking" *Volia Rossii* publication, and sent a letter in his name to the journal requesting that they cease printing the novel, which they refused to do. One negative review of *We* by the influential critic Iuly Aikhenval'd (Marc Slonim's uncle), based on the *Volia Rossii* publication, appeared in a Berlin journal, *Rul'* (*The Helm*). This was in fact almost the only printed reaction to this publication in the West, which is particularly ironic given the heated accusations that would later be made against Zamiatin about its "subversive" impact. Aikhenval'd argued that in his writing of the novel the author had become infected by the very dreariness of the monotonous society he was seeking to depict, "…despite the pointedness of the satire, despite the intelligence and talent of the author, and despite the brilliance of certain details. The writer has been defeated by his own subject-matter." In private correspondence, Gor'ky made it clear that he was not impressed by what he had read in *Volia Rossii* either.[59] Another reviewer at the other end of the continent, in Chinese Khar'bin, praised the *Volia Rossii* publication that July, not so much for its artistic qualities as for its timely warnings about the future of socialism.[60]

During the first half of 1927, Zamiatin could continue to feel that his work was being taken seriously only abroad. On 4 May, Sergei Prokof'ev wrote to him from Paris, using the address of "Grandes Editions Musicales." He had read *Attila* with the thought of basing an opera on it "with great interest and even enthusiasm. But I didn't find its ending pleasing." One problem was that Honegger's 1925 opera *Judith* ended in almost exactly the same way (with a twitching tent-flap and voices off, preceding a murder), and so it would be unthinkable for him to write another opera on such a similar theme. In any case, said Prokof'ev, he would be engaged on his current projects for at least a year. However, he added, "before then I hope to be back to spend some time in the USSR again, and then you and I could meet."[61] A letter from Erenburg in Paris that spring brought news that Zamiatin's reputation had spread even further afield, since his story *The Lamp* (*The North*) was one of several works to have been published recently in Spanish (Erenburg did his best to extract some money from the Spanish publishers for him).[62] In an apparent reference to the "row" over the publication of *We*, Erenburg added: "Although it was unpleasant for me, I did write to Prague. I hope it will have an effect."[63] This sounds more like someone who was going through the motions, rather than genuine indignation on Zamiatin's behalf. On 10 June, Akhmatova's common-law husband, the distinguished art critic Nikolai Punin, who accompanied an exhibition of Russian art to Japan that summer, wrote to him about the possible translation of his work into Japanese.[64] That November Isida Kiodzi, who had met Zamiatin earlier that year in Leningrad, wrote to him from Moscow asking him to send him *Attila* and the stage version [as yet uncompleted] of *The Cave*, and offered to try to get hold of the American text of *We*. He explained that Kuroda had just left for Japan, and was intending to translate his work shortly.[65]

That spring, Boris Kustodiev began to feel much weaker. Plans were made to send him for an operation to Berlin (with the assistance of Petr Kapitsa, whose portrait Kustodiev had painted in 1921, shortly before he left for Britain to work with Rutherford at the Cavendish Laboratory in Cambridge). However, Kustodiev developed pneumonia. He died on 26 May 1927 at the age of 49.[66] Zamiatin was invited, along with Benois, Gor'ky, Dobuzhinsky, Nikitin, Fedin, and others, to contribute to a memorial volume. He would continue to work on what would become his piece "Meetings with B.M. Kustodiev" for the rest of the year, and into early 1928.[67]

At the beginning of July he set off on a different kind of summer trip, this time heading north past Lake Onega. Three days later he had reached Aleksandrovsk (now called Poliarny), a small coastal settlement about 1,000 km due north of Leningrad in the Murmansk region, on a latitude well beyond the Arctic Circle, parallel with the very north of Finland. In February 1926 he had proposed a film script, *Northern Love* (based on his story *The North*), to the Lenfil'm studios, and this was where the filming was to take place.[68] Aleksandrovsk was on the mouth of the Kola Bay, surrounded by steep, snow-covered cliffs even in the warmth of summer. This far north the sun set only for

15 minutes or so each night. He was putting up in a fisherman's attic, and had been eating nothing but salmon and fish soup, which had an unaccountably good effect on his digestion, and he felt well in the salty ocean air. They spent long days filming at a bay with a beautiful waterfall, some two hours away by boat. On 17 July he told Liudmila that most of the film crew were leaving that night (it was a 5-hour boat ride inland to Murmansk), but he was inclined to stay on for a few days in order to spend time with the local fishermen. The weather had turned autumnal already, with beautiful mists, and it was chilly enough for him to sleep in his sweater. He was disappointed that they had not adopted some new waterfall scenes he had proposed, and that they were going to finish filming in Leningrad: "So be it—but without me, I've had enough." In the meantime he felt inspired to write a new—and very simple—story.[69]

The story Zamiatin conceived on 17 July in Aleksandrovsk was *The Yawl*, which he continued to work on over the next six months. It is the tragic tale of a fisherman who scrapes together the money for a boat of his own, only to have it wrecked by a sudden storm as they tow it back from Murmansk, with the fisherman leaping to his death as the boat founders. The piece is clearly shaped by Zamiatin's first-hand experience of the local fishermen's work on the boats during a herring catch, and the landscape with which he had become familiar during his stay in Aleksandrovsk.[70] Now that he had turned forty, this creative moment seems to reflect a weariness with the self-consciousness of neo-Realism, and a new inclination towards traditional realism, which he had already begun to explore through his historically-grounded Attila projects.

This moment of relative serenity did not last long, however. By 21 August he had left Leningrad again, this time for the south. He wrote to Liudmila from Tiflis (Tbilisi) after a spectacular drive over the mountains of the Caucasus from Vladikavkaz, during which he got his nose thoroughly sunburnt. He was heading for the spa town of Borzhomi in Georgia, about 150 kilometres to the west of Tbilisi, to undergo a course of treatments. Borzhomi turned out to be rather dull, and in mid-September he moved to try the waters of a different spa, Essentuki, which was situated further north, back on the Russian side of the Caucasus. In Essentuki he found a clean room, better food, and a doctor "with a good surname" (Akhmatov), and he agreed to a whole series of treatments, including enemas and mud baths. "The mud baths are a very exhausting business—you feel so weak. But I believe in them more than in anything else." Liudmila herself was on holiday up the coast, at the Russian resort of Gelendzhik. By 7 October, Zamiatin had moved on to yet another spa, Kislovodsk, and was rather wistful to hear what a good time she had been having. He was living in a house and playing tennis with Aleksei Tolstoy and Tikhonov, and Zoshchenko also came to stay, but he did not feel strong enough to work.[71] Chukovsky called on Zoshchenko after his return from the Caucasus, and recorded the latter's opinion that Zamiatin was essentially unhappy: "He dimly feels that his career hasn't quite worked out, and he sleeps badly and is suffering. We travelled back here together: he always had to drape the lamp in order to get to sleep." The following week Chukovsky, happy as ever to gloat over any criticisms of Zamiatin, dropped in to see Tynianov and found Shklovsky there. They had a frank conversation, in which they talked "sadly" about how weak Zamiatin was as a writer, and Tynianov recalled that it was Chukovsky who had first pointed out that he was no good.[72]

There were further, ominous public attacks on him as well. In September 1927, an article in *Na literaturnom postu* reviewed his writings since the Revolution, and concluded that, as a representative of a dying class, the reactionary Zamiatin found it impossible to write about real life, taking refuge even in his best work in history (*The Fires of Santo Domingo*), or (as in *We*) in fantasy. The same journal published a sardonic ditty about him in a section expressing their wishes to writers on the 10th anniversary of the October Revolution, in which "Sir" was recommended to change his habits and establish himself somewhere closer to the USSR, rather than living "in the back of beyond."[73] On 14 October, Zamiatin's play *The Fires of Santo Domingo* figured alongside Bulgakov's *Days of the Turbins, Zoika's Apartment,* and *The Crimson Island* on a new list of 498 plays banned by the literary authorities.[74]

At least there was some slightly more cheering news from the theatres. Ruvim Shapiro, director of the BDT in Leningrad, gave newspaper interviews in late September in which he confirmed that *Attila* was scheduled for production that autumn after all, with a première planned for 15–20 December. The BDT and the Vakhtangov theatre in Moscow were also both proposing to stage Zamiatin's adaptation of Saltykov-Shchedrin later in the season. At the end of the year, very unusually for him, Zamiatin himself performed on stage, taking the part of Baron (an aristocrat who has fallen on hard times) in scenes from *The Lower Depths*, at an evening organised by the VSP and the Academy of Sciences to celebrate Gor'ky's 35 years of literary achievements. Other actors on that occasion included Fedin, Tolstoy, Tikhonov and Marshak.[75]

An aspiring young Russian writer, Irina Kunina-Aleksander, formerly one of Zamiatin's neighbours in the house on Mokhovaia Street, had written from Yugoslavia to propose that she should translate *At the Back of Beyond* and *A Provincial Tale*. She was trying to negotiate with publishers to overcome the problem of there being no copyright convention between the two countries. Now married to a Yugoslav, she had not seen Zamiatin for nearly two years. On 15 January 1928 he replied, referring to the characters from *At the Back of Beyond* as his children, and teasing her about the dubious relationship that might imply between them if the stories were to be reborn in Serbo-Croat through her. "If this book comes off, let's arrange the translation of the novel after that: it hasn't appeared in Russian, but it's been published in English in New York, it's been translated and published in Czech, and it's being translated into German. And here the convention would be in force." He told her she should now be able to obtain a copy of *We* in Russian from the publishers "Petropolis" in Berlin. Kunina-Aleksander had also been giving lectures on contemporary Russian literature, in which she had controversially tried to draw attention to the merits of Soviet, as well as émigré Russian writers. She had therefore asked her father (who still lived in the old house) to call on Zamiatin for advice, to help her choose materials for her next lectures on Soviet poetry and theatre and on proletarian writers. He told her he had spoken to her father, but added that there was very little good new literature that year—even Leonid Leonov's *Thief*, of which much had been expected, had "turned out to be dull and long-drawn-out."[76]

In 1927 he had been negotiating with a couple of publishers about the possibility of a new collected edition of his writings. V. Narbut from "Zemlia i Fabrika" (ZiF) warned him that he would have to exclude certain works which might not be to the taste of their firm's "new, wider readership," and that for the same reason he would have to make the edition cheap, which meant he could not agree the terms requested.[77] So Zamiatin explored options for his collected edition with "Nikitinskie subbotniki" instead.[78] The outline he drew up in November 1927 was for 6 volumes: *Provincial Life*, *At the Back of Beyond*, *The Islanders*, X (to include the *Impious Tales* and some newer stories), a volume of drama, and a volume of articles and memoirs (of Blok, Andreev and Kustodiev).[79] By now the possibility of publishing *We* was not even discussed.

In February 1928, Chukovsky called on Zamiatin at home:

> We hadn't visited one another for about two years. I liked his place very much. I had gone to ask about Gor'ky, whether Zamiatin had any materials about Aleksei Maksimovich dating from the time of "World Literature." It turned out that he hadn't. "And I'm tired of memoirs. I've only just finished Kustodiev [...]. I'm not corresponding with Gor'ky at the moment, he seems to be angry with me about something." He has comical posters on his walls from *The Flea*, a wonderful carpet on the floor, and he showed me his stories translated into Spanish and his novel *We* in Czech. [...] He showed me some fascinating illustrations by Kustodiev for *The History of the Flea* [sic] in which, despite the stylisation, he has created the best portrait I've seen of Evgeny Ivanovich. She, that is Evgeny Ivanovich's wife Liudmila Nikolaevna, has become kinder; she's not wearing lipstick any more, and she's become simpler.

This warmer attitude towards Zamiatin prompted a frank letter from Chukovsky shortly thereafter, when he himself ran into serious trouble. On 1 February, Nadezhda Krupskaia, Lenin's widow and head of the children's literature organisation, had published an article in *Pravda* in which she described Chukovsky's popular children's poem *The Crocodile* as "bourgeois muck." Chukovsky, shattered, took refuge in a former monastery three hours away from Leningrad, and wrote to Zamiatin to show him the article and his reply to it, and to ask his advice — he evidently still respected him as someone with useful experience of standing up to the authorities. He was aware that Krupskaia was deliberately trying to destroy him, and indeed this did lead to a temporary ban on any publication of Chukovsky's works for children.[80]

February 1928 was also the month when the film of *The North* came out. On 13 March, Zamiatin wrote to the editors of *Zhizn' iskusstva* (*Life of Art*) to register a protest: the Soviet cinema authority ("Sovkino") in Moscow had made cuts and changes to his script, and he had already asked for his name to be removed from a work which he now considered to be a travesty of his original. However, the film had just been released with his name still attached, and so he wanted publicly to renounce any association with it. This was just like his earlier unsatisfactory experience with the film *The House in the Snowdrifts* (based on *The Cave*).[81]

The admiration Zamiatin felt for Mikhail Bulgakov's early writing had evidently become the starting-point for a warm friendship; intellectually, and as personalities, they had a great deal in common. On 17 March, Liudmila wrote to reproach Bulgakov for neglecting them: perhaps he had retreated "to some uninhabited, uncrimson island" (a reference to his hilarious skit on Soviet history in 1917–21, *The Crimson Island*, which was then in rehearsal in Moscow). "But we—I—do want to be involved with you, and we would like to see you here with us, as before." A couple of weeks later, Bulgakov was back in Leningrad: Liudmila sent him powders for his headache, and invited him round that evening. During this stay, Zamiatin extracted a promise from him to contribute an article on "The Dramatist and the Critics" for a volume to celebrate the 25th anniversary of the theatre organisation "Dramosoiuz." Bulgakov wrote on his return to Moscow that he was already missing "your enchanting city," and was feeling ill and melancholy; he had also left his black and lilac scarf behind, and asked them to send it on. On 15 May, Liudmila (who became their main correspondent) wrote a mock-indignant letter to Bulgakov, complaining that Zamiatin and the painter Nikolai Radlov were undermining the rules of their favourite game (probably the game of verse improvisation called *bouts-rimés*): "Isn't it time you came to St Petersburg to restore order?"[82] Radlov may have drawn his elegant cartoon of Zamiatin around this time. That year he also made a portrait in oils of Zamiatin in a three-piece suit with a bow tie, his left hand in his jacket pocket and a cigar in the other.[83] It was just as provocative an image for Zamiatin to present of himself to Soviet society as the notorious photograph Bulgakov had had taken of himself a couple of years earlier sporting a monocle, at the time of the controversial staging of *The Days of the Turbins*.

Early in May he drafted another of his "autobiographies," this time as an introduction to the first volume of his collected works, where it appeared—after some censorship interventions—in 1929. He recalled his childhood and early reading, and then reviewed the course of his busy career over the previous decade, since returning to Russia from Newcastle:

> I no longer had time for drafting designs—practical technology dried up in me and fell away like a yellowed leaf (all that remained of technology was teaching at the Polytechnic Institute). Instead, I was giving courses of lectures on the most

recent Russian literature at the Herzen Pedagogical Institute (1920–21), and on techniques of fiction at the House of Arts Studio, as well as working on the editorial board of "World Literature," on the board of the VSP, on the House of Writers committee, the Council of the House of Arts, the "Historical Drama" section, and for various publishing houses—Grzhebin's, "Alkonost," "Petropolis," "Mysl'"; and editing journals—*Dom iskusstv, Sovremennyi zapad, Russky sovremennik*. During those years I wrote relatively little; amongst my most significant things was my novel *We*, which came out in 1925 [*sic*] in English, and then in translation into other languages: the novel has not yet appeared in print in Russian.

He went on to mention his "betrayal" of prose in 1925 in favour of drama; but suggested that, having briefly had recourse to verse form in his play *Attila*, there was now nowhere further for him to go, and he was turning back toward the novel and short stories. "I think that if I hadn't returned from England in 1917, if I hadn't lived alongside Russia through all these years, I wouldn't have been able to write any more. I have seen a great deal: in Petersburg, in Moscow, in the backwoods of Tambov, and in villages in the Vologda and Pskov districts, and in heated railway freight trucks. And so I have come full circle. I don't know, and I can't tell, what twists and turns there will be in my life after this."[84] A further glimpse of his thoughts about his writing that year came in a fragment he wrote called "About my work": "Altogether, I will be turning back from drama towards prose for the foreseeable future, and I think I will return in a new way: after very great complexity, very great simplicity. Such, for example, is the story *The Yawl* which I completed recently."[85]

At the end of May 1928 Gor'ky returned to Russia on his first visit since leaving, ostensibly for health reasons, in the autumn of 1921. Zamiatin had just been discussing the celebratory volume of articles for "Dramosoiuz" with his friend, the publisher Aleksandr Krolenko, when, on 26 May, a personal and savage attack on Krolenko and his scholarly publishing house "Academia" appeared in *Leningradskaia pravda*. Krolenko's outraged friends, including Zamiatin and Gor'ky, signed a collective letter a few days later, drawing attention to the outstanding quality of the work of "Academia" over the previous seven years, and to Krolenko's personal contributions to that success. The publishing house was eventually saved, but Krolenko himself was charged with minor abuses of his position and initially sentenced in July 1929 to two years in jail, although this was then commuted to 4 months in a very mild house of correction.[86]

Good news then arrived from France. Erenburg had become more hopeful now of success in placing *We*, and in March he once again sent an urgent request for a copy of the novel in English, which he needed in order to secure the French translation, and also asked for a power of attorney. Six weeks later he confirmed that he had received the English version from Prague (perhaps he had lent it to Roman Jakobson a couple of years earlier, and now got it back again). He delivered this to the "Nouvelle Revue Française" publishing house, who then agreed to publish *We* that winter: he had found a good translator, and the terms would be the same as he, Erenburg, received for his works in France, i. e. 5% of the sales. "If the book is a commercial success, you'll get something, and if not, then it's money for matches, plus the glory." Towards the end of July Erenburg sent him a cheery message from Slovakia, where he was on holiday, and passed on greetings from his companions there, Jakobson and Ovady Savich. He added that he had signed the contract for *We* with "NRF" before he left France.[87] On 10 October Erenburg wrote again, complaining that he had not heard from him for a long time, and inquired whether he was happy with the contract, which he had asked Nikitin to pass on to him.[88]

In February 1928, the much-delayed rehearsals of *Attila* had finally begun at the BDT. At this point Blok's widow Liubov' Dmitrievna, the "Beautiful Lady" of his early poetry, sent Zamiatin an effusive letter to tell him that she had now got over her feelings of rancour towards Russian literature, which she felt had damaged her life and Blok's. She believed that his *Attila* was the literary and theatrical event she had been waiting for, and particularly the part of the romantic heroine Il'degonda, Attila's noble hostage. She could not believe that she had irrevocably aged in his eyes and those of the theatre (she was in her late 40s): "I feel obliged to offer myself to you for the role of Il'degonda; there is no other actress [...] and I will overcome my appearance of age." She begged him to give her a frank reply, promised that she was hardened to reverses, and asked him in any case to accept her request "as a homage [...] to your beautiful tragedy."[89] Zamiatin presumably found some graceful way of declining her offer. But he soon had more serious problems to deal with, as he told Gor'ky furiously at the end of May, when it emerged that *Attila* had suddenly been banned: "The BDT in Leningrad has been working for several months on this play, [...] and yesterday I heard that 'Gubrepertkom' [the Leningrad censors] were not going to permit the play to be staged. [...] I apologise for burdening you with this. But this is a serious matter for me: can I go on living and working in Russia, or is that now impossible?" He sent Gor'ky a copy of the play's text, and begged him to provide a short review of it to support him in his protest.[90]

In early June 1928, he went down to Moscow to see if anything could be done to save *Attila*. He dined more than once with Bulgakov, who had returned early from a holiday in the Caucasus because of the similar banning by Moscow's "Glavrepertkom" [the Chief Repertory Committee] of his own new play, *Flight*, which had already been accepted for production by MKhAT. From now on the lives of the two friends, and their professional difficulties, would run along strikingly parallel tracks.[91] Gor'ky read *Attila* and was very complimentary, as he would be later that summer about *Flight*, and insisted that it ought to be put on. Perhaps he preferred the new, more "realist" Zamiatin to his earlier modernist mode of writing? After persistent lobbying by Gor'ky, "Glavrepertkom" finally agreed to license *Attila* for production, but only in a limited number of theatres, and only if a number of changes were made (the Huns were to behave more politely, etc.). The BDT insisted that Zamiatin should stay in Moscow and make the alterations immediately: "I can't tell you how difficult and unpleasant it was to do it," he told Liudmila (22 June).[92] Gor'ky promised to arm the BDT with a copy of his own review of the play, especially since the Leningrad branch of "Repertkom" was still insisting "categorically" that the play was not to be staged.

While in Moscow, Zamiatin was also trying to decide whether to sign a contract for the proposed 6-volume edition of his works with "Federatsiia," or to confirm the deal he'd set up previously with "Nikitinskie subbotniki." One way or another he expected to get some money, so Liudmila was not to be anxious about the costs of the redecorating they were planning (new curtains, telephone sockets, a shower and a washbasin). This was probably for the new home they moved to that year, apartment 16 at 29 Zhukovsky Street, which would be his final Leningrad address. Eventually he signed a contract with "Federatsiia," even though they only accepted the volume of articles provisionally, and had tried to beat him down over the price.[93] In any case, that meant that the refurbishment could go ahead. "And tell Rostislav (and let him say it back to you) that there's no reason for you to be sad" (22 June). He had also attended some of the sensational hearings in the case mounted against 53 mining engineers accused of industrial sabotage, which was effectively the first major Stalinist show trial. As the decade drew to a close, Stalin had decreed an end to NEP and was moving to consolidate centralised control over the economy in the form of the first Five-year Plan; but at the same time, he was eliminating all political opposition and beginning to establish exclusive—and fearsome—personal control over cultural and ideological matters. Zamiatin told Liudmila: "I've been twice to the Shakhty trial. It's really horrible. Altogether I'm fed up with everything here, and I can't wait to get away" (18 June).

On 9 July Tikhonov wrote to say that the first volume of Zamiatin's collected works had passed the censors, apart from the sentence in his "autobiography" where he mentioned having been in prison in 1922: "I agree with comrade A. Fadeev that maybe it would indeed be worth leaving that phrase out." In his reply, Zamiatin commented: "Fadeev has disappointed me: I thought he had less of a pro-Marxist brain." In fact Aleksandr Fadeev, author of the 1927 Soviet classic *The Rout*, would go on to become the post-War Chairman of the Union of Soviet Writers, and a notorious apologist for Stalin. Zamiatin continued: "I don't feel the least bit awkward writing about it; and if someone feels awkward reading it, then I'm not to blame. And if I were to keep it entirely quiet, then a false light would be cast on the entire autobiography, where I speak in some detail of my earlier Bolshevism—and I don't want that." Instead, he proposed a somewhat more elliptical way of phrasing the information. Even so, it still didn't get published in the form he wished. In January 1929 Tikhonov wrote to him to explain that it had not been the fault of the "Federatsiia" publishers, but the censors had simply removed the offending phrases all over again.[94]

By mid-July, Zamiatin was becoming fretful that the promised written permission for *Attila* seemed to be so slow in coming through. In deference to "Glavrepertkom" certain alterations had been made: "some 'minuses' have been glued on to a number of the Roman characters." Nevertheless, he feared that the BDT would still be nervous of antagonising the Leningrad "Repertkom."[95] Two weeks later he was finally told: "Your play *Attila* has been licensed by 'Glavrepertkom' in your most recent version, without further corrections and without any cuts whatsoever." However, the question of which license category it should be assigned to (i. e. how wide a range of theatres would be permitted to stage it) would be left open for the time being.[96]

Meanwhile, Bulgakov was still wrestling with the authorities over his own play, and on 1 August Liudmila sent him more powders for his headaches, and asked him to make sure to bring a copy of *Flight* with him when he came to visit. That the campaign for *Attila* was still worth fighting was demonstrated by the fact that at this very moment news reached Zamiatin in Leningrad that Bulgakov had at least won a different battle, and had received permission for his Revolutionary and theatrical satire *The Crimson Island* to be performed. He congratulated Bulgakov on 13 September, and reminded him about the article he was due to contribute for the "Dramosoiuz" almanac.[97] Two weeks later, however, Bulgakov replied from Moscow to say that he had written 20 pages of his "Dramosoiuz" article about theatre critics, but that the previous day he had burned the lot "…in that same stove you have sat next to more than once. And it's a good thing I came to my senses in time. Given that I am surrounded by living people, there can be no question of committing this *opus* to print. […] and I'm quite confident when I say that you wouldn't have printed it in any case. […] After your congratulations a feeling of (reverential) horror was added to the love I bear for you. You congratulated me two weeks before *The Crimson Island* was permitted. Which means you're a prophet. As for the permission, well, I don't know what to say. I wrote *Flight* and submitted it. But it's *The Crimson Island* that's been passed. It's mystical. Who? What? Why? For what purpose? The thickest of fogs has enveloped my brain. I hope you won't deprive me of your prayers."[98]

Zamiatin's own situation was less cheering. On 26 September the Leningrad "Repertkom" told the BDT that they were again refusing to recommend that *Attila* should be staged, even despite the "Glavrepertkom" recommendation. This amounted to a renewed banning of the play. In the October edition of the "Repertkom" bulletin Pavel Novitsky stated that *Attila* had nothing new to offer either in content or in form, and that the tragedy of clashing cultures had been reduced by Zamiatin to personal issues. "The tragedy is written in a splendid literary language. But it offers no other achievements."[99] Zamiatin wrote indignantly to the BDT to demand an explanation for their craven response: they immediately caved in to the Leningrad "Repertkom," and ceased work on the play.[100]

The dispute over *Attila* then moved into the courts, with Zamiatin accusing the BDT of breach of contract, so he began to cast around for influential support.[101] He approached Gor'ky again in late October (he had recently returned to Italy) to see if he would write a few more lines with his opinion of the play, for use in court. Gor'ky sent these on 4 November, and told him he was writing at the same time to Aleksei Rykov, Chairman of the Council of People's Commissars of the USSR. "Be so kind as to let me know how this nonsense resolves itself." Once again the very highest politicians in the land were being drawn into literary debates. In his comments, Gor'ky described *Attila* as "highly valuable both in a social and a literary sense. I see its value in the fact that the Huns, led by Attila, go to destroy Rome, which used to enslave people. I also consider that the heroic tone of the play and its heroic subject are acutely useful in the present day, when bourgeois philistinism hisses at us ever louder." He added that he found the Leningrad banning of the play in the face of the positive ruling by "Glavrepertkom" quite scandalous.[102]

Something of the agony Zamiatin suffered over this whole issue is perhaps reflected in a piece he drafted on 23 December, "For a volume about books": "When my children go out into the street badly dressed, I feel upset for them; when little boys chuck stones at them from behind the corner, I feel pain; and when the doctor approaches them with pincers or a knife, I feel as though I would rather be cut open myself. My books are my children—I have no others." On 8 January 1929, Zamiatin wrote to Gor'ky to thank him for his support: "From the very start it was clear that the court was on the side of the author. But your letter, which was read out in court, undoubtedly made a huge impression. The verdict was that the theatre was found guilty of failing to fulfil its production contract, and was obliged to pay the author 1,500 roubles or so. [...] All the same, the play is dead and buried."[103] Accepting his defeat, he had already begun work during 1928 on transforming the failed drama project back into a prose piece about Attila, which became the unfinished novel *The Scourge of God* (1928–1935).[104]

In the spring of 1928, Zamiatin had also completed *The Flood*, the last really substantial new work he would write before he left the USSR.[105] The following January, he wrote to Sergei Obradovich, one of the editors of the almanac *Zemlia i Fabrika* [*ZiF*], to complain about a number of alterations he had discovered in the proofs of the text. In this novella, a stylistic tour de force, he once again explores the themes of infertility and sexual desire, the violation of innocence, and violence (an axe murder). The text is shaped by the rhythm of the floods which afflict the city, a recognisably Dostoevskian St Petersburg. However, the narrative is essentially driven by a different kind of flooding, that of Sof'ia's menstrual cycle, the increase in tension in her as her menses approach, which is compounded by her dread of them as evidence that once again she has failed to conceive. In a complex and prophetic dream which is best interpreted using Freud's notions of condensation and displacement, she anticipates the murder of Gan'ka, her young rival, in terms which link her menstrual bleeding to the blood in which she finds her hands are covered after the crime. This linkage is then developed through the suggestion that her fertility, the conceiving of a baby girl, is actually dependent on Gan'ka's death. Zamiatin conceded to Obradovich that the censors might object, for example, when the young girl Gan'ka mangles a Soviet term such as "Sovnarkom" (Council of People's Commissars), but he protested vehemently about the apparently prudish cuts the editors had presumed to make. "It's fine if the editors of the *ZiF* almanacs decide to correct young authors and teach them how to write. But I think I have already got beyond that age, and can take responsibility myself for the artistic aspects of my writing; under no circumstances will I permit 'aesthetic' alterations to be made to my works." He invoked also the new law on authors' rights which had been passed in 1928, and insisted the cuts be restored, or he would withdraw the story.[106] *The Flood* was duly published early in March 1929, and Grebenshchikov arranged for him to read it at a literary evening a month later.[107]

During the summer of 1928, when he had not managed to get away on holiday at all, and which had largely been taken up with his losing battle on behalf of *Attila*, one entertaining distraction for Zamiatin had been his collaborative work on the libretto for Dmitry Shostakovich's new opera, based on Gogol's story *The Nose* (1836). Shostakovich had decided to turn to this classic short story because he felt it would suit his satirical purposes better than a Soviet-era text could. Zamiatin was listed as one of the authors of the published libretto (1930) alongside G. Ionin, A. Preis and Shostakovich himself.[108] In another new musical dimension of Zamiatin's career, the composer Iury Shaporin's music for *The Flea* was performed that winter as a suite at a symphony concert, and was scheduled to go on sale as a score the following year. After all the disappointments of 1928, Zamiatin next turned his hand to a short comic sketch, *The Martyrs to Learning*. A wealthy widow sacrifices herself and marries her former coachman Iakov in order to acquire the working-class genealogy now required in order for her son Rostislav (the choice of name is obviously a private joke) to enter university, only for Iakov to start demanding that she should look after him like a proper working-class wife, and bring him his tea.[109]

The eighth anniversary of the Serapion Brotherhood was celebrated on 1 February 1929. In the rapidly changing circumstances, and as intellectual freedoms in the USSR diminished, there was much to mourn. Gruzdev described the occasion to Gor'ky: "On the surface there was much merriment, but in essence it was rather gloomy. There is something solid and settled now in their literary reputations. [...] At the celebrations Zamiatin read out an epitaph to each of the Serapions, and there was a lot of bitterness in them." These four-liners addressed to Fedin, Gruzdev, Slonimsky, Zoshchenko, Tikhonov, Nikitin, and Polonskaia do indeed seem to dwell on the constraints they had encountered, and the collapse of their dreams.[110] That same month, the youngest Serapion, Vladimir Pozner, who had left for Paris with his parents shortly after the group was formed, sent copies of two books he had published there in 1929 about modern Russian literature. Zamiatin figured prominently in both, and they carried affectionate inscriptions.[111] Another pleasing message from France came from Erenburg in March, to announce that the French translation by B. Cauvet-Duhamel of *We* [*Nous Autres*] was already being advertised, with a publication date a month or two away. He was delighted to hear that Zamiatin had embarked upon another long work (*The Scourge of God*), and was expecting much of him.[112]

In mid-September 1928 Zamiatin had learnt of the straitened circumstances of his former editor Viktor Miroliubov, who was sometimes even going without meals, and so he did his best to find him an income.[113] On the sunny afternoon of 20 February 1929, he met Krolenko at the outdoor ice-rink, and they skated together for a while. Perhaps not unconnected with that conversation, Zamiatin wrote to Miroliubov shortly afterwards to invite him to look in at "Academia" (where Krolenko still worked), to have a word about some work there: "I press your hand firmly. Your sincerely loving Evg. Zamiatin." During these weeks Zamiatin was also involved, as a member of the VSP committee for resolving disputes, in an argument over authors' rights, and Miroliubov was suddenly appointed as another member of the same panel.[114]

In mid-April, Zamiatin wrote to Iarmolinsky in New York: "I haven't written to you for a long time, because I didn't want to write misanthropic letters, but none others seem to come out at the moment. Somehow life is not much fun. Although materially, and seen from outside, everything is fine: my play is on, this winter four volumes of my complete works (although not very complete, in fact) have appeared, and this autumn the fifth volume will probably appear.

I haven't written much that's new: just a few stories. I'm currently embarking on a novel, and as for that, maybe I'll talk to you about a translation by next spring." However, Tikhonov wrote a fortnight later to let him know that the prospects for publishing the fifth volume of his works (the collection of articles and essays) had worsened.[115] Zamiatin had little to recommend to Iarmolinsky in the way of new novels: perhaps Fadeev's rather earnest Civil War narrative *The Rout*, and Tynianov's more experimental biographical account of the final years of the playwright Griboedov, *The Death of Vazir-Mukhtar*.[116]

The opening salvo in a sharper attack by the proletarian writers on the fellow-travellers and "bourgeois" writers appeared on 2 May 1929, in the form of extremely hostile ditties directed against Zamiatin and others, on the pages of the Leningrad edition of *Literaturnaia gazeta*. They were composed by the poet Aleksandr Bezymensky, a leading member of RAPP. Under the title "Certificate concerning social eugenics," he had written:

> Type: Zamiatin.
> Genus: Evgeny.
> Class: bourgeois.
> In the village: a kulak.
> The product of degeneration.
> Footnote: an enemy.[117]

Zamiatin was livid. Feeling betrayed by the VSP, for whom he had worked for so many years, and which was responsible as a member of the Writers' Federation (FOSP) for publishing the offending newspaper, he wrote a letter of resignation from its board the very next day: "A political denunciation—even one which rhymes—is still a political denunciation; that is the literary genre to which Bezymensky's 'epigram' belongs. What Bezymensky thinks of me doesn't bother me in the slightest; and what countless Bezymenskys print about me in official publications doesn't upset me; but the fact that in this case the denunciation has appeared in a newspaper of the Writers' Federation entirely alters the matter. My comrades from the VSP belong to the Federation; my comrades from the board of the VSP are some of the editors of *Literaturnaia gazeta*; and the official seal of the VSP stands on Bezymensky's publication."[118]

At a meeting three days later, the VSP board deplored the publication of the epigrams, and described the one attacking Zamiatin as "slanderous, irresponsible, and defamatory of him as a Soviet citizen." For the rest of May there was a flurry of meetings, resolutions, and exchanges about the issue between the board of the VSP and that of the Federation, but nothing appeared in the way of a public retraction. The VSP chairman wrote to Zamiatin, emphasising that their representative on the newspaper had not been shown the epigrams for approval: and in view of the value the board placed on Zamiatin's work, he asked him to withdraw his resignation. But this was not enough to placate him. He replied that their failure to issue a public statement meant that the situation had not been remedied, and it was now too late. So his letter of resignation remained in force. Further negotiations between the literary organisations ensued, and on 25 June the national edition of *Literaturnaia gazeta* finally published a cautious admission that FOSP had allowed the "unacceptable" publication of "non-literary" materials. Unfazed, on 8 July Bezymensky simply republished his original epigram, along with a selection of quotations from articles on Zamiatin, attacking him as an enemy of the Revolution. Zamiatin never rejoined the VSP board, and by the end of 1929, the VSP itself had become the target of RAPP attacks.

After a rather bruising few months, he wrote to Vengerova on 5 July about some new prospects for *The Flea* abroad. In a comment reflecting his renewed urge now to get out of Russia, he told her that he was not too concerned about the financial terms, "but rather the possibility of travelling and being present during the work on the play. So you can agree to any terms for it—what I really need is for the theatre to summon me to work on the production." Vengerova had evidently been suggesting a new collaboration to him too, in the form of Ben Hecht and Charles MacArthur's 1928–29 Broadway hit *The Front Page*, which she had posted to him to see if he could interest Soviet theatres in it.[119] On 22 July she wrote back from Paris that she was glad that he liked *The Front Page*; she was about to start work on a translation into Russian, which she hoped to send him before the end of August. She also enclosed another American play for him to consider, Elmer Rice's *Street Scene*.[120]

Over the summer of 1929 Zamiatin started work with a group of authors on an anthology of insights into the writing process called *How We Write*, which was published in Leningrad in 1930. During 1926 he had written two drafts of an article "Behind the scenes. How we write (on the psychology of creative work and mastery as a writer),"[121] and this became his own contribution to the volume.[122]

Gor'ky sent Zamiatin his piece—with which he was not very satisfied—for *How We Write* during his second visit back to the USSR that July. He also made one further attempt to help over the *Attila* dispute, which was still dragging on, by writing to the RSFSR Prosecutor N.V. Krylenko, pointing out that by now Zamiatin had obtained three verdicts in his favour, all of which had subsequently been overturned. "This is how the course of events has been relayed to me, and if it's really so... then of course this severely compromises the Soviet courts." But even after an intervention by Krylenko things did not go Zamiatin's way, and on 6 October 1929 the appeal court set aside all the earlier verdicts and exonerated the theatre entirely from the charge of breach of contract.[123]

That summer Zamiatin wrote a comical letter to Bulgakov: "I quite understand that every reminder of the city where you were obliged 10 (ten) times to eat humble pie at the billiard table is not particularly pleasant to you. Believe me, only extreme necessity constrains me to subject you to this unpleasantness. As you know, I have given up writing plays. But I would urgently like to offer the Moscow theatres one good American play [*The Front Page*]. And for that I need to know which theatrical folk are in Moscow at the moment." He sent greetings to Bulgakov's wife, Liubov' Evgen'evna (in fact, Bulgakov had been having a passionate affair since February with the woman who would eventually become his third wife, Elena Sergeevna Shilovskaia). In his reply on 19 July, Bulgakov retorted: "As far as eating humble pie at the billiard-table is concerned, there exists a well-known phrase: 'My turn today, but tomorrow it's yours, mate!'" He explained that most theatre directors had left Moscow for the summer, and mentioned that he had been talking to people about *Attila*, and that there still seemed to be a little ray of hope for it. "But what if that ray is lying? O, Tempora, o Mores!" That month Bulgakov had written a desperate letter to Gor'ky, Stalin, and other members of the Government imploring them to expel him from the country, since after ten years all his literary and theatrical work had been banned.[124] Liudmila let him know that they would be passing through Moscow on the 28th, on their way south for the holidays. They would have less than an hour there, but would be delighted if he would drop by to chat to them at the station.[125]

Although the Zamiatins travelled down to the Crimea together, they actually holidayed separately: he headed back to Voloshin's at Koktebel', while Liudmila stayed about 20 miles along the coast at Sudak. In his first letter to her on 8 August he told her he had found a number of musical, acting, and literary acquaintances there, and was hoping to start playing tennis, only he did not have the right shoes. He was smoking only a moderate 5–6 cigarettes a day.[126] Zamiatin wrote to thank Gor'ky for his "very interesting" contribution to *How We Write*, which had arrived on the day of his departure, and for his good advice about other writers to include—in fact one of them, Vikenty Veresaev, turned out to be at Koktebel' too, so they had already spoken.[127] In the meantime, Pasternak wrote him a very courteous letter, thanking him for the invitation to participate in the collection, and suggesting they should use extracts from the first part of his *Safe Conduct*, which was just about to come out: "I know, and I can guess, how difficult things are for you, and I cannot overcome a feeling of causeless and unnatural shame at the awareness that relatively, and with certain reservations, things are much easier for me now than in the years when we used to meet at Pil'niak's and at [*Russky*] *sovremennik*. You know how much I love and value you."[128]

A few days later, Zamiatin wrote Liudmila a relaxed letter (to "Much-respected Milochka"), in which he comically described how his landlady's (dog's) suitors were keeping him awake at night. He was planning to play tennis that evening, since the Bulgarian tennis shoes he'd ordered had arrived the previous day, but he was still feeling too tired to travel even as far as Sudak. He signed it—almost uniquely—"I kiss you." Liudmila was staying, along with Natalia Krandievskaia-Tolstaia (Aleksei Tolstoy's wife), at the dacha of the composer Aleksandr Spendiarov, whom Zamiatin had met during his 1923 visit to Koktebel'. On 13 August he sent her a telegram to let her know he had decided to visit her that day, signing it "Epikhodov" (Chekhov's "walking disaster" from *The Cherry Orchard*). Evidently he then brought some of the young people of her household back with him to Koktebel', and he reported on them entertainingly to Liudmila. They had been duly punished for being "so unfeeling about his tears at leaving her," because when they arrived they had to endure a lengthy poetry reading by Voloshin in the hot sun before getting any supper. In a second installment of Epikhodov's adventures, he described how he was lying naked on the beach when two acquaintances appeared, and spoiled his solitude for two days. He had lost his purse and the key to his room, and left his swimming trunks on the beach. He then spent a whole day moving into a better room in Voloshin's own villa. On the 27th, he reported that he was sleeping well in his new, cool accommodation, even after staying up late to dance the foxtrot; he had been out on a motorboat excursion to admire the mountains and the eagles; and he had managed at last to get hold of some sugar. On the other hand, he had lost weight (he now weighed just under ten stones), and he was smoking 10–12 cigarettes a day because he was surrounded by smokers. He had found a psychiatrist with whom he had discussed hypnosis, and a historian who told him of two new books about Attila.[129] Altogether, he was enjoying a proper holiday, such as he had missed the previous year.

The journalist I. Basalaev recalled him in Koktebel' in those final tranquil days of that summer: "Evgeny Zamiatin, a tall man with a small head [...] walks through the yard to the kitchen. He has well-established relations with the kitchen. He goes there to fetch water for shaving, to order a meal, or to have a chat with the woman in charge. [...] In his cool room there is a brick floor, a low, hard iron bed, a stool and a window heaped with boxes, newspapers, and scraps of paper. Evgeny Ivanovich sits there without a shirt (a slim, tanned torso, strong muscles) in front of a folding mirror, and unhurriedly, patiently—as ever, whatever he is doing—he shaves with a safety razor. [...] By the way, there is a widespread opinion of Zamiatin as a dry, unfeeling man. In my opinion that's wrong. He's a passionate man, who knows how to live, and he lives through every dimension of his physical being."[130] He was going to need all of that strength and unhurried patience in order to deal with the next trials he would face.

21. Portrait of Zamiatin by Boris Kustodiev (1923, © René Guerra).

22. Cartoon by Boris Kustodiev of Zamiatin (1927), for the latter's *Biography of a Flea*.

23. Cartoon of Konstantin Fedin by Nikolai Radlov.

24. Cartoon of Aleksei Tolstoy by Nikolai Radlov.

25. Photograph of Zamiatin (1920s?).

26. Photograph of Zamiatin (Leningrad, 1929).

27. Photograph of Zamiatin in his study in Leningrad by A.A. Krolenko (1931).

28. Zamiatin wearing plus-fours, playing with the monkey Whisky at Boris Grigor'ev's house in Haut-de-Cagnes (1932).

29. Photograph of Zamiatin (1930s?).

30. The Zamiatins' home at 14, rue Raffet, Paris (XVI).

31. Irina Kunina-Aleksander (1957).

32. Konstantin Fedin and Maksim Gor'ky (1934).

33. The grave of Zamiatin and his wife Liudmila in the cemetery at Thiais (Paris).

CHAPTER 7:

FROM KOKTEBEL' TO THE WARSAW STATION (1929–1931)

Zamiatin's relaxed holiday in the Crimea was thrown into complete disarray at the end of August 1929, in the middle of a meal: "During lunch today (I always eat here, at Voloshin's dacha) Veresaev dashed over, scrambled over the flowerbed (to Voloshin's horror) and thrust into my hands a copy of *Komsomol'skaia pravda* (*Komsomol Truth*) from 27 August. A few minutes later Adrianov rushed over with copies of *Literaturnaia gazeta* and *Vecherniaia krasnaia* (*The Red Evening Paper*) from the 26th. There was general panic. Everywhere there are articles concerning Pil'niak and me: why has Pil'niak's novel *Mahogany*, which was banned by the censors, been published by 'Petropolis' [i.e. in Berlin], and why was the novel *We* published in *Volia Rossii*?"[1] Pil'niak's 1929 novella *Mahogany* had conjured up a nostalgic feeling for old Russia, and presented a distinctly ambivalent picture of events post-1917. The blatantly coordinated publication of these articles signalled a sharp worsening of Zamiatin's situation, and the attacks on him and Pil'niak that year would escalate to become one of the most notorious episodes in Soviet literary life during the 1920s.[2] "On the occasion of these sensational newspapers, I bought a watermelon today and stuffed myself after lunch: I don't know what will happen."[3] The articles criticised Zamiatin for not publicly denouncing Slonim's Russian-language publication of *We* in Prague, and suggested he was guilty of actions which had compromised Soviet literature and drawn the sympathy of the Russian emigration towards writers like himself, Bulgakov, Zoshchenko and Pil'niak. "Every copy of a newspaper was literally torn apart, and every new piece of information was heatedly discussed by everyone. Zamiatin himself, to give him his due, behaved calmly."[4] He rightly understood straight away that this all formed part of a concerted campaign by RAPP against the VSP, whose board he had until so recently belonged to in Leningrad, and whose Moscow branch had just appointed Pil'niak as their Chairman.

He decided to leave Koktebel' and join Liudmila, arriving at Sudak on 6 or 7 September. On the day of his departure, he wrote an inscription in a volume he presented as a gift to Voloshin, in which he compared himself to a monk being assailed by demons.[5]

During September the campaign intensified. The attacks on the VSP for its supposed lack of political principle were targeted on Zamiatin and Pil'niak, with groups of writers and workers being called upon to express in print their condemnation of the pair's "culpable" actions. The Leningrad VSP wrote to *Krasnaia gazeta* to protest against this discrediting of one of its members. The Moscow VSP, meanwhile, hastily tried to distance itself from the two writers, proposing on 6 September that Pil'niak should stand down as Chairman, and referring Zamiatin's case back to the Leningrad section. Three days later, FOSP, the umbrella organisation of which the VSP formed a part, published a resolution condemning the two authors' publication of their works abroad as "an example of the sabotaging of the interests of Soviet literature, and of the entire Soviet nation."

Pil'niak had already been in touch with him by telegram from Moscow, and on 8 September Zamiatin posted him the draft of a letter he proposed to send to the editors of *Literaturnaia gazeta*. In it, he pointed out that they had omitted to mention that *We* had been written 9 years previously ("the novel was completed in 1920"), and that its publication in *Volia Rossii* (which he had never seen) had not only taken place more than two years before, but had been prefaced with the editor's explanation that the extracts had been translated back into Russian from Czech. Perhaps disingenuously, he claimed: "Using even a modicum of logic, it's obvious that such an operation on a work of art could not possibly have been conducted with the knowledge or consent of its author. I will say more: the author made an attempt to stop the operation, but unfortunately was not successful."[6] Meanwhile, Pil'niak had pointed out that in publishing *Mahogany* with "Petropolis" in Berlin he had done nothing different from other well-respected Soviet authors such as Aleksei Tolstoy, Konstantin Fedin, and Mikhail Sholokhov. He emphasised that he had publicly complained about émigré interpretations of his work, and affirmed that henceforth he only wished to dedicate himself to the cause of Soviet literature.

The Leningrad VSP urged Zamiatin to return in haste from the Crimea. In response, he sent them a copy of his proposed letter to *Literaturnaia gazeta*, together with a more detailed account of the whole affair. He explained that he had quite simply posted the manuscript to Berlin in 1920 or 1921, with the reasonable expectation that it would be published in Russian simultaneously there and in Petrograd. The novel had subsequently been published in translations into English and Czech, and he had never disguised the fact, nor received any objections to this. He had read the novel in public meetings of the VSP in 1923–24, and nobody had protested at the time. He also pointed out that he had asked Erenburg to try and get *Volia Rossii* to stop the 1927 publication, and claimed he had asked Slonimsky to approach them as well. "I am mentioning all these chronological details so as to demonstrate to what extent the question of my novel *We* has been artificially attached to the campaign that has been mounted against the VSP."[7] He complained that he had been condemned at a meeting in Moscow even before his own explanations had been solicited, and asked how his comrades from the VSP who were present could have allowed such a thing. On 12 September, Zoshchenko told Slonimsky: "I feel sorry for Zamiatin. It's an ugly spectacle, when a 'European' and 'Anglophile' is dragged face-down through the dirt. It's a vulgar sight. And if they start shouting at me too much, then I'll just lay down my arms. I'll write a letter to the newspapers to say that I'm giving up all literary work for the time being."[8]

On 21 September, just after Zamiatin reached Moscow from the Crimea, both Pil'niak and Pasternak resigned from the newly purged Moscow VSP. Fedin was one of those who had attended the meetings of the Moscow VSP, and he had now returned to Leningrad. Zamiatin wrote to him that same day:

> Today I've learned that you'll be holding a general meeting of the [Leningrad] VSP, and that members of the new board (of the new?) VSP have set off from Moscow with the purpose of bringing the Leningraders to heel. [...] Evidently the question of the novel *We* will be raised at this general meeting. [...] I've decided not to come back for tomorrow's meeting: if the Leningraders turn out to be just as feeble as the Muscovites, then I have no desire to see that shameful sight. If the meeting is like the one in Moscow (Gor'ky accurately described that as a "lynching"), then nothing I say will change by one iota the resolutions they pass, which have been prepared well in advance [...]; and if the general meeting in Leningrad turns out to be different, then my presence will be superfluous, since I can add nothing to the explanations I asked N. V. Tolstaia[-Krandievskaia] to pass on to

you. What's more, if I were to start speaking myself, then I would start saying such harsh things that no good would come of it.[9]

He explained that Pil'niak had not delivered his *Literaturnaia gazeta* letter in the end, because they both now agreed that it was not detailed enough, and so he planned to write a new one, which to some extent would be shaped by the outcome of the next day's meeting. He suggested adding one more point to those he had sent Fedin already: "The utopian novel *We*, written in 1919–20, is above all a protest against every kind of mechanisation of man, against turning him into a machine; the American critics in their reviews of the novel *We* called to mind the system which has been applied in America in the factories of Henry Ford. Reflections of the epoch of War Communism can be found in this novel, but it is of course impossible to connect it to the present day."[10] In other words, he denied again that the Soviet system had been the main satirical target of the novel.

The decisive VSP meeting of 22 September was indeed a humiliation for the Leningraders, as Fedin reported back to Zamiatin: "Yesterday probably differed very little from the VSP's 'eventful day in Moscow.' The disarray and the confusion of the board were terrible to see. Decisions were taken in haste, and under such monstrous pressure, that by the end everyone felt quite crushed. […] The 'work' went on from three in the afternoon, when the board's meeting began, until midnight, when the general meeting ended. The only difference between things in Moscow and in Leningrad was that the old board remains in place here, to conduct a purge and then hold new elections in October. […] As for your own case, the board was unanimous in disagreeing with the Muscovites." Nevertheless, they had been unable to sway the outcome: "What that boils down to in essence—setting aside the rhetoric—is the following: 1) your giving permission for a translation into English is deemed a political error; 2) it was noted that you hadn't acknowledged this error in any of your explanations; 3) you haven't renounced the ideas expressed in the novel *We*, which our society considers to be anti-Soviet. The fourth point concerns a ban on publishing abroad works which have been 'repudiated by Soviet society'—I think that's it. […] I don't know what will be published about it, and altogether I don't know what will happen next. But I have decided that question as far as I myself am concerned."[11]

Zamiatin later observed that many of those present at the Leningrad meeting of 22 September knew nothing of the novel other than its title, while those who had previously heard readings of it had met it enthusiastically at the time; and in any case, of the 200 people present at the start of the meeting, only 42 ultimately voted. He also made the point that he was incapable of changing his ideas retrospectively: "For me ideas are not like a tie, the colour of which you can change according to the day's fashion."[12] Three days after the disaster, Fedin commented in his diary: "The board castigated itself, and offered itself up for castigation. To act in any other way, that is to preserve its dignity, proved impossible. [...] The significance of this campaign against the VSP is to subordinate it to the directives of the leaders of the proletarian writers, [...] to deprive the VSP of the illusion of internal democracy, and to deprive it of 'the right to silence'. [...] The writing community will have to pass other people's words off as their own. We are to stop thinking once and for all. Others will do our thinking for us. [...] I was crushed by the drubbing we writers received on 22 September. Never have I as an individual been so humiliated. On the 23rd I resigned from the board of the VSP [as Chairman], with the intention never to return for any reason, or under any pressure."[13] Fedin's principled stand on this occasion would secure Zamiatin's friendship for many years to come.

At a meeting of RAPP in Moscow on 22–25 September, speakers complained that the Leningrad VSP, and Zamiatin in particular, had still got off lightly. Fadeev commented: "Zamiatin is a much more specific figure than Pil'niak. In every speech he makes, and in all his work, without concealing the fact, he declines to accept our cause. [...] They're really protecting him. He is one of the figures upon whom the democratic intelligentsia depends to a large extent, and they're closing ranks behind him. Even now they're reluctant to deny him, because he represents the fulfillment of those high-flown ideas they have about themselves."[14] Zamiatin, who was still in Moscow, wrote his new letter to *Literaturnaia gazeta* on 24 September (it was published on 7 October); he repeated many of his earlier points, simply adding that he was now resigning from the VSP altogether. He told Liudmila he was hoping to see Gor'ky in the next day or so. Since he was feeling very tired and rather unwell he thought he probably would not go down to Lebedian'; and he sent his greetings to her "and to the orphaned children."[15]

When Zamiatin saw Gor'ky on the 27th, he presented him with an entirely new and far more challenging request: "He was very nice and courteous; I was nice too, on the occasion of having slept properly. I handed Gor'ky two documents: my letter to the editors of *Literaturnaia gazeta*, and an application—fully motivated—to go abroad. In three days or so he is going to speak about my application to some highly-placed personages."[16] Over the previous twelve years, Zamiatin had worked hard to find a role for himself in Soviet culture. Initially he had supported Gor'ky to the hilt in all his projects. After the disappointment of not being allowed to emigrate in 1922–23, he had thrown himself energetically into fostering and defending the new Soviet literature, fighting from within the system for freedom of speech. But the reverses over *Attila* had shown him that not even the repertory committee, nor the courts, could protect his interests. And now, with the launch of this all-out personal attack on him, he was throwing in the towel.

His friend Bulgakov had recently reached the same conclusion, and had written to his brother in Paris that August: "I must inform you that I'm in a bad way. All my plays have been banned from the stage in the USSR, and they will not print a single line of my prose. During 1929 my annihilation as a writer has been effected. I have made one final effort and submitted an application to the Government of the USSR, in which I have asked that my wife and I be allowed to go abroad for whatever period they decide." He too had approached Gor'ky, asking him on 3 September to support his application.[17] Zamiatin and Bulgakov must have discussed their plight at length in Moscow during these weeks, and for the next couple of years their determination to escape Russia after the destruction of all their literary ambitions would dominate their lives.

On 30 September, presumably at Gor'ky's suggestion, Zamiatin wrote directly to Aleksei Rykov, head of the Soviet government, noting that every work he had written over the last eight years had been met with hostility, and telling the story of his frustrations over the *Attila* play: "This cannot be called anything other than persecution. The consequences of this persecution are such that all possibility of literary work is out of the question for me in the future. This recent episode has finally convinced me that, at least at present, my presence in Soviet Russia is superfluous, both for Soviet Russia and for me. For that reason I request permission to go abroad (together with my wife), if only for a year."[18] He added that the immediate purpose of his trip would be to work on a New York production of *The Flea*, in Vengerova's translation. In October he sent a further letter to the Council of People's Commissars [the government]:

> I have understood that for the moment, for as long as the views on literature which have become established here don't change, or until I change myself, I am not needed in Soviet Russia, nor in Soviet literature. It's absolutely clear, given the situation which has developed, that to remain here would mean literary death for me, i. e. silence. All the same, it seems to me that I haven't deserved the death sentence, and that a few things—at least in my past—give some grounds for mitigating this sentence. And for that reason I once again turn to you with an insistent request to permit me, together with my wife, to leave and go abroad for one year. I have no intention of engaging in political activities— I just wish to continue my life as an artist of the word.[19]

On 1 October, before at last leaving Moscow for home after his protracted absence that summer, he left a note for Gor'ky asking him not to pay attention to his apparent cheerfulness: "To tell the truth, things are hard, and I don't know what I shall do if I don't manage to leave for a while."[20]

On 2 October, Bulgakov also resigned from the VSP, followed soon after by Akhmatova, Veresaev, and others. A meeting of the Leningrad VSP on that day was attended by a heavy-weight delegation from Moscow including Fadeev and the RAPP leader Averbakh: this concluded the reorganisation of the Leningrad VSP, the entire board of which had in any case already stepped down. In *Literaturnaia gazeta* on 14 October, what had now become the VSSP (The All-Russian Union of *Soviet* Writers) declared: "Zamiatin's great artistic talent does not give him the right to forget the interests of the country of which he is a citizen as well as a writer." The following day, Averbakh described *We* in *Krasnaia gazeta* as a "lampoon against socialism."[21] A constitution for the new VSSP, which by now had lost a third of its original members, was approved on 30 December 1929. It declared that the former organisation, united through professional and practical concerns, had become obsolete; its new purposes were now to be specifically political, as an instrument of socialist construction.

Aleksandr Galushkin has provided a persuasive explanation of the real background to this apparently arbitrary and manifestly unjust sequence of actions directed so aggressively against Pil'niak and Zamiatin during the second half of 1929. He looks beyond the specific attacks by certain proletarian writers on these two individuals, and views it as just one facet of the drastic new directions taken by Stalin's government during that crucial year in his consolidation of power. 1929 was the year of purges within the Party to eliminate any remaining opposition to Stalinist hegemony, and saw the introduction of the first Five-year Plan, together with collectivisation, to replace NEP; the Shakhty trial of 1928 had served as an ominous prelude to the Terror to come. Much of this was part of a move to discredit the policies supported by Bukharin and by Trotsky (expelled from the country in January 1929) during the previous few years: these had been characterised by tolerance towards "bourgeois specialists" (in literature this included "fellow-travellers"), who had been allowed during the NEP period to co-exist with, and operate alongside, official Party cadres. Throughout these months there was discussion of a "new resolution" as regards Party policy towards literature, to replace the Central Committee's relatively liberal resolution on literature dating from 1925. In July 1929 the Central Committee agreed "to liquidate organisations whose existence did not serve political purposes," with the VSP named as a prime example, being the largest organisation of "fellow-travellers," and with a history of defending writers against government restrictions. This would be achieved through the co-ordinated actions of loyal Communist writers, and the campaign was to be orchestrated and conducted through the pages of the Communist press.

The protests and widespread resignations which followed upon these actions, together with the objections raised in articles such as Gor'ky's "Waste of Energy" (published on 15 September), inevitably attracted much comment in émigré circles. In the following weeks Marc Slonim published a piece in Berlin, "Why they are persecuting Pil'niak and Zamiatin";[22] Damanskaia published a review of the French translation of *We*, the novel "about which there is so much fuss in Russia at the moment," (she also described it in fact as being "far from this author's best work");[23] Remizov, writing to Postnikov in Prague, expressed concern about Zamiatin's plight.[24] On 17 October an article in *Poslednie novosti* in Paris observed: "The Bolsheviks' innovative and not insignificant assertion of their rights over books has now extended to claims over their authors. [...] The power of the censors over books has now been replaced by the individual enserfment of the author: that which is not pleasing to the authorities may not be printed anywhere."[25] However, it turned out to be less easy than anticipated to impose hegemonic rule on the writers, and for the moment people like Anatoly Lunacharsky, who had just been removed from his post after

12 years as Commissar of Enlightenment [Minister of Culture], continued to protest against the primitive formula which presumed that "if you are not with us, you are against us." The Party continued to work on a new resolution concerning literature until March 1930, but nothing was concluded at that point, perhaps because of internal disagreements or perhaps, as Galushkin suggests, because of the shock of Maiakovsky's suicide in April 1930. All of this was moving towards the setting up of a monopolistic Union of Soviet Writers during 1932–34.

By the morning of 21 October 1929 Zamiatin had gone back down to Moscow again to press his case for an exit visa; he tried ringing Gor'ky, but the household wasn't yet awake. However, he managed to see him on both the following days, and achieved a degree of success before Gor'ky departed again for Italy: "He was courteous—very. These are the results: on Tuesday he spoke to Stalin and gave him a copy of my letter [to Rykov]. And he had spoken (for a second time) to Iagoda. In the end the latter said: 'Well, if he's going to insist, we'll probably let him out, but we won't let him back in again afterwards…' Getting this business under way (as Gor'ky explained) still has to be done according to normal procedures."[26]

While he was in Moscow he was also dealing with some of his other affairs. Vengerova had written from Paris to let him know that *The Front Page* had just become a successful film in the States, and she was wondering whether the director Pudovkin might be interested in making one in Russia, using their text? She sent him a couple of other plays for consideration, including R.C. Sherriff's *Journey's End* (1928). Unfortunately, the plan for a New York production of *The Flea* had fallen through.[27] Zamiatin was meanwhile working on some final adjustments to *The Front Page* for the Vakhtangov Theatre. He spent an evening with Bulgakov, who had had no success whatsoever with his own request to leave the country, and was very downcast: "He's having heart palpitations, he was drinking tincture of valerian and lying in bed." Towards the end of October Zamiatin "seized himself by the collar" and bought a ticket to Lebedian', where he spent three days. On the 29th he told Liudmila that he was back at Pil'niak's after a trip which, despite two sleepless nights in the train, had been pleasant—lovely weather, good sleep and food, a walk through the fields—and he regretted that she had not been there with him. And he wrote about their future "travel plans" with apparent confidence now: "It would be good if for the moment you could get hold of the application forms for travelling and start gathering together the necessary documents—there's probably a mass of them."[28] Meanwhile, Pil'niak had been celebrating with champagne because his novel (the reworked *Mahogany*, now transformed into a politically acceptable production novel under the title *The Volga Flows into the Caspian Sea*) had been passed by the censors. He had written a public recantation, been forgiven, and before long was allowed abroad again.[29] On 1 November, Zamiatin was taking a couple of Americans [one of them perhaps the UPI correspondent Eugene Lyons], together with Pil'niak, to see *The Flea*.[30]

Later that month Pil'niak came to visit them in Leningrad. Afterwards, he wrote affectionately to the Zamiatins, asking whether they had submitted their travel application yet. He also thanked Zamiatin warmly for his suggestions about the manuscript he had just sent off, presumably of the revised *Mahogany*. On 24 November Fedin (whom Frezinsky plausibly presents as never having been an entirely trustworthy friend of Zamiatin's) made some rather acid remarks in his diary about this visit:

> All this is rather comical and pitiful—Boris [Pil'niak]'s wish to see the *Mahogany* business as a triumph. He thought he'd be met in Petersburg with fanfares, but people were avoiding him because he'd behaved so stupidly during the notorious discussions at the VSP. It was more complicated as far as Zamiatin was concerned, and of course he is more complicated and subtle than Pil'niak. He is losing his significance as a writer not because he has fallen under an official "anathema," but because he is undergoing a severe artistic crisis, which could end in his death. The other day he gave a reading at home of the beginning of his novel about Attila (Akhmatova, Slonimsky, and Pil'niak were there). With every line you could see how artificially the fabric of words was constructed, what an effort it took him to drive out that reliance on imagery which formed the basis of Zamiatin's earlier works. It's all created with his head, without the slightest motion of his spirit. The chapter about Rome was like a prolix textbook of ancient history.[31]

So while waiting for his future to be determined, Zamiatin had evidently returned to his writing. He applied to the Public Library to borrow books for his work on *The Scourge of God*, and was granted permission to take out ten at a time.[32] On 29 November he signed a contract with the "Leningrad Writers' Publishing House" for the publication of *The Flood* in book form. Early in December, the Vakhtangov Theatre let him know that *The Front Page* had been approved and they were planning to première it in the first half of April 1930, with Ruben Simonov as director.[33] In January 1930, Vengerova wrote to thank him for the good news about *The Front Page*, and offered to send him some more new plays, including Sean O'Casey's 1927 *Silver Tassie*.[34]

Zamiatin and Liudmila finally submitted their applications to go abroad on 4 December. However, the issue was clearly still a matter of dispute in government and OGPU circles, and on the 12th they were told to their surprise and dismay that their request had been turned down. A few weeks later Zamiatin sent an appeal to Rykov, as well as writing to Iagoda, now Chairman of the OGPU: "Gor'ky informed me, on the basis of his conversation with you, that if I were to insist on the necessity of a trip abroad, then permission would be granted to me accordingly. [...] Allow me to remind you of M[aksim] Gor'ky's conversation with you about my trip abroad, and to ask you not to refuse to contribute to a positive resolution of this matter." Nevertheless, in January 1930 the OGPU informed Zamiatin that the decision not to allow him out had been reconfirmed.[35]

At the end of this difficult year, he was grateful to receive a note from the literary historian Leonid Grossman, explaining that his signature had been appended to an attack on Zamiatin in *Literaturnaia gazeta* without his permission.[36] And on 9 January 1930, Andrei Bely wrote to thank him for the invitation to contribute to *How We Write*, adding: "And in the meantime—I've never thought so much about you, with an anxious heart, never have I wanted so much to see you and have a talk with you, although all our meetings and conversations live on vividly in my memory; and I would often like to enjoy your company as a person (as a writer—well, that doesn't need saying, since I joined the ranks of your admirers from your very first book)." He promised to provide a contribution for the book, and urged him to come and visit him in the country.[37]

By 19 January Zamiatin was in Moscow again, partly in order to attend a run-through of *The Front Page* at the Vakhtangov Theatre, the play having been passed for performance by "Glavrepertkom" "without any enthusiasm ('it's a bourgeois play, no light is cast upon issues of class' etc.)." Certainly this satire on American journalism does seem an improbable choice for a Soviet theatre, notwithstanding its attack on corruption in Chicago, and on the city authorities' paranoia about "the Reds." The Aleksandrinsky Theatre in Leningrad now offered him a contract for it too.[38] Three weeks later he'd been listening with people at the Vakhtangov to American songs and foxtrot tunes for the first act. That evening he went to hear Bulgakov read his own latest play [presumably the one for MKhAT about Molière, *The Cabal of Hypocrites*, which was banned by "Glavrepertkom" on 18 March]. He himself had been flirting with MKhAT about an idea for a new play.[39] *The African Visitor* is one of his feeblest works, a light-weight domestic farce involving a young man who dresses up as a visiting African in order to get the girl he loves. The play seems to have been composed in an apparently conciliatory spirit in the immediate aftermath of the crisis of 1929.[40]

Zamiatin had been hoping for a meeting with Vasily Shmidt, Deputy Chairman of the Council of People's Commissars, but he waited in vain. In the meantime, he was obliged to cancel his teaching commitments: in 1928 he had finally given up teaching maritime engineering and taken up a post as a Foreign Languages Instructor at the Leningrad Shipbuilding Institute, which had broken away from the Polytechnic. At Pil'niak's, where he was staying, there was a busy social whirl, with late night dancing. He was invited for a meal by Gor'ky's first wife Ekaterina Peshkova, who would be seeing Iagoda, (the OGPU Chairman was known to be rather smitten with Gor'ky and Peshkova's daughter-in-law Timosha), and she undertook to put in a word about his plight. While he was in Moscow he also tried to lobby on behalf of Akhmatova, whose "academic" ration status was under threat because of a new pressure on "non-active" individuals. Shchegolev gave him the news that the eminent historians Evgeny Tarle and Nikolai Likhachev had been arrested on 28 January, as part of a new government purge of the Academy of Sciences: "What a business!" A month later, Nikolai Marr, the distinguished philologist and Director of the Leningrad Public Library, would be refused an exit visa to give a series of lectures at the Sorbonne.

On 24 April a report by "Gulliver" (Khodasevich and Nina Berberova) in the Paris newspaper *Vozrozhdenie* (*Rebirth*) observed that the campaign against Zamiatin had not let up, and quoted extensively from a recent *Krasnaia nov'* article (Voronsky had been dismissed from there a couple of years earlier), in which *The Fires of Santo Domingo* and *Comrade Churygin* had been denounced as lampoons of the revolution, alongside *We*, and he had been challenged to declare his political beliefs: "These are decisive days at present: each person has to take a look at himself and make an irrevocable statement, and Zamiatin is someone who will need to make that statement louder and more clearly than most."[41]

Towards the end of February 1930 it was Liudmila who went down to Moscow for a month, while he stayed behind in Leningrad. Her nephew Andrei was ill, and she had gone to be with her sister Maria. Zamiatin sent her frequent, chatty and supportive letters during this difficult period, describing an outing to go skating, a visit to Fedin and the Tolstoys, billiards with Zoshchenko, a concert by Maria Iudina at the Philharmonic, and an evening with guests at home (Agrafena cooked crab). As it became clear that Andrei was gravely ill, he was full of sympathy. He remembered having heard Christian Scientists talking the previous winter about miraculous cures, and offered to try and track them down. In these gloomy circumstances it was difficult to sit down and "write a merry comedy," but he had been working on *The African Visitor*. He was also writing an article about the wharfs at the Putilov factory. He suggested she should bring a kilo or so of pressed caviar back from Moscow, along with some turkey, oatmeal, cigarettes, and half a kilo of mints. In a first echo of the new campaign of collectivisation in the countryside, he also told her of the mother of an acquaintance, who had been entirely dispossessed as a *kulak*. "And this morning I received a letter from Lebedian', from Varvara Aleksandrovna [Platonova: his aunt Varia]. All they've got is black bread, there's hardly any sugar, and there's no paper—they've nothing to write letters on... I'd like to send them some rusks and some sweets." He did manage to contact the Christian Science doctor, who said he could only offer long-distance treatment with the consent of the patient, so that there was nothing he could do to help Andrei. On 20 March Zamiatin wrote: "It's impossible to write or to imagine what's happening where you are—human words stumble against it, as against a wall."[42]

He and Liudmila were back in Moscow for the première of *The Front Page* at the Vakhtangov Theatre on 29 May 1930. Ruben Simonov had refused to allow alterations to the main text, despite pressure from "Repertkom" to sharpen up the ideological content of the work: instead Zamiatin had had to create some "interludes," brief episodes staged in front of the curtain, which would touch upon themes such as the persecution of the USSR and the threat of war.[43] By 10 June, Liudmila had gone back to Leningrad, while he continued working on *The African Visitor* for readings of it at MKhAT and the Vakhtangov

Theatre: "What will come of all this is not clear, but at least they're talking about the possibility of a production." He'd been dining with Iury Olesha and with Bulgakov, who liked *The Front Page* as a play, but wasn't very impressed with the acting.[44]

Zamiatin decided to begin his summer break early that year, and in July 1930 he persuaded his friend Krolenko from "Academia" to go with him, to stay in a village in Ukraine. Their conversations planning the trip gave Krolenko his first opportunity to meet Liudmila, whom he found very courteous. Zamiatin left Leningrad on the 6th.[45] He did not sleep much on the train, but passed the time drinking tea and eating wild strawberries bought en route, and reading Galsworthy. Kiev was Bulgakov's hometown, which he had described so lovingly in his novel *The White Guard* and the play based on that novel, *The Days of the Turbins*. Zamiatin stayed there with a writer friend, Vera Gedroyts, and explored the city with an artist, Leonid Povolotsky, whose wife Irina Avdieva was to recall that "Zamiatin was telling my husband that there were only two ways out for him: suicide, or fleeing abroad…"[46] In the context of Maiakovsky's shocking suicide just three months earlier, this must have seemed a particularly chilling remark.

Krolenko joined him on the 9th, and they then travelled on together to Olefirovka, east of Kiev and not far from Poltava and Sorochintsy.[47] There they stayed in a *pension* with a number of theatrical and musical acquaintances, including the musicologist son of Rimsky-Korsakov. Zamiatin was given a small flea-ridden room in a peasant hut, but it was an attractive village with a pine forest, a meadow, tennis, croquet and a river 20 minutes' walk away. He urged Liudmila and her friend Zoia Nikitina to join him: "I think you would like it here. […] Several times a day I think of you, and regret that you're not here: a mushroom in the woods—how you'd love to pick it! flowers—for you! I'm baking in the sun—why me? now if it were you… And the water in the river is so warm, about 20 degrees."[48] It was very difficult to get the kind of food he wanted, even eggs [perhaps a consequence of collectivisation?], he was short on sugar and kerosene, and had been forced to borrow half a candle.[49] But he slept well and was smoking just 6–7 cigarettes a day. There had been lots of bathing and chatting, often about literary affairs, and Krolenko quizzed him about his relations with Fedin. "Zamiatin and I talk on political themes. He considers that the Five-year Plan is just a publicity campaign for Europe's benefit, that nothing will come of it, and it will lead to a drop in the quality of life; socialism is senseless, since it increases the sum of human suffering. But he doesn't believe it's heading towards disaster."[50]

A couple of weeks later Zamiatin told Liudmila: "The popular view is that I have put on weight and look much better than when I arrived. And now—about you: 'I've decided not to go anywhere… I've had a rest already.' I don't like all this. Really, Mila Nikolaevna, why deprive yourself of the little that we can get out of life? After all, I know that you love sunshine and water. And after all we have money for the moment—there's enough. So don't, please, come up with such hasty decisions, and instead put your mind to the question of where to go. And then I might spend at least part of the summer with you, like last year." He asked her to send various books, as well as sugar, candles, collar-studs, medicines (*Pulsatilla, Arsenic* and *Nux vomic.*), a bar of chocolate, and a stone for cleaning his white shoes. He was considering moving on next to a writers' sanatorium in the Crimea, at Batiliman (there was no room at Koktebel'), although that depended upon the key issue of whether he could be guaranteed a single room: "I would die of insomnia if I had to sleep with someone else."[51]

By mid-August he was on his way to Batiliman, although the journey was very exhausting, and in the end his train was 22 hours late. A week later he was feeling depressed about the way things had turned out over the year since the campaign against him had been initiated: "Well, Mila Nikolaevna, I will admit to you what I don't want to admit even to myself: I'm no longer the same person, I'm finding things hard, and I don't want to get up and go. But I still hold the reins in my hand, and I drive myself on." In Batiliman, his "single room" turned out to be divided only by a thin partition from the next room, which contained three women and two children. It was stony and arid after the lush Ukraine, and very windy too—and there was a long and steep walk down to the sea. But the food was much better than at Olefirovka, and he was being provided with a special diet (tea instead of ersatz coffee, white bread, eggs, chicken), and they had some wine and good tobacco on sale too. Eventually he began to enjoy the place, since he had mostly been left in peace and had done lots of reading. Early in September he managed to move into a small house, and gained a little weight. He thought he would be able to bring her "and the children" some grapes, even though they were hard to obtain. He returned to Leningrad on 21 September.[52]

One of the letters which would have been waiting for him on his return was one dated 17 July from Babette Deutsch in New York, who was evidently out of touch in more than one sense: "Altho [sic] you have not heard from us in so long, we often think and speak of you, and of the charming fashion in which you played host to us during our Russian visit. What are you writing now, I wonder? Plays, short stories, a novel? Or are you perhaps editing a magazine? I have an ineradicable mental picture of you designing a cruiser with one hand and writing a very modern and moving story with the other." She mentioned that they now had a second child, a little boy, "who would like to play with Rostislav."[53] There was also news that the Guild Theatre in New York had taken an interest in *The Bellringers* (they turned it down later that year).[54]

A year earlier Vladimir Podgorny had written to Zamiatin on behalf of MKhAT to say that, at the request of "Glaviskusstvo" ["Chief Directorate of the Arts," which had absorbed the functions of "Glavrepertkom" during 1928], it was felt that some "political interludes" needed to be inserted into the text of *The Flea*, which had temporarily been taken off. He asked him to draft something suitably topical (references to the Labour party in the English scene, for example). That autumn he wrote to let him know that *The Flea* was due to be revived in December, and asked him again to provide some new materials to "refresh" it.[55]

On 23 October Zamiatin (describing himself as "formerly a writer, and now a lecturer at the Leningrad Shipbuilding Institute") wrote to Bulgakov, addressing him as a "respected director" and "master of dramaturgy." This was because Bulgakov had received a personal telephone call that summer from Stalin, who asked him whether he really wanted to leave the USSR; caught unawares, Bulgakov had hastily decided that the safer course would be to say no, and as a result he had been offered work at Stalin's behest as an assistant director at MKhAT and as an adviser at the Moscow Young Workers' Theatre (TRAM).[56] Zamiatin had not benefited from any such direct intervention from on high, and his own new career move was somewhat more prosaic. On 4 November he was confirmed as Head of the Foreign Languages Department at the Shipbuilding Institute. In a reference, his erstwhile fellow student V. Pozdiunin noted: "He combines a knowledge of shipbuilding disciplines and their terminology with a knowledge of languages, both of a technological and a literary nature. Furthermore, E.I. Zamiatin has extensive pedagogic experience and has worked at the Shipbuilding Faculty of the Leningrad Shipbuilding Institute since 1911." During the year he was in charge there, Zamiatin drew up the academic programmes for the Department, and appointed the staff who would succeed him and remain in post there for the next 30 years or more.[57]

As for literary undertakings, Zamiatin signed a contract in November with Krolenko's "Academia" to edit and provide an introduction and commentaries to Sheridan's *School for Scandal*.[58] That month, Pil'niak wrote his last surviving letter to Zamiatin, in which he asked for help in getting his most recent work published, including the book he had worked on that summer as a token of his "obedience," based on his travels around Tadzhikistan. He was hoping to come and see him in Leningrad, and sent greetings to Liudmila and to Akhmatova. Zamiatin did indeed help to get the book published in Leningrad in 1931.[59] During 1930–31 he received a number of enthusiastic letters from an Italian translator, Konrad Perr'e, to whom he sent several volumes of his work. Perr'e also expressed interest in Pil'niak's *The Volga Flows into the Caspian Sea*. It doesn't appear that many of Zamiatin's texts did get translated into Italian at this juncture, but Perr'e did his best to promote Zamiatin's reputation with two men who would go on to become leading Italian Slavists, Renato Poggioli and Ettore Lo Gatto. Professor Lo Gatto travelled to Russia in April 1931, and met Zamiatin on that occasion.[60]

In mid-December the translator Charles Malamuth, who was in Moscow, wrote: "Mr Ray Long has informed me by cable today that he has accepted for publication in the *Cosmopolitan* magazine your short story *Martyrs to Learning*, entitled by him in English *Martyr to Education*, and translated by me. Please accept my congratulations! I hope that other stories of yours will find their way into American magazines." He told him this would earn him $75, and offered to select another story to translate shortly.[61] The following January, Malamuth's friend, the UPI correspondent Eugene Lyons, sent a letter to Zamiatin, who had presumably asked him to make some purchases on his behalf with the dollars he had earned. Lyons was already back from Germany, but Malamuth was "going out soon, so he will obtain those few things you mention. [...] Incidentally, I brought some Dunhill tobacco for you and Aleksei Tolstoy. How shall I transmit it? With all kind regards, cordially yours..."[62]

On 31 December 1930, Zamiatin (but not Liudmila) joined Krolenko and the theatre scholar Stefan Mokul'sky for New Year celebrations, and eight of them sat down together to a splendid dinner and stayed up until 4am. During the next few weeks, and throughout that spring, he enjoyed several further parties with Krolenko and the Mokul'skys, together with the Tikhonovs and Radlovs, but usually without Liudmila—perhaps due to her frail health. They went skating, and took turns to host dinner and late-night poker. On 24 January 1931, together with Krolenko, he attended the funeral of his fellow pupil from Voronezh, Pavel Shchegolev.[63]

Zamiatin had from time to time been pressing to know the fate at "Federatsiia" of his "fifth volume," the collection of literary and biographical essays under the title *Litsa* [*People*].[64] But an internal review there concluded that it was "a profoundly idealistic book, with concrete political attacks on the Revolution in a number of places. [...] The book ought not to be published." All this was regretfully reported to him in a letter in late April from E. Nikitina, who explained that, despite her best efforts, it had not been possible to accept the book for publication.[65] Zamiatin responded: "To tell the truth, as things stand at present I wasn't expecting any other reply from 'Federatsiia.' I would have been not a little surprised if it had proved possible to publish those articles, which are of course far from 'Orthodox.'" And so he asked for the materials to be returned to him—especially pieces like "Robert Mayer," of which he had only the one copy.[66]

During this time he was working on four successive versions of another new play, *The Birth of Ivan*.[67] It survives as an outline, tracing the destiny of a village boy called Ivan who overcomes superstition and disadvantage to lead the workers when revolution comes. Like *The African Visitor*, it feels like a deliberately uncontroversial work, designed to get past the censors at all costs. On 2 April, Podgorny wrote from MKhAT to say they were enthusiastic about the outline he had sent them, but the censors had told them that, given Zamiatin's reputation, they wouldn't consider the play until they had received a complete text. MKhAT's other news was that the revival of *The Flea* had had to be delayed until the start of the following season.[68] Other new ventures Zamiatin attempted at this difficult and frustrating time include a draft for a comic opera in 3 acts, completed early in May, which survives only in an 8-page version called *The Surprise*.[69] That month he also completed a 20-page draft of a new film script, *Hunton Colliery*, in which he drew on his experience of the north-east of England to create a drama about oppressed miners.[70] This was in reality a version for the cinema of an English novel, *Goaf*, by a coal-miner and writer, Harold Heslop, sharing its fictional setting (Hunton Colliery), its characters and main plot lines. The novel had been translated into Russian by Vengerova in 1926, and had sold half a million copies in the USSR. Heslop received an invitation to the Soviet Union in 1930, and Vengerova asked him to call on Zamiatin during his visit. Apparently Zamiatin was fascinated to hear his accent, and repeated his pronunciation with fond nostalgia: "South Shields... Sooth Sheels! I never learned to sing the Tyneside speech."[71]

In the second week of May he finished drafting a further "autobiography" for a proposed *Dictionary of Dramatists* (which never appeared).[72] He still wrote nostalgically about the Lebedian' of his youth: "The horse fairs, the gypsies, the card-sharps, the landowners in their tight coats and nobles' peaked caps with red cap-bands. The church festivals, when during prayers in the cathedral the police chief stood right at the front, with behind him the town officials, and the school teachers in full uniform with swords, and the merchants with medals round their necks. At Shrovetide the rides along Main Street in colourful 'carpeted' sledges, straight out of the 17th century." However, after a little more of this he exclaims: "But enough! did all this really happen? It's so far away—entire centuries away—from the present, that you can scarcely believe it yourself. And all the same, I know that it was like that, and it all took place only forty years or so ago."[73]

The "present" was proving so frustrating and dismal that when Gor'ky decided to visit the USSR again in May, after an 18-month absence, Zamiatin resolved to try and take advantage of the influence he still wielded, in one final attempt to get permission to leave.[74] Gor'ky may have been disenchanted with him as a writer at certain points over the previous decade, but he was still prepared to help him as a man, perhaps remembering his loyalty after 1917. His advice was that Zamiatin should write to Stalin directly, and he would then deliver the letter in person. This lengthy letter of early June 1931, addressing Stalin as "Respected Iosif Vissarionovich," appealed for him to intervene directly in Zamiatin's fate: "My name is probably known to you. Being deprived of the possibility of writing is truly for me, as a writer, a death sentence, but circumstances have combined in such a way that I cannot continue my work, because creative work is unthinkable if I am obliged to work in this atmosphere of systematic persecution, which only increases from year to year. I do not in any sense wish to portray myself as an injured innocent. I know that during the first 3–4 years after the Revolution, amongst the things I wrote were some which might provide grounds for attacks. [...] In particular, I have never concealed my attitude towards literary servility, obsequiousness and opportunism: I considered—and I still consider—that this degrades the writer just as it degrades the Revolution."

He described the way in which he had been increasingly demonised, and his works misrepresented—so often anachronistically—as anti-Soviet. As a recent example, he cited his work on *The School for Scandal*: that March the censors had not only banned his introduction to Sheridan's life and works, but also refused to allow his name even to appear as the editor of the translation: these decisions had been reversed only after an appeal to Moscow. He also rehearsed the ever-painful story of *Attila*, citing Gor'ky's recommendation of the play and several positive comments made about it by workers' representatives—adding, with a touch of humour, that "perhaps the worker comrades went a bit over the top in invoking Shakespeare." He mentioned that ever since the RAPP campaign against him and Pil'niak, libraries had been forbidden to lend out his books; that *The Flea* had been taken off after four successful seasons; and that publishers who tried to publish him had come under attack. He therefore appealed to Stalin for his "death sentence" to be commuted to a slightly milder punishment, in this case exile for himself and his wife:

> If I am not in fact a criminal, then I request permission for myself and my wife to go abroad temporarily, even for a year, in order to return again as soon as it becomes possible in literature to serve big ideas without being servile towards little people, as soon as attitudes to the role of the literary artist change, at least in part. And I am confident that this time is already near, since after the successful construction of the material base, inevitably the question will arise about the construction of the superstructure—of an art and a literature which will truly prove worthy of the Revolution. I know that it will be far from easy for me abroad as well, since I cannot join the reactionary camp over there—this is convincingly enough shown by my past (membership of the RSDWP (b) in Tsarist times, prison at that same period, two sentences of exile, and being charged during the war with writing an antimilitarist novella).

He mentioned that he had other reasons for wishing to travel—for treatment for his long-standing colitis, and the need to work on productions abroad of his plays. "But I don't wish to conceal the fact that my main reason for requesting permission for me and my wife to go abroad is my hopeless situation as a writer here, and the death sentence which has been pronounced on me here as a writer. The exceptional attentiveness which other writers have met on your part when they have appealed to you allows me to hope that my request too will be treated with respect."[75]

Towards the middle of June, Zamiatin went down to Moscow yet again, to follow up on arrangements to deliver the letter to Stalin. He was in regular contact with Gor'ky's secretary Kriuchkov, trying to arrange a meeting with Gor'ky (who was in poor health), and there was a lot of waiting around. He went shopping for shoes for himself and for Liudmila, and presented her sister Maria with some stockings, cigarettes, a little tea and coffee, and some cheese.[76] On 14 June he got to join Gor'ky for a lengthy meal, together with Tikhonov, and the old man was "very courteous," but they only managed half-an-hour of conversation alone about his affairs: "The result was that he undertook to do his best on my behalf, and today or tomorrow he would convey my letter 'into his own hands.' At first he tried to dissuade me from leaving, and proposed that I should delay my final answer for a day, that is until yesterday. Yesterday at about 3pm I had another meeting with him, and again I landed right in the middle of dinner there. After dinner, at about 4, I asked him to hand the letter in and we bade each other farewell."[77] Zamiatin knew that Bulgakov had written a similar letter to Stalin on 30 May 1931, just days before his own, and apparently told him he'd approached it the wrong way: "You made a mistake, and that's why you were refused. You didn't construct your letter right—you embarked on discussions about the revolution and evolution, and about satire. But meanwhile what you have to do is write crisply and clearly—that you're asking to be allowed out—and that's all! No, I'm going to write to him the right way."[78] By 22 June he heard that his application had reached "the authorities," but there was still no response. Gor'ky was going to be in Moscow the following day, and he was hoping to see him and find out if there was any news. That morning Andrei Bely came and spent several hours drinking tea with him. Bely had come to Moscow to campaign for the release of his wife Klavdia, who had been arrested on 30 May and taken to the Lubianka.[79] Zamiatin was fed up of being stuck in Moscow, but Kriuchkov kept telling him not to leave, because his case could be decided any day. A copy of *Attila* had been delivered to him as requested, but Zamiatin couldn't visit Gor'ky because he was seriously ill and had been coughing blood.

He had been discussing since 1929 the possibility of making a film version of *The Yawl*, which was now due to be submitted to "Sovkino."[80] He'd also been negotiating with a film company about *Hunton Colliery*, but the plan fell through: "they concluded that the social elements weren't shown very clearly, and that the controversial personal intrigue pushed them even further into the background." There was better news from MKhAT, where they told him *The Flea* was definitely going to be revived in the autumn. He was contemplating trying to get away briefly for a boat trip along the Moskva and Oka rivers.[81] However, on 9 July he was still in Moscow, and complaining that despite the beautiful weather he had to stay indoors and finish work on *The Yawl*.[82] "Because of this work, and because of Gor'ky, who keeps feeding me meals but keeps deferring any proper meeting with him, I haven't gone anywhere, and I'm stuck here. Today there was a telephone call: there'll probably be a meeting the day after tomorrow (on the 11th), and probably there'll be a reply by then. Today at dinner Aleksandr Nikolaevich [Tikhonov] gave me the news that there were rumours that I hadn't succeeded in pulling off my affair — but for the moment these are just 'corridor rumours.'" On 10 July he added a note to say that there had been a further call to say that the "audience" would be the following evening out at the *dacha*; and supposedly there would be a reply by then. "I'll try to ring you on the morning of the 12th, before 2 or 3pm. By then, I imagine, I shall have a clearer idea (at last!) of the date when I can leave Moscow."[83] Zamiatin would later write a memoir of Gor'ky in which he described the course of that fateful meeting, and Gorky's role as a "very skilful diplomat" on behalf of so many Soviet writers:

> At that time he no longer lived in St Petersburg, but in Moscow. In town he had had placed at his disposal that famous house which used to belong to the millionaire Riabushinsky. Gor'ky would only drop in there on visits, and spent the majority of his time at his *dacha*, about 100 kilometres away from Moscow. There, not far away, Stalin also had his *dacha*, and he began to visit his "neighbour" Gor'ky with increasing frequency. These "neighbours," the one always with his pipe, the other with a cigarette, would go off on their own, and over a bottle of wine they would talk about something or another for hours… I think I am not mistaken when I say that the straightening out of many "sharp lurches" in the policies of the Soviet government, and

the gradual easing of the régime of dictatorship, were the result of these friendly conversations. This role of Gor'ky's will be evaluated only some time in the future. [...] In those years it was not an easy matter for a writer with my reputation as a "heretic" to get a passport for foreign travel. I turned to Gor'ky and asked him to mediate. He began to try and persuade me to wait until the spring (of 1931). "You'll see—everything will change." Nothing changed that spring. And then Gor'ky, rather reluctantly, agreed to try and get permission for me to go abroad.

One day his secretary rang me to say that Gor'ky was asking me to visit him for dinner that evening, at his *dacha*. I remember very distinctly that unusually hot day, the thunderstorm, and the tropical downpour in Moscow. Gor'ky's car whisked us, the several guests who had been invited that evening, through a wall of water. The dinner was a "literary" affair, and there were 20 or so people at table. At first Gor'ky sat looking weary, and was taciturn. Everyone was drinking wine, but he had a glass of water in front of him, because he was forbidden wine. Then he rebelled, poured himself a glass of wine, then another and another, and began to be more like his usual self.

The storm ended, and I went out on to the enormous stone terrace of the *dacha*. Gor'ky promptly came out there too and said to me: "Your passport business has been settled. But you could, if you like, hand the passport back and not go abroad." I said that I would go. Gor'ky frowned and went back in to his guests in the dining-room. It was already late. Some of the guests were going to stay at the *dacha* for the night, and the rest—including me—were going back to Moscow. When we were saying our farewells, Gor'ky said: "So, when will we see one another again? If not in Moscow, then perhaps in Italy? If I'm there, then you come and see me there without fail! In any case—until we meet again, eh?" That was the last time I saw Gor'ky.[84]

Zamiatin had at last achieved the freedom to go abroad he had sought for a decade. It had been a close-run thing this time as well: the majority of the Politbiuro had apparently been opposed to the request when it was tabled for discussion, but Stalin had decided to support Gor'ky's recommendation on this occasion.[85]

During the early part of August he spent some time in a sanatorium out at Petrodvorets, not far from his home in Leningrad, perhaps to recover from the previous stressful weeks: he managed to bathe every day, but the food was terrible, and he had been reduced to preparing eggs, cocoa and oatmeal porridge for himself, using a spirit-lamp. "Today for the first time since you left I dined at home, and that was a wonderful meal: rice soup, salmon and cauliflower."[86] Liudmila and her sister were in Moscow and planning to go down to Lebedian' if they received confirmation from Zamiatin's sister Aleksandra that this would be convenient. He also suggested that Liudmila should try to see Bulgakov, who was holidaying on the Volga. "By the way: what do you mean, he's 'in a trance'? Is he envious, or what?" Bulgakov's renewed request to Stalin to go abroad had indeed failed where Zamiatin's had succeeded—he simply never received a reply—and Bulgakov described his mood at the end of July that year in a letter to Veresaev: "My wing has been broken. [...] I suffer from one tormenting unhappiness. And that is that my [further] conversation with the General Secretary [Stalin] never took place. What that means for me is horror, and the darkness of the grave. I have a frantic desire to see other countries, if only briefly. I get out of bed with this thought every morning, and I go to sleep with it."[87]

Zamiatin had instructed Liudmila in Moscow that she was to be ready to telephone Kriuchkov if nothing had come through about their passports by 14 August. He now went back down to Moscow himself, to start to make the practical arrangements for going abroad. One of the people he contacted was Vladimir Pozner, the youngest Serapion Brother, who was still living in Paris. By 26 August he was able to write to him, proudly announcing: "This letter is being written to you by a man who has a passport for foreign travel in his pocket. In just over a month I'm hoping to be sitting with you in some nice Paris café, so long as a French visa is lying in my pocket alongside the passport by then. This is my request to you: could you put pressure on somebody in Paris to help ensure that there's no delay over the visa (for myself and for my wife Liudmila Nikolaevna)? Since you're on the spot you'll know who could be most useful for this." He had already submitted an application for their visas to the French Consulate in Moscow, citing in support of his application "Nouvelle Revue Française" (NRF), who had published *We* in 1929, together with another publisher "Kra," the publisher of Pozner's books, as well as the left-wing French dramatist Charles Vildrac, who had visited Zamiatin in Leningrad. While he was drafting this application, he had been staying in Moscow with Vsevolod Ivanov, who was the one who advised him to put down Pozner's address as his contact in France.[88] Pozner replied helpfully a week later, reporting on his own visit to "NRF," and on his fortunate encounter there with an official who had promised to put in a word on Zamiatin's behalf.[89]

The process of obtaining a French visa dragged on, and Zamiatin wrote again to Pozner at the beginning of October, as they were hoping to leave soon after the 20th: "And then we will see one another, I hope, at the beginning of November: I'm not intending to stop in Berlin for more than a week, as I have almost nothing to do there, and anyway I don't like Berlin. At the end of November Vsevolod Ivanov and Slonimsky are planning to come to Paris: it will be fun for us all to meet up there!" Zamiatin explained that he had been giving Pozner's address to people such as his Italian translator and his New York publisher, and asked him to keep any correspondence from them until they met.[90] Again Pozner replied promptly, to tell him that according to his contact permission had recently been granted for the Zamiatins to come to Paris, and that any delay was now with the French Consulate in Moscow. Pozner added that two other Soviet writers were planning to be in Paris as well, Tarasov-Rodionov and Kataev: "Can you imagine what a hubbub there'll be!"[91] Zamiatin was also receiving help from other quarters. Erenburg wrote to him on 13 October to let him know that Benjamin Crémieux, secretary of the PEN Club, had firmly promised to obtain a visa for him, and reassured him: "Altogether things have become somewhat easier with visas here at the moment, and I think that if you haven't already received it, then you will obtain it in the very near future." Erenburg was going to be away until 15 November, when he hoped to find Zamiatin already in Paris.[92]

On 25 September, Boris Grigor'ev sent him a typically contradictory letter from his place in the south of France, Villa Borisella in the beautiful village of Haut-de-Cagnes: "Dear Zamiatins, come to stay with us as if it were your home, and know that we are bound to you in spirit and are waiting for you with open arms; and then take me back with you to the Motherland. I don't like anything I have seen, I don't agree with any of it, and haven't learnt anything, except perhaps misanthropy. I only love all that is Russian, and dream of returning home once and for all—and I will die there. I have written about you to a few people in Paris, but everything is difficult here. There's chauvinism and envy of the Russians, of their strength and their talents..."[93]

They were now mostly occupied with settling all their affairs and tying up loose ends. On 13 October Zamiatin received a certificate for the customs authorities, to confirm that as a writer travelling abroad he needed to take with him books and manuscript materials for his historical novel *The Scourge of God* and for other works including *The Birth of Ivan*, *The African Visitor*, and *The Martyrs to Learning*.[94] Krolenko visited them the next day: they had "pre-departure" conversations, and Zamiatin read him his letter to Stalin. They spent an evening together with many of the usual friends, but didn't play poker.[95] Zamiatin inscribed the newly-published *School for Scandal* "To that respected foreigner Rostislav, for when he will have learned to read, but in the meantime, because of his illiteracy, to his mama Liudmila Nikolaevna. Evg. Zamiatin. 16-X-1931. Rostislav's name-day."[96] On 1 November Zamiatin obtained a certificate from the Leningrad Shipbuilding Institute, to confirm that he was still employed there.[97] Meanwhile Podgorny wrote to him from Moscow to let him know that the first performance of the revived *Flea* at MKhAT had been scheduled for the 15th.[98]

Zamiatin's aunt Varia, still living in the family home in Lebedian', was now very unwell and being looked after by his sister Aleksandra. He sent Varia an emotional letter in those final weeks, reflecting on the difficulty of reconciling oneself to a universe which allowed her to endure so much physical pain for no apparent reason:

> And it's upsetting not to be able to think of anything which could spare you this. It's upsetting, because you are not any old Varvara Aleksandrovna, but someone who is close to me. And that's not at all because you are my mother's sister (my mother's brother, for example, is nobody to me), but because I always knew that you understood what I was talking about, and I understood what you were talking about. Anyway, enough philosophising! It's because I'm sitting at home today, and there are no outsiders here. That happens rarely these days: all sorts of people come and go, in connection with my departure, or I have to go out to places for the same reason. Today it's warm outside, it's autumnal and damp and I don't want to leave the house, and in such weather even thinking about travelling, about homelessness, brrr! that's not very agreeable. Everyone around me is envious, as though I had won two thousand roubles, but I can't feel it yet. Either it's because we have got out of the habit of such unusual journeys, and become settled—or have I just got old?[99]

On 26 October, Bulgakov wrote to tell him that he had at last received a piece of good news: with Gor'ky's help, his Molière play had been licensed for performance at MKhAT, despite the earlier "Repertkom" ban. He was clearly not bitter about Zamiatin's good fortune: "And what sort of way of carrying on is this—not writing to your old friends? When are you going abroad? I was told that you'd be coming to Moscow at the end of October or at the beginning of November. Dash off a line to tell me when. [...] It will be pleasant for a provincial like me to admire the pipe and the suitcase of a real tourist."[100] Zamiatin replied two days later: "And so, hurrah for the three Ms: Mikhail, Maksim [Gor'ky] and Molière! This splendid combination of three Ms should turn out very profitably, and I'm very glad for you. So it seems you are going to join the ranks of the playwrights, while I join those of the Wandering Jews… My distant travels will begin, probably, on 14 November. So that means I should be in Moscow on the 4th or the 5th: that depends on our hearing that we've got the visas (which we still don't have yet, the devil take them!). And on 15 November MKhAT is relaunching *The Flea*, which I'll probably not have time to see. That's a pity. But we'll see one another in any case." Bulgakov responded on the 31st: "Dear Wandering Jew! when you get to Moscow let me know that you're here and where to find you, by whichever means you prefer—even, say, with a note at MKhAT, because my telephone—blast it—is giving no signs of life."[101]

In the event, they set off from Leningrad, initially for Riga in Latvia, on 15 November 1931. The French visas never did come through before their departure, so for the time being they were planning to travel as far as Berlin. Krolenko described how that afternoon he "…left home for the Warsaw Station, to see off the Zamiatins. It took me a long time to find them on the platform. Amongst those seeing them off were Rabinovich, Korchagina-Aleksandrovskaia, Aliansky, Zoia Nikitina, Akhmatova, Nad. K. Radlova, Grebenshchikov, Sergeev. I didn't succeed at all in chatting to them. I handed over some photographs, which the Zamiatins were very pleased with. In order not to have to talk to anyone, after the train had left I took the tram."[102]

Chapter 8:

From Riga to Cagnes (1931–1932)

On 16 November 1931, Zamiatin and Liudmila reached Riga, the capital of Latvia, which had gained its independence from Soviet rule over a decade earlier. Liudmila wrote that very day to Fedin, who was undergoing treatment in a sanatorium in the Swiss town of Davos for the tuberculosis he had recently developed. She told him that she had spent her penultimate evening in Leningrad in his flat, playing poker with his wife Dora, and their very last evening with "the three Mishas" [Sergeev, Slonimsky and Aliansky—the latter having changed his name from Samuil to Mikhail in view of the increasing persecution of Jews in the USSR]: they had exchanged heartfelt words and drunk a lot of wine. The couple were planning to travel onwards to Berlin on the 18th. "EI was utterly exhausted before our departure, he's very weary. At the moment he's asleep. And I'm going out to wander about this unfamiliar town—I like doing that, and I'll post this letter." In his own letter to Fedin from Riga, Zamiatin commented: "I don't know where I am: it's not quite Russia, nor quite abroad, nor quite some sort of Finland. I'm trying to extract some money (*"laty"*) from the local Russian theatre. The devils have been performing my *Flea* for five seasons (!) and my *Society of Honourable Bellringers*, but as for money—well, so far all I've had is lunches. Perhaps I'll give them another play—if the lunches turn into good dinners. [...] I'm leaving for a great nation—Germany—in a day's time. There, by all accounts, theatrical and other affairs are in such a dire state that after a week or so I'll go on from there to Paris. Altogether everything is very wonderful and—in all honesty—difficult (for me!). [...] I'll write again when I've come to my senses."[1]

In his account of an interview with Zamiatin printed in one of the local Russian newspapers, *Segodnia* (*Today*), Boris Orechkin observed that the people of Riga already knew him well, since the success of his

Flea had been rivalled only by Bulgakov's *White Guard* [*The Days of the Turbins*] in the local Russian theatre. "Zamiatin has now left the USSR entirely legally with his wife, on a foreign passport valid for one year." At a meeting with the actors he had explained that he'd been granted a year's leave from the Shipbuilding Institute, and that his ultimate destination on this trip was America, where he hoped to work on the staging of his plays, and to collaborate with Cecil B. de Mille, whom he'd met and enjoyed talking to the previous August in Moscow. His first destination was Berlin, where he was hoping to get some of his plays staged, perhaps by Max Reinhardt; and then to go on to America after a holiday in the south of France. Orechkin seemed to view his arrival as evidence of a certain relaxation in Soviet culture, citing the examples of both Bulgakov and Erdman, whose recently banned plays now seemed likely to be staged.[2]

After they moved on from Riga to Berlin, Zamiatin reported to Pozner on 22 November that he was now at last in possession of a French visa, and had embarked on an attempt to get one for the USA. The French writer Drieu la Rochelle may have been instrumental in finally helping them to obtain the French visas. Zamiatin had been discussing some possible theatre projects in Berlin, and was hoping to be in Paris a week or so later.[3] However, on the 27th Liudmila told Zoia Nikitina that they now expected to remain there a further week. "What can you say, it's a fine town. EI is rushing around being busy — this instead of that rest which he needs so badly. My one hope is the south of France — Paris, of course, won't help at all." For the moment letters sent to them in Paris were being forwarded to their address in Berlin. Zoia had undertaken to look after their affairs in their absence, and Liudmila asked her to deposit Zamiatin's royalties in a savings account for Agrafena Pavlovna to use, and to make sure she understood that these were his instructions. She had found Berlin to be clean and tidy, brightly lit and full of smart people and flowers and fruit — but very expensive, and the economic crisis was all too apparent in the unsold goods and the high unemployment.[4]

Zamiatin was soon writing ruefully to Fedin: "Yes, yes, dear Kosten'ka, it's already 1 December, I'm already getting frozen in my light coat, and the opiate of the people has already appeared in the shop-windows — Christmas trees; and I'm being asked from Paris whether I'm proposing to sit here until the Hitlerites form a government, and I still haven't budged. Berlin has turned out to be partly an international literary stock market, partly a gathering of international sharks. In any case, each one of the local imperialist sharks (who intend to feed on my skinny flesh) assures me that the others are swindlers, and I'm already utterly confused as to *'wer ist wer'*." He described how the publisher Ullstein had arranged for a speedy translation of *The Flea*, which was to be revised by the German playwright Carl Zuckmayer, "who they say is the most fashionable dramatist here. And meanwhile I'm being ruined, marks tumble out of my pockets like slogans from a good Soviet newspaper… " But eventually this plan fell through.[5] One memoirist recalled how Zamiatin's hopes of getting anywhere in the German cinema were also frustrated, even if he was politely received: "You're so very Russian, it's impossible to adapt you to our lives."[6] On 25 November he drafted an idea for a film script based on *At the Back of Beyond* called *Marusia. Siberia*, and he also started his article on "The Future of the Theatre" in the course of these weeks.[7]

That December, sad news reached him in Berlin from Lebedian', of the death of his loving aunt Varia, who had been so ill before his departure. Shortly after this loss his sister Aleksandra decided that it would be wiser for her, as the close relative of a politically controversial writer living abroad, to make a discreet departure from the two adjoining family homes in Lebedian'. She moved to the larger town of Tambov, where fewer people would know her history. This completed the final break with Lebedian' for Zamiatin. Aleksandra lived mostly in Tambov until her death in 1957, her husband Vladimir Volkov having died in 1942. A couple of surviving letters written to a friend towards the end of her life reflect her deep and continuing religious faith, and her extensive knowledge of folk remedies for a whole series of ailments.[8]

Meanwhile Zamiatin's friends in Czechoslovakia were keen for him to visit Prague, but in the light of the recent scandal over *We* it was important that this should not be seen as politically provocative. Abram Kagan, owner of the "Petropolis" publishing house in Berlin, wrote to Postnikov on 1 December: "He has limited means, and therefore despite his desire to spend some time in Prague, is unable to take advantage of your kind invitation. But if you were able to send him a free visa and money for the journey there and back, then he will come with pleasure. […] … however, you need to do this without particularly publicising it. You understand perfectly well why this is so. Many proletarian and non-proletarian writers arrive here from Russia, but Zamiatin represents a brilliant exception: he has not lost that courage and pride which are as characteristic of him now as they were ten years ago."⁹ On 6 December, Zamiatin told Iarmolinsky that there was now a plan for them to travel to Prague the following week; he also asked him whether attempting to get to New York by February would seem a good idea, and whether the support of Ray Long and Cecil B. de Mille would be sufficient to gain a US visa.¹⁰

The Zamiatins evidently arrived in Prague in the middle of December, and he contributed some readings to a literary evening there on the 19th. Apparently he had always wanted to visit Czechoslovakia, and had even once studied Czech. Ten days later he gave a public lecture on "The Russian Theatre Today." His public appearances were warmly received and widely reviewed, and the lecture was published in Czech translation the following month.¹¹ One person who attended the lecture was Al'fred Bem, who noted in his diary: "It was unexpectedly sharp in relation to the official line. It would seem that he doesn't intend to return to Russia." Another person present was A. Kizevetter: "Arosev and the other gents from the Villa Terezia [i.e. the staff from the Soviet embassy] were enthroned in the front row. But unexpectedly Zamiatin read his lecture in such a tone that the Soviet audience was squirming, and the rest of the audience was extremely satisfied. —'In the USSR the writer is not required to think, the government has thought everything through for him already.'—that's a sample of the spirit in which the lecture was put together. […] He went on to say that all that was valuable in the theatre had been created before the Bolsheviks. All this had a very strong whiff of 'non-returning.'"¹²

That same day Zamiatin wrote to his young friend and translator Irina Kunina-Aleksander, who had evidently invited them to visit her in the Tyrol: "A holiday in a charming place and in charming company would of course be wonderful. And I really need a holiday after the month in Russia before we left and the six weeks abroad since… I'm tired to death. But we have to see through to the end the hospitality of the Czechs (not an easy thing). I'm being interviewed and photographed and translated, I'm setting up deals with theatres, and I've given readings in various places. Today I have a public lecture on the modern theatre." He asked her to consider what theatrical prospects there might be in Yugoslavia, and proposed again that she should have a go at translating *We*, since he could do with some money: "Of course they let me out of Russia almost naked, without any foreign currency." He was now expecting to be kept in Prague until 6 January, and then hoped to leave Berlin for Paris around the 15th.¹³

On 31 December Zamiatin wished Fedin a happy New Year from Prague. "It's a wonderful city, and the people are really 'like us.' [...] It turned out that the ambassador here is Arosev. The day after tomorrow I'm going with him to Marienbad. It would all be good, only I'm very tired."[14] That day he read two acts of *Attila* at the home of Tsvetaeva's friend Anna Tesková, in the presence of Postnikov, A. Bem, P. Savitsky and members of the Prague Linguistic Circle including Roman Jakobson and Jan Mukařovský.[15] That evening they celebrated the New Year at a literary club, the Umělecká Beseda. He was supposed to join Liudmila and Nadezhda Mel'nikova-Papoushkova for a drink earlier in the evening, but he was late. They left him a menu with a cartoon of three parrots on a perch, ticking him off: "We waited for you until 22.10 and went off cursing. These are the barbarian ways of an Attila! [...] Decadent Europe will be waiting with impatience for the advance of the Attilan (this year, please!) in the Umělecká Beseda."[16]

While the Zamiatins were making merry in Prague, another lively New Year's party was taking place back in Berlin. The poet Ovady Savich was one of those writers who still got published in the USSR as well as abroad. He and his wife Alia had emigrated to Berlin in 1924, then Paris in 1927, and they spent regular holidays with Erenburg and Roman Jakobson in Brittany or Slovakia.[17] It was this group of old friends who decided to meet up in Berlin. The Erenburgs arrived from Paris at the last minute, in full evening dress; Jakobson had travelled directly from Prague, where he had heard Zamiatin reading *Attila* earlier in the day, and was distributing lavish kisses.[18] One topic of conversation must surely have been the newly-emigrated Zamiatins, their mutual friends, who had also recently travelled between Berlin and Prague, and were shortly to move to Paris themselves. Some of these people seemed to be able to travel fairly freely in and out of the Soviet Union, and to mix socially with self-exiled émigrés abroad, without the paranoid fears that would accompany such actions only a few years later. The difficulties of getting a visa for foreign travel were still viewed by them as an irksome bureaucratic rigmarole, rather than a state policy of isolationism and imprisonment. When leaving Russia, Zamiatin had by no means necessarily closed the door behind him, and the question of whether to return remained a matter of judgement and choice. In these circles his permission to travel abroad might be viewed as a privilege and a great stroke of luck, but not necessarily as some dramatic opportunity to escape. His friend Slonimsky, for example, did not get a visa to Paris in November 1931 after all but, as so often, it only took an intervention from Gor'ky, writing personally to Stalin from Sorrento, for everything to be sorted: "I would ask you earnestly to give instructions for the writer Mikh[ail] Slonimsky to be allowed out to come here, as he is travelling to do some work on a new novel" — and sure enough Slonimsky was permitted to travel, and went to visit Fedin in Germany the following summer.[19]

The Zamiatins seem to have returned to Berlin in the second week of 1932. He was certainly still in Prague on 7 January, when he drafted an indignant letter to the Paris émigré newspaper *Poslednie novosti* (*Latest News*), complaining that they had published without his permission an interview he had given to the journalist V.M. Despotuli in Berlin in December. This newspaper of the White emigration was just the sort of publication the Soviet authorities would frown upon.[20] Galushkin cites Ivan Gronsky, the *Izvestiia* editor who was very close to Stalin: "When E[vgeny] Zamiatin was permitted to go abroad (no-one had sent him into exile), the majority of the members of the Politbiuro were opposed to this decision. Stalin spoke in favour of granting this permission, and declared in this connection that Zamiatin wouldn't write anything against us over there. And he turned out to be right."[21] During his years abroad Zamiatin avoided contacts with Russian émigré publications, just as Voronsky had recommended in 1922–23, and largely avoided émigré cultural figures, apart from his friends Aleksei Remizov, Vladimir Pozner (who was becoming more and more left-wing anyway), and the artists Iury Annenkov and Boris Grigor'ev.

They left Prague around 8 January, having been seen off at the station by their Czech friends: a photograph of the occasion shows Zamiatin wearing a natty tweed suit with plus-fours.[22] But their onward journey from Berlin to Paris was then delayed for a further month, while he pursued various theatrical and cinema projects, all of which came to nothing; and it was probably the imminent expiry of their German visas which finally forced them to move on. He had asked Vladimir Pozner to look for some quiet rooms, preferably near his own flat, where they could stay in Paris. Initially, he was planning to spend only a short while there, before heading off for a month to Grigor'ev's villa in the south of France, to rest. He was delighted when Pozner invited them instead to stay in his own home at 36 rue Desaix, in the 15th *arrondissement*: "It would of course be charming to live in your flat instead of trailing around hotels, where for nearly three months now I've been completely unable to catch up on my sleep."[23]

The Zamiatins finally arrived in Paris on the morning of 9 February 1932.[24]

As it happened, the 26-year-old Vladimir Pozner had arranged to travel to Italy that same day, to spend 10 days visiting Gor'ky in Sorrento, so they would barely have glimpsed one another before he left. Pozner probably travelled with the American publisher Ray Long (who had recently published one of Zamiatin's stories), to discuss with Gor'ky plans to publish books about the Soviet Union; indeed, Pozner published an upbeat book, illustrated with photos reflecting the comfortable life of the Soviet people, later that same year. Gor'ky had been forewarned of Long's visit by a man named Barkov at the Paris Embassy, and in a letter to Stalin soon afterwards he described Ray Long as: "A thoroughly 'decent' man, to the extent that this is generally possible for an American bourgeois who is fully aware that his country is in danger, and that this danger could be averted by a decisive change of policy among the group around Hoover — which is to say, primarily, diplomatic recognition of the Soviet Union by Washington."[25] The regular and frank correspondence between Gor'ky and Stalin at this time reveals the extent to which Soviet policy aims were pursued abroad through the establishing of sympathetic contacts with potentially influential figures such as Long. Even when he was living in Italy, Gor'ky still remained a crucial point of reference for many Russians in the West — certainly amongst Zamiatin's friends — and he continued to have a significant influence on Soviet cultural policies. It is rather remarkable to think that Zamiatin, who saw both Pozner and Long on their return to Paris, may have gained first-hand intimations of these imminent shifts in diplomatic relations, with the long-sought US diplomatic recognition of the USSR being achieved the following year. Pozner himself remembered that visit to Gor'ky as a hugely memorable event decades later.[26]

Zamiatin and Liudmila were greeted at the station in Paris by the Erenburgs and the Saviches. As Alia Savich wrote: "We met him in triumph. Ovady Gertsovich [Savich] considered Zamiatin the most serious contemporary writer of prose. Il'ia Grigor'evich [Erenburg] also held him in very high regard, and was proud of Zamiatin's review of his *Julio Jurenito*. Zamiatin came with his wife, a beautiful, plump woman, a true Russian beauty. Everyone loses weight in Paris, and after a certain time she became rather desiccated, and it was sad to remember how she was when she arrived. Soon after his arrival, we arranged a formal dinner in his honour. There was a lot of fuss and agitation about arranging this occasion, but I think it went off very successfully." Zamiatin described this same meal to Fedin in Leningrad: "The atmosphere is troubled, and there's a mood of crisis… Although if for example you go to have a meal with the Saviches—what crisis? Oysters on ice, artichokes, cheeses, and God knows what besides. By the way, we drank vermouth and talked about you." Liudmila's first impressions of Paris, after just five days, were certainly enthusiastic: "Paris fills me with joy, I can tell you… It's a marvellous, wonderful city. There is so much that is fantastical. And the entire history of French literature has become real." They had visited the playwright Charles Vildrac, whom Zamiatin had met in Leningrad in 1929, and been to the Comédie Française, where they had sat in the front row to watch a play by Vildrac, which he found rather light-weight and provincial by contrast with Reinhardt's opulent staging of Offenbach's *Tales of Hoffmann*, which he had seen two weeks previously in Berlin.[27] Boris Grigor'ev had written to welcome the Zamiatins shortly after their arrival in the West, in a characteristically emotional letter:

> Dear Zamiatins, at last! Well, we congratulate you wholeheartedly—that is, if you have not yet become disappointed by Europe! I believe you are a bit tardy with your departure—this is the third year the crisis has been undermining life in Europe and America, until you can hardly recognise it. How easy everything was, and how hard it has become! […] Will you still stay for long in Paris? I wish you every success, but you should know that even the slightest, trifling achievement in your affairs is now considered a miracle—successes are a thing of the past. […] Our true happiness lies in the fact that we live in our own house, and there's the sun, the scent of verbena and heliotrope and pine—all these grow in our garden: oranges ripen here, flowers bloom, the carrots are coming up, and doves fly about. The sea, the mountains, walks and work. You'll like it here. Write to tell us the day and the time of your arrival, and we'll come and meet you. […] What joy. […] So, we're expecting you. I embrace you both as dear friends.[28]

His wife Elizaveta added: "There is a chaise-longue ready for Liudmila Nikolaevna under an orange tree, and for Evgeny Ivanovich an enormous Louis XIV writing desk." She also told them about nearby Nice: "…and 20 minutes in the other direction the famous Juan-les-Pins, a modern-day Babylon, where they preach nudism and pyjamism, and where all the world's 'stars' gather every summer." They themselves lived quietly, two kilometres from the sea, in a not too luxurious villa high up in the village of Haut-de-Cagnes.[29]

The Zamiatins decided that Liudmila should go on down to join the Grigor'evs in the south of France almost immediately, while he stayed on in the capital for some weeks—in the end it would be a couple of months—to try to get contracts for work. Writing to Fedin on 22 February, Zamiatin told him that he was attempting to establish contact with three different theatres. He had seen Remizov and his wife since his arrival, and was struck by how stooped Remizov had become—"a hunchback, a wizard."[30] On the following day, the eve of Liudmila's departure, the Erenburgs gave a dinner in order for him to meet some influential French people. As Liudmila started relaxing in the south, he began to pursue all possible leads to establish himself professionally. He was the guest of honour on 4 March along with Henri Barbusse, Erenburg and Savich at a dinner given by the "Groupe des Ecrivains Prolétariens de Paris."[31] This new group was associated with Barbusse's *Monde* newspaper, which for several years had been engaged in heated polemics against the more hardline pro-Moscow groups on the French left and in the Comintern.[32]

But concrete projects were hard to secure in France, as elsewhere, as the economic crisis worsened. That March, Zamiatin composed a letter from La Rotonde on Boulevard Montparnasse, using writing paper which advertised its "Brasserie, Restaurant, American Bar, Dancing, and Permanent Exhibition of Modern Art." This letter was to George Reavey, a Russian-born Irish poet, translator and literary agent acquainted with James Joyce, who would be the key figure in his attempts to get noticed in the British literary market. Zamiatin had commissioned him to translate *Mamai*, and asked him to find out whether a stage adaptation of *The Cave* might be of interest to the new American Theater in Paris.[33] His plays *The Flea* and *The Bellringers* had already been translated into French, and he now proposed some stories, including *At the Back of Beyond*.[34] He arranged for Pozner to get *The Cave* and *Mamai* translated into French as well.[35] But one of the first of his stories to appear in the French press, in *Monde*, was X, under the title *L'aventure du diacre Indikoplev*, illustrated by the well-known avant-garde artist Mikhail Larionov.[36] A few weeks later *Lu* published a French translation of *The Martyrs to Learning*.[37]

Above all, he was waiting to hear whether his ultimate plan of moving on from France to the United States would have any chance of success. One contact he approached for support in obtaining a US visa was Cecil B. de Mille, who had visited the USSR in 1931—the UPI correspondent Eugene Lyons commented that de Mille "typified another side of foreigners' uncritical enthusiasm for the Soviet experiment."[38] De Mille replied from Hollywood to the request Zamiatin had sent him the moment he reached Paris: "I have this day written to the American Consulate in Berlin, as you requested, and am hoping that we shall have the pleasure of seeing you in our part of the world. We are in need of good dramatic brains more than ever." Perhaps the mention of Berlin rather than Paris was just a slip of the pen on de Mille's part, but in any case his intervention seems to have had no success.[39]

Towards the end of March, Zamiatin wrote again to Fedin in Davos, describing how he had spent the previous stormy day winning at poker in the snug apartment of Vladimir (Vova) Pozner's mother-in-law: "In the other room Vova (a man who is much more serious and businesslike than me) was playing bridge... This was one of my few idle days in Paris, but otherwise it's a constant round of more or less purposeful meetings, meals, visits, and the devil knows what—I'm getting fed up with it. Amongst other things, a dinner with the [Soviet] Ambassador and a formal reception there with some *Deputés*, and Erenburg and I were sat there like the generals at a wedding... The food was bourgeois, and top quality. And the wine... A waiter asked me: 'Which vintage would you prefer, sir?'"[40] It appears then that Zamiatin, still the bearer of a Soviet passport, was close enough to the Soviet authorities at this stage to be invited to social occasions at the Embassy, just as he had been included by Aleksandr Arosev, the Soviet Ambassador, on an excursion to Marienbad during his recent stay in Prague. The Soviet Embassy in Paris at the time was known for being more lavish and sophisticated in its lifestyle than most other Soviet Embassies around the world, and indeed over the next couple of years the Party would take steps to do something about what was felt to be the relatively lax ideological discipline which prevailed there at the time.[41] Zamiatin seemed to be quite comfortable at the beginning of his life in France to move in these more liberal circles of those who sympathised with the USSR.

In his letter to Fedin he continued: "There are much better prospects here than in Berlin, where everything is doomed. I'm heartily tired. Maybe I'll get away at the end of this week, finally, to the south (where L[iudmila] N[ikolaevna] has been sunbathing for the past month). In the evenings I go around the bars with Annenkov."

Iury Annenkov, who later described Zamiatin as his "very greatest friend," did a number of wonderful sketches of Parisian night-life, and Zamiatin's own *Notebooks* from the Paris period describe the scandalous Kiki at La Coupole, the cafés of Les Halles, and the sexy dancing in the streets on the 14th of July.[42] Zamiatin's closeness to Annenkov was regarded with some suspicion by the Saviches. Ovady Savich became the Paris correspondent of *Izvestiia* and *Komsomol'skaia pravda* that year, and they remained identified with Erenburg and the more loyal pro-Moscow circles. Having welcomed Zamiatin so warmly, the Saviches evidently came to find him a bit eccentric. Observing him in a domestic context, Alia noted "…Zamiatin's oddnesses and fussiness: when his wife was obliged to go away somewhere, we invited EI to live with us for a while. He bought some enormous sheets of black paper, and each evening he would pin them to the window-frames with drawing-pins to screen all the windows (all the frames ended up covered in little holes). He would only brew coffee and tea using Vittel mineral water, which was completely tasteless, but he bought it in cases." With time they drifted apart: "In Paris Zamiatin somehow lost himself. He kept working on his Attila without being able to finish it. He grew closer and closer to the Russian émigrés, and became friendly with Iury Annenkov. We saw one another more and more infrequently."[43] Annenkov had settled in France in 1924, at the point when diplomatic relations between France and the Soviet Union were established. He managed to remain on friendly terms with the Soviet Embassy, attended social events there, and continued to exhibit in Moscow—for example at an exhibition of French art in 1928: "This was at the time when the 'iron curtain' had not fully descended. Writers who arrived from the USSR were kept under observation, but not on a very short lead. They would visit Annenkov, who was considered a Soviet citizen, although he had absolutely no intention of limiting his contacts among émigré or indeed French circles of society."[44]

Marc Slonim has left a detailed account of how Zamiatin viewed his situation with regard to the Paris émigré community at the beginning of his stay: "Early in 1932 I discovered from the artist Iury Annenkov that Evgeny Ivanovich Zamiatin would soon be arriving in Paris with his wife Liudmila Nikolaevna, and that he had asked about me in a letter and wanted to find out my address, so that we could meet straight away. I must admit that I awaited this meeting with him with some trepidation: after all, I had been the literary editor of the Prague monthly *Volia Rossii*, and in 1927 I had printed in it nearly all of Zamiatin's novel *We*." Slonim was all too aware of how drastic the consequences of this publication had subsequently been for its author:

> We sat down in my workroom, which polite guests referred to as my study. It overlooked the inner courtyard, with a double window on the corner—you could see through the neighbours' windows, and the curtains were drawn back. Zamiatin looked somewhat askance at them. I drew them, and jokingly remarked that "no-one's watching here." He shrugged—"an inbred reflex" and smiled. [...] EI hastened to dispel my anxieties. He said that I was not at fault as far as he was concerned, that I hadn't done him any harm, and reminded me that the publication of the novel in the émigré journal in 1927 had been met by silence in Moscow and Leningrad and, as he put it, "they dragged it back out into the light of day two years later, when it became necessary to open fire with all possible weapons. It was not about *We*, [...] but about excluding me from literature and calling down an anathema upon me." From that moment on the conversation ran very smoothly, and we sat together in lively conversation for three hours, until dusk fell. [...] EI asked me at length about the Russians in Paris, not out of curiosity, but he was concerned as to how he should behave with the émigrés; and at our subsequent meetings he constantly returned to this question. Not only because of his Soviet passport, but also because of the fact that his whole cast of mind and his political views made him alien to the émigrés, he didn't conform to émigré norms, and he was distinctly aware of that. He could not and would not work for their newspapers and journals abroad: he was too left-wing for them. He did have several old friends in Paris who felt dispassionately about politics: Iury Annenkov, Mstislav Dobuzhinsky, Boris Iakovlev, and Vladimir Ivanovich Iurkevich, his friend from the Polytechnic, who was also a shipbuilder. He was planning to see Remizov and Osorgin, and to make the acquaintance of Bunin. But in general his attitude to the émigré community—with a few exceptions—was restrained and cautious. And indeed the so-called cultural circles of the Russian emigration manifested a certain chilliness towards him, at times a mistrust. In any case, EI quite correctly understood that as far as establishing his new life was concerned, he had no reason to suppose that he could count on any help from influential émigrés. And after all he did now have to set himself up abroad, and earn a living.[45]

These were indeed the two major problems he had to face in France. The first was how he would be regarded in the complex and suspicious political and social world of the Russian emigration. Tensions had been exacerbated since 1927, when the Soviet Embassy banned citizens travelling abroad from frequenting the milieux of the White emigration.⁴⁶ It is not clear whether Zamiatin did in fact meet Bunin, for example, although Bunin reputedly had the highest regard for his writing, and rated him above Remizov.⁴⁷ The second challenge, as Slonim was aware, was how he was to make a living. In one respect at least, the Zamiatins were in an advantageous position: this had been explained to them the previous December by Elizaveta Grigor'eva: "You have Soviet passports, and we are émigrés—these are two different camps, and it will be easier for you [to obtain visas to enter France] than for us émigrés, because émigrés are unemployed, and the French are concerned that you might take their jobs away from them, and so they are unwilling to hand out visas, whereas you, who have your own homeland, a place you can always return to—you offer no threat to the unemployed."⁴⁸ On the other hand, they did now have to start securing an income.

For as long as he was in Paris, Zamiatin could keep up with the newspapers from home: and so it was that during February he discovered in *Literaturnaia gazeta* translations into Russian of articles which had been printed in the Czech Communist newspaper *Rudé právo*, denouncing him for his Prague lecture on "The Russian Theatre Today." As he complained to Fedin: "*Literaturnaia gazeta* uses filthy language about me—the usual thing. [...] In a few days I'm going over there [to the Embassy], and I'm going to kick up a row over those little articles you wrote to me about. What are those hotheads trying to achieve? Do they want me to lose patience entirely? They'll achieve that one day. I'm going to send an insulting 'Letter to the Editors,' which of course they won't print."⁴⁹

On 30 March he composed that exasperated open letter, which he sent to Moscow via the Soviet Embassy. As he said, he could have had little expectation that it would in fact be published; but he must have judged that it was not an entirely reckless gesture for him to undertake as a new arrival from the USSR, not a burning of his boats in emigration, if this was something he had discussed with, and even delivered through the hands of the Soviet diplomats in Paris who had recently entertained him to lavish meals. Was it possible that they— and Zamiatin himself—had some inkling of the apparently liberal imminent changes in the air on the Soviet cultural scene? In these early months of his exile, it is certainly clear that he still saw himself playing an ongoing role in Soviet culture, was still absorbed by the debates and struggles about who was to control literature, and he still felt that it was worthwhile—and not too dangerous—to send an outspoken expression of his views to the leading literary publication of the day in Moscow. In his letter he complained about the republication of the articles from *Rudé právo*, and the commentaries on them which implied that he was a class enemy. He sent Fedin a copy of this letter, "for his entertainment": "Of course they won't print it, the lily-livered devils, because I don't wear sackcloth and ashes. Read it and send it on to those of our friends who share my anxieties in our socialist fatherland (if you've acquired a typewriter, could you be so kind as to type it out?)."[50] He was altogether determined that his letter should be known about at home: he sent Zoia Nikitina a further copy, "for her entertainment" and that of "all the Mishas" (including Slonimsky and Zoshchenko), reiterating tactfully that it had been submitted "officially," via the Embassy.[51] On 21 April Slonimsky was told in confidence that *Literaturnaia gazeta* had received Zamiatin's "elegant refutation" of the accusations against him, but that it would indeed not be printed.[52]

Zamiatin was naturally also concerned about the reputation he would make for himself in French circles. He gave his first two brief interviews to the French press in mid-April, just before leaving for the south.[53] For the next, more substantial ones, he selected the publications with care: the first was to *Les Nouvelles Littéraires*, an influential but independent weekly, and the second to Barbusse's *Monde*.[54] In different ways, however, both were destined to misfire. The interview with Frédéric Lefèvre, editor-in-chief of *Les Nouvelles Littéraires*, appeared on 23 April. Zamiatin had prepared it in detail, even to the extent of drafting some of his answers in advance for Pozner to translate, for this was a prestigious series. During 1932, Lefèvre would publish similar interviews with Stefan Zweig, André Maurois and others. This was therefore a significant opportunity for Zamiatin to introduce himself to French readers.[55] He focused on his best-known work in France, the novel *We*, and commented on its similarities with Huxley's *Brave New World*, which had only just appeared:

> Shortsighted reviewers saw in my text nothing more than a political pamphlet. That is of course incorrect: this novel sends

out a signal about the dual threat which humanity is facing: that of the hypertrophied power of machines as well as the hypertrophied power of the state. The Americans, who wrote a good deal some years ago about the New York edition of my novel, rightly saw in it a critique of the methods of [Henry] Ford. In his most recent novel the English writer Aldous Huxley develops almost the same ideas and plot situations which you will find in *We*. Recently Drieu la Rochelle told me that when he met Huxley he even asked him whether he hadn't read *We*; it turned out that he had not. Which just goes to show that these ideas are simply circulating in the menacing air which we breathe these days.[56]

In fact Aldous Huxley, then also living in France, did at least become aware of the author of *We* soon after the publication of *Brave New World*: on 23 July he wrote a review of Zamiatin's article on theatre which had appeared in *Le Mois*, commenting: "At the moment the Russians are probably the people best qualified to be prophets."[57]

Perhaps in order to enhance the hopes he had of breaking into the theatre scene in Paris, Zamiatin laid particular emphasis when talking to Lefèvre on his recent experience as a dramatist: "In recent years I have mostly been involved with theatre. If you have only once in your life seen a theatre auditorium in a state of excitement about your play, you'll never forget it. Especially if that takes place in our times, in Russia, where the theatres are full not just of the usual audiences, but of the common people, to whom only now the doors of the theatre have been opened, and who respond in a particularly lively and fresh way."[58]

However, when this interview was actually published, Lefèvre embellished it with a highly provocative title and sub-titles, such as: "Writers in the USSR: there's money, but there's no freedom." Zamiatin wrote to Pozner in some dismay: "I am bitterly disappointed by our '*cher confrère Lefèvre*': despite all my warnings, he has managed to stir up trouble for me with his headings. [...] The material I gave him, which I believe to have been reasonably objective and restrained, has been used in a way which I didn't want. He fulfilled his promise to send me the material to proofread, but afterwards he sprinkled on such a lot of pepper that I'm still sneezing. If you get the opportunity, and if you meet Barkov [from the Embassy], will you attempt, by the by, to find out what impression this pepper of Lefèvre's has made, and tell them that it came as a complete surprise to me."⁵⁹ In the event, it seems there was little reaction in official Soviet circles to this, his most significant interview outlining his literary position as he established himself in France—perhaps not least because the First Secretary, Barkov, was very shortly thereafter transferred to China, apparently having contributed to "violent personal animosities" within the Embassy because of his anti-Semitism.⁶⁰

Zamiatin had prepared a second interview text in advance: this time it was with Pozner himself, and intended for publication in Barbusse's *Monde* shortly after the appearance of the Lefèvre interview. Here he argued that the ethos of the Five-year Plan had proved inappropriate for Soviet literature, not least because most authors lacked any understanding of industry and technology—unlike himself, of course. Instead of the topical themes favoured by the proletarians, literature should be tackling other matters:

> One of these themes, as yet only tentatively addressed in Soviet literature, is the question of the relationship between the individual and the collective, the individual and the state. In practice this question has been decided entirely in favour of the state, but that can only be a temporary solution: in a state which has set as its ultimate goal the dwindling of state power to nought, this question will undoubtedly arise sooner or later in a very acute way. [...] The other, very relevant theme for Soviet literature [...] is the theme of the position of the artist in a society organised according to new principles. This is less dangerous, less explosive than the first theme, and what's more it concerns the writer more directly just at the moment, when attempts are being made by the state to regulate "the literary industry."

He also observed that in general Soviet literature was not much concerned with the "eternal triangle" which so dominates the plots of European literature—nor indeed did the Soviet state intervene to a significant extent in matters of sex and the family. However, he could anticipate a time when the state would turn its attention to these matters, developing its concerns with perfecting the human race, and therefore with eugenics—and he expected this topic to provide fascinating material for the artists of the future.⁶¹

He was now rather alarmed about the possible repercussions of the Lefèvre interview, and hastily wrote to Pozner: "This is what

I think: would it not be better in the circumstances to hold back the material I sent you for *Monde*, in order not to pour oil on the flames?" Alternatively, he suggested publishing it with a rather bizarre additional section, where Pozner would "ask" him some question about the successes of industrialisation, and he would respond—presumably with sincere pride—by describing the remarkable increase in ship-building productivity at the Soviet Putilov wharfs between 1926 and 1931.[62] This would of course have seemed entirely incongruous alongside the rest of the piece. But evidently Pozner agreed with him that altogether it would be wiser to hold the piece back, and this entire "interview" remained unpublished in Zamiatin's lifetime.

He renewed his efforts to make an impression on Western readers with a further extensive interview he gave when he came back to Paris for a period that summer. This time it was not for a French, but a British audience, and it was conducted by Alexander Werth, the Paris correspondent of the *Manchester Guardian*. As Zamiatin noted, this was just about the only English newspaper it was possible to find at the time in Soviet public libraries and reading rooms. Werth commented that Zamiatin looked no more than 35, despite his 48 years, with flashes of irony gleaming constantly in his grey eyes. He gave the impression of being very active and enormously competent, with nothing about him of the "dreamy Slav." He described to Werth the privileged life that writers can lead in Russia, acknowledging that he and Liudmila had been unusual by Soviet standards in having a 3-room apartment to themselves in Leningrad:

> Successful writers, and especially successful playwrights, are in an exceptional position. The successful playwright, who gets 5 or 6 per cent of box-office receipts, is the only "legitimate bourgeois" in Russia today; and nobody interferes with his wealth. [...] Besides, authors are given a specially generous ration card, which entitles them to receive butter and cheese and all the other "luxuries" unknown to so many ordinary mortals. The Soviets are very good to authors in that way. All the most important professional writers receive these rations. There must be seventy-five such authors in Leningrad, and about a hundred in Moscow.[63]

It would seem, then, that during his first months in the West Zamiatin was relatively fearless about what he would submit for publication back in the USSR, as evinced by his furious letter to *Literaturnaia gazeta*; if anything, he was more circumspect about what he was prepared to say in print in France, where he assumed that the Embassy was keeping a close eye on his public statements. Clearly he had no intention of jeopardising his passport. Joining the émigré community so late on, a decade after most of the White emigration, not only marks the difference in his political views and experience; it also sets him apart, because of his close involvement with all the struggles Soviet literature had experienced in the 1920s. In his essays and interviews we get the overwhelming sense of how much he still cares about the development of Russian literature in the new Soviet state. In the absence of any children of his own, the progress of those he regarded as his special protégés, the Serapion Brotherhood, preoccupied him constantly. He keenly followed the twists and turns of Soviet literary politics from France, constantly updating his assessments of how things were progressing, and looking for signs within the political turmoil that true literary values were re-emerging. Soviet Russian literature was his literature—and it would take several more months and years of life abroad before this direct sense of identification with its travails would fade to disappointment and powerless regret.

Meanwhile, however, he had at last succeeded in escaping Paris for his much-deferred holiday. The Grigor'evs had acquired their villa, which they named Borisella, in 1927. It is an enchanting house high on the slope of the small medieval hilltop village of Cagnes-sur-Mer near Nice, approached along steep and winding cobbled lanes draped with wisteria. Now known as Haut-de-Cagnes, it used to be frequented by many painters, and is situated close to the property at Collettes where Renoir had lived until his death a decade or so previously, as well as Vence, where Matisse would work on the chapel a decade later. Liudmila had arrived to stay at Villa Borisella on 25 February. Her visit was a success, at least at the start. Boris Grigor'ev, away on a visit to Prague, wrote in early April to Zamiatin, who was staying by then in Grigor'ev's Parisian *pied-à-terre*: "I'm very happy to hear from Elizaveta Georgievna that Liudmila Nikolaevna is such an unusual and sensitive woman, someone with whom it is both easy and pleasant to spend time. That is very valuable, for Elizaveta Georgievna has become very nervy, and even difficult." Grigor'ev reported that all their mutual friends in Prague had spoken warmly of Zamiatin, while he himself was longing to get back to France: "I will probably get naturalised, and very soon, as a Frenchman. […] I am 100% certain about this. I'm finished with Russia. That's how it must be. Some time you and I will get to New York, and you'll see for yourself that it is the West, not the East which will thrive. [...] I have been telling everyone here that I'm not giving you back to the Bolsheviks, not even for a short stay. [...] I'm so glad that you've both come, and that you will stay a long time. I embrace you, Evgeny, and wish you many successes in my dear and unique Paris."[64]

On 6 April, Liudmila reported very happily on her stay in Cagnes to Zoia Nikitina: "Right now it's 6 o'clock in the evening, I'm writing in the garden, without stockings, wearing only a light summer dress, and the sun is warming me; to the left you can see the sea (it's 20 minutes' walk from here), and straight ahead and to the right are the Alps. And sitting next to me is a charming little monkey, Whisky, my friend and jester. During the month and a half I've been here, I've really been able to rest. My friends are pampering me, the sun is baking hot, and I've turned brown. Soon I'll be bathing. It's very sad that EI has got stuck in Paris, but it seems that he will be turning up here in a few days' time. EI is moving in the *grand monde*, meeting French writers, artists and actors." A couple of weeks later she added more details for her friend to enjoy: "While I was still in Paris I had a few summer dresses made. For the spring the fashion is for light wool."[65]

Shortly after his own arrival there in the middle of April, in one of the stream of letters he wrote that summer to his friends all over the world, Zamiatin told Fedin: "I have finally got away from the Babylon which is Paris, I've spent three days catching up on half a year's sleep, and I'm beginning to feel like a man instead of a hollow jacket. I'm going to spend about a month here, and after Easter (*kulich* cakes and other such superstitions are all guaranteed!) I'll go back to Paris to conclude my business. There are some serious projects under way, and if it weren't for this blasted crisis I would already be a Rothschild."[66] He wrote in a similar vein to Zoia Nikitina: "I have been recovering from all those Parises and Berlins for about a week now on the Côte d'Azur. It's so hot and bright and blue that I am sitting on the terrace and writing you this letter wearing dark glasses. However, I won't be able to rest for long. Three articles hang around my neck like a millstone — one for a Prague University journal, one for Berlin, and one for *Le Mois* in Paris (where an article by Gor'ky came out recently). And then I'll have to go back to Paris, because of theatre matters and other things. There's the hope of pulling off some fairly serious projects, but the whole question now is just whether the theatre will be able to raise funds for the production. That's the French, if you please, who are already short of money—how do you like that?"⁶⁷ By mid-May he had completed the article on "The Future of the Theatre," begun soon after leaving Russia, which was published later that month in *Le Mois*, and was working on another for *Ost-Europa* in Berlin, while the one for *Slavische Rundschau* in Prague (closely associated with Roman Jakobson) would be completed some time later.⁶⁸

While he was relaxing in Cagnes, a sensational event took place in Moscow. Quite unexpectedly, a Resolution passed on 23 April by the Central Committee of the Party liquidated his old enemy RAPP, along with other proletarian cultural organisations, as a preliminary move towards the creation of a single Union of Soviet Writers. Gor'ky had written to Stalin in exasperation a month earlier: "These endless factional arguments and rows within RAPP, in my opinion, are extremely harmful, especially since it seems to me that their grounds lie rather in personal motives than in ideological ones."⁶⁹ Zamiatin welcomed the news of the Government's closing down of RAPP in an uncompleted essay, "En URSS":

> The leaders of this group had resolved, without the slightest compunction, to "re-educate" other writers. [...] These impatient conquistadors began to accomplish their task with, so to speak, artillery methods, taking advantage of the fact that in effect they held monopoly rights over literary criticism. Their critical bombs almost always contained one and the same suffocating gas: accusations of political unreliability. The results of this education by artillery fire were, of course, entirely lamentable: some of those being "educated" fell silent for extended periods of time, while in the works of some of the others you began to hear unbearably false notes, which offended even the ears of the uncritical.⁷⁰

To Fedin he wrote: "RAPP has gone up in a puff of smoke. Which is just what you thought would happen."⁷¹ This confirms that it was likely to have been the well-informed insider Fedin who was the main source of Zamiatin's relative optimism about Soviet literary policies in his writings during the preceding weeks. In his interview with Werth he went on to express the hope that the proletarian writers and the fellow-travellers would now come together in the new organisation, to everyone's benefit.⁷²

To Postnikov, whom Grigor'ev had seen in Prague, he wrote that he was continuously engaged in correspondence "in three languages, Russian, French and English. I have cast my hooks towards several countries, the fish are biting, and in Paris there's a large one—but as for landing any, well I've hardly managed to land anything at all so far: just small fry." There was to be a dinner in the second half of May, where he was to make a speech on the theatre in Russia, and deliver a public lecture—both of them in French. He was also planning an evening where he would read his stories. Then, he added, "the sun peeped out, and I was hauled away to go for a walk. [...] At the moment there are frogs shrieking down below, an eagle owl calling, and nightingales singing. And above, there are lights stretching up as if on a staircase: this is a tiny little medieval town, with narrow lanes, gates, arches, and a small castle right in the middle. It's a wonderful spot. The only pity is that it's quite a way from the sea; for the summer it would be good to be a bit closer to the water. Although a lot of water will flow under the bridge before we get to the summer—I'm trying not to look too far ahead."[73] On 29 April he told the Remizovs that he had become utterly weary of new people and impressions over the previous six months, so was particularly enjoying the peace and quiet. On the following day they were planning to go into Nice, to attend the early morning Easter service at the Russian Orthodox Cathedral.[74]

Almost as soon as he arrived in the south, Zamiatin asked Pozner to try and place the essay he had recently written called "On my wives, on icebreakers and on Russia."[75] The piece did not appear until 4 January 1933, in *Marianne*, but it was evidently one of the fruits of Zamiatin's first weeks in Paris. One of his most delightful essays, it opens with a confession that he has two wives: technology and literature. This is again a conscious echo of Chekhov's well-known dictum that he had two wives, literature and medicine. "Today I'm going to cheat on literature with my old, technological wife: I want to write… about icebreakers." These were peculiarly Russian vessels, of which only twelve had ever been constructed, mostly abroad, and they had fulfilled the purpose of opening up a path between Europe and Russia. Since he himself had frequently played a direct part in their creation, they too had become his "children." He gave an affectionate description of the way icebreakers force their way through the ice, using their heavy, blunt bows, which he saw as epitomising the typical features of Russia itself: "Russia moves ahead along a strange and difficult path, which does not resemble the path of other countries; its way is uneven and juddering, the icebreaker rears up and then immediately crashes down, all around there are thunderous, cracking sounds, and it moves forward, destroying as it advances. [...] And it seems the Russian people too have needed specially sturdy ribs and an especially thick skin, so as not to be crushed by the weight of that unprecedented burden which history has placed upon their shoulders."[76]

By early May, Zamiatin felt able to write a short letter to Pozner entirely in French, and although it was not absolutely correct he certainly came to acquire a more than competent level of fluency.[77] This is borne out by one of the little notebooks he kept, in which he jotted down French vocabulary. We cannot tell the dates of these entries, of course, but it is notable for containing only fairly advanced phrases (*un guet-apens*; *préconiser*; *escamoter*), together with some racier terms, perhaps reflecting his evenings spent with Annenkov in the bars of Paris (*les fesses*; *nichons*; *la grue*; *un aspect niais*; *un peu gris*; *l'aigrefin*; *s'amouracher*; *couchable*; *elle est bonne pour coucher avec, mais...*).[78]

During May they visited Monaco, just along the coast, and he sent a first postcard back to Bulgakov in Moscow: "Dear Molière, we're sitting in a café in Monaco, and thinking of you. What faces! What material for your pen! I'm delighted that you're not working to no purpose (I read about the revival of the Turbins). [...] I'm soon going back to Paris—for a month in the first instance. Then I'll probably come back here. And from here, perhaps on to America."[79] In these words, Zamiatin celebrated not just the apparent success Bulgakov had had in getting his Molière play approved for the stage in October 1931, just before their departure, but also the extraordinary news—perhaps yet another indication that literary life in the USSR was getting a little easier?—that in January 1932 Bulgakov's *Days of the Turbins*, banned in 1929 after Stalin had criticised some of his other plays, had been permitted again. The première of the revival took place on 18 February. Meanwhile Zamiatin himself was making his own jottings in his notebooks, possibly with a view to using them in later writings: reflecting conversations with Russian émigrés he met in Nice, Monte Carlo, and so on, these anecdotes are largely tales of how the Whites escaped the clutches of the Cheka and fled Russia.[80]

That same month he penned a letter (now in rather less fluent English) to Iarmolinsky, describing his experiences since leaving the USSR, including the collapse of funding for theatres in Berlin just when he was hoping to get *The Flea* staged in German. With things looking difficult in Paris too, he asked about the possibility of coming that October to New York to give lectures on contemporary Russian culture: "This I have been advised to do by Ray Long, whom I met six weeks ago in Paris and who promised to arrange for me something in this way. What is your opinion about the chances of this enterprise?"[81]

At the very end of May Liudmila wrote again from Nice to Bulgakov, who had suffered a set-back in his love life, and was also gloomy about the slow progress of the production of his Molière play:

> I don't believe, and I don't want to believe, that you've aged. I'm sure you may have become weary. But still, you'll relax over the summer and become your previous self, that brilliant, witty, and charmingly merry person that you were sometimes in Leningrad, when I always used to laugh such a lot. Yes, *mon cher ami*, the paths of destiny are unpredictable—and here I've been enjoying myself for nearly three months now on the Côte d'Azur. [...] *Mon mari* has dashed back to Paris again. It's the height of the spring season there. I've already sent your letter on to him. Paris is entirely fantastical. It's nothing like Berlin, which is so dull and clean and regular, nor is it like Prague. It's an astonishing and beautiful city! I'm very happy to think that I'll return there and am going to live there. [...] I won't say *adieu* to you, no—*au revoir, au revoir*, wherever you like—in Moscow, or in Leningrad. Have you been up there without us? I'm fiercely jealous.[82]

Zamiatin wrote to Kunina-Aleksander from Paris on 1 June to see if she could get any of his plays staged in Zagreb or Belgrade, adding: "I've been back about a week and I've already managed to get exhausted. It was wonderful in the south, but unfortunately I was compelled to spend more time writing articles than having fun."[83] That spring he was also in correspondence with Ettore Lo Gatto, who was glad to hear direct news of him from Renato Poggioli, who'd seen him in Prague the previous winter; however, he was not very encouraging about the idea of an Italian translation of *We* (he eventually undertook this project in 1954, and published it in 1955). During the following weeks Zamiatin worked on a cinematic adaptation of the novel. Under the title *D-503*, the film-script was written for "Features Productions" and completed on 15 July.[84] Unfortunately, it was rejected that December.[85]

He was also making vigorous efforts, through George Reavey, to get some publications in England, pressing him to get ahead with his translations of *The Cave* and *Mamai*.[86] When *Mamai* was finished Zamiatin sent it to London, to Gor'ky's ex-wife Moura Boudberg, who remained very close to her former husband and was regarded with much suspicion by the British authorities as a possible Soviet agent. He urged Reavey to visit Boudberg in London and to ask her to suggest publishers for *Mamai* and for his *Tales for Grown-up Children*. However, she doesn't seem to have achieved anything for him. "Perhaps it was a mistake to have relied upon a woman for up to date I had no reply of her. [sic]" He also had hopes for *We*: he suggested Reavey should pick up a copy of the French translation in Paris to facilitate negotiations in Britain, the American edition of 1924 evidently being difficult to obtain in London. "And if you succeed to arrange the publishing of it in London, it will be marvellous. It's very desirable to edit this novel in a new translation for the American one has been rather poor, or at any rate to correct this American text, and of course I should be very please[d] if you make one or the other. [sic]" Charles Malamuth would later describe Zilboorg's version of the novel as "hideously-translated."[87] Zamiatin also offered Reavey "The Future of the Theatre," his "rather merry" article about icebreakers, his stage adaptation of *The Cave*, and *The Dragon*.[88]

On 21 June, Fedin wrote from Germany about the upheavals in Moscow: "The confusion in the ranks of the RAPPists [...] is much more profound, of course, than is apparent from the newspapers." He mentioned that the "fellow-travellers" were much cheered by what had happened, adding: "I've been included in the organising committee to draw up the constitution for a new Union. But I only found out about this from the newspapers, and I've no details about how things are going." This nomination had presumably been proposed by Gor'ky, who had returned to Russia in order to assist with plans for the new Writers' Union immediately after the April Resolution dissolving RAPP was published.[89] "Zhenia! About your letter to the editors of *Literaturnaia gazeta*. Dora Sergeevna [Fedin's wife] has this to tell: Zoia [Nikitina] asked Averbakh (who is now a fallen angel), whether the letter had been received. Averbakh replied: 'It's been received, but it won't be printed. Zamiatin writes about the things which he didn't say. But he doesn't write about what he did say.' Zoia sent your letter on to Aleksei Maksimovich [Gor'ky], since he hadn't had a copy from you." In Fedin's opinion the letter would still not be printed, despite the defeat inflicted upon Zamiatin's persecutors, and like Averbakh he urged Zamiatin to make his political views clearer: "This time, as before, you leave open the most important question: how you view the Revolution? [...] I fear that this question, as far as the sphere of your own existence is concerned, belongs to the category of eternal questions, and that on this matter you'll never say anything decisive. But is it something about which it is possible to remain silent?"[90] This is typical of the "friendly" pressure Fedin would continue to put on him to declare his sympathies with the Revolution.

Zamiatin gave a public reading of *The Flood* and the last act of *The Flea* at the Salle du Grand Orient (Paris IXème) on 24 June. According to the not always reliable memoirist Annenkov, Liudmila may have come up to join him, for he describes lending them his second apartment in rue Duranton for a few weeks before they went back south.[91] Zamiatin sent invitations to several friends, including the Remizovs and George Reavey. The poet and literary critic Georgy Adamovich, who had worked for "World Literature" before emigrating in 1923, commented that the evening was attended rather more by the émigré community than by Soviet representatives, and noted that Zamiatin was a marvellous reader.[92] Despite this manifestation of interest in him, some émigrés felt that he never integrated properly in France. Zinaida Gippius in 1934 would dismiss him rather cattily as "a semi-Soviet semi-émigré."[93] In *The Italics are Mine*, Nina Berberova expressed the not entirely convincing view that "He didn't get to know anybody, didn't consider himself an émigré, and lived with the hope of returning home at the very first opportunity." She apparently only met Zamiatin once, spending a couple of hours with him in a café during July 1932. She was irked by what she perceived as his rather superior, patronising tone, and put off by what he apparently told her about his intention to "sit things out quietly." "I suddenly understood that he had nothing to live for, he had nothing to write about and no-one to write it for, that he detested them [the Bolsheviks], and rather scorned us. [...] Those [final] six years were a gift to him from Stalin."[94] These sorts of comments have hitherto largely shaped posterity's understanding of Zamiatin's somewhat subdued and enigmatic last years in Paris, and they clearly raise questions about his political position and his integrity in that regard.

By the end of July he managed to get away, and was back in the south of France again. He wrote to Nikitina:

> Paris is not Berlin, nor Moscow; as far as telephones are concerned things are rather inadequate, not many people have them, and I spent half my life in the metro. [...] I'm as tired as a shock-worker. Especially since I wasted half of July over the business of extending the French visas for myself and Liudm[ila] Nik[olaevna] (the visa expired on 5 August). I have a good number of distinguished French acquaintances, and I started, as I can tell you, with the Minister—but by the time you've gone from the Minister to the passport office in the *préfecture*... [...] But in any case, that's all behind me now, and I'll be here until the middle of October. [...] And maybe I'll be able to make a trip to America later in the autumn. One way and another my American friends have made quite a stir about me there, and I've had a heap of enquiries from American publishers.

He was careful to suggest to his correspondent in Leningrad that he might return to Russia before the end of 1932, "but in any case I have leave of absence from the Institute until 1 January, and it would be good to make use of that to the full." He therefore entrusted Nikitina with a couple of practical tasks: extending the tenancy agreement on his flat from the beginning of October for another six months "or maybe another year, to be on the safe side"; and passing the royalties for *The Flea* on to Agrafena Pavlovna, who had been poorly and had still not managed to find a new job. He also told Nikitina about the cultural scene in Paris: "The spring season in Paris was served with a Russian sauce this year: the Russian opera with Chaliapin, the Russian ballet, and an exhibition of Russian artists. [...] And then to complete my education there was the Grand Prix. Now that was a spectacle! Rothschild's trotters prancing about, the ladies, the President in top hat and white gloves. This was already the closing of the season, and at the final curtain, on the 14th of July, there were patriotic foxtrots on the streets and in the cafés, and a sky [...] full of wonderful fireworks... And that was the end of my season and of my visa affairs, and I climbed into a car (not mine, alas), and sped down south—via Grenoble and through the Alps. A marvellous journey." He had also been attending one of the two most significant Russian art exhibitions to be mounted in Paris during his years in France. Partly organised by Boris Grigor'ev, it reflected to a large extent the artists of the "World of Art" group, many of them now living abroad.[95] It was the son of one of these artists, Aleksandr Benois, who was driving from Paris to southern Italy and gave Zamiatin a lift to the Riviera. To this long letter Liudmila added a brief note: "I've been swimming and sunbathing until I can take no more. We eat grapes, which we steal from the vineyards. We do the same for figs and peaches, since it's acceptable to do that here."[96]

Zamiatin complained to Reavey that in the latter part of July he'd been working "…as a galley-slave over some scenario for talkies. It was a very urgent and I should add—not very pleasant work. [sic]"[97] This was another indication of the rather unwelcome shift towards writing for the cinema which would occupy more time than he wanted over the next few years. That summer and early autumn he also corresponded with the choreographer Leonid Miasin [Massine] in London, in the hope of getting him to accept two scripts based on Russian *"byliny"* [heroic tales] for the ballet, possibly using Borodin's 2nd Symphony. Unfortunately this project came to nothing.[98] By September he reported to Postnikov that so far his endeavours had amounted to: "More fireworks than francs: several interviews, 5–6 stories in newspapers and magazines (French), a fairly pointed article about the theatre in *Le Mois*, and a larger more "academic" one in *Mercure de France* (probably in their next, October number). *The Flea*, translated into French, had already been taken on by a fine theatre, the Pigall [sic], but cruel fate decreed that the theatre should go up in a puff of smoke and be turned into a cinema… *The Bellringers*, also now translated, are still doing the rounds of various theatres. Something more definite may come of the one-act play I made from my *Cave*, which will evidently go on this winter in the Montparnasse Theatre, but even that is progressing like a snail, and goodness knows when it will finally get there…"[99]

For the second phase of their stay in the south the Zamiatins had decided to move out of Villa Borisella, down to the nearby seaside resort of Cros-de-Cagnes, where they rented a place of their own in a small street leading directly down to the sea-front, the Villa Simple Abri. It seems that the move down to Cros-de-Cagnes was accompanied by some sort of cooling in the relations between the two couples. A month later Grigor'ev wrote in a moment of exasperation to a mutual friend in Prague: "In such difficult times, apart from anything else, the Zamiatins 'moved in' in Soviet fashion, and took over my house. We have become entirely disappointed in them. Thank God, it seems they've fixed themselves up somewhere else!"[100] Grigor'ev, whose letters reflect a certain taste for melodrama, seems not to have borne a grudge for too long, but in any case their lives began to follow separate paths soon thereafter, when he started to travel more frequently abroad. On 5 August Zamiatin told Fedin:

> Liudmila Nikolaevna and I have rented the top floor of a small villa here: [...] two rooms, a kitchen, a bathroom, and a space on the roof for *dolce far niente* and sun-bathing. [...] For the time being all this has been rented (very cheaply) for a month: in a month's time we may move to St-Tropez, not far from Toulon. [...] We're trying not to look far ahead: I've already lost the habit of living on firm foundations, in a settled way, with a tomorrow and a day-after-tomorrow. It's most likely that I will spend quite a long time in the south, or so it seems—I have to continue a novel [*The Scourge of God*] which I have begun to work on here. [...] And just visible in the distance, like the mountains here [...] is my America. And perhaps that's where it will remain—neither Mohammed to the mountain, nor the mountain to Mohammed. And equally far away lies my step-mother, Russia. I don't think I will get there earlier than the New Year. Let's see which way our literary cart turns next—just in case it turns off the highway down a narrow path again, where your eyes and ears become so covered in Averbakhian dust that you can't breathe. *A propos d'*Averbakh: I was almost certain that they wouldn't print my letter. And that's fine.

He also asked Fedin to tell his wife that "all the women here go around in trousers, never any other way, and they call them pyjamas—but they're trousers."[101] The idea of moving to St-Tropez had arisen because Vladimir Pozner's father Solomon, with whom he was also very friendly, had taken a villa there, and Zamiatin was hoping he might allow them to stay there cheaply for a while.[102] A week later, Liudmila wrote again to Nikitina: "We walk a lot and we go out in a car. But the constant greenery, the constant sunshine, the tranquillity of nature, the quiet and the ease are somehow beginning to pall. And I'm thinking with pleasure about our return to Paris. For me it remains still an almost unknown city." She thanked Nikitina for all the tasks she was carrying out on their behalf, and added: "I'm greatly in your debt—I will somehow repay you, when I return."[103]

Zamiatin and Liudmila stayed on in Cros-de-Cagnes rather longer than the month initially projected: "Firstly, I was obliged as soon as I'd arrived here to draft a fairly long interview in English for London, about Russian literature. And then various cinematic acquaintances started to get at me, which ended with my being signed up to do a scenario for a large French film company [Gaumont]. It was very hurried and exhausting work, and it would have been much more interesting and useful for me to write my novel, but I needed francs urgently, and this all the same was a more or less frankish business."[104] He now intended to stay in the south until about 20 October, but in the meantime he began to feel ill "with something like flu, or malaria."[105]

On 27 September, Fedin wrote to him again from Germany, asking whether he'd been following events in the Russian papers, such as the build-up to the celebration of Gor'ky's achievements. This event, marking forty years of Gor'ky's literary activity, was acidly reported as the "apotheosis of Gor'ky" by Eugene Lyons: "The Bolshoy Theater was the setting. All the important political leaders, from Stalin down, were on the stage; all the kosher men of letters, the goose-stepping artists, the successful flatterers were there." This was the occasion when Gor'ky's home-town of Nizhny Novgorod, and the main street in Moscow, Tverskaia, as well as the Moscow Arts Theatre, Chekhov's theatre, were all renamed after Gor'ky. "Everything that an all-powerful dictatorship could do to exalt and flatter and overawe the shaggy and rather pathetic old man was done. [...] When he rose to speak his voice was curiously sad, self-deprecating. 'No mortal man,' he said, 'could possibly deserve all this.' But he did not find in himself the strength to utter words like 'freedom' and 'idealism' and 'beauty'— words that were the keynotes in the symphony of his genius."[106]

Fedin went on to bring Zamiatin some more, really startling news about the indignant letter he'd written to Moscow at the end of March: "I'm sending you a wonder of wonders: your letter, printed in *Literaturnaia gazeta*! Without any commentaries, without annotations, without references, without any cuts, without any promises by the editors to 'return to this question,' without any 'by and larges,' without 'howevers' or 'buts.' And they say there are no mysteries in the world. How can there not be! There certainly are…"[107] The letter had been published in *Literaturnaia gazeta* ten days previously, and was even reprinted the following day in *Izvestiia*. That paper's editor, Ivan Gronsky, later recalled how Stalin had again taken a very close, personal interest in Zamiatin's affairs, and given him a dressing-down for his initial reluctance to publish it: "You acted wrongly. It's very easy to create an enemy. If you offend someone, you turn him into an enemy. But turning him into a friend is more onerous, and turning a person into one of us is even harder."[108] The project of bringing

Zamiatin back into the fold was evidently by now a specific ideological target in Stalin's eyes.

The couple now hoped to return to Paris by 1 November. Zamiatin started asking Annenkov for advice about where they might live — would the small flat on rue Duranton be available?[109] Unfortunately, Annenkov had let the flat go by then. In mid-October Zamiatin wrote to Reavey, comically grumbling that he had lost track of him: "I am started a long and difficult fight with a new novel. What a mess! Never write any novel—that is my testament to you. [sic]"[110] In fact, their stay in the south dragged on, and on 11 November Zamiatin wrote to Fedin:

> Even four days ago it was summer, and now it's the devil knows what. And I'm feeling dismal accordingly. I am staying here until the middle of next week because of various cinema commitments, and then Liudmila Nikolaevna and I will go together to Paris. Annenkov and Savich write to me that Babel' is there, and Erenburg has returned as well. It will be interesting to meet up with them. It's such a nuisance that you can't get the newspapers here, and from the Paris-based Russian papers you only get a very distant impression of what's going on in Russian literature.

He was curious to know how the plans for the new Writers' Union were shaping up: "If you still have any *Lit[eraturnaia] gazeta*, any recent copies […], and if you don't need them, please send them to me. […] A couple of weeks ago I wrote to the Embassy about extending our passports. They've promised to do it, and meanwhile we are quietly living on expired ones… Yesterday L[iudmila N[ikolaevna] and I were playing poker with some friends (after a long abstinence). We came home, and she sighed: 'No, it was more fun playing with Fedin and Aliansky…' And that's true."[111] This, then, was the moment when their allotted "one year" abroad came to an end. It does seem astonishing that the Russian (and the French) authorities were content for Zamiatin and his wife simply to let their passports expire, and he shows no sign of anxiety over this matter, clearly believing that he still continued to be regarded benevolently by both sides. This was in any case a moment when diplomatic relations between the two countries were particularly cordial, culminating in the signing by the French and Soviet governments on 29 November 1932 of a Pact of Non-aggression and Non-interference.[112]

It was presumably due to Kunina-Aleksander's efforts that translations of "Behind the Scenes" and *The Yawl* appeared in *Ruski arkhiv* in Yugoslavia during 1932. She was also trying to arouse interest in *We* in Ljubljana, and he told her that it wasn't worth trying to get a copy of the novel from "Petropolis" in Berlin, "since they don't have any more copies of the text in Russian, and you'll be able to obtain the French version from me more quickly."[113] On 15 October came his most significant publication in France to date, when *The Flood* appeared in *La Revue de France*, followed there in November-December by "Le théâtre russe contemporain," based on the lecture which he'd given in Prague a year earlier.[114] Almost his final publication that year was his piece on childhood in the Soviet Union, "Enfants Soviétiques," about the humourless, vocational focus of Soviet education, which had substituted the dogma of Communist ideology for the precepts of religious faith; this appeared in *Marianne* on 21 December.[115] After the Zamiatins had returned to Paris, a couple of new publications appeared, which extended the process of introducing him to the West. Marc Slonim included a section on him in his new book, *Portraits of Soviet Writers*. And Werth published further pieces on him in the *Manchester Guardian* (6 and 7 December), based on interviews he had conducted with him down at the little villa in Cros-de-Cagnes. This time the subject matter was specifically the theatre in Soviet Russia, covering Stanislavsky and Meierkhol'd as well as more recent significant theatrical figures.[116]

Zamiatin wrote to Fedin, who was now in Berlin, thanking him for sending the newspapers he'd asked for. He'd attempted to imagine himself at the meetings of the organising committee for the projected new Union of Writers, which had taken place in October and November, "and I must admit, it didn't come off, my imagination couldn't encompass it, just as I couldn't imagine Bely or Pasternak there…" He then described the difficulties of their return north: "The first week after our arrival in Paris went by in the most disagreeable fashion, in hunting for a flat. At last we've moved in—and, it seems, we've been caught out, because it's rather cold. I'm now sitting and with great urgency I'm writing an article for an English newspaper about… shipbuilding in Russia. And then simultaneously it'll be the turn of a scenario for Gaumont and my novel, which is progressing at an unbearable, tortoise-like pace, because all the time I'm obliged to be distracted by various small-scale tasks."[117] On 12 December he told Kunina-Aleksander that their apartment was at 22 rue Lamblardie, in the 12th *arrondissement*: "I'm tired—there's been a lot of rushing around, not just for business, but also for fun—I'd become very monastic in the south, and had got fed up with that. But soon I'll be getting back down to work."[118] On the same day he told Postnikov that their two weeks in Paris had felt cold and grey after the south: "And unfortunately Liudmila Nikolaevna has rather succumbed: that old business with her bronchial glands has flared up, she needs treatment and to have massages with oil and so on. I'm mobilising my finances for this business."[119]

In the closing days of 1932, the Zamiatins wrote letters to Bulgakov in Moscow and to Postnikov in Prague. Liudmila wrote first to Bulgakov, on Christmas Eve: "Some *Réveillon*, when it's 15 degrees above zero [...]! No, for Christmas Eve I prefer frost, snow and bright stars, and to see in the New Year not in a restaurant in Montmartre, but in Moscow or in Leningrad—and with you, dear Mikhail Afanas'evich. That's the wish I'm making for myself for 1933. [...] We got shamelessly stuck down on the Riviera, and only came back to Paris about a month ago. EI was doing a filmscript in Nice, then he was writing his novel, and I bathed and bathed, and maybe I overdid it, because I haven't been feeling too well in Paris. And Paris is so beautiful and dynamic and fantastical, and I'm constantly, every day discovering something new for myself." On Christmas Day itself, Zamiatin added his own message, complaining comically about the cacophonous radios he could hear from all over their building, and reporting that they were living reasonably well, because just before Christmas he had managed to collect the various sums he was owed for his work:

> In one of the editorial offices (*Revue de France*, which is their "thick journal"), an incident occurred which can only be described as mystical: before me there appeared Marcel Prévost, who I had assumed to be dead, but he is alive and even, as it turns out, an immortal [he was elected a member of the Académie Française or *immortel* in 1909]. Our acquaintance came about on the basis of *The Flood*, which they had printed, and which had gripped the old man. Well, he's a *demi-vierge*. [Prévost had written a scandalous play, *Les Demi-vierges*, in 1895]. But I did once spend some time sitting with Maurois—and then I thought of you—that's someone you would enjoy talking to, there's a man with an attractive mind. God knows I'm missing you and your wife, but we are unlikely to see you before the spring: various projects have been started and are not yet completed, and so our

passports have been extended for another six months for the time being. The other day I saw that Muscovite of yours, Babel'. Uh-huh, your lives over there are certainly full of excitement at the moment...[120]

Four days later he wrote to the Postnikovs, revealing a rather less buoyant mood as he and Liudmila settled into life in their new flat:

Dear friends, I thank you for your letter. These are not just words, they are genuine. It's easier to live when you know that somewhere, even in a far-off land, there are good people who think well of you. Although I have a reputation as a "tough" person, oh Lord, sometimes it happens to me too that I strip off all my outer garments and stand naked — and then, when I find myself all alone among the rocks, it feels fairly chilly in this wide world... However, it is not worth continuing further on this unholidayish theme. Over these last days I've been sitting writing a film-script for a French company [*Sten'ka Razin* for Vandor Films, intended for Chaliapin, but never realised] — instead of carrying on with my novel, so I was writing and spitting at the same time. As a result, there is a kind of dreary slush in my heart, like the Parisian winter [...] But for the moment things are not too bad: we can eat and drink, pay for the flat, and travel in the metro. As for what happens next, well, we'll see; we've already learned not to try to guess more than a month or two ahead. [...] In Paris we're living in a kind of seclusion, we have hardly any acquaintances nearby, and often you don't feel like dragging yourself into the metro, and so I rarely see anybody. I saw Babel' and I saw Erenburg.[121]

The year actually closed with events reflecting his original profession. First, there was the publication on 31 December of an item in the *Trade Review* of *The Glasgow Herald* by "Professor Eugene Zamiatin of the Leningrad Shipbuilding Institute," entitled "Russian Shipbuilding: Problems following the Revolution. Recovery from Industrial Paralysis. Second Five-Year Plan."[122] On that same day, the authorities at the Shipbuilding Institute sent him a telegram to tell him that, in response to his letter received on 21 December, he was granted permission to extend his period of leave from Leningrad further, until the autumn of 1933.[123]

Chapter 9:
Paris (1933–1937)

After an entire year abroad, the Zamiatins had finally settled in Paris, more self-sufficient now with their own apartment, but in some respects perhaps feeling a little more isolated, rather less closely supported by the friends who had welcomed them on their first arrival. Their Soviet passports would continue to be renewed, each time apparently without difficulty, but they were still far from clear about their future. The dilemma about whether to return eventually to the USSR would continue to loom over them.

The first extant letters they wrote in 1933 were to Elena, Annenkov's ballerina wife, who had already gone back to Russia for family reasons. Zamiatin repeated to her the story of their search for an apartment: "You know that in this respect I'm a fussy chap, I have to be somewhere that's very quiet, and this, and that. And then in the end we were so exhausted that we took the first thing which turned up: *appartements meublés*, two very nice rooms, a bathroom, hot water, gas, a lift and even a telephone in the apartment. A minute and a half from the metro, although it's true that we're not close to the centre." His shifting over towards writing film-scripts was at least providing them with an adequate income: "The cinema is the only thing at the moment where they pay people of our sort decently. Quite a few of my stories have been translated here and printed, but you don't get francs for those, just 'franclets.' Which, as you well know, trickle out of your pockets here extremely quickly. And time passes quickly too: it's been almost a year now, and it's as though it had never happened! Then there was the New Year, which I saw in fairly thoroughly—and came home at half past seven in the morning; my last stopping-point was La Coupole in Montparnasse, where a somewhat tipsy Kiki—whom you know well—was doing such things!" Elsewhere he described how Kiki, the artists' model, singer, and companion of Man Ray during the 1920s, had taken offence at the bourgeois customers in the restaurant that New Year's Eve, and flashed her naked breasts and bottom at them while the barmen looked on with indifference. Liudmila added to Annenkova: "Paris is beautiful and elegant and lively. But I don't need to write that to you—you know this very well yourself, and remember it. [...] I think you are glad to have moved back to Moscow; you're happy there, is that right? I'm glad for you and for your mother."[1]

In February, Liudmila complained to Bulgakov that she'd received no reply to her December letter. "So what about you, are you planning to come to the West? When? This spring? This summer? *Au revoir, mon cher ami*, I don't want to think that you have already said *adieu* to me."[2] These last remarks, from someone who had succeeded in leaving Stalin's Russia to one who had desperately and vainly attempted to do so for several years, could have seemed insensitive; but perhaps they reflect the ongoing belief the Zamiatins still had that travelling to the West might largely be a matter of timing, and of good luck. After all, Babel' had recently arrived (in September 1932) with the intention of living in Paris for a whole year. That stay of his included six weeks in Italy visiting Gor'ky in the spring of 1933, until the latter's final—as it turned out—return to Russia in May; the comic writers Il'f and Petrov would also visit Paris during 1933. Liudmila makes another, tantalising remark in this letter, where she mentions that she'd hoped to see Bulgakov's photograph in the New Year's edition of *Literaturnaia gazeta*, adding: "I didn't find my first husband there either. And I so wanted to have a look at you both." This is the only surviving reference to a "husband" Liudmila may have had before she settled down with Zamiatin, and it isn't clear to whom she's referring (perhaps her early fellow-revolutionary Boris Krylov?). She also mentioned that Zamiatin had been very busy with his latest filmscript, a talkie of *Anna Karenina* commissioned by Fedor Otsep for Pathé-Nathan.

Over several months, Bulgakov kept starting replies, which have been preserved although they were never sent; on 10 April 1933 he explained that he had divorced Liubov' Evgen'evna and married a woman they had not met, Elena Sergeevna Shilovskaia, who was to become the prototype of his heroine in *The Master and Margarita*. He had been dreaming of Paris because he was working on a biography of Molière, and he too had been adapting Tolstoy, but for the theatre: "And so you've tied the knot with Anna Karenina? My God! The very word 'Tolstoy' inspires horror in me! I wrote a stage adaptation of *War and Peace*. And now I can't walk past the shelf where Tolstoy stands without a shudder; may adaptations be cursed forever and ever, amen! And you ask when I am planning to come to the West? Just fancy, many people have been asking me that question over the last three months..."[3] To a close friend in Moscow at this time Bulgakov wrote: "My heart misses a beat at the thought of rivers, bridges, seas. There is a gypsy moan in my soul. But it will pass."[4]

The work on his own Tolstoy adaptation took over Zamiatin's life during the ensuing weeks, as he complained to Nikitina in March: "At the moment I'm quarrelling and arguing with Lev Nikolaevich Tolstoy: I'm doing a screen version of *Anna Karenina*. For the French version (there will be German and English ones too) the dialogues will be polished up by André Gide. Not long ago Liudmila and I went to see the Hollywood (silent) version of *Anna Karenina*: now there was a peculiar business! Well, let's hope that I'll turn out something a little less sprawling. It's very interesting work, but to tell the truth it's devilishly difficult. [...] I'll probably spend another month or so on it, and then I'll try to go away somewhere and get a holiday—if of course I don't tie myself down in the meantime with another new job, which is very likely. [...] From the beginning of the summer I'm hoping to get back down to my novel."[5] The silent version of *Anna Karenina* they saw was probably the 1927 MGM film with Greta Garbo; the Otsep version which Zamiatin worked on for the rest of 1933 never did make it into production, however, probably because it was eclipsed by MGM's own 1935 talkie remake, starring Garbo once again and released that August.[6]

During the spring or early summer of 1933, they seem to have managed to get away to the seaside, to Brittany, one of the favourite holiday destinations of the Erenburgs. They also moved house some time after mid-March, abandoning rue Lamblardie, which is in one of the eastern districts of Paris, for 14 rue Raffet in the elegant 16th *arrondissement*, in the west. Populated by the more affluent Russians, this was where a number of their closest friends lived, including the Remizovs and Annenkov, who were just 5 minutes' walk away on rue Boileau. Although initially they seem to have viewed it as a temporary move, this third-floor flat on a quiet street sloping steadily up towards the Bois de Boulogne would become the Zamiatins' home for the rest of his lifetime.

At the very end of June he wrote both personal and official letters to the Director of the Leningrad Shipbuilding Institute, requesting permission to extend his leave yet again, and to renew the tenancy on his flat, citing both his work and his health in justification. They had shown remarkable patience with him back in Leningrad, but on 20 October he was finally dismissed from his post in charge of foreign languages at the Institute, for his failure to return from leave—by which time he had been away from his duties for about two years.[7]

During the summer, and again in December, Zamiatin was working on articles under the title "Moscow-Petersburg." These were the pieces he'd been trying to make a start on the previous year in Cagnes, commissioned by Roman Jakobson in Prague for the Berlin/Leipzig journal *Slavische Rundschau*. In an analysis of the way literature had developed during the Soviet period, he extended the elegant distinction originally drawn by Gogol', in which he characterised Moscow and Petersburg as having respectively feminine and masculine characteristics, shaped not only by the accident of the grammatical gender of their names in Russian: "Moscow gave herself up to the Revolution in a more impetuous fashion, more recklessly, and more unquestioningly than St Petersburg [...] and that's understandable: St Petersburg has to bear the heavy burden of cultural traditions, which are especially apparent in the sphere of art. Lacking this heavy baggage, travelling light, the Muscovite muses dashed ahead, overtaking not only St Petersburg, but also Europe and sometimes common sense at the same time. [...] Petersburg remains a window into Europe, towards the West; while Moscow has become a door through which 'America' has flooded into Russia from the East, across Asia." Reviewing here not only painting, architecture and music, but also theatrical design and drama, he saw the "American" impulse towards the unusual, the sensational and the shocking epitomised in the work of the Muscovite Meierkhol'd, although Stanislavskian traditionalism was now beginning to reassert its hold in the theatre again. Zamiatin considered the moves towards creating a single Soviet Artists' Union over the previous year as a largely positive development, presaging an end to the wrangling for legitimacy over avant-garde and revolutionary status in art.[8]

By the middle of August he had retreated for his summer holiday to Clamart, as he told Kunina-Aleksander:

> I'm writing this to you, fortunately, not from Paris, but from a *dacha* outside Paris, near the woods of Meudon. There's a storm outside the window, a downpour, and the old trees in the park have been rejuvenated and are breathing as deeply as they can. [...] I've been living here for about a week, or rather I lie in the

park with a book (or else just the sky) in front of my eyes, and I've already recovered a little from Paris, the asphalt, the petrol, the heat, the bustle and the rush. One way and another I got worn out there recently, and was feeling really rotten—and so instead of all sorts of distant travels I decided to drop my anchor somewhere not too far away for 2–3 weeks, and for the moment I don't regret it. And then later we can see. There are various "foreign" plans: I'm being enticed to go to Italian Switzerland,—to Como, and to Spain, and, by the way, to Yugoslavia.

But shortly afterwards he had to report to her the utter collapse of his schemes: "I had various plans for travelling, and even two weeks ago I was sure that I'd soon be on Lake Como, and had already obtained the visa—but then everything changed." One reason was the exciting news of a plan to stage *The Flea* in French: "I'll need to keep an eye on the production, so that it doesn't turn out too peculiar (if it goes on at all: these days you always have to allow for the likelihood, right up to the very last, that the whole business will fall through for some reason). And the second thing is that I'm writing to you lying down—I'm ill, and very unpleasantly so: the pains are such that I probably wouldn't even be frightened of childbirth right now. It's an acute attack of sciatica, or maybe something worse."[9]

He wrote in a similar vein three weeks later to the wealthy V.P. Krymov, one of several new Russian arrivals in Paris from Berlin that year, in the aftermath of Hitler's appointment as Chancellor and the Reichstag Fire: "I'm so upset that I can't come to you on Sunday—I really can't tell you. Over the two or three days since our telephone conversation I've managed to be transformed into a fixed object, and I'm writing you this letter lying down. In the best case it's an acute attack of sciatica, but the doctor is inclined (because of the intensity of the pain) to reckon on something worse: an inflammation and infection of the hip joint." The prime mover in the project to stage *The Flea* was an actor, Paul Oettly, and after a meeting at the café Les Deux Magots on 28 August, Zamiatin was asking Krymov, at Oettly's behest, whether he might be prepared to invest about twenty thousand francs in the show. "This production of *The Flea* has acquired a particular importance for me, because I'm afraid my doctor may be right, and ill-health may put me out of commission for several months."[10] Oettly was intending to open his new youth theatre with *The Flea* that autumn.[11] Rehearsals were soon under way, and Zamiatin, who had returned to

Paris on 19 September, was at least fit enough now to attend them: "I'm not very satisfied with it for the time being, and of course it's a far cry from Moscow."[12] Early in November he described his play to Bulgakov as something quite alien to the French: "my *Flea* hops right outside the inevitable adulterous canon here." He was still expecting the production to première at the end of the month, with sets for which Annenkov had made preliminary sketches.[13] Within days, however, it emerged that Annenkov would not be able to complete them after all: he had unexpectedly been offered a four-month film contract, and had left Paris. This was probably an important break for Annenkov, who like Zamiatin was coming under financial pressure to switch over from the theatre to the cinema. Starting from that year, Annenkov would go on eventually to create the sets and costumes for over 60 films.[14] By late November it had emerged that the première would take place not in Paris at all, but in a Brussels theatre, La Gaîté, on 5 December, with the one in Paris due to follow a fortnight or so later.[15]

By now his literary life in emigration was beginning to settle into a fairly unassuming routine. Apart from the filmscripts and translated stories there were occasional articles for the British press. On 21 September, *The Glasgow Herald* contacted Alexander Werth in Paris, asking him to negotiate with Zamiatin over a further article on Russian shipbuilding for their *Trade Review*: "The returns from Russia always present a difficulty, and I am rather doubtful as to their accuracy, and it would be a great advantage to have a note from Mr Zamiatine [*sic*] giving the details of the year's work by the various Russian shipyards. [...] The payment for the Russian contribution would be 7 guineas."[16] We may wonder, incidentally, how the Soviet Embassies in London and Paris felt about Zamiatin providing "more accurate" statistics about this strategically important arm of Soviet industry than were readily available in official publications during the 1930s.

The later part of September 1933 brightened for the Zamiatins with the visit to Paris of Irina Kunina-Aleksander together with her husband Bozhidar, whom they had not met. While they were there, Zamiatin inscribed a copy of the German text of "Moscow-Petersburg" to Bozhidar Aleksander, "as a token of the beginning of our friendship."[17] The article came out in Dutch that month, and Kunina-Aleksander's translation into Serbo-Croat appeared in October. That year, she also arranged for the publication of "The Russian Theatre Today" in Yugoslavia. In a letter after their visit he thanked her "...above all for yourself: here you so rarely meet people with blood inside them rather than petrol, with a heart rather than a little motorised pump." Liudmila added an affectionate note to Irina and to her "Bozhii dar" [God's gift]. Kunina-Aleksander sent sleeping pills soon afterwards, for which he was very grateful: "Once again I've slept like a child for two nights. My sciatic torments, for my sins, are not yet over, but all the same they have eased. I'm now applying a 'sweating system' as a treatment: every second day they place me in a wooden cage (with just my head poking out) and they cook me for half-an-hour with hot steam. These are preparatory classes for entering hell, which squeeze every drop of sweat out of you. But they seem to help. I need a copy of 'Moscow-Petersburg' for translation into English. Would you kindly send me the text you have—I don't have any left."[18]

In early November, they both wrote to Bulgakov, Zamiatin to congratulate him on his new family. "Dear Molière Afanas'evich, […] ah, you young folk, you young folk, such a flighty lot! […] As you can see, my flea affairs, as well as certain prospects for another play and film, unfortunately still delay me here, so our meeting will have to be put off again. Well, what's to be done, what's to be done! Don't forget me, and do write." In her letter, Liudmila explained about their visit to Brittany that spring: "And then there was all the business of trying to get visas for Italy, and frequent excursions to places around Paris (which are charming!). And then in September *mon cher mari* fell ill." She reproached Bulgakov for not having written to them sooner, and declared playfully: "You can be glad—thanks to you I've become more indifferent to my homeland, and have begun to think less and dream less about it… We live near the Bois de Boulogne […]. In the spring and the summer we often went for walks there, and now we go by car—we have French acquaintances who have cars, and so they come by to pick up the poor invalid, and give him a chance to breathe some fresh air. I've got very weary during EI's illness, both physically, and in terms of morale. So I'm not responding well to Paris at the moment, although I love it very much and have got used to it. […] Let Elena Sergeevna keep her promise and bring you to Europe."[19]

Konstantin Fedin as ever seemed to have no difficulty getting permission to travel (admittedly on medical grounds) abroad. He wrote from Italy in October about his plan to visit Paris, hoping that Zamiatin or Pozner might help him obtain a French visa, and then again in November, with a long and frank letter full of news of Russia: "Where shall I start? Perhaps with the fact that they hear too little about you over there, at home, and that everyone I meet always questions me as to whether I know about your plans, whether you're writing and so on." He had heard that Agrafena Pavlovna had found a job, and was still managing to keep their flat for them, although there were always anxious moments when the tenancy came up for renewal; and that Nikitina had been energetic in protecting Zamiatin's interests, although she too was wondering about his plans, especially since she was quizzed about them whenever she went to collect his royalties.

Fedin described the ways the cities had changed externally, with St Petersburg now flooded by electric light and Moscow becoming covered in asphalt. He also talked about how difficult life had become back home—allowing himself this liberty, presumably, because he was writing from Italy rather than from within the USSR. Policing was oppressive, and there were shortages of food and petrol, and epidemics of typhus. "The people are underfed and tired, and they drink too much. [...] I'm writing all of this, it goes without saying, for you personally. That is, for sensible and private use only. When we meet (which I'm hoping for very much), I'll tell you about many other things, about the bottomless contradictions, which are becoming deeper and deeper. [...] It would be difficult to run through all our mutual friends, and in some cases it would be too sad. Again—until we meet." He described attending Pil'niak's birthday in Moscow before he left: "now there's a man who's strongly suffering from loneliness, in a literary sense." And he mentioned having visited Gor'ky more than once since the latter's return, including an occasion when the guests of honour had been Stalin, Lazar Kaganovich (one of Stalin's most loyal henchmen) and Nikolai Bukharin. "Our brother-writers behaved despicably. Alesha [Aleksei Tolstoy] played the jester and clown all night. [...] An utterly sad picture but, so to speak, a revealing one. Around Alesha there's a whole lot of riff-raff, he sees that perfectly well, but he's given up even worrying about it." Fedin also commented on the recent award of the 1933 Nobel Prize for Literature to Ivan Bunin, now living in Paris, which he felt Bunin deserved both in literary and personal terms.[20] The Prize was awarded "for the strict artistry" with which he had maintained "the classical Russian traditions in prose writing." In his acceptance speech, Bunin observed that it was the first time the prize had been awarded to a man in exile, and he used the occasion as an opportunity to reiterate his belief that civilisation itself depended on freedom of speech and conscience. This sensational event was widely seen as an aggressively defiant gesture towards Moscow, and a triumph for the White emigration.

In reply, Liudmila told Fedin they had already heard about the current hardships in Russia: "And we're living in such a bourgeois fashion that sometimes it's rather repellent and unpleasant to think about how people who are close to us are having to live over there." In his own letter to "dear Kosten'ka" Zamiatin told him about his health problems: "I've become so important that the policemen stop the traffic when I'm crossing the street: they take me for a distinguished veteran of the Great War. For I walk with a stick, and mostly using only one leg… I've begun making jokes about this only now; but a month ago, and before that, it was no laughing matter. Just imagine that instead of your left leg you had a painful tooth a metre long, and that unfortunately there was no possibility of going to get that tooth pulled out. This nasty business is called sciatica, and I've never experienced anything worse in my entire life. During the whole of September, when I was at a *dacha* not far from Paris, I slept only 2–3 hours in 24. My nurse Liudmila Nikolaevna has worn herself to a rag fussing over me. All our plans for the summer foundered because of this (and we had visas for Italy actually in our pockets!). Since October I've moved back to Paris—or rather back to my bed in my Paris apartment. It only began to ease during November, and now I've begun to 'get about' a little. […] Last season was a cinematic one for me, and this one, it seems, is going to turn out theatrical."

He was looking forward very much to Fedin's visit, and boasted that he would be able to pull some strings on his behalf, using the Interior Minister's secretary, "who seems to be a fan of mine," and Benjamin Crémieux, Head of the Press Section at the Foreign Ministry. Reminding him that he'd also need two French sponsors, he recommended André Maurois and Drieu la Rochelle: "They are both very nice people, and I know them both well: I'll ring them, and I'm sure they'd be delighted to stand guarantee for you."[21] Evidently he had become quite friendly with Maurois, who addressed him in one letter as *"mon cher ami,"* and invited him to come and have a meal to discuss his play (presumably *The Flea*): *"J'ai lu les deux premiers actes ce matin et les aime beaucoup."*[22] Soon Fedin told Zamiatin that, thanks to his help, he was now able to plan a visit to Paris for the New Year, and he asked Liudmila to find out where he could get the pneumothorax treatment he would require while he was there.

Zamiatin also explained to Fedin that he would gladly have asked Pozner to help over the visa, especially given his own limited mobility, but he feared that by now this might prove counter-productive. Pozner had joined the French Communist Party in 1932, moving to become very close to the hardline, pro-Moscow Paul Vaillant-Couturier, editor of the Party organ *L'Humanité*. He was therefore likely to be regarded with suspicion in French government circles.[23] Pozner thereby aligned himself directly with those who, like Erenburg and the Saviches, seemed unabashed in promoting Soviet interests abroad. Interestingly, no correspondence appears to have survived between Zamiatin and Pozner after 1932, and although he and Pozner's father Solomon continued to exchange friendly messages up until the end of 1933, including plans to meet socially, that correspondence also ceased.[24] This apparent parting of the ways helps us to understand better the limits of Zamiatin's own sympathies with pro-Communist groups in 1930s France. While he was never going to find common ground with the White émigrés, given his own Socialist Revolutionary convictions between 1905 and 1917, he continued to feel comfortable with more moderate left-wingers such as Barbusse, or indeed Annenkov, rather than with outright Soviet propagandists.

Towards the end of November he wrote again to Kunina-Aleksander, this time with some comments on her own work—a translation of Blok's *The Twelve* which he thought excellent (as far as he could judge the Serbo-Croat), as well as a story she had written. He went about this in a very systematic way, praising her prose but identifying weaknesses in the narrative structure, and moments when the main character was a little too dry or knowledgeable.[25] There was a generous pedagogic dimension, which Zamiatin took very seriously, in their relationship—perhaps because he had no other literary pupils to lavish attention on any more?

He had now managed to obtain a visa to travel to Brussels for the première of the French production of *The Flea*. As Zinaida Shakhovskaia explained, it was quite common at the time for Paris shows to be "tried out" in Brussels. She wrote about it for a left-wing newspaper, *Le Rouge et le Noir*, and gave a frank account of it in her memoirs: "*The Flea* was a flop—here in Brussels at least. The actors were desperately bad. And the text had become utter nonsense in translation, and was completely incomprehensible to the locals, as it would have been even to me, had I not known Leskov's flea story." She tried to say something consoling to Zamiatin as he came out gloomily after the sparsely-attended show: "In front of me stood a wiry, very upright man who seemed younger than his 49 years, and who somehow didn't look that much like a Russian; and yet if you looked closely—and despite his straight parting and a certain stiffness in his expression—he was definitely a Russian. I had already seen Russians like him, with fairly high cheekbones and narrow, almost Asiatically narrow eyes. Probably a more emotional man would not have liked to meet afterwards with someone who had been a witness to what for him had been such an unpleasant occasion. [...] Zamiatin turned out to be very charming and intelligent. At first he was rather reluctant to visit us, since he was apprehensive about having relations with White Russians. [...] On his subsequent visits he used to stay with us in our attic, where Vladimir Sirin [Nabokov] stayed, and [...] Marina Tsvetaeva, Marc Slonim, Don-Aminado and Teffi." It was at Shakhovskaia's that Nabokov first got to know Zamiatin, asking her on one occasion to pass on his warm greetings ("he's extremely likeable").[26] She clearly found Zamiatin intriguing, and subsequently offered a very persuasive analysis of his character, emphasising that duality which he was so aware of in himself:

> I've rarely seen in anyone else such energy and such an appetite for work, and I've also rarely met amongst Russians someone who had such a well-rounded education. [...] Puffing at his pipe, Zamiatin would read us his stories, delighting us with his language, and occasionally irritating us with the self-consciousness of his style. He was a kind man, and he was always concerned about the welfare of his friends who had stayed behind in Russia, and in particular about Anna Akhmatova. But he didn't have the lightness of character you associate with kind people. It was as though something was weighing him down, and it was not humour that he had, but a sarcasm born of scepticism, or possibly from despair. [...] Zamiatin commanded respect not just because of his profound decency, but also because of his very carefully concealed kindness. Perhaps he concealed it because it was a feeling he could not rationalise, and he believed in technology, in progress, in science, and in a creativity which could be strictly controlled and subjected to well-known laws, whereas his life and his own emotions didn't obey any laws that he could understand, and eluded analysis and precise definitions...[27]

Despite praise for the performance of Oettly in the part of "Leftie," *The Flea* received dreadful reviews in the Belgian press.[28] Zamiatin returned from Brussels to Paris on 10 December, and wrote Kunina-

Aleksander a surprisingly cheerful account in the circumstances, reporting that there'd even been talk of getting the play translated into Flemish: "The Paris première, it seems, will be next week." Prompted by some remarks Fedin had made about Akhmatova's financial difficulties, he urged her to send a gift for her to Leningrad, either in the form of a parcel or a Torgsin (foreign-currency store) credit.[29] The next day he asked Shakhovskaia to do the same, preferably by sending something to Agrafena Pavlovna, who would then deliver it to Akhmatova in person.[30] He gave Fedin one explanation for his relatively buoyant mood: "When I returned from Brussels it was already as a biped: it's not clear why, but my sciatica has disappeared almost without a trace (touch wood!), although I didn't keep to any special diets and even had a great deal to drink on a couple of occasions."[31]

In mid-December, Zamiatin completed the second part of the essay "Moscow-Petersburg," in which he again vaunted the élite status of St Petersburg in pre-Revolutionary days as the capital of Russian literature, looking down its nose at the perceived provincialism and brashness of Moscow. He described the April 1932 resolution of the Communist Party, which had dissolved RAPP, as a reaffirmation of the "Petersburg line" in the arts, and one which should inaugurate a new, significantly more promising chapter of Soviet literature, with a revival in the historical novel and a resurgence of the lyrical in poetry. It was possible, of course, that these gains would not remain secure. "But there are grounds for hoping that the vigour and youth of Soviet literature will win through. Over the last year there have been enough symptoms to justify such a hopeful diagnosis."[32]

The last week of 1933 was taken up with last-minute correspondence about Fedin's plans to come and stay in Paris in time for New Year's Eve, with Liudmila joyfully letting him know that the visa had finally been sent off: "You'll see how rich France is, how charming the French are, and how wonderful Paris is. [...] Come to us first of all, and then we'll think where to lodge you."[33] Zamiatin wrote to various friends with seasonal greetings, and thanked Kunina-Aleksander for sending a Torgsin credit to Akhmatova: "I've been suddenly cured of my sciatica, although the only curative waters in the spa town of Brussels were wines (which had been strictly forbidden to me by my doctors). After the Brussels performances, which were effectively dress rehearsals, it became apparent that it was vital to make a few changes in the cast; and for that reason the première of the play in Paris has been deferred." To the very last then, he remained determinedly hopeful about the Paris *Flea*. Liudmila added a note too: "You are a darling, for having sent money to Akhmatova. [...] We're expecting Fedin for the New Year (from Italy). And we will of course talk a lot together about you. I'm feeling less well than usual, but EI is already back on his feet, and is cheerful."[34]

In 1933 the flow of Zamiatin's publications slowed quite noticeably, with very little coming out that was new. In December, two further translations of his stories appeared—*Comrade Churygin Takes the Floor* in *La Revue de France*, and *Ten-minute Drama* in *Paris-Soir*. The first of these was prefaced with a note by "MP" describing Zamiatin as one of the greatest of young Russian talents, and reminding readers that he was the author of *The Flood*, published in the same journal a year earlier: "The story you are going to read is no less virtuosic, and what's more I don't think anyone has ever traced with a firmer or briefer hand the trajectory of the Russian Revolution."[35] Given the remarks Zamiatin had made to Bulgakov a year previously it seems likely that "MP" was in fact Marcel Prévost, whose public endorsement here must have given him considerable satisfaction. In January 1934 a couple of other pieces appeared. One was his humorous story *The Protectress of Sinners* in *Les Nouvelles Littéraires*.[36] The other was a completely contrasting publication, the piece commissioned by *The Glasgow Herald* on Russian shipbuilding, with the headings: "Higher Production at any Price—Watershed of the Two Five-year Plans—The Search for Higher Productivity—Intolerable Delay—The Cost of Production—Not According to Plan—the 1933 Programme—Recent Products of the Soviet Shipyards."[37]

On New Year's Day 1934, Remizov sent a note in his characteristic fantastical calligraphy encouraging them to visit, and reminding them that the house he lived in (at the same address as the theatre director Nikolai Evreinov), just along rue Boileau from Annenkov, was indeed "only a step away" from rue Raffet.[38] A requiem service for Andrei Bely, who died in Moscow on 8 January, took place in Paris on the evening of the 20th, so another planned meeting was put off. Zamiatin responded on the 30th with a return invitation.[39] Fedin was presumably involved in these gatherings as well, since the lodgings Zamiatin found for him were on rue Pierre Guérin,[40] the road which runs straight on from rue Boileau; in fact the house lived in by Remizov and Evreinov was directly visible from Fedin's own front door. A long letter at the end of January from Zamiatin to Kunina-Aleksander indicates that Fedin stayed in Paris for about six weeks in all:

Don't blame me, but blame Fedin for having hindered me from replying to you promptly. He landed on us on the evening of 31 December, and by 11pm he and I and Liudmila Nikolaevna (who was still suffering slightly from flu) set off to see in the New Year with one of my friends. […] We went on to Montparnasse, and only got home at around 7 in the morning. And so it went on for a couple of weeks or so… […] He's cheerful and happy, and has finished a novel (*The Rape of Europe*). […] In about 10 days' time he's planning to return to St Petersburg. Every two weeks here he has to undergo a pneumothorax procedure, but he has evidently got used to this by now. In any case, the other morning they pumped the air out of his lungs, and by 6 that evening he was already with me at a large cocktail party. He's just been here (he's living almost next door). […] I'm really sorry that he'll soon be leaving: he's one of the few Russian writers with whom I have truly friendly relations. And it was a pity that you weren't with him in Paris at the same time: we would have made up a cosy St Petersburg group. […] I'm already fed up with Paris. My affairs have turned sour. There are Stavitskys everywhere, including the theatre: that charming man and good actor who was staging *The Flea* also turned out to be a little Stavitsky. It's emerged that when he received the takings in Brussels, he didn't pay the actors, so the actors have now scattered in all directions, and *The Flea*, at least for the time being, is currently in a state of anabiosis here.

What I want to do is to abandon everything and sit down to the continuation of the novel I began long ago, and which I know is an interesting one. But—capitalism, capitalism! I simply cannot manage to balance my budget in such a way as to sit somewhere peacefully and write the novel. And for the moment I keep having to write various articles. I've made an agreement with *Marianne* in Paris (have you seen that magazine? It's published by "NRF"), that I'm going to provide them with a regular feature on "Lettres russes," about Russian literature. Maurois does a "Lettres anglaises" for them. What do you think of the possibility of using this material for the press in Yugoslavia? I'm sending you a brief article about Andrei Bely. I would like to mark his death in the foreign press. In Paris, for example, people don't know about him at all; but in Yugoslavia, as a Slav country, I think they will know him better.[41]

Later that year, he would describe Andrei Bely as "the Russian Joyce," and someone who had had a considerable influence upon himself.[42] Before they parted on 12 February, he presented Fedin with a photograph of himself, inscribed "To Kostya and to Russia, with great love, Evg. Zamiatin."[43]

His misspelled reference here to Paul Oettly as a "Stavitsky," in the sense of a conman, reflects an enormous scandal in French political life, which over the following fortnight was about to come to a head. The Russian Jew Alexandre Stavisky was being sought by the police in connection with a financial scam which threatened to compromise a number of local politicians in the town of Bayonne, and he was then found dead in a chalet in Chamonix. Even before his death, which may or may not have been suicide, the controversy was seized upon by a coalition of xenophobic right-wing groups who organised demonstrations in Paris on 6 February 1933, which turned very violent and led to many casualties; this was followed three days later by a counter-demonstration organised by the socialists, which left a further 9 people dead and over one thousand injured. Vladimir Pozner described accompanying Elsa Triolet there with Louis Aragon, who was reporting on the events for *L'Humanité*, and Triolet's horror when the police began to fire upon the demonstrators.[44] This became a major crisis in the life of the shaky Third Republic, leading to the fall of the government and catalysing the left wing to unite against Fascism. All of this drama, happening in Paris at the end of Fedin's visit, must surely have been something they followed closely.

Towards the end of that month Liudmila wrote somewhat mournfully to him, now that he was back home in Soviet Russia: "The door has swung firmly shut... Ah, if you only knew, dear Fedin of ours, what fierce misery I felt after your departure. The first two days were particularly painful. My heart ached intolerably. I didn't feel up to going out anywhere (the tickets for the Comédie Française were wasted), nor to seeing anyone. [...] Today you'll probably be back in Leningrad — maybe it's still wintry, but it will be beautiful as ever. [...] We spent a long time sitting in a café (outdoors, in the sunshine) on the Champs Elysées, and regretted that you weren't with us. And tomorrow we'll eat pancakes, and again we'll feel sad."[45] She had spoken to Erenburg the day after his departure, which is in fact one of the few references we have to any further contact between them and Erenburg after his initial welcome in 1932. Fedin's friendship with Pozner, Erenburg, and the Saviches probably meant that the Zamiatins had met up with this more pro-Soviet circle again during these weeks. Zamiatin added his own note to her letter: "The Etoile and Concorde are lonely without you, and so am I. I've again started sleeping not too well [...] I sat for two days writing an article about Soviet war novels. [...] I've become sufficiently cheeky to write it directly in French. [...] They're soon going to broadcast my *Churygin* over the radio ("Colonial") —you'll be able to hear it in Piter. When will it become possible to talk to you over this radio? In the absence of the radio, could you let Agrafena know that I'll send her the confirmation of the extension of my passport. If you get the chance, find out why she needs it and let me know."

Some weeks later Fedin replied, recalling what a happy and convivial time they'd spent together in Paris: "Everyone here asks after you a great deal, because they remember you very warmly and well, and are waiting for you. On your behalf I promised everyone that you would definitely come back this summer. And really—do plan to come. [...] Your letter truly touched me, because once again I was convinced how much you miss Leningrad and how much you belong to Leningrad. From all my conversations with you I understood that despite all the connections and friendships, interests and tastes that you have acquired in Paris, you are still 90% living with us."[46] This exchange of letters about Zamiatin's situation seems to go well beyond the conventional noises each party needed to make for the benefit of the official eyes that might be scrutinising their correspondence, offering a glimpse perhaps of the real hesitation that he felt at that moment, and the genuine conviction of Fedin that they would be better off returning to the USSR. It is difficult not to feel that Fedin's pressing invitation must have been the subject of much discussion in rue Raffet.

In mid-February 1934, Zamiatin wrote to the theatre director Fedor Kommissarzhevsky (Evreinov's former collaborator) in London, to ask whether he might be interested in staging *Attila*, or *The Flea*, or *The Society of Honourable Bellringers*, all of which he had sent him three months previously.[47] At the same time, he sent Reavey a rather desperate-sounding list of requests concerning his forthcoming trip to London: to retrieve the texts of his plays from Kommissarzhevsky if he was not interested; to call on Allen Lane to find out their intentions regarding *We*, as well as to offer them *Siberia* and ask advice about trying to place *The Flea*; he also wanted Reavey to show to the film company that had adapted H.G. Wells's novels the synopsis of the screenplay of *We (D-503)*, and to mention to them *Attila*, *Siberia*, and *Sten'ka Razin*, alongside a range of potential screen adaptations—of Dostoevsky's *Idiot*, his *Gambler*, or Turgenev's *Spring Torrents*.⁴⁸ His mood of anxiety was also reflected in a letter to Kunina-Aleksander three weeks later. By now she had become the correspondent to whom he revealed himself most frankly, evidently because of her sympathetic character, and because there was no need for constraint with her, as there was with his friends still living in the USSR:

> "*L'écriture c'est moi*," and if you were a skilled graphologist you'd be able to tell from the handwriting of this letter that there's something wrong again with its author (I myself know the differences in my own handwriting very well). Between the middle of December and the middle of February I felt wonderful. [...] But now insomnia has taken over again, and my nerves are jangling. It never comes at a good moment, and that's especially true now—there's work waiting for me on my desk. [...] After my Stavitskian adventures with my flea [...] I have a few [...] cinematographic prospects and *espoirs*, but unfortunately there's no bank that will exchange even the rosiest of those for francs. [...] In Paris it's already spring, there are mimosas and violets in the streets, and lovers kiss shamelessly in all the metros... Poor Fedin had no luck: while he was living here the weather was dreadful throughout. And now he's keeping warm by his stove in St Petersburg. [...] By the way, about St Petersburg: read the novel by B. Temiriazev called *A Story about Trifles*. It'll be pleasant for you to recall your Petersburg years, for it's a novel about St Petersburg, about our city. I think I told you about the author: he's a mysterious person, and no one has seen him in the flesh. But he does exist. The other day this book was left with the *concierge* for me, bearing a dedication from the author (although I don't know the author). [...] It's a very curious book.⁴⁹

This was a bit of playful mystification, for he knew perfectly well that *A Story about Trifles*, recently published in Berlin under a pseudonym, was by the artist Iury Annenkov. The work was received with some suspicion, apparently, by the émigré community: "This novel about the Revolution was perceived as Soviet, thanks to its narrative, full of emphatic 'devices' and based on the technique of montage, and to its language, evocative of Soviet-style 'ornamentalism.' Some saw in it a provocation, suggesting that the novel had been authored by a Soviet writer."⁵⁰ This example of the growing literary antagonism between the conservative aesthetics of the emigration and those of the first generation of Soviet-era writers may perhaps also help to explain why Zamiatin's *We* had received a relatively unenthusiastic reception in France five years previously.

He sent Kunina-Aleksander his unpublished "Lettres russes," the article he had drafted directly in French, even before it was published in *Marianne* on 15 April.[51] He justified his choice of Russian war novels as a topic for his French readership by sardonic reference to the current political atmosphere: "We evidently find ourselves on the eve of a brilliant demonstration of the latest achievements of human genius: stratospheric missiles, death-dealing rays etc. Everyone is preparing for war, they're talking and writing about it everywhere, even in the USSR, which was the first to insist upon immediate disarmament, and which through an irony of history may become the first country to be drawn into the war. Recently a whole series of novels has appeared there on the subject of war, and if Freud is correct when he says that dream and art serve equally as an escape from ideas that preoccupy us, then this fact is extremely significant." Acknowledging that the Russian works he was going to consider were relatively primitive compared to masterpieces like *All Quiet on the Western Front*, he observed that, nevertheless, "these books provide reliable testimony about the current mood in the USSR, where alongside fervent internationalism a new form of patriotism has come into being."[52]

Kunina-Aleksander was still sending him her own writings for comment. In a detailed response on 7 May, Zamiatin observed: "your greatest vice is that you're too intelligent, whereas poetry, as you know, 'has to be a little bit foolish.' It's all very well for Pil'niak or [Aleksei] Tolstoy, who were granted this fortunate foolishness at birth, but what are the likes of you and me to do?" In other words, the hero of her tale *Red Fez*, set in Sarajevo, was too rational in his motivations and actions. "I didn't reply for a long time, because I was so busy I was in a daze: I've been baked in a layered pie made of three different cinematographic jobs, all of which landed on me simultaneously, and all—as is always the case—urgent, and needing to be done in a hurry." Kunina-Aleksander was evidently somewhat dismayed by his criticisms, and two weeks later he had to write back to her with kindly reassurances.[53] Meanwhile he was still faintly hoping that something useful might come of the staging of *The Flea*. On 16 May he wrote to Shakhovskaia in Brussels, mentioning that there was talk of making a new French adaptation of the work for a production the following season, and asking her to enquire about the progress of its translation into Flemish. "My great friend Fedin visited Paris for a couple of months. Naturally, those months were full of fun, especially because there was a lot of fun to be had on the streets of Paris, including even gunfire." Two weeks later he welcomed Shakhovskaia herself on a visit to the French capital.[54]

Back in Moscow, the chain of events inaugurated by the banning of RAPP in April 1932, and the decision, as reported by Fedin, to create a new unitary writers' organisation, was reaching a climax. From 6 May, applications were invited for membership of the new Writers' Union from "those who supported the platform of Soviet power and were participating in socialist construction." The Commission to review applications included several of Zamiatin's friends, such as Fedin and Vsevolod Ivanov, who were joined later by Tikhonov and Slonimsky. The first new member was Gor'ky, and of course Zamiatin was close to many of the others who signed up, and whose names he saw printed in *Literaturnaia gazeta*. Bulgakov sent in his application on 29 May. Like Bulgakov, Zamiatin would have been aware that many practical advantages were going to be associated with membership, such as access to publishing outlets and institutional protection for copyright and royalties. In due course, these would extend to privileges such as access to restaurants, shops, and holiday trips—as savagely satirised by Bulgakov in the Griboedov House scenes of *The Master and Margarita*—and even to supplies of writing paper.

Zamiatin, still living in Paris with his Soviet passport, and still—perhaps—agonising about whether to return to the USSR, made the decision not to pass up the opportunity to apply for membership, and sent in a request by telegram from France. This evidently caused some consternation to the members of the Applications Commission, who were unsure how to handle this approach from abroad, and they decided to refer it to Stalin himself for his opinion. In a remarkable document of 14 June 1934 (discovered by Aleksandr Galushkin in the Archive of the President of the Russian Federation), Pavel Iudin, secretary of the Commission, reported directly to Stalin: "Zamiatin's application has received strong support—and expressions of satisfaction at this action of his—from the non-Party writers Konstantin Fedin, Aleksei Tolstoy, Nikolai Tikhonov, Mikhail Slonimsky, Boris Pasternak and others. Inasmuch as Zamiatin's admission to membership of the Union raises questions which are beyond the remit of the Union of Writers, I request your instructions." A handwritten response was appended to this document with a flourish: "I propose that Zamiatin's request should be granted. I[osif] Stalin." What this meant was that he was accepted into the new Writers' Union on Stalin's say-so, without going through the usual procedures (neither the application nor any list of publications were formally considered by the Commission), and no announcement about his membership ever appeared in print either.[55] Of course, the news became known to his friends. Just a week later, on 21 June, Fedin wrote the Zamiatins a brief note and asked: "When are you planning to come? Do you already know that Zhenia is a member of the Union of Soviet Writers? I've just received a telegram from Moscow that he's been accepted. Please write."[56] We may even speculate that Fedin had been urged to encourage Zamiatin to apply, and was later disenchanted when Zamiatin did not follow through by returning to the USSR, so that this represented a "failure" in Fedin's mission.

Why did Stalin decide to accede so magnanimously to Zamiatin's request on this occasion? The weeks running up to the First Congress of the Writers' Union that summer are very eventful and contradictory in respect to Stalin's own interventions in the fates of writers. On the night of 13–14 May Osip Mandel'shtam was arrested for his poem denouncing Stalin; his flat was searched and he was taken away from the very same building Bulgakov had recently moved into. Three weeks earlier, Bulgakov had submitted an application to travel to France for two months; on 18 May he actually glimpsed the foreign passports which had been prepared for him and his wife, but permission was nevertheless withheld and they were not handed over. Bulgakov was cast into a state of utter despair, exacerbated when he learned on 1 June that Pil'niak and his wife had, once again, received passports for travel. By contrast, on 25 May, to everyone's amazement, the "oppositionist" Nikolai Bukharin was nominated to speak about poetry at the Congress. After a suicide attempt by Mandel'shtam in his place of exile in the Urals, Stalin telephoned Pasternak at home at the end of the first week of June and had a conversation with him about Mandel'shtam's fate, which is generally held to have led to the poet being allowed to switch his place of exile from Cherdyn' to the more bearable Voronezh. The call was probably not common knowledge, but Pasternak talked about it to Erenburg, who had just arrived in the USSR with André Malraux for the Congress.[57] On 10 and 11 June Bulgakov drafted letters to Stalin protesting about his harsh treatment, but received no response. The Commission's enquiry about Zamiatin's application was submitted on 14 June, and the outcome had been decided personally by Stalin by the 21st. In the immediate run-up to the Congress then, it would appear that Stalin was choosing to demonstrate that his authority, however absolute and arbitrary, could be used occasionally for benign purposes. The "taming" of Zamiatin was still a propaganda prize he wanted to obtain.

Back in France, Zamiatin would have been unaware as yet of most of these dramatic events. Writing to Kunina-Aleksander on 24 June, he told her: "My address, unfortunately, is still the same: Paris. I'm sitting by the cinematographic sea and waiting for good weather. When I'll get away, and where to—I don't know. Most probably it'll be the middle of July—and to somewhere not far outside Paris, in order to wait in more agreeable surroundings. I have some interesting projects, three of them at once, but what will emerge from them is harder to predict than a win on the National Lottery. And in between times I've begun to write a few new short stories (all the previous ones that were suitable have been translated)." He asked her this time not to send him medicines, but maybe some treat from Zagreb such as light tobacco, sherbet or Turkish delight.[58] This seems to have been the first moment since arriving in France that Zamiatin felt in the mood for writing new fiction, although the results, it must be said, are somewhat tame. In *The Watch*, for example, a hapless bureaucrat makes a fool of himself in front of his attractive secretary; but the Civil War setting adds little to the intrigue, and the piece amounts to no more than a humorous anecdote. This was perhaps the manuscript Marcel Prévost turned down that July for *La Revue de France*, exhorting him to submit something more like his earlier contributions.[59]

Fedin's note about his Union membership seems to have reached Zamiatin by 25 June, and he and Liudmila sent him a postcard that day of the rue de Rivoli. Liudmila told him they'd recently visited the Champagne region by car, and seen Rheims Cathedral as well as visiting the champagne cellars, where they enjoyed some tastings. Zamiatin promised Fedin more news shortly: "The long letter to you which I've begun will be finished and sent off in a few days' time. And until then—*salut!*"[60] It would be another six weeks, however, before that long letter was completed. One problem was that Zamiatin had started to feel unwell again—was this induced by the stress of trying to decide what to do about the question of going back to the USSR, now that he had been officially accepted into the ranks of the Soviet literary establishment? In a letter to Kunina-Aleksander a month later, he wrote: "I've been feeling awful, to such an extent that at one point I was living my life in a predominantly horizontal position. And with a mood to match. I'll probably sit it out in Paris until the end of next week, and then I'll most likely go somewhere on the outskirts—that will be clarified over the next few days. [...] Maybe it'll be possible to arrange some distant journey... for example to Yugoslavia. This will have to be decided with arithmetical simplicity: by the quantity of francs."[61]

However, none of his more recent endeavours for the cinema were proving very successful. Negotiations had been undertaken in Britain during 1934 to create a consortium, in which some Labour Party MPs took an active interest, to include "Sovkino" and four English film companies. Amongst the first films planned were Zamiatin's script for *Peter I*, based on Aleksei Tolstoy's novel, and his own *Attila*.[62] In January 1934 the film actor Valery Inkizhinov, who had played the role of a descendant of Genghis Khan in Pudovkin's 1928 *Storm over Asia*, and was now living in Paris, had also sent off the synopsis of *Attila* to a Swiss firm which had expressed interest. That summer Inkizhinov enthusiastically offered himself for the title role.[63] During the same period, Zamiatin was also exchanging letters with an engineer, Paul Sicault, who reported to him that, as instructed, he had submitted four film scripts to British Gaumont: *Attila, Scourge of God*; *Taras Bul'ba*; *Goya*; and *The Condemned Men*. Little was achieved by all these negotiations, except that *Taras Bul'ba* did appear in 1935, directed by Aleksei Granovsky.[64]

On 7 August, he finally wrote his long letter to Fedin from Bellevue: "It's up on a height above Paris, and the view from here really is wonderful. We have an entire villa at our disposal." They were staying in the house of the doctor and writer Aleksandr Rubakin, son of the well-known bibliophile N. Rubakin.[65] Zamiatin was enjoying the flowers, the trees, and the eagle owl that you could hear every evening:

> I could have a really good rest here—unless, foolishly, I were to sit down and start working. Not long ago I revived my old self and wrote a couple of stories (in Russian... for the French). But I should really rest: I've felt absolutely rotten recently—my old friend colitis. But I'm already recovering, and if I stay here, as I intend to, until the beginning of September, then I'll put on weight. [...] *A propos*, Iury [Annenkov] is threatening to come...

in his new car: he bought it not long ago, after he'd designed the costumes for a certain film with which I was also partly associated. Thank you for the news that I've been "unionised." Was it a tricky business? Write and tell me. Three days ago I spent half a day here in the company of Sergei Prokof'ev. [...] I imagine you will receive this just before your departure for Moscow, to the Congress of world-historical significance?[66]

Prokof'ev had recently returned from a fascinating journey, travelling in Russia through places very close to Zamiatin's heart, from Moscow to Ufa, along the Moscow Canal, and up the rivers Oka, Volga, Kama and Bela. He was now spending July and August in Paris working on some piano pieces before joining his family in the south of France. In a decision which must greatly have preoccupied Zamiatin, and which they may even have discussed during this visit, Prokof'ev would uproot his family from Paris eighteen months later and move back to settle in the Soviet Union, where he believed his art would be more fully appreciated.[67] Later in 1934, Isaak Babel' would also be pressing his mother and family to move back from Paris to Russia with him.

Another guest Zamiatin received that August was A.— F. Pottecher, who published an account of their conversation entitled "Three Hours at Bellevue with the Russian Writer Evgeny Zamiatin": "Some of his stories that have been printed in our journals are true masterpieces. Listening to him is a great pleasure. He speaks French very carefully, not entirely confident about his vocabulary — but on his face there is such a determination to be understood, that you listen to him, so to speak, and get absorbed. His words carry you far away and oblige you to think. With every phrase Zamiatin sets a problem. But he doesn't exhaust you, because he is articulate, precise, and witty." Pottecher had been intrigued by the newspaper reports from Moscow that summer about the First Congress of the newly-created Writers' Union, and the articles written about it by the French delegates Jean-Richard Bloch and Louis Aragon. Zamiatin talked to him about the enormous appetite there was in the USSR for both classical and contemporary literature in Russian, as well as for foreign classics such as Shakespeare, Molière, Racine and Balzac. The turn that literature had recently taken back towards realism, and in favour of a clearer, more approachable style, was very well suited, he felt, to the millions of new readers in the country.[68] This would, incidentally, turn out to be Zamiatin's last published interview.

The First All-Union Congress of Soviet Writers had opened in Moscow on 17 August 1934 and lasted for two weeks: this was the event which established the Writers' Union, and promulgated Socialist Realism as the official method of Soviet literature and criticism. Despite the confusing signals of the previous weeks, there was still a largely optimistic mood about the future of Soviet literature after the taming of RAPP in 1932. Gor'ky gave a long and dull speech; Babel' spoke candidly of his recent lapse into silence. But Bukharin used his keynote speech on poetry to call for diversity and quality, singling Pasternak out as a master of the age. Jean-Richard Bloch, translated by Erenburg, spoke of the necessity of nurturing a number of writers who would be read only by 5,000 readers, alongside the mass bestsellers. Erenburg echoed these sentiments, calling for diversity, tolerance, and an art which would appeal to the intelligentsia, and spoke in defence of both Pasternak and of Babel'. Far from being denounced for this, Erenburg was subsequently invited to join the Presidium of the Union and awarded a *dacha* at Peredelkino. Pasternak's position and status were considerably enhanced by the 1934 Congress, and for a few months he felt a sense of rapprochement with the régime. We tend nowadays to think of the occasion as having brought Russia's writers to heel through the imposition of Socialist Realism, but those were not necessarily the aspects most evident at the time.

Early in September Zamiatin wrote again to Fedin, this time reflecting upon the impressions of the Moscow Congress he had gleaned from the newspapers. He and Liudmila had been in Bellevue for over a month, enjoying the scented air and the opportunity for indolence:

> As usual I brought a whole lot of books with me so that I could work, but... it's such bliss here that I haven't had the courage to spoil it with ink and tobacco. I've done almost nothing, but on the other hand I've not had a bad rest, and have got myself better. And that, if you like, was the most important thing, for by the end of the season, before our departure, I felt rotten (always the same thing: my sensitive guts). Whereas now I'm devouring bananas, pears and so on every day. And I entertain myself by reading the stenographic records of our brother writers! My goodness, you've cooked up... not a Congress, but a school of oratory! But the orators were so-so. Best of all (don't be cross) seemed to me to be... the Parisians: Jean-Richard Bloch spoke

genuinely, and Erenburg was interesting. And maybe the most notable thing was the panorama of the literatures of the national minorities, such as the Georgian, the Armenian, the Tadzhik etc. That wasn't empty talk, but real practical work.

He then asked Fedin for help again with his domestic affairs: "I have a request for you: if our Agrafena Pavlovna comes to you for advice, could you help her through the Union (of which I am, as you well know, a member) to secure my rights over the apartment? At the moment the tenancy agreement is until 1 October, but our passports have already been extended to a later date. [...] It would be good if it could again be for a year, and if that's really out of the question, then at least for a term of pregnancy—9 months—or even 6." By now, however, Zamiatin's implicit promises to Fedin that he would eventually return were beginning to sound increasingly hollow. He added: "The other day Sergei Prokof'ev was here at our *dacha*—and he told us about his visit to Detskoe." In other words, Prokof'ev had called on Fedin at home during his trip to Russia—and presumably discussed with him too the question of whether to return to live in the USSR.[69]

After Bellevue they moved on to spend some time in Chartres before returning to Paris. On 8 November, Liudmila sent a lengthy account of her life as a non-working wife to Elena Annenkova:

> My life here is [...] settled and comfortable, with oil, gas, and hot water, a morning bath without fail and often one in the evening (you just turn on the tap and your bath is ready), with as much as you want of milk and bread etc. Our housekeeping is very straightforward, and if we do sometimes need to do something at home (more often we eat out), you yourself know how simple and convenient it is here to buy things and cook them. We live in a beautiful *quartier*, and the proximity of the Bois de Boulogne is a great pleasure for me—I rarely let a day pass without going for a little trot there. And since I have plenty of time, I don't need to hurry anywhere or for any reason. I love Paris, I've grown accustomed to it, and I call our *quartier* my "second home." You of course know this district—Auteuil— with its gardens and avenues and good air, which is very clean in comparison with other districts of Paris. [...] I know you received my postcard from Chartres. I returned from there at the end of October, having spent plenty of time wandering

through the fields and the woods (I found so many white mushrooms there!), I breathed enough fresh air there to last me the whole winter, I put on weight, and emancipated myself from EI. And now I'm back to my Paris existence, not without pleasure. EI is working at the moment with a certain film director (at his house), so I'm taking advantage of the freedom: I'm visiting friends, [...] going to the shops, and have been to several exhibitions—this autumn's Salon was spectacular. [...] EI has put on some weight, and had a good rest over the summer. During the spring he was not well. His mood is good. He sends you all greetings, and I give you a big kiss. [...] *The Flea*, alas, never did get to hop about here.[70]

The impression we gain here of a happy and confident Liudmila chimes in well with an account that Kunina-Aleksander later provided, of the way she felt that the couple's relationship had gained in strength between the early 1920s in Leningrad, when she first got to know them, and the 1930s:

Zamiatin knew how to be merry, more often than not when he was not at home, where, as it seemed to me in my youth, there was the slightly dismal devotion of his companion, as though she felt herself guilty for the child she had failed to give him, or as though some non-existent child's grave separated the two of them. And maybe for that reason Liudmila Nikolaevna used to go about, until she went abroad, with her gaze lowered and slightly to one side, fixed on some spot between her own comical old-fashioned boots with their white kid uppers and black buttons, and Evgeny Ivanovich's sturdy English footwear. In the final years of his life in Paris there was nothing of this any more; maybe the difficulties of life in a foreign land, and the heart ailment from which he turned out to be suffering, bonded together these two people who were so different, and equally unsuited for life abroad? It was also the case that in foreign parts Evgeny Ivanovich no longer had his friends' magnificent homes, where literary beauties with elegant legs and a good knowledge of foreign languages held court. Whereas in Russia they were there, and he knew, even in the difficult years, how to tease and be witty and laugh, not just with those intelligent Asiatic eyes of his, but also with his voice and his shoulders, even just by removing the pipe from his mouth.[71]

In other words, when Zamiatin was no longer such a literary star, eclipsing his wife in social situations and easily tempted into flirtations, he and she found themselves able to rediscover the closeness that had first drawn them together thirty years previously. It was as if they had left some of the tensions in their marriage behind when they emigrated from Russia. There is no further mention of the dolls Rostislav and Misha in any of their letters after 1931 either, and perhaps they were left behind in Leningrad too, as the issue of childlessness came to seem less important.

Towards the end of November, D.S. Watt of *The Glasgow Herald* replied to an offer from Zamiatin of a further annual update on the Russian shipbuilding industry. Watt promised him another seven guineas for an article of 1,000–1,500 words, to be submitted by 10 December: "You understand that the project of our Trade Review is to outline the work done in 1934 and give some indications of the prospects for 1935. Your article will be of particular interest in view of the fact that there is little authentic information published in this country regarding the shipbuilding activity of the U.S.S.R." This article by "Prof. Eugene Zamiatin" appeared on 29 December under the title "Shipbuilding in Soviet Russia. Efforts Towards Better Production. Turning Point in Industry. Projected Ice-breaking Flotilla."[72]

The last few weeks of 1934 are reflected in just a handful of letters written from Paris by the Zamiatins. Two of these were rather gloomy ones to Kunina-Aleksander, in one of which he thanked her for introducing him to the Yugoslav artist Ivan Tabaković, who had designed the cover for her 1931 translation of *At the Back of Beyond*, and whom he had found charming:

> It was all the more pleasant for me to see Tabaković because I'm fed up with the local Parisians: I hardly see anyone, and mostly I'm plunged in self-absorption and misanthropy. [...] Over the summer I spent a month and a half just as misanthropically near Paris, in Bellevue, with a subsequent fortnight's epilogue near Chartres. I hardly did anything during all that time, I had a very good rest and acquired the misleading appearance of a good *rentier* (misleading, because I have some doubts about my goodness, and secondly because I'm not a *rentier* but a proletarian, who even lacks chains: at least those are possessions!). I can move about in a way that's completely different from last year: I run around as much as I like, and I'm even eating the salami

you sent; and I've been working very hard over the last two months. Unfortunately, it's a film again; and unfortunately it's with Otsep again (he's very difficult to work with—he's as stubborn as Hitler); and unfortunately it still hasn't provided any francs, so that I'm having to tighten my belt. [...] It's so unfair that it's only states or corporate entities who are allowed to run their budgets on a deficit, whilst for individuals that is, alas, impossible! And for that reason I find myself glancing towards my *Islanders*: it's not impossible that during 1935 I might find myself somewhere in London, if various cinematographic schemes I have with them come off.[73]

Despite the flippancy of his remark about Fedor Otsep, with whom he and Annenkov had previously spent long evenings working on *Anna Karenina*, Zamiatin was perfectly aware what a sinister threat Hitler could pose. In his *Notebooks* he had jotted down: "Hitler's programme includes 1. castrating all Jews, and 2. if any German girl should sleep with a Jew she is liable to suffer harsh punishment." With this letter he sent two of his new stories, *The Watch* and another called *The Meeting*, which he had finished only the previous day; he also asked whether she might be interested in his recent "Lettres russes" piece on historical novels. Overall, 1934 had once again proved a thin year for publications, which amounted to just a handful of very short and rather unadventurous stories. He was, however, finally moving back towards work on his Attila novel, *The Scourge of God*.

He was grateful for the affectionate responses he received back from Kunina-Aleksander and her husband: "After such letters it becomes easier to live, and I don't feel so lonely. Paris for me is a desert inhabited by phantoms, and I live here like a hermit. [...] With what pleasure would I find myself in your parts! But there you are, my financial sins won't allow me into your paradise. However, as soon as one of my larger projects comes off—my first trip will be to see you. [...] At the moment there's a lull for the festive season, all the wheels of business have ground to a halt, and people have gone away. After some pleasant work—a few brief stories—I've returned again to my chores: film scripts."[74]

The shocking political event at the end of 1934, which completely dashed the liberal hopes raised by the Writers' Congress, was the murder of the Leningrad Party leader Sergei Kirov on 1 December. Other Old Bolsheviks such as Bukharin were devastated; Zinoviev and Kamenev were arrested two weeks later and sentenced to death by mid-January 1935; and other arrests and executions on a massive scale soon followed. These events inaugurated the purges, show-trials and executions of Stalin's Great Terror. Kamenev had been particularly close to Gor'ky, and his disgrace also seems to have marked the beginning of the real decline in Gor'ky's influence over cultural life.[75]

On the last day of 1934 the Zamiatins sent Fedin New Year's greetings, regretting that they had not heard from him for some time, and recalling fondly how they had met up in Paris precisely one year earlier. This year, in unusually mild and sunny weather, they would be raising a glass of champagne to him in Annenkov's home.[76] Zamiatin had a streaming cold when he wrote again to Kunina-Aleksander at the very end of January 1935: "I'm running a temperature of 39 degrees, and it's flu, with a hurricane-like, point 12 cold." He had been reading her draft of a novel while confined to bed, and once again he criticised her writing (and her hero) for being too rational and cold: "I know (and this from my own experience), that what is 'true' is achieved when your work is guided by your sub-conscious—the conscious, like various kinds of ideology, can only play a subordinate part. (Oh, how they would have roasted me over there for this 'heresy'! And in fact they did roast me! What blockheads!)"[77]

At the end of January, *The Watch* came out in *Les Nouvelles Littéraires*.[78] Zamiatin decided to build on his return to fiction and make a modest attempt to boost his literary profile. Invitations were sent out for a *soirée* on 18 February 1935, where he proposed to read a new piece called *"Le ballet et la révolution"*—presumably the basis for what he later proposed as a film script called *"Le Dieu de la Danse,"* which anachronistically amalgamates something of Nijinsky's story with a melodramatic Civil War love intrigue. This event was to take place, appropriately, at the Salle des Archives Internationales de la Danse.[79] Also on the programme were some other new stories, slight and humorous anecdotes, including probably *The Vision*, *The Lion* and *The Meeting*. A month or so afterwards he told Kunina-Aleksander:

> We live, as you know, in a country where capital—or the lack of it—determines everything in life. And I, naturally, was suffering from its lack. I was obliged to take urgent measures; so I organised an evening of readings of my new works. I organised the evening as a private occasion, and I read extracts from my new novel (*The Scourge of God*), which is as yet unfinished,

as well as a number of new stories. As a result I've patched up my budget. Later on I'll probably arrange another *soirée*, this time a public one. [...] To tell the truth my mood, like Liudmila Nikolaevna's, is not wonderful. She had a very nasty flu, which she was unable to shake off for a long time. Once her flu was over, and my rushing around with the *soirée*, we launched out for a week or two into "society life," to patch over the hole in our hearts. On one occasion I squeezed into a dinner jacket and even went to a ball—I've never yet seen a ball in Paris, and I wanted to have a look. As you perhaps know from your own experience, all these entertainments function like morphine—they have an effect only for a brief while, and then the pain starts up again. [...] I don't know about my future yet: the waters are dark... It's possible that during the coming month I'll make a visit to Belgium, in order to hold a *soirée* there in Russian, and possibly give a talk in French. And I've begun discussions with Amsterdam about giving a talk there. But all of this is again really from the realm of "distractions."[80]

A week or so later he wrote to Shakhovskaia, asking whether she might help him to organise a reading in the Russian Jewish Club in Brussels, and mentioning that he'd heard from Marc Slonim that there would be enthusiasm in Antwerp for such an occasion as well.[81]

On 27 March his second "Lettres russes" article was published in *Marianne*. His main theme here was the recent revival of interest in historical narratives, with Soviet authors apparently less nervous than they had been hitherto of tackling historical topics which predated 1917. The most conspicuous success in this genre was Aleksei Tolstoy's novel *Peter I* (Parts 1 and 2, 1929 and 1933): Zamiatin explained the appeal of this Soviet "best-seller" by the obvious parallels that could be drawn between the dictatorial Tsar imposing a technological and industrial revolution from above during the early 1700s, and the situation of Soviet Russia in the 1930s. He also praised Ol'ga Forsh's recent novel about the eighteenth-century radical Radishchev, which he described as one of those "books for 5,000 readers," novels for the intellectual élite whose right to existence had been so vigorously defended by J.-R. Bloch at the 1934 Writers' Union Congress.[82]

In a further letter to Kunina-Aleksander three weeks later, written while Tabaković was sketching him shortly before leaving Paris, Zamiatin commented wistfully: "I now regret that I met with him relatively infrequently. A passing thought: when our last day comes, how many things left undone will we regret, and how many people whom we have lost..." But at least his finances had taken a turn for the better: "The (muddied) source as ever is still the cinema. At the moment I'm busy with a screenplay for Granovsky: may Nikolai Vasil'evich Gogol' forgive us for our desecration of *Taras Bul'ba*!" He was hoping to save enough for a trip to Yugoslavia, although he had heard that Kunina-Aleksander might be visiting Paris herself soon. He had this information from a Mme Heilbronner, who had asked him via Tabaković "to recommend to her and a friend *'un professeur intelligent de la langue russe.'* I recalled that in Russia, by the way, I had once been a *'professeur de langue anglaise'* and recommended myself." He had opened his "new university" the previous evening. "All of this is quite amusing, but meanwhile the unfinished novel still languishes in my desk drawer, and waits for its turn. Could it be that it's destined to be completed in Yugoslavia? Yugoslavia is turning into the promised land..."[83]

In mid-May he wrote a long and revealing letter to his translator friend Charles Malamuth, who had shared with the UPI correspondent Eugene Lyons his most famous scoop, an interview with Stalin in the Kremlin in November 1930:

> I am turning red. I'm turning red—alas!—not politically, but simply from shame at replying to you only after four months. [...] I began this letter several times—and each time it remained unfinished: either visitors interrupted me, or work, or my horrible mood, which it would have been disagreeable to spit out on to paper. And finally I decided to start it again, not in English this time, but in Russian. After all, why not indulge myself occasionally with Russian? I write quite enough letters in English, and especially in French, but Russian ones only rarely. And so, as you see, I'm alive. But to be honest, I don't at all like the way I'm living. There's not bad capital in my head, and I waste it on *Ersatz*, on the scribbling of various film scripts—just because it's the only not too miserably paid work here. Although even so, it's terrible pay by your American standards. I simply cannot manage to get on top of my budget for six months or so, in order to settle down to my novel. The greatest luxury that I can permit myself is to write a few new short stories, in order for them to be printed in French, or Dutch, or English—just not in Russian. [...] Living like this is senseless, of course. I have to attempt to undertake a *coup d'état*. But of what kind? Should I return to my

homeland? But up until now my homeland has rather proved a step-mother than a mother to me. It's true, it seems, that the situation there has changed—but not for me, I fear. Writers live there, singing with happiness. But when I read, in *Literaturnaia gazeta* for example, their "songs"—that shameless flattery addressed to all the bosses—then I begin to experience a sharp attack of nausea. Were I to return, I wouldn't join the ranks of the flatterers, and so that would mean I'd remain a writer "outside the ranks," and I'd be condemned to complete or near silence.

This letter is perhaps the most explicit reflection of Zamiatin's dilemma by this stage: while others such as Prokof'ev were taking the plunge and returning to the USSR, he still resisted the blandishments of Fedin, and continued to trust the instinct which warned him against the dangers of such a step for someone like him, who would never really be "Red" enough. Instead, he was wondering about travelling further West: "And so—should I not perhaps seek my fortune in the United States? Boris Grigor'ev, who returned from America recently, told me all sorts of tempting things. I have a good mind. I know the language. I have friends in America—first among them Charles Malamuth (Lyons has fallen silent, and didn't reply to my letter). There has even been a certain artillery barrage in preparation for such an assault (have you held in your hands Max Eastman's book *Artists in Uniform*?) So, in a word, I'm coming back to the idea of a visit to America, starting with a lecture tour. Do try to make some serious enquiries in this direction. The themes of the lectures could be: Soviet theatre, Soviet literature, or Soviet children. Maybe you could get in contact with Eastman about this, if you're acquainted with him?" Eastman's book, published in 1934, had included an entire chapter devoted to Zamiatin and his persecution by RAPP. Once again, nothing came of this plan to travel to the USA.

He was still busy with *Taras Bul'ba* during April 1935, as it was due to go into production that summer. With that same letter he sent Malamuth proposals for a number of other film-scripts: *The Captured Tsar* (about Tsar Alexander II and his mistress Iur'evskaia); *Goya's Great Love*; *The Queen of Spades*; and finally, his Attila project. "*Attila* is a theme for Cecil de Mille, naturally. Would it not be possible to offer it to him? I'm sending all these materials to you since, to be honest, I see more friendly helpfulness in you than, say, in Lyons (there is much of the business man in him). And judging by your letter, my *Razin* is already in your hands. [...] I'm completely exhausted. Today I'm resting, and then tomorrow it's back to work: I have to sketch out the text for a lecture on 'Soviet Theatre' which I'm going to give (in French) in Amsterdam on 7 June. From there I'm travelling to Antwerp and to Brussels, to give readings of my stories in Russian. Apart from that, they're proposing that in Brussels I should read a lecture in French on the role of the theatre in education in Russia—this is for a Congress organised as part of the Brussels Exhibition."[84]

On 7 June, Zamiatin did indeed give his lecture in Amsterdam on "The Russian Theatre Today." The text of his talk, claiming European supremacy for the Russian theatre, was based on the lecture he'd given in Prague at the end of 1931, and he evidently assembled it fairly hastily, since its 17 pages are made up of a mixture of handwritten sections, pasted-in bits of typescript, and even newspaper cuttings.[85] During his stay in Amsterdam he apparently found time to go and see the red-light district, as he noted down a brief description of the women sitting in the windows in his *Notebooks*.[86] From there he wrote to Shakhovskaia, asking whether he could stay with her for three days or so on the way back—as well as the lecture at the Congress he was hoping to give a reading at the Russian Jewish Club on the 15th, if she could help out with getting tickets sold and advancing money to the Club's manager if necessary. The lecture he read in Brussels was the piece called "Theatrical Parallels."[87]

In 1934 and 1935, Erenburg had also been travelling extensively around Europe, and on his visits to Alsace and the Low Countries he had been horrified by the success of Nazi propaganda in aggressively promoting German nationalism. He therefore wrote directly to Stalin in the autumn of 1934, calling for the creation of a movement to oppose the Nazis. As a result, he was entrusted with the task of organising an anti-Fascist Congress in Paris in the summer of 1935. This was the "*Congrès International des Ecrivains pour la Défense de la Culture*" held on 21–25 June in the Palais de la Mutualité, attended by an audience of 3,000 and involving 230 delegates from 38 countries. These included Brecht, Musil, Anna Seghers, Lion Feuchtwanger, Heinrich Mann, Hemingway, Aldous Huxley, H.G. Wells and E.M. Forster, as well as the French and Russian delegates. Its character was largely shaped by the role played by the French Communist Party and the Soviet authorities in its organisation, with the dual goal of creating a united anti-Fascist front and promoting a positive image of the USSR as the defender of Europe against Nazism. French and Soviet diplomatic relations had recently been cemented by a further treaty of mutual assistance signed on 2 May 1935. The threat of Hitler inevitably presented a dilemma to those who had misgivings about Stalinist Russia, and many people attended who were perhaps convinced by the first purpose (to unite against Hitler), even if they had reservations about the pro-Soviet propaganda exercise.[88]

Erenburg's role was to organise the Congress along with Gide, Malraux, Jean-Richard Bloch and others. The meeting was presented as an affirmation of the significance of the intellectual, and a rallying call to defend the core values of European civilisation. Erenburg, Savich and Pozner were all engaged to report on the proceedings for different Soviet newspapers. Five days before the opening of the Congress, Malraux was told that Gor'ky, who was to have led the Soviet delegation, "was unwell" and would not be coming (he had already, ominously, been refused permission earlier in 1935 to travel as before to the West for medical treatment). On Erenburg's advice, Gide and Malraux went to the Soviet Embassy to ask that Babel' and Pasternak be included in the Soviet delegation instead, to lend more distinction to the proceedings. In a grotesque episode, Pasternak received a call from Stalin's personal secretary instructing him to set off immediately, and he was bundled into a train along with Babel', protesting, straight from the sanatorium where he was being treated for nervous depression; they arrived in France only in time for the end of the Congress. Just a year after the Writers' Union Congress, Pasternak had been traumatised by what he had recently seen of the consequences of collectivisation in the Russian countryside, and by the waves of arrests amongst the literary intelligentsia. He was in a terrible state in Paris, ill and clearly frightened. He received acclaim after a brief speech on the final day defending the aesthetic value of poetry (according to Babel', he was the one who had cobbled this together for Pasternak in a Paris café, with Erenburg's help). Babel' spoke fluently in French, but no record of his speech survives.

There was a catastrophic "non-meeting" for Pasternak with the poet Marina Tsvetaeva, whom he had not seen since 1922, although they had had a passionate exchange of letters in the interim. Presumably fearing that his words would be reported back to the security organs, an apparently terrified Pasternak babbled some banal and cryptic remarks about whether Tsvetaeva should agree to return to the USSR, as her husband Sergei Efron and daughter Ariadna were pressing her to do. She was left baffled and furious.[89] Zamiatin was with Annenkov when he drove Pasternak around Paris and out to St-Denis in his car: we may wonder whether they perhaps elicited a clearer picture of the real state of affairs in Moscow from Pasternak than Tsvetaeva had succeeded in doing. As the Congress ended an exhibition of Russian art opened in Paris (26 June-10 July). This second major exhibition which Zamiatin saw in Paris by Russian painters overlapped very little with the "World of Art" one he had seen in 1932: this more "Soviet" exhibition was organised by Tsvetaeva's husband Sergei Efron on behalf of the "Union for Returning to the Motherland" (commonly held to be a GPU front organisation), and displayed works by Annenkov, Goncharova, Larionov and Chagall.

It has been suggested that Zamiatin may even have counted as an official member of the Soviet delegation—or perhaps he was simply automatically entitled to attend as a full member of the Soviet Writers' Union? In any case his Paris acquaintances, such as the Erenburgs and Saviches, were much involved in the organisation of proceedings, and he got the opportunity to meet up with old friends from the USSR. Nikitin related Aleksei Tolstoy's impressions of seeing him there; and Tikhonov, abroad for the first time in his life, recalled that, like Tsvetaeva, he came regularly to the sessions. He noted that Zamiatin no longer carried himself like a confident English gentleman, but rather as someone who had endured many reverses.[90] It is intriguing to think of Zamiatin perhaps making the acquaintance of Aldous Huxley, or saying hello again to H.G. Wells. He was likely also to have been one of the 5,000 people who, like Babel', attended the official opening on 30 June of a new road, the Boulevard Maxime Gorki in Villejuif, a working-class district in the south-east of Paris.[91] He would have had ample opportunity to observe his fellow-writers from the USSR during these days, and to reflect on their situations: clearly nothing emerged from his conversations to persuade him that he ought to be returning to Leningrad, and indeed this whole episode may have been what finally decided him against that option.

That autumn there were further sinister developments in Russia. Akhmatova's son and husband were arrested, and then released.[92] In October, Alia Savich's mother and sister both fell ill; she rushed back to Moscow to look after them, but was then refused permission to leave again, remaining trapped there. Erenburg would do his best to help the Saviches, and he and Savich worked together as journalists in Spain in 1937, but she remained parted from her husband until 1939, when he finally joined her in the USSR.[93]

After the anti-Fascist Congress, Zamiatin considered going to the Belgian countryside for his holiday, but was unable to find anywhere to stay.[94] The couple went back for six weeks to Bellevue, where they had been happy the previous year. On 17 August, Annenkov went out to visit them at Dr Rubakin's, and Zamiatin, who had been reading through the literary journals, made scathing remarks about the current state of Soviet culture. He was having a lazy time after finishing some work for Otsep (further alterations to *Anna Karenina*), and with nothing new started.[95] As he told Kunina-Aleksander: "We've been in Bellevue since the beginning of August […]. The weather, the air, the lack of people, the quiet and the woodpeckers in the park are all wonderful! We'll be here until the beginning of September, and then there's a project to travel to the south somewhere, with Annenkov."[96] A few weeks later he reported to Shakhovskaia: "The summer's over and my plans for the Ardennes turned to dust… […] Now I'm back in the old flat in Paris. Unless I get tied down with new cinema jobs, it's just possible that I might run away from here somewhere to the south, to sit there in some Mediterranean lair and write."[97] Those southern travel plans never materialised, although Liudmila seems to have got away for a while, leaving him to fend for himself. Slonim recalled that "in the fall of 1935 he shared my apartment, and we had long, intimate talks almost every evening. To my admiration of the writer was now added my affection for the man."[98] On 6 September, Zamiatin's story *The Lion* appeared in *Paris-Soir*, while on 9 October a more substantial publication appeared in *Marianne*, in the form of the French translation of *The Cave*.[99] After the film-scripts for Otsep and Granovsky, he completed a further one for Strizhevsky on 10 September.[100]

Over the ensuing months Zamiatin plunged into work on *The Scourge of God*, his most sustained period of composition of the novel. Like his fellow-writers in the USSR, he too was revisiting the pre-1917 history of the Russian lands, shaped around the life of Attila, who as a young hostage witnessed the declining years of the Roman Empire. His story is interwoven with that of the 5th-century historian Priscus, who charted the period when Rome succumbed to barbarian invasion. The novel hinges on the clash of West and East, and the collapse of an effetely degenerate civilisation in the face of the youthful virility of the primitive Goths and Slavs—a subject not without modern resonances. Seven chapters of *The Scourge of God* were completed—they were edited by Marc Slonim and published posthumously in 1939— but work on it effectively ended in 1935. The surviving chapters are beautifully written, poised, far less angular than some of Zamiatin's more neo-Realist writing. In the context of his growing "impatience" with life in the West, Liudmila's reiterated yearning for the snow and the cold, and her sense of awkwardness about the bourgeois comforts of their lifestyle, the most striking and sensual images of this historical novel emerge as the young Attila dreams in Rome of the physical traits of home: raw sweat, coarse food, rough fabrics, wolves, wild horses, and snow. One of the very last entries Zamiatin made in his *Notebooks* was an exhortation to his protagonist: "Oh, Attila! oh courteous philanthropist, when will you finally return, with your four hundred thousand horsemen, and when will you put a torch to this beautiful France, this nation of shoe-soles and trouser-braces?!"[101]

At the very end of the year, Zamiatin and Liudmila were invited by Tsvetaeva, together with the distinguished philologist Boris Unbegaun and his wife, to a social occasion. Also present were her husband Sergei Efron (probably a Soviet agent), and the children Ariadna and Mur, all three of them now to varying degrees pro-Moscow in their views, and determined to return to the USSR. Tsvetaeva herself, whose circle of acquaintance overlapped in Paris with Zamiatin's through a range of figures such as Khodasevich, Charles Vildrac, Prokof'ev and Marc Slonim, was much more doubtful about the idea. Their tragic fates when the family did travel back, first Ariadna and then Efron (covertly) in 1937, and Tsvetaeva with her son Mur in 1939, were of course to prove her right. When Tsvetaeva reached Moscow she learned that her sister was already in a labour camp; Ariadna was arrested soon afterwards, as was Efron, who was probably shot; Tsvetaeva herself committed suicide in 1941, and all traces of Mur vanished during the War.

On 11 January 1936, Zamiatin wrote to Kunina-Aleksander: "This winter I've been feeling a great deal better than I did last winter. [...] Not long ago I finished one film-script and now, when I've sent off this letter, I'll get down to another one."[102] The first script he mentioned was probably his adaptation of Gor'ky's play *The Lower Depths* for Jean Renoir.[103] He clearly meant what he said about getting down to the next one straight away, because the 30-page version of his *Mazepa* is dated the 15th of the same month.[104] The day before he finished it he sent a jocular, but also practical letter about his financial affairs to Aleksei Tolstoy, who had been visiting Paris again. Perhaps it is significant that it is now no longer Fedin whom he asks for help:

Dear comrade-sinner, [...] write to me about that business we discussed in Paris, the question of my royalties [probably for *The Flea*]. [...] In order to receive that money I sent a power of attorney to our Agrafena Pavlovna, which had been witnessed at the Soviet Consulate in Paris—and nevertheless they wouldn't hand over the money on that basis, saying that the validity of the power of attorney had expired, although I remember perfectly that it wasn't given for a fixed period. I'm getting fed up with all this tiresome nonsense. My royalties belong to me, and "Dramosoiuz" has no right to withhold the payment of them. I need this money. I explained to you in Paris why I needed it. Above all, I don't want Agrafena Pavlovna to be going hungry while she awaits my arrival. I also need to purchase a number of Soviet publications—and so on. In other words, be a good fellow, get into your car, go and visit "Dramosoiuz" and collect my money. I enclose a new power of attorney (dated 10 January). From the money you receive give Agrafena a thousand, say, for the time being. And write and tell me how much you have left. [...] I spent half the winter sitting writing my novel, but since December I've been swamped with cinema commissions one after another. There are some interesting jobs taking shape, and it looks as though I'll travel soon to London.[105]

On 15 April Zamiatin's third "Lettres russes" feature appeared in *Marianne*. Perhaps reflecting what had now become an irrevocable decision on his part never to return to the USSR, it is much more sardonic and more openly critical, even of Gor'ky. It opened with this comment: "At the end of 1935 in the Soviet press reproaches were piled upon fictional writing for 'lagging behind' the general line of the machine of state. In all probability, the muses are indeed not capable of keeping up with the new fashion of 'Stakhanovism.' And indeed, last year's harvest in the grain-fields and the steel foundries turned out much more abundant than those in the field of literature. So far we've not seen a single work equal in power to Sholokhov's *Virgin Soil Upturned* or to Aleksei Tolstoy's *Peter I*." Authors who Zamiatin felt had retained their individual voices included Prishvin and Ianovsky: "We find one common trait in almost all Soviet writers: the distinct preference which they accord to mechanical civilisation, of course in its Soviet interpretation. Nature is viewed by them primarily as an object to which the city-dweller can apply his energy. Rousseauist impulses towards communion with nature or the flight from city life are only encountered these days as rare exceptions: Prishvin is one of these. [...] There is no other contemporary Soviet writer who can see and observe trees, animals and birds and understand their language as he does." Ianovsky's book was more in the style of a heroic epic, containing lyrical descriptions of the steppes: "As we see, neither book [...] addresses topical themes, those themes which authors are called upon to address not just by the ruling party but also by the 'high-priest of Soviet literature,' Gor'ky, as well as by a portion of their readers."[106]

At the beginning of 1936 a further clamp-down on artistic freedoms in the USSR was inaugurated with the publication in *Pravda* on 28 January of a devastating attack on Shostakovich, the notorious editorial "Chaotic Din instead of Music." A savage denunciation of Bulgakov followed soon after, and a renewed banning of his works. On 9 April, Gor'ky responded with his last major article, a defence of "Formalism."[107] Meanwhile Zamiatin followed up his third "Lettres russes" piece with a further, even more explicit critique of Soviet cultural politics. By 24 May, he had completed "Actualités soviétiques," originally intended for the left-wing *Vendredi*, although it remained unpublished until it appeared in New York in 1990.[108] This was his own response to the discussions initiated by the attack on Shostakovich: "The most recent *mot d'ordre* in Soviet literature is the struggle against 'Formalism.' The signal for the attack was given by the article in Moscow, in *Pravda*. [...] The all-out battle was fought at several writers' meetings in Moscow in the middle of March. At the same time, blood was also shed in battles against 'Formalists' which took place at meetings for artists, architects, theatre directors and musicians." He then provided an explanation of the term "Formalism," looking back through the sensation-seeking but original work of Meierkhol'd to the linguistic investigations undertaken by Shklovsky, Tynianov and Eikhenbaum. But, he pointed out, the term had been used in the recent disputes to lump together all "left-wing" forms in art. And why? "You have to remember that literature in Soviet Russia is a form of state employment, and they hold that the writer is obliged to serve the same goals as the state has set for itself." In other words, the "Formalists" were simply those who did not subscribe to the utilitarian view of literature. "The 'Formalists' displayed very little courage in defending their positions: they didn't justify themselves, but rather repented of their 'errors.' Masochistic repentance, it seems, should be listed as one of the fundamental characteristics of the notorious *âme slave*. Epidemics of public breast-beating have already taken place within Soviet literature over the years since the Revolution, often appearing as something like the medieval processions of flagellants. It's always surprised me that the old, true revolutionaries should stand and watch these processions calmly." Pasternak alone had shown dignity in speaking out against the arguments of the critics of "Formalism." Zamiatin invoked again Bloch's defence in 1934 of a literature "for the 5,000," texts which might not suit the wider mass of readers. And citing the phrase Stalin had famously applied to writers during a meeting in October 1932, he pointed out: "If writers are the 'engineers of human souls,' then laboratory experiments are still a vital condition for the work of an engineer. And even if only one experiment out of 1,000 proves successful, the other 999 are no less necessary than that one."[109] In Moscow, however, the persecution continued, and Pil'niak, his fellow-victim from 1929, was once again subjected to public humiliation at the hands of the literary establishment on 28 October, when his novel *Meat*, co-authored with S. Beliaev, was publicly denounced at a meeting of the Writers' Union.[110]

Annenkov noted that Zamiatin came to visit him on 22 May with Ol'ga Glebova-Sudeikina, Akhmatova's close friend, who had shared an apartment with her in 1921–23 before emigrating to Berlin and Paris in 1924.[z] Two days later, Zamiatin's next long letter to Postnikov in Prague demonstrated that he continued to be very preoccupied with literary developments back in Russia:

> Today is the first really spring-like day, it's warm and sunny. That lifts the spirits, although it doesn't seem as though there's anything to be cheerful about. There are some people who are glad that in Russia there is sausage, and that there are hierarchies and awards, although the very word 'award-winning' is enough to turn my stomach. Amongst respected writers there's just the same toadying. It's just a disgrace: it's got to the point where even *Pravda* remonstrates with them for excessive zeal! […] But this remonstrating is a good sign—will they perhaps educate them to become people rather than slaves there? And then it'll be a place where I can work too (if it's not too late). But for the moment I just sit here, although I'm already fed up with Paris. […] For the greater part of the winter there was work on the novel (still my old Attila), and the first part is written, but as a result, you will understand, the treasury is empty. And

so—cinema again… I get published little by little by the French, the Dutch, the Serbs, and the Americans. Mostly by the French. […] Liudmila Nikolaevna is flourishing in Paris, where she's got even more fed up than me.*

Liudmila inserted the asterisk in the text above, adding a note of her own: "As a writer of fiction, EI is inventing: I'm not in the least fed up with Paris, on the contrary I love it more and more with each passing year."[112] On 1 June, being as usual the one who kept in touch with Bulgakov, she wrote to him: "Nearly two years have passed (just think—2 years!), since I received your last letter. In it you wrote that Elena Sergeevna was planning 'to take you around all these Europes.' And Elena Sergeevna has still not carried out her intention, and you still haven't come." She was apparently unaware of Bulgakov's recent fall from official grace: "More than once we've dreamed of how we would give you a worthy welcome. To the sound of a guitar, like Nikol'ka's in *The Days of the Turbins*, a cantata would be performed in your honour (how splendidly your Nikol'ka sings!), and we would drink a heavy, scented Burgundy. […] We read the reviews of *Dead Souls* [Bulgakov's stage adaptation of Gogol's novel] and of *Molière*, since we get almost all the Moscow papers and journals. […] We don't live badly. With every spring I like Paris more and more. And when EI raises the question of a possible move to London, I protest. I have no desire to part with this astonishing city, with 'la belle France.' But Paris began to get on EI's nerves long ago."[113]

That summer Gor'ky died suddenly, in circumstances which are a matter of some controversy to this day, with some commentators suggesting involvement by Stalin or the security organs. Gide was visiting Moscow at the time, and gave a funeral oration in his honour.[114] Apparently Zamiatin and Annenkov were the only Russians to participate in a memorial evening organised in Paris a few days after his death (and even Annenkov considered that Zamiatin was a little naïve about the extent of Gor'ky's 'good offices').[115] In July, Zamiatin wrote a memorial essay to honour him, which was published as "Maxime Gorki" on 1 August in *La Revue de France*.[116] By coincidence, Jean Renoir finished the filming of his *Lower Depths* that autumn from the screenplay drafted by Zamiatin and Jacques Companeez, starring Jean Gabin, Louis Jouvet, and Suzy Prim. The official premières of *The Lower Depths* [*Les Bas-Fonds*] took place from early December, and received a very good press.[117] By the end of December, Renoir's work had already been awarded the prize for the "Best Film of 1936."[118] It must have been gratifying for Zamiatin, after so many years of what he felt was drudgery for the cinema, to be associated at last with a project that had received widespread recognition in France for its artistic merit.

On 7 October he telephoned Annenkov, and they went out to eat prawns and mussels together in a restaurant. However, Marc Slonim recalled how his friend's health deteriorated that year: "In the fall of 1936 I was summoned by his doctor, who told me that Zamiatin was incurably ill and that his days were numbered, a heart ailment, which kept him in bed for weeks, making his end imminent."[119] On 16 November, he told Kunina-Aleksander that he was unable to work much. By now his hopes of publication seemed to rest principally on her and Yugoslavia: "I sent you the dramatisation of *The Islanders*—that is, the *Bellringers* play—on Saturday, by special delivery. That's the last copy I have, and I think the only one in Europe. *A propos*: at the beginning of 1937 *The Islanders* will appear in one of the Paris journals in French, and *The North*, which you are planning to Serbianise or Croatise—has already been Frenchified and will also soon get printed." He concluded this letter: "For about three months now I've been plagued by some sort of *crises du coeur*, and I'm having to mess about with doctors—I'm fed up with it, and it doesn't fit in with my plans."[120] The doctor Slonim mentioned may well have been Bulgakov's own younger brother Nikolai Afanas'evich, who had emigrated at the time of the Civil War and been working in Paris for many years. Nikolai told his brother that he and Zamiatin had met during the spring of 1934, and Bulgakov, whose intermittent attempts at keeping in touch with the Zamiatins had petered out at that point, wrote back asking him to send their address. Nikolai sent further brief greetings from Zamiatin in 1935. On 9 December 1936 he wrote to Bulgakov: "Evgeny Ivanovich is complaining of his heart, I'm visiting him and treating him: he and his wife send you their greetings."[121]

On 11 December, in a missive to New York written on a postcard of the gargoyles of Notre Dame, Zamiatin wrote in English to Malamuth: "Contemplating Paris like these chimeras, I am asking myself why you did not write me a line all the last year. I am writing you this to remind [you] I am still existing. [...] Have you read *Le retour de l'URSS* by Gide? [sic]" Gide's book, written after his summer trip, had appeared that November and created a sensation with its unexpected denunciation of the totalitarian nature of the Soviet system, just as his sudden turn towards Communism had done four years previously.[122] Zamiatin's English was less fluent and confident now than in previous years—perhaps overlaid now by his French, or because ill-health was affecting him? In his reply a fortnight later Malamuth commented: "I have not yet read André Gide's book *Le retour de l'URSS* but I judge from the vicious attack on it in *Pravda* that it is a fairly intelligent account of conditions in the land of the joyous Stalinist life. I hope to read it soon." Malamuth then provided a detailed account of his own energetic participation in the "American Committee for the Defense of Leon Trotsky": "Although I am not a Trotskyist, I have done whatever I could to secure ordinary human rights for him. [...] It is our Committee that secured asylum for him through the intercession of Diego Rivera and others." He described the contradictory mood of the American proletarian audiences at mass meetings, which booed Stalin, but hissed Max Eastman when he attacked the Stalinist bureaucracy. He also reported that: "Lyons is now writing his *Autobiography*, which is really a confessional on his Russian experiences. It is a kind of apology to all decent people for his share in creating a good reputation for the Frankenstein monster that is now devouring Russia. I have read all that he has written so far, and I find it a very honest book."[123] On 15 December, Zamiatin wrote a long, reflective letter to Kunina-Aleksander:

> I'm having a day today when I'm resting and occupying myself by paying off my "epistolary debts." I'm starting with a letter to you, and then there are 3 letters to New York in the queue, one to Amsterdam, one to Prague... to everywhere except Russia, as you see. I scarcely write "There" any more: the atmosphere there is such that it's better to leave them in peace. I had a letter from Fedin at the beginning of the summer (or rather not from him, but from his wife). He was planning to come here to spend the late summer and autumn in France. But evidently the trip didn't come off for him. [...] Apparently his health has settled, but as for his spiritual well-being—that's not too good, I think. His novel *The Rape of Europe* is a failure, of course: it's a boring, dull and lifeless thing. The Soviet critics tried to cover it up to start with, but now the verdict of "failure" has been passed on it even "There." That's pretty much what Aleksei Tolstoy told me, when he spent a few days in Paris at the end of September. [...] Tolstoy! He's a cynic, and politically he's shameless—he just swims along like a fish in water. He has set aside the completion of his *Peter* in order to write a more "topical" novel, *The*

> *Defence of Tsaritsyn* (which, as we all know, was led by Stalin). So all is perfectly clear... Tolstoy and I did agree over one thing: our opinions of the latest "achievements" of Soviet literature. It's a failed harvest, a drought! Olesha is drinking like a horse and not writing; Babel' and several others are simply not writing, and as for those who are writing—well, it would be better if they didn't. *The Rape of Europe* is dull, Leonov's *Road to the Ocean* rings so false that it makes your teeth ache, it's the weakest thing he's written; [...] Pil'niak... I don't know whether you've read anywhere that not long ago, at an editorial meeting at *Novy mir* (*New World*), he publicly turned to the comrades with a serious question: would he not do better, in their opinion, to abandon literature and "requalify as an honest Soviet official." Not long ago I wrote for *Marianne* (here in Paris) my regular feature on Soviet novels, and with difficulty found only one that was worth writing about—German's *Our Friends*. [...] In the New Year, 1937, I'm hoping to do more journalism (French, of course).

He told her that he wasn't seeing much of Slonim, although he often spoke to him on the telephone. "And as for me—this winter I've rarely left the house because of the state of my health: it isn't a life-threatening business, but it's very unpleasant. It's not so much my heart as the 'sympathetic nerve', in other words it's what the doctors call *fausse angine de la poitrine*. And no one really understands the causes. It's principally brought about by getting overtired, 'excessive smoking' etc. I'm very proud: I've not smoked for 3–4 months now, and I imposed that ban all by myself, even before the doctors did. It's not too bad, but it is very difficult to work without cigarettes: over the years it's developed as a 'conditioned reflex.' I don't like being ill—and do you know, I'm rather ashamed of it?"[124]

The article for *Marianne* Zamiatin mentioned here was the fourth in the series "Lettres russes," and Zamiatin's last piece of writing as a critic, although it was not in fact published at the time. He described Iury German's novel *Our Friends* as a breath of fresh air in the pompous world of Soviet literature written during 1935. He welcomed the unheroic, straightforwardly realistic nature of the heroine Antonina, in whom "there is that witchcraft which in film-heroines is called sex appeal." German had succeeded in making the Communist protagonists plausible characters, although even in this novel the GPU man was presented as an absolutely ideal figure. Zamiatin also reviewed Nikolai Ostrovsky's *How the Steel was Tempered*, which in due course would be held up as an exemplar of Socialist Realism. He observed that in Ostrovsky's case, fame was bestowed upon him from above: "...the Moscow authorities, quite exceptionally, awarded him a medal, and he received congratulations signed by the top people in the Kremlin — including even Stalin himself." He characterised Ostrovsky's literary style as a coarse version of Gor'ky's manner; his renown, therefore, was principally due to the tragic heroism of the author's own life (he was a Party activist despite being blind and paralysed by illness), which Gide had sketched in touching terms in the Appendix to his *Retour de l'URSS*. Zamiatin noted that both of these authors belonged to a younger generation: "But where are the writers of the older generation, who had already, it seemed, established themselves firmly on the Soviet Parnassus—Babel', Olesha, Pil'niak, Leonov, Fedin, Lidin and others? Babel' and Olesha, probably the most talented and interesting of this group, have remained long and stubbornly silent, despite the fact that Soviet critics are constantly reproaching them for this. Others cannot be reproached for their silence, but... perhaps it would have been better if they'd stayed silent: the books of the 'older generation' published this year are a series of failures." This, then, was the bitter fate of the Serapion Brothers, whom he had nurtured, and of their contemporaries. He cited again the attacks on Pil'niak which had driven him to ask whether he should change profession. "When a talented writer asks himself a question like that—there's something to make you stop and think."[125] In fact, at the beginning of 1937 Pil'niak was to undertake an action in Moscow which was a far cry from his humiliating behaviour the previous October. At a writers' meeting to denounce "Fascist-Trotskyites," Pil'niak dared to speak up in defence of Zamiatin's former sparring partner Aleksandr Voronsky, who was already under arrest. Pil'niak himself would be arrested on 28 October, and was shot on 21 April 1938.[126]

Zamiatin's final months are only really reflected for us in his further letters to Irina Kunina-Aleksander. On 4 February 1937 he wrote her a fond and exceptionally lengthy missive, in which he offered a detailed critique of the play about Pushkin's life she had written for the centenary celebrations which were being prepared that year in all Russian-speaking countries. He also drew amusingly on his own experiences of the travails of the playwright: "Dear authoress, be calm: your cold sweat, despair and so on—are all well-known symptoms of that illness known as *morbus authorica*. It's just as unpleasant, but just as harmless, as sea-sickness: and as soon as you've sailed through the première, you'll immediately forget about all these disagreeable sensations and you'll feel wonderful. But until then, you'll be drenched in a cold sweat, more than once. You'll come away from the dress rehearsal in a state of utter despair. After the first scenes, which the audience will greet in a restrained way, you'll be sitting in your box as though on a bed of needles. But towards the end the audience will start to blow their noses and wipe their eyes, and then they'll start to clap and summon the author (or Pushkin), and then the author herself will be wiping her eyes—from the sweet tears of success…" He concluded: "That's all. And so then—farewell, or—*au revoir*? God knows we live in such times that it's hard to know. And in addition—I'm feeling absolutely wretched. […] I send heartfelt greetings to Bozhidar, and sincerest wishes for your success." Just two weeks later, Zamiatin wrote Irina the last letter of his life, from which it was clear that his health had worsened. He did not even prefix this letter with the standard courteous "Dear…," but launched straight into an account of his mood:

> The dull light of Paris in February. Some sort of noxious greyness is creeping into the room through the window. If I were a dog—I'd be howling with misery. But instead of me, there's a radio howling somewhere downstairs. I'm waiting for a call: the doctor's due to visit at any moment, in order to say various comforting phrases which I don't believe… There's a ring—and suddenly, instead of the doctor—Renée Heilbronner, with an enormous package in her arms—and with hugs "*de la part de Irotchka.*" You cannot imagine how timely this was for my morale, to force my mood to change, and to force me to remember that things aren't quite so bad in the world for as long as you have friends. My thanks to you, dear "Irotchka"—above all, for nothing other than you yourself, for your friendship and your concern. It's very difficult for me to allow myself to be overwhelmed by my emotions, or especially, to speak about this, but my goodness, you've triumphed […]! Yesterday morning I began to write you an answer to your letter of 10 Feb., but only had time to write a few lines about "business," about the calculation you suggested based on my future royalties in Yugoslavia. In all conscience I'd prefer to manage without this advance. There are some hopes that in the next few days some of the cinematic projects I've been working on will be decided upon, and then, at least for a while, everything should be all

right. But it's a game of roulette, like the Lotterie Nationale: my hopes may deceive me (or, more likely, I may be deceived by those "respectable" people who work in cinema; they are, with the very smallest of exceptions, gangsters, for whom the prison-cells are crying out). In any case, I was writing to you to say you should wait before sending the money until my next letter, which I was expecting to send in a few days' time. But now that your Renée has brought *un beau billet de cinq cent francs* and deposited it on my desk—declaring that she has a categorical mandate from you to leave the money with me—then I took it, to which I hereby solemnly append my signature. But all the same: what's this for? What is it that's proposed for translation and publication? A book of stories? The novel *Nous autres*? As soon as this becomes clear, please write and tell me: what, who, how much, when? (*A propos*: the novel is coming out this spring in Spanish—in South America, in Santiago) —so that I can work out the accounts concerning my "advances" from you. But still, you've no time to think about this at the moment, at the height of your theatrical excitements: your Pushkin is probably already walking up and down the stage and speaking. [...] Greetings to you, to Pushkin and to Bozhidar. EvgZ.[127]

As Annenkov recalled: "Zamiatin's health became significantly worse at the beginning of 1937. I visited him for the last time a few days before his death. Zamiatin received me lying on a sofa, and of course with a smile on his weary face."[128] Slonim visited too: "Zamiatin became thin, almost transparent; he talked with difficulty, and his only joy was to listen to music, especially to Musorgski, whom he always admired as the greatest expression of Russian genius. He listened to *Boris Godunov* on the day of his death."[129] He was found dead early on the morning of 10 March 1937. Tsvetaeva told Bunin's wife that they had been due to meet at a friend's on the 11th, "...and he said: if I'm well enough..."[130] Damanskaia reported people's astonishment, because so few knew he was ill, let alone seriously—when he occasionally appeared somewhere in Paris amongst Russian writers, he was always immaculately turned out:

E.I. Zamiatin, in the opinion of the doctors, died of heart disease (*angina pectoris*) complicated by flu. [...] On the morning of the 10th it was planned that he should be transferred to a clinic, where he was to have a blood transfusion. He firmly believed in the successful outcome of this operation. But he was not fated to live to see that morning. He passed away between 4 and 6 in the morning, without waking, from heart failure in the opinion of some, from a brain haemorrhage in the opinion of other doctors. It was hard to reconcile oneself to the thought, as one looked at the closed eyes and sharp features of his face, on which there was frozen his subtle, very slightly mocking smile, that this was the face of the already dead Evgeny Zamiatin.[131]

The funeral took place on Friday 12 March, and friends gathered beforehand at his home. In Annenkov's words: "On the day of the funeral I climbed up to the floor of Zamiatin's flat at no. 14, rue Raffet, but I lacked the courage to enter the flat. I remained on the landing, outside the open door. A few minutes later Mstislav Dobuzhinsky came out of the flat, in tears, and leaned against the wall next to me. He told me that Zamiatin's face had preserved its smile." After a short funeral service at 9am in the flat, performed by Father Nikon, the coffin was carried out. Zamiatin—or Liudmila—was evidently sufficiently reconciled with his religious upbringing to want a priest to officiate after his death, and indeed memorial services would be held for him on the anniversaries of his death in 1938 and 1939 in the St Alexander Nevsky Russian Church on rue Daru. Annenkov continued: "Five minutes or so later they carried the coffin out on to the staircase. The stairs in the house were steep, winding, and too narrow, so the coffin had to be taken down in an upright position. There were a lot of people there, but I was so upset that I can't recall their faces or their names."[132] The interment took place at the cemetery at Thiais, which is located in the south-east of Paris, and can now be reached from the nearest metro stations at Villejuif, named after the left-wingers Louis Aragon and Paul Vaillant-Couturier: to get there you come out on to Boulevard Maxime Gorki, that new road inaugurated in this workers' district eighteen months previously, and you keep going along avenue de Stalingrad. There was no Père Lachaise cemetery for Zamiatin, nor indeed the Russian Orthodox cemetery at Ste Geneviève-des-Bois, where 10,000 other Russian émigrés are buried, including distinguished figures such as Bunin, Remizov, Gazdanov, Merezhkovsky, and Gippius.

There was some disagreement amongst Zamiatin's acquaintances after the event about just how many people were present for the funeral itself that morning in Thiais, but all accounts concur that it was a sparsely attended, perfunctory and thoroughly bleak occasion, on a cold day in driving rain, and that the grave was already filling with water when the coffin was lowered into it. Definitely present were Slonim, who had organised things, Tsvetaeva, Damanskaia, Manukhina, Roman Gul' and, presumably, Liudmila. It's not certain whether Annenkov and Dobuzhinsky were there, and Gul' disputed Berberova's claim to have attended. Remizov was unwell with a fever. "There were no funeral speeches. Not a word…"[133]

These were traumatic days in any case for Tsvetaeva, whose daughter Ariadna would leave France for the Soviet Union just three days later, "without a backward glance."[134] The day after the funeral, Tsvetaeva wrote reproachfully to Khodasevich and his wife: "I am one of those who is <u>neither</u> ours <u>nor</u> yours. I was thinking about this with bitterness and gratitude yesterday at the fresh grave of Zamiatin, and I threw a pinch of clay on to his coffin with those words (in my head). <u>Why were you not there?</u> I was the only author there—and for that matter I'm an authoress. There was one other authoress, Damanskaia. It was terribly, searingly <u>meagre</u>—both in people and in flowers.— It was rich only in clay and in winds—from all four corners. […] He died on the 10th, on Wednesday, at 7 in the morning—alone. That is, he was discovered dead at 7am. I feel <u>wild indignation</u> on his behalf."[135] Tsvetaeva had always felt a deep personal affinity with Zamiatin the heretic and independent spirit, with the émigré who never quite fitted in to the Paris emigration and died with an enigmatic smile on his face. "It's a terrible shame, but there is a consoling thought, that he spent the end of his life in spiritual peace and in freedom. We didn't meet frequently, but it was always good: like me, he too was—neither ours, nor yours."[136]

CONCLUSION

During the weeks following Zamiatin's funeral on 12 March 1937, Liudmila naturally received affectionate letters of condolence from close friends (the Grigor'evs,[1] the Fedins[2]), and also some from literary figures she knew less well, from across a wide range of political sympathies within the Russian emigration. The historical novelist and chemist Mark Aldanov offered his deepest sympathies: "I didn't know your late husband well in person, but much admired him as a great writer and a bold, independent man."[3] The writer Boris Zaitsev, a close friend of Bunin's, told her that although they had never met her, they had known Zamiatin himself years before and had great affection for him.[4] In fact, the Zaitsev family would become some of Liudmila's closest friends over the following years and decades. Back in Moscow, Bulgakov heard of his friend's death by 21 March. In a continuation of the coincidences which marked the trajectory of the two writers' lives, he would spend the summer of 1938 relaxing at a *dacha* on the very street in Lebedian' where Zamiatin had been born and brought up (Elena Sergeevna had a connection there through her first husband). Bulgakov was perhaps fortunate to escape arrest during Stalin's Terror, dying in his own bed three years to the day after Zamiatin, on 10 March 1940.[5]

There were one or two tributes from French admirers: André Pierre in *Les Nouvelles Littéraires* referred to Zamiatin as "*Cet excellent écrivain, qui s'était fait beaucoup d'amis dans les milieux littéraires français*", while B. Cauvet-Duhamel, the translator of *We* [as *Nous autres*], declared to Liudmila: "*J'aimais beaucoup M. Zamiatine, dont le talent et la sincerité étaient si éclatants.*"[6] Kunina-Aleksander was too distressed to write straight away: "I believe that among Evgeny Ivanovich's friends and pupils, readers and admirers there are still many who, like me, will carry to the grave his every word, every kindness, reproach, lesson, counsel and joke. His magnanimity, courage, bravery and foresight—those noble, distinctive features of his free and heretical spirit—rendered him solitary amongst other people." She was planning to visit Paris with Bozhidar in early June, and pressed Liudmila to go back with them afterwards for a rest.[7]

On 24 April an announcement appeared in *Poslednie novosti* that a memorial evening was to be held on the 26th, with Marc Slonim presiding. The plan was for Drieu la Rochelle and Jean Renoir to take part: Paul Oettly and Maria Reinhardt would perform a portion of *The Flea*, and Jean Gabin and Suzy Prim would perform part of *Les Bas-fonds*. The paper reported on 28 April that in the event Sirin (Nabokov) had given a reading of *The Cave*, and Bunin read *The Dragon*. This rather remarkable line-up again attested to the fact that Zamiatin was actually far from being ostracised or despised amongst the entire White emigration. Maria Reinhardt read *April*, while Drieu la Rochelle reminisced about the many fascinating conversations he'd had with Zamiatin in bistros, despite his sometimes hesitant French.[8]

Some of the obituaries laid emphasis on the difficulty of his final years. Damanskaia claimed that "in reality he died of misery, of spiritual loneliness, of the fact that he'd not found in emigration what he'd counted on, probably, when he parted with Russia five years ago: he didn't find a readership."[9] Mikhail Osorgin, who described him as "a great Russian writer, a rare stylist, and an educated and clever man," also mentioned his "very straitened circumstances."[10] There were those who seemed keen to exaggerate his failures. An article in *Vozrozhdenie (Rebirth)* by "Gulliver" declared that he had died "hungry and destitute." "Gulliver" was the pen-name adopted by Nina Berberova (sometimes with her partner Khodasevich), and this aggressively inaccurate remark reflects again the hostility towards Zamiatin she'd felt on first meeting him in 1932. Liudmila was deeply offended (the comment was also underlined in red in Remizov's copy of the article), and she succeeded in forcing *Vozrozhdenie* to print a retraction.[11] The poet and critic Georgy Adamovich concluded: "There can be differences of opinion about Zamiatin as an artist. But this is what should be precious to everyone about his personality: he was the only one of the significant Soviet writers who didn't capitulate, didn't consent to irrevocable actions, who found in himself the strength and the courage to say 'no.'"[12]

In May 1938 Liudmila moved out of rue Raffet to a smaller apartment a mile or so to the south, at 14 place du Dr Paul Michaux, where she lived as a *"réfugiée russe (Nansen)"* until her death in 1965. She was buried alongside Zamiatin in the cemetery at Thiais. For nearly thirty years she had done her best to defend his posthumous legacy and promote his works, fighting loyally and determinedly against what must at times have seemed like insuperable obstacles. For the truth is that by the 1930s Zamiatin had already faded into obscurity as a writer. The publications of *We* abroad — in the stilted translation into English in 1924, followed by versions in Czech and French which had gone virtually unnoticed — had failed to establish his international reputation. A trickle of other publications in various languages and countries during the 1930s had not been enough to change that, and it took all Liudmila's tenacity to overcome this apparent oblivion during the years after his death.

To start with, there was the question of creating and preserving his archive. Just before they left Leningrad, Zamiatin had asked Sof'ia Esenina-Tolstaia on 11 November 1931 to look after some of his papers. She worked at the State Literary Museum in Moscow, and eventually she ensured that many of the materials were transferred to the Moscow literary archives at IMLI and RGALI (formerly TsGALI). It is thought that a portion of these materials may have gone missing, perhaps including the draft versions of *We*.[13] As for the papers and books which came out with them to the West, or which accumulated there during the 1930s, it was Liudmila who looked after those. "Fortunately Liudmila Nikolaevna was notable for her rare care in relation to Zamiatin's entire literary legacy, and she took great trouble to preserve all that he'd written — right down to the briefest notes, notebooks, and all his drafts and letters. And these were not only preserved, but at the same time they were sorted according to chronological and other indicators, with precise indications of dates and other explanatory remarks. Zamiatin's archives survived."[14] Like Bulgakov's widow Elena, and Mandel'shtam's widow Nadezhda, Liudmila accomplished this heroic feat in very difficult circumstances.

Three years after Zamiatin's death, Paris fell to the Nazis. In some haste, Liudmila packed up his archive and entrusted it for safekeeping to the historian Boris Nikolaevsky, who had undertaken to conceal a number of archives for Russians in France. But when the War ended, Nikolaevsky was not at first able to remember where he had put it: in August 1946 he explained that her suitcase had reached him at the last moment, and it was not with the other archives, which were hidden in a basement and had recently been dug up. He asked her to remind him what it looked like, and to send him a key if she had one. Only in November 1947 was he able to reassure her that it was safe, and that he had unpacked it himself; but there would be a delay in sending it because of Dutch postal regulations (it must have been hidden in the Netherlands). In fact, it took until September 1950 for the archive finally to reach her, a full decade after it had been handed over.[15]

Back in Russia, the books and papers Zamiatin had left in his home were also miraculously saved. Shortly after the death of the faithful Agrafena Pavlovna at the height of the siege of Leningrad, the literary scholar A.P. Mogiliansky visited the apartment at 29 Zhukovsky Street on 8 August 1942, as part of a systematic attempt by the library authorities to rescue abandoned collections. Books in Russian, French, English and German were scattered on the floor, together with papers: he filled three sacks with these materials, which included the 334 pre-emigration letters to Liudmila from Zamiatin. The very fact of these letters having been left behind when the couple emigrated in 1931 seems to provide further evidence that they hoped eventually to return. Mogiliansky had everything taken to the Public Library, to preserve the archive for posterity.

After the seminal 1950s publications of Zamiatin's works in Russian in the USA, Liudmila was approached by L.F. Magerovsky, Curator of the Bakhmeteff Archive at the University of Columbia in New York, to donate her archive to them. The acquisition took place in 1957; but Liudmila wrote to Magerovsky that the archive was "unfortunately far from complete: one part perished during the Occupation." Liudmila kept back the personal part of the archive, and she typed out copies of many of the literary texts and drafts before sending them to Columbia. After she died, the remaining collection passed to Boris Zaitsev's daughter Natal'ia, who presented it in 1995 to the Bibliothèque de Documentation Internationale Contemporaine (BDIC) at the University of Paris X at Nanterre.

In the meantime, Liudmila had been doing her best to get Zamiatin's works into print as well. The first significant publication was the unfinished Attila novel *Scourge of God*, which came out in Paris in 1939 in a text edited by Marc Slonim.[16] The publishers "Petropolis" in Berlin were apparently on the point of publishing *We* in 1939, but the outbreak of the Second World War put a halt to what would have been a crucial first publication in Russian.[17] After the end of the war, the two figures who played an absolutely vital role in retrieving the fortunes of Zamiatin's novel—and securing his modern reputation—were Gleb Struve and George Orwell. While the war was still at its height, on 17 February 1944, George Orwell wrote to Struve, then a Lecturer at the School of Slavonic and East European Studies at the University of London, thanking him for his book *25 Years of Soviet Russian Literature*: "It has already aroused my interest in Zamyatin's *We*, which I had not heard of before. I am interested in that kind of book, and even keep making notes for one myself that may get written sooner or later." Orwell was lent a copy of the novel in its French translation during the summer of 1944, and wrote a review of it in *Tribune* on 4 January 1946, describing it as:

> [...] one of the literary curiosities of this book-burning age. [...]
> ... it is astonishing that no English publisher has been enterprising enough to reissue it. [...] Aldous Huxley's *Brave New World* must be partly derived from it... [...] The atmosphere of the two books is similar, and it is roughly speaking the same kind of society that is being described, though Huxley's book shows less political awareness and is more influenced by recent biological and psychological theories. [...] It is this intuitive grasp of the irrational side of totalitarianism—human sacrifice, cruelty as an end in itself, the worship of a Leader who is credited with divine attributes—that makes Zamyatin's book superior to Huxley's. [...] What Zamyatin seems to be aiming at is not any particular country but the implied aims of industrial civilisation.

A couple of weeks later, at Orwell's invitation, the two men met for lunch in London, and Struve told Orwell about his plan for getting a new English translation of *We* made, for which he was proposing to write an introduction. Struve pursued this idea by sending a letter on 7 April 1946 to Remizov, to ask whether Liudmila Nikolaevna had survived the war, and where he could obtain a copy of the work in English or French. Presumably Remizov then put him in touch with Liudmila Nikolaevna, to whom Struve wrote two weeks later to express gratitude for her offer to send copies of the novel in English and French (this despite not having her archive at the time), and for suggesting Marc Slonim as a contact. Remizov was able to provide Struve with some Russian proofs (perhaps from "Petropolis"?) in May. That autumn Struve set off for America, and was soon offered a professorial chair in California. Between December 1946 and July 1949, precisely the period of the writing and publication of *1984*, Orwell wrote at least nine letters to Struve, and to a number of British publishers, in his determination to see *We* printed in a new translation.

On 24 January 1947, announcing inaccurately that it was about to be reissued, Orwell made a further attempt in *Tribune* to draw readers' attention to Zamiatin: "Look out for this book." Two years later, in the spring of 1949, Orwell wrote to Fredric Warburg, (the publisher of *1984*): "I just think somebody ought to print it & that it is disgraceful that a book of this kind, with its curious history as well as its intrinsic interest, should stay out of print when so much rubbish is published every day." By now Orwell was in hospital, terminally ill with tuberculosis, and his letter to Struve about *We* of 27 July 1949 was the last letter he was ever able to type for himself. He died in January 1950.[18]

The unwavering determination of Orwell and Struve eventually paid off, not with a new translation of the novel into English, but with the first ever full publication of the novel in Russian in 1952. This was achieved when Vera Aleksandrova of the Chekhov Press in New York approached Liudmila in 1951 with the proposal, which she readily accepted.[19] While there is no actual evidence that Struve had brought this about, letters from Remizov to Liudmila in September 1952 expressing confidence that Zamiatin's second book—his volume of literary portraits called *Litsa* (*People*) —would also get published by the Chekhov Press, and that "Gleb Petrovich" [Struve] would be sure to help, certainly suggest that this was very likely to have been the case.[20] It seems somehow pleasingly appropriate that in the end it should have been an Anglo-Russian impetus which at last saw this Russian Anglophile's greatest work into print. It was especially apt since, as Michael Glenny has argued, it was precisely Zamiatin's Russian novel which had provided a key link in the development of British anti-utopian science-fiction, bridging the gap between H.G. Wells on the one hand, and Huxley and Orwell in the following century.[21]

The 1952 publication of *We* in Russian, followed by his *People* in 1955, generated an entirely new wave of interest in his writing. Translations of *We* into several other languages, including Italian and German, followed during the 1950s, together with a reprint of the Zilboorg translation in 1959 and a new English version by B.G. Guerney in 1960. University departments of Russian across Europe and the United States enthusiastically adopted the text, which, largely ignored and disparaged in the author's lifetime, had now revealed itself, after Stalinism and the Second World War, as one of the most prescient pieces of fiction in its century.

At the University of California at Berkeley, this new interest in Zamiatin's writings was reflected in a 1965 doctoral dissertation by

Alex Shane, which he developed into his seminal study, *The Life and Works of Evgenij Zamjatin*, in 1968. Shane's supervisor for this project was—of course—Professor Gleb Struve, and even though he had no access at the time to archives in Russia, Shane was able to consult with Liudmila herself before her death, as well as with Zamiatin's friends Charles Malamuth and Marc Slonim. Malamuth told Shane: "He was a man of great courage, great integrity; hence, uncompromising in his devotion to certain basic principles and standards. [...] There was no self-deception, no flight from reality in Zamyatin's stance on issues and principles."[22] It was then this same devoted group of his friends who, with the assistance of Orwell and Struve, succeeded in carrying Zamiatin's reputation intact into the second half of the century, where it would grow and flourish.

Back in Russia, Zamiatin's name had become virtually unmentionable after the mid-1930s, except very occasionally as "a bourgeois writer who had maliciously slandered the Soviet state in his novel *We*."[23] Despite the immense contributions he'd made to the early years of Soviet literature, his role was almost entirely airbrushed out of Soviet literary history. There is scarcely a mention of his name, for example, in the memoirs and correspondence Fedin and Erenburg published during their lifetimes. There was a moment during the Thaw, in 1966, when the Public Library in Leningrad ventured to compile a bio-bibliographical catalogue of Zamiatin's works, but it was not published at the time—the censors simply had it removed from volume 7 of the encyclopaedia of *Russian Soviet Writers*.[24] His rehabilitation came only in the dying days of the USSR, when the policy of *glasnost'* led in 1988 to the first publication of *We* in his native land, in the journal *Znamia* (*The Banner*). In the absence of any archival holdings of manuscripts or drafts of the novel, this publication (like all subsequent publications in Russia until the new edition of 2011) was obliged simply to reproduce the Chekhov Press text published in 1952.[25] Since the 1990s a series of conferences and important publications in Russia by scholars in Moscow and St Petersburg, as well as in the provinces, and the opening of a museum in his former home in Lebedian', have established Zamiatin as a Russian writer of the foremost importance, his inclusion in school and university syllabuses alike now qualifying him without question—if belatedly—as a Russian classic.

It seems fitting, nevertheless, for two of Zamiatin's admirers outside Russia, writing in English, to sum him up. The first is Charles Malamuth: "Throughout the 53 years of his life (1884–1937) Eugene

Zamyatin was the only Russian writer of Soviet citizenship whom the Kremlin could not force into its livery. He lived and died true to the high civic standards set for Russian letters by its great masters during the nineteenth century. [...] He welcomed the liberation from old oppressions in the Revolution of 1917, but he resented its blighting dogmatism and regimentation, and fought against it at once."[26] Marc Slonim, looking back at the man whose life he had so nearly wrecked in 1927, and whom he had escorted to his grave 10 years later, summed him up as follows:

> Alexander Blok called him with friendly mockery "the Englishman from Moscow." Lean, clean-shaven, with reddish hair parted on the side, always wearing tweeds and with an "unextinguishable" pipe in his wide generous mouth, he indeed resembled an Englishman. He spoke in an even voice, hardly changing his inflections when throwing out a sarcastic hint or an ironic allusion; his manners were reserved, and to those who knew him but little he seemed all "buttoned up," a man who kept an "unmelting icicle" inside—some hard core of perfect self-mastery, strong will and keen intelligence. But this gentleman was an independent artist and a fearless thinker. He combined logic and imagination, precision and fantasy. The technician who preached "functional expressionism" and taught young men how to write a compact, economical prose, was a man of strong passions. Under his balanced exterior were national traits of intensity and deep inner life. Like many people with a scientific background, he loved dreams and irrational flights, and glorified man's desire to overcome all limitations. An enemy of conventional rules and dogmatic structures he had a romantic devotion to freedom and individualism, and exposed whatever endangered them.[27]

CHAPTER 1

1. Letter to Liudmila, 26 March 1906, *RNZ*, 13, 14, 15; 334 letters written by Zamiatin to Liudmila Nikolaevna Usova (Zamiatina) between 1906 and 1931 were first published in this annotated edition, and the volume has become a vital source for any biographical study of the writer.
2. Zamiatin himself gives the date as 19 January in his 1920 and 1923 autobiographies (RGALI, F. 1776, op. 2, 3; *Ia boius'*, 3) and his military service registration document of the same year confirms this (BDIC, dossier 124), while his student file gives the date as 20 January (TSGIA, F. 478, delo 765, op. 1). His 1916 foreign passport includes certificates offering both dates (BDIC, dossier 133). But the Lebedian' Register of Births for January 1884 confirms that he was born on the 20th and christened on the 21st (page from *Metricheskaya Kniga na 1884*, reproduced in the Zamiatin Museum).
3. Strizhev, 103; Komlik, 109. Aleksandra Ivanovna Zamiatina (Volkova) was born on 7 May 1885.
4. Zamiatin's brief autobiographies of 1922, 1923, 1924 and 1928 are to be found in *Ia boius'*, 2–12, and provide much of the information drawn upon in these pages. Another important source for this period is *Zamiatinskaia entsiklopediia*. See *RNZ*, 422 for Zamiatin's letter to "Katia" of 26 February 1892.
5. Letter to S. A. Vengerov, 27 January 1915, "Perepiska E. I. Zamiatina s S. A. Vengerovym," M. Iu. Liubimova, T. A. Kukushkina and E. Iu. Litvin (eds.), in *EZ*, 186.
6. *RNZ*, 420–421.
7. Strizhev, 103; 1931 autobiography, *Katalog vystavki*, 5.
8. Certificate reproduced in the Zamiatin Museum.
9. Letter to A. I. Zamiatina, 13–14 November 1901, reproduced in the Zamiatin Museum.
10. 1922 autobiography, in *Ia boius'*, 2; Briukhanova, 24.
11. 1923 autobiography, in *Ia boius'*, 3; Golikova, 2.
12. Student file, TSGIA, F. 478, op. 1, delo 765.
13. 1931 autobiography, *Katalog vystavki*, 5.
14. Golikova, 2.

15. Letter to A.I. Zamiatina, 7/20 October 1902, N.N. Komlik and N.S. Zamiatina, "'Predaniia russkogo semeistva' (Novye materialy k biografii E.I. Zamiatina)," in *Literaturovedenie*, 434–435.
16. The term, which describes someone who was not of noble birth according to the Tsarist "Table of Ranks," is used on a document of 13 November 1905 indicating that Zamiatin had made himself available for military service (BDIC, dossier 128).
17. 1931 autobiography, *Katalog vystavki*, 5, 6; letter to Liudmila, 22 April 1906, *RNZ*, 30–31.
18. Student file, TSGIA, F. 478, op. 1, delo 765; Briukhanova, 26.
19. Student file, TSGIA, F. 478, op. 1, delo 765.
20. 1928 autobiography', in *Ia boius'*, 9.
21. Ibid.; 1931 autobiography, *Katalog vystavki*, 6.
22. 1923 and 1924 autobiographies, in *Ia boius'*, 4, 5.
23. For an account of the friendship between Zamiatin and Grebenshchikov, see M.Iu. Liubimova, "Ia.P. Grebenshchikov i E.I. Zamiatin: Perepiska (1916–28)," in *EZ*, 252–270. Liudmila's tax return for 1963 gives her date of birth as 20 October 1889 (BDIC, dossier 209), whereas information privately supplied by Marina Liubimova about her medical student record gives 5 September 1884, which seems more plausible. Other sources suggest 1883.
24. Zamiatin made notes about these early days of their relationship, which he then sent to Liudmila as an enclosure with his letter of 9–10 May 1906, *RNZ*, 38–41.
25. Liubimova (a), 98–99; this source provides much of the material in these paragraphs.
26. Letter to Liudmila, 26 March 1906, *RNZ*, 16, note 1.
27. 1928 autobiography, in *Ia boius'*, 9.
28. Strizhev, 104.
29. M.Iu. Liubimova, "Evgeny Zamiatin—avtor romana *My*" in *My* (2011), 5.
30. M.Iu. Liubimova, "Biografiia E.I. Zamiatina: istochniki dlia rekonstruktsii," in *EZ*, 8–36 (12); this analysis is further developed in her "Evgeny Zamiatin—avtor romana *My*" in *My* (2011), 37–38.
31. Letter to Liudmila, 9 April 1906, *RNZ*, 23.
32. Quoted in letter to Liudmila, 9–10 May 1906, *RNZ*, 37.
33. Letter to Liudmila, 9–10 May 1906, *RNZ*, 36.
34. Much of the material for the remainder of this chapter is drawn from the following letters from Zamiatin to Liudmila, and the accompanying notes: 26 March; 6, 9, 15, 17, and 22 April; 5, 9–10,

and 20–23 May 1906, *RNZ*, 13–43. The relevant dates will be given after quotations in the text.
35. The code has been deciphered by Buchina and Liubimova (*RNZ*, 17). On 22 April 1906 he told Liudmila that his letter of 10 April had probably been intercepted, since a policeman who knew him had watched him delivering it to the postal carriage at the station (*RNZ*, 30).
36. M. Iu. Liubimova notes that this paraphrase indicates that Zamiatin had been reading Nietzsche's *Beyond Good and Evil*, which had been translated into Russian in 1905 (*RNZ*, 21, note 2). For a discussion of the philosophical and political works Zamiatin was reading during 1906 see M. Iu. Liubimova, "Biografiia E. I. Zamiatina: Istochniki dlia rekonstruktsii," in *EZ*, 8–36, and her "Evgeny Zamiatin—avtor romana *My*," in *My* (2011), 37–82.
37. 1928 autobiography, in *Ia boius'*, 10.
38. Student file, TSGIA, F. 478, op. 1, delo 765.
39. Letter to Liudmila, 1 July 1906, *RNZ*, 45–48; 1928 autobiography, in *Ia boius'*, 10.
40. Seton-Watson, 624.
41. E. Zamiatin, "L. Andreev" (1922), in *Litsa* (New York: Inter-Language Literary Associates, 1967), 53.
42. 1928 autobiography, in *Ia boius'*, 10.
43. Seton-Watson, 599–600.
44. Student file, TSGIA, F. 478, op. 1, delo 765.

Chapter 2

1. *Katalog vystavki*, 13; Briukhanova, 28–29.
2. Golikova, 3; BDIC, dossier 185.
3. BDIC, dossiers 133b/120 (3).
4. 1928 autobiography, in *Ia boius'*, 10.
5. Letter from Boklevsky, 19 June 1911, Nechiporenko, 71.
6. *Katalog vystavki*, 13.
7. 1928 autobiography, in *Ia boius'*, 10–11.
8. "Zhurnal dlya pishchevareniya," in *Ia boius'*, 14–16.
9. Traces survive in the archives of preliminary sketches from 1907–08 for short stories entitled *Morning and Evening, In the Crowd,* and *A Snowy Window,* and for a cycle of four novellas with names of flowers, planned under the collective name of *The Flowers Speak*

to Me at Twilight or *A Mirror of Flowers*. He followed these in the summer of 1909 with *The Tale of a Sweet Young Lady*, a "parable" in verse called *Ngabami the Wise*, and a miniature called *Smiles* (IMLI, F. 47, op. 1, ed. khr. 11, 5–7, 8–9, 12–14, 18).

10. Letter to A.I. Zamiatina (Volkova), 19 November 1908, in N.N. Komlik and N.S. Zamiatina, "'Predaniia russkogo semeistva' (Novye materialy k biografii E.I. Zamiatina)," in *Literaturovedenie*, 436–437.
11. Letter to Liudmila, 27 July 1910, *RNZ*, 66–68.
12. Letter to Liudmila, 14 June 1909, *RNZ*, 51; *RNZ*, 439.
13. Letters to Liudmila, 27 and 29 July 1909, *RNZ*, 52–54.
14. Letters to Liudmila, 30 December 1909; 22 July 1910; 15–16, 19–20, 25, and 27–29 June 1911, *RNZ*, 62, 65–66, 79–85.
15. Letters to Liudmila, 2 August 1910, 5 June 1911, *RNZ*, 69, 74–76.
16. Letter to Liudmila, 5 July 1911, *RNZ*, 86–88.
17. Letter to Liudmila, 21–22 August 1911, *RNZ*, 94–95.
18. Letter to Liudmila, 9–10 January 1912, *RNZ*, 109–110.
19. Letters to Liudmila, 25 August and 13 September 1911, *RNZ*, 97, 99–101.
20. Letters to Liudmila, 7–8, 13, and 21 September 1912, *RNZ*, 123–126.
21. 1924 autobiography, *Ia boius'*, 5; "Zakulisy," in *Ia boius'*, 160.
22. Briukhanova, 32; 1922 autobiography, in *Ia boius'*, 2–3.
23. Letter to Liudmila, 29 January 1912, *RNZ*, 115–116.
24. See letter to Liudmila, 5 June 1909, *RNZ*, 51, note 1.
25. S. Postnikov, "Stranitsy iz literaturnoi biografii E.I. Zamiatina," (ed. R. Iangirov), *Russ. Stud.* II, 2, 516–520 (on p. 517, Postnikov mistakenly dates this first encounter to 1912).
26. Strizhev, 104.
27. Letter to Liudmila, 22 June 1913, *RNZ*, 130–132.
28. Letter to Liudmila, 30 June 1913 (letter 1), *RNZ*, 133.
29. *Zapisnye knizhki*, 16–27.
30. Letters to Liudmila, 3 and 26 July 1913, *RNZ*, 134–137, 141–143.
31. Letter to Liudmila, 21–22 July 1913, *RNZ*, 139–141.
32. Ibid.
33. "Perepiska E.I. Zamiatina s V.S. Miroliubovym," N.Iu. Griakalova and E.Iu. Litvin (eds.), *Russ. Stud.* II, 2, 422.
34. "Zakulisy," in *Ia boius'*, 163.
35. "Perepiska E.I. Zamiatina s V.S. Miroliubovym," N.Iu. Griakalova and E.Iu. Litvin (eds.), *Russ. Stud.* II, 2, 422–425.
36. Letter to Liudmila, 7 September 1913, *RNZ*, 148–150.

37. *Katalog vystavki*, 14; the invitation is reproduced in *RNZ*, 159.
38. Letters to Liudmila, 23 and 24 September 1913, *RNZ*, 151–153.
39. BDIC, dossier 210; S. Postnikov, "Stranitsy iz literaturnoi biografii E.I. Zamiatina," ed. R. Iangirov, *Russ. Stud.* II, 2, 517–518.
40. Letters to Liudmila, 20, 28, and 30–31 October 1913, *RNZ*, 162–163, 164–167.
41. BDIC, dossier 210; for a useful discussion of the influence of Remizov see Cavendish's chapter "Zamiatin and Literary Populism," 9–32.
42. "Perepiska E.I. Zamiatina s V.S. Miroliubovym," N.Iu. Griakalova and E.Iu. Litvin (eds.), *Russ. Stud.* II, 2, 417–18; I have translated the title of the story *Uezdnoe* as *A Provincial Tale*, but it seems appropriate to translate the title of the identically named collection of stories as *Provincial Life*.
43. RGB, F. 9, kart. 1, ed. khr. 49.
44. Annenkov, 1, 252–253; BDIC, dossier 126.
45. Letter from A.I. Volkova, early April 1914, *RNZ*, 541.
46. See first letter to Liudmila of 17 May 1916, *RNZ*, note 2, 203.
47. Letters to Liudmila of 13, 14–15 and 16 April 1914, *RNZ*, 171–173; and see "Steamer-icebreaker Suur Tõll" at http://www.meremuuseum.ee/?op=body&id=43 (accessed 19 August 2010).
48. Letters to Liudmila, 1, 2, 3, 4–5, 6 and 8 June 1914, *RNZ*, 173–176.
49. Letters to Liudmila, 14–16 and 28 July 1914, *RNZ*, 178, 180.
50. Letter to Liudmila, 25 July 1914, *RNZ*, 179.
51. *The Town of Alatyr'* was completed on 28 January 1915, after 3 drafts, and published in *Russkaia mysl'* 9 (1915); see T.A. Kukushkina, "Materialy E.I. i L.N. Zamiatinykh v sobraniiakh Pushkinskogo Doma. Annotirovannyi katalog," in *EZ*, 411.
52. Letters to Liudmila, 12, 14–16, 25 and 28 July 1914, *RNZ*, 176–181.
53. Letter to Liudmila, 13 November 1914, *RNZ*, 184.
54. IMLI, F. 47, op. 3, ed. khr. 62.
55. Zamiatin supplied the biographical information on 27 January, but failed to provide the additional bibliographical information Vengerov requested on 10 September 1916, half-way through his stay in England, and so his entry did not in the end appear in the volume; see M.Iu. Liubimova, T.A. Kukushkina and E.Iu. Litvin (eds.), "Perepiska E.I. Zamiatina s S.A. Vengerovym," in *EZ*, 186–187.
56. Letter to S.A. Vengerov, 15 December 1916, M.Iu. Liubimova, T.A. Kukushkina and E.Iu. Litvin (eds.), "Perepiska E.I. Zamiatina s S.A. Vengerovym," in *EZ*, 191.

57. IMLI, F. 47, op. 2, ed. khr. 43, 44; and see notice in *Den'* for 8 October 1915 in BDIC, dossier 210; also the letter of 4 October 1915 to P. Shchegolev, IMLI, op. 3, ed. khr. 17.
58. *RNZ*, 522.
59. P. Tikhanov, *Kriptoglossariy*; D. K. Zelenin, *Velikorusskie skazki permskoi gubernii; Kurioznoe i kratkoe iz'iasnenie liubopytstva dostoinykh nauk fiziognomii i khiromantii*; the 18th-century author P. S. Mogila's book for children about the Orthodox faith; and S. V. Maksimov's *Nechistaia sila*. See M. Iu. Liubimova, "Ia. P. Grebenshchikov i E. I. Zamiatin. Perepiska (1916–28)," in *EZ*, 255.
60. IMLI, F. 47, op. 3, ed. khr. 88.
61. BDIC, dossier 210.
62. IMLI, F. 47, op. 3, ed. khr. 142.
63. *RNZ*, 529.
64. A. Remizov, *Ukrepa: Slovo k russkoi zemle, o zemle rodnoi, tainostiakh zemnykh i sud'be*; RNB, F. 292, ed. khr. 43.
65. "Perepiska E. I. Zamiatina s V. S. Miroliubovym," N. Iu. Griakalova and E. Iu. Litvin (eds.), *Russ. Stud.* II, 2, 432.

Chapter 3

1. "Russian Shipbuilding: Problems Following the Revolution. Recovery from Industrial Paralysis. Second Five-Year Plan," by Professor Eugene Zamiatin of the Leningrad Shipbuilding Institute, *Glasgow Herald Trade Review*, (31 December 1932), quoted in Tejerizo, 70.
2. *RNZ*, 193–94, note 1.
3. BDIC, dossier 133.
4. French and Smith, 40–43; Keys and Smith (a), 18–29; McGuire, 12–15; Kitchen, 6–7.
5. Letters to Liudmila, 28 March and 12 June 1916, *RNZ*, 194, 205.
6. BDIC, dossier 133.
7. Letter to Liudmila, 3–4/16–17 April, *RNZ*, 195–196.
8. 1928 autobiography, in *Ia boius'*, 11.
9. Letters to Liudmila, 30/17 April and 11 May/28 April 1916, *RNZ*, 197–198, 200.
10. Letter to Remizov, 22/5 May 1916, Buznik (a), 178.
11. Letters to Liudmila, 21/8 and 23/10 June 1916, *RNZ*, 207–208; the Zamiatin scholar Alan Myers obtained the support of Iosif

Brodsky in his successful campaign to have a blue plaque attached to Zamiatin's Sanderson Road home in 2002.
12. Letter to Liudmila, 30/17 April 1916, *RNZ*, 198.
13. Ellis, 3.
14. Letter to Liudmila, 9 June/27 May 1916, *RNZ*, 204.
15. Telegram to Liudmila, 18 June 1916, *RNZ*, 208.
16. Letter to Liudmila, 27/14 July 1916, *RNZ*, 209–210.
17. Letter to Liudmila, 1 August/19 July 1916, *RNZ*, 211.
18. Letter from Liudmila to Zamiatin, 15 July 1916, *RNZ*, 541–542; she numbered this as the 8th letter she had sent him.
19. Letters to Liudmila, 24/6, 24/7 [sic], and 27/9 August 1916, *RNZ*, 212–214; Zamiatin numbered this last one as the 23rd letter he had sent her.
20. Telegram to Liudmila, 9 August 1916, *RNZ*, 215.
21. Letter from Liudmila to Zamiatin, 10 August 1916, *RNZ*, 543.
22. Letters from Liudmila to Zamiatin, 17 and 23 August 1916, *RNZ*, 544–545.
23. Telegram to Liudmila, 1 September 1916, *RNZ*, 216.
24. 1928 autobiography, in *Ia boius'*, 11.
25. Draft letter quoted by M.Iu. Liubimova, "Ia.P. Grebenshchikov i E.I. Zamiatin. Perepiska (1916–28)," in *EZ*, 256–258.
26. Letter to Liudmila, 9 June/27 May 1916, *RNZ*, 205.
27. Telegram to Liudmila, 10 August 1916, *RNZ*, 215.
28. "O moikh zhenakh, o ledokolakh i o Rossii," (1922), in *Ia boius'*, 182.
29. 1923 autobiography, in *Ia boius'*, 4.
30. 1922 autobiography, in *Ia boius'*, 3.
31. Kaznina, 200–01.
32. Parish, 22, 28, 31, 33, 75.
33. IMLI, F. 47, op. 3, ed. khr. 4.
34. IMLI, F. 47, op. 3, ed. khr. 12.
35. N.Iu. Griakalova and E.Iu. Litvin (eds.), "Perepiska E.I. Zamiatina s V.S. Miroliubovym," *Russ. Stud.* II, 2, 432–433.
36. Letter to Remizov, 22 April/5 May 1916, Buznik (a), 177–178.
37. Letters to Liudmila, 11 May/28 April and 30/17 May 1916, *RNZ*, 200, 202.
38. Letter to Liudmila, 30/17 May 1916, *RNZ*, 202–203.
39. Primochkina (a), 148; BDIC, dossier 210.
40. Primochkina (b), 181.

41. Letter from S. A. Vengerov, 10 September 1916, in M. Iu. Liubimova, T. A. Kukushkina and E. Iu. Litvin, "Perepiska E. I. Zamiatina s S. A. Vengerovym," in *EZ*, 188–190.
42. Ibid., 190–192.
43. IMLI F. 47, op. 1, ed. khr. 38.
44. Letter to Grebenshchikov, 28 August 1916, in M. Iu. Liubimova, "Ia.P. Grebenshchikov i E. I. Zamiatin. Perepiska (1916–28)," *EZ*, 257.
45. IMLI, F. 47, op. 1, ed. khr. 39–42.
46. IMLI, F. 47, op. 1, ed. khr. 33–36; op. 1, 32: this version is dated 1916 in error.
47. For an account of the respectable upbringing of a typical middle-class child in the period, centred around the wholesome amusements approved by the local Church, see Peacock.
48. This is one of the many discoveries made during his research on Zamiatin in the North-East by Alan Myers, who wrote a number of important articles on the subject (see Bibliography); on Sir Andrew Noble see Dougan, 93.
49. *Victory Meeting*, 58, 95.
50. Ellis, 95.
51. Tyne & Wear Archives, *Register of Aliens*, DS/WS 23.
52. Letters to Liudmila, 27/14 and 30/17 May, 12 June/30 May and 17/4 June 1916, *RNZ*, 201, 204, 205, 206.
53. I derived some of my information for this section from the very useful website constructed by the late Alan Myers, "Zamyatin in Newcastle," http://www.seaham.i12.com/myers/zamyatin.html, (now no longer available); there is a good illustration of the *Sviatogor* in French & Smith, 40.
54. 1923 autobiography, in *Ia boius'*, 4.
55. Heywood, 53, 61, and 87, note 20.
56. 1928 autobiography, in *Ia boius'*, 11.
57. Tejerizo, 67.
58. "O moikh zhenakh, o ledokolakh i o Rossii," in *Ia boius'*, 178–183.
59. Tejerizo, 79.
60. Letter from Liudmila to Zamiatin, 23 August 1916, *RNZ*, 545.
61. Dougan, 132.
62. Kaznina, 202–203.
63. Letters to Liudmila, 21/8 April and 12 June/30 May 1916, *RNZ*, 197, 205.
64. 1924 autobiography, in *Ia boius'*, 6.

65. BDIC, dossier 133.
66. Keys and Smith (b), 12–14.
67. 1922 and 1928 autobiographies, in *Ia boius'*, 3, 11.

CHAPTER 4

1. A. Merich [Avgusta Damanskaia], "Vstrechi s E.I. Zamiatinym," in R.M. Iangirov, "Sovremenniki o E.I. Zamiatine. Po materialam russkoi zarubezhnoi pechati 1920kh–1930kh godov," in *EZ*, 393–396.
2. Barratt and Scherr, 175.
3. "M. Gor'ky" (1936), in *Ia boius'*, 224–226.
4. "Prezentisty," in *Ia boius'*, 23.
5. Zamiatin presented the journalist Louise Bryant, John Reed's lover, with a copy of *Thursday* early in 1918, and she published it in her book *Six Red Months in Russia* (New York: George H. Doran Company, 1918). See Chapter 22, "Free Speech," http://www.marxists.org/archive/Bryant/works/Russia/ch.22.htm (accessed 24 May 2013).
6. "Elizaveta angliiskaia," in *Ia boius'*, 21–22; see also the helpful commentaries to this and other articles in this volume by A.Iu. Galushkin.
7. Gor'ky, 125, 143.
8. "O lakeiakh" and "Bunt kapitalistov," in *Ia boius'*, 38, 43.
9. See the uncut version of *Kheruvimy* published in Zamiatin, (Munich), vol. 3, 361–362.
10. "Posledniaia stranitsa," in *Ia boius'*, 45–46.
11. "Besedy eretika. 1. O cherviakh," in *Ia boius'*, 48.
12. "O ravnomernom raspredelenii," in *Ia boius'*, 39–42.
13. "Domashnie i dikie" and "Skify li?," in *Ia boius'*, 35–38 and 26, 27.
14. "Zavtra," in *Ia boius'*, 48–49.
15. "Vospominaniia o Bloke," (1921) and "Rech' na vechere pamiati A.A. Bloka," (1926), in *Ia boius'*, 114–123, 145–146.
16. IMLI, F. 47, op. 3, ed. khr. 171.
17. R. Iangirov, "'Zavetnyi drug' Evgeniia Zamiatina. Novye materialy k tvorcheskoi biografii pisatelia," *Russ. Stud.* II, 2, 478–482, 494.
18. IMLI, F. 47, op. 3, ed. khr. 86; E.Iu. Litvin, "A.A. Akhmatova i E.I. Zamiatin—Perepiska (1922–1924)," in *EZ*, 240; *Neizdannyi Sologub*, 385.

19. Buznik (a), 178.
20. Frezinsky (a), 136.
21. "O sluzhebnom iskusstve," in *Ia boius'*, 34–35.
22. "O belom ugle," in Zamiatin (Munich), vol. 4, 549–51.
23. IMLI, F. 47, op. 1, ed. khr. 51–52.
24. IMLI, F. 47, op. 1, ed. khr. 53–56.
25. *Vdova Polivanova (Nadezhnoe mesto)* [*V Zadonsk na bogomol'e*].
26. Letter to Viacheslav Polonsky, 30 June 1918, RGALI, F. 1328, op. 1, ed. khr. 147.
27. A.Iu. Galushkin, "E.I. Zamiatin i K.I. Chukovsky—perepiska (1918–28)," in *EZ*, 193, 199–201.
28. Letter to Liudmila, 3 September 1918, *RNZ*, 218–219.
29. This visit to Lebedian' is described in his letters to Liudmila of 29–30 August; 3, 9, and 24 September; 6/19 October 1918, *RNZ*, 216–226. The relevant dates are given after quotations in the text.
30. "Sovremennaia russkaia literatura," in Zamiatin, (Munich), vol. 4, 348–365.
31. Veidle, 104.
32. Chukovsky, 117.
33. "Zavtra," in *Ia boius'*, 48–49; BDIC, dossier 96.
34. Contract of 16 May 1918, IMLI, F. 47, op. 2, ed. khr. 51.
35. "Psikhologiia tvorchestva"; "O iazyke"; "O siuzhete i fabule."
36. "Aleksandr Blok," in Zamiatin, (Munich), vol. 3, 143.
37. Gumilev was arrested from here in 1921 after being escorted home by a group of his devoted poetry students.
38. In Ol'ga Forsh's 1930 novel about the House of Arts, *Sumasshedshii korabl'*, Zamiatin appears in the guise of Sokhatyi.
39. "Aleksandr Blok," in Zamiatin, (Munich), vol. 3, 142; Chukovsky, 141, 143–144.
40. Strizhev, 105 dates this event to 1918; but Primochkina (a), 150 cites a telegram from Gor'ky of 1919.
41. N.Iu. Griakalova and E.Iu. Litvin (eds), "Perepiska E.I. Zamiatina s V.S. Miroliubovym," *Russ. Stud.* II, 2, 418.
42. Grigory Faiman, "'I vsadili ego v temnitsu...'—Zamiatin v 1919, v 1922–24 gg.," in *Novoe o Zamiatine*, 80.
43. Buznik (b), 176.
44. Pyman, 332–333.
45. Primochkina (b), 182.
46. Shane, 37.
47. RGALI, F. 1776, op. 2, ed. khr. 3.

48. George Orwell, "Freedom and Happiness," in *Tribune*, 4 January 1946, 16.
49. George Orwell, letter of 16 June 1949 to Francis Henson, quoted in J. Myers, 24.
50. Galushkin (a), 12.
51. 11 October 1919, IMLI, F. 47, op. 1, ed. khr. 69; 8 November 1919, Chukovsky, 139.
52. IMLI, F. 47, op. 1, ed. khr. 166; in November 1919 Zamiatin borrowed a book by N.N. Marakuev on Robert Mayer from Grebenshchikov—see *EZ*, 255.
53. Flat 4, 19 Karpovka Embankment (see *Russ. Stud.* II, 2, 434 and II, 3, 366); Briukhanova, who says he lived here until 1921, describes it as his wife's parents' flat (typescript version of Briukhanova article).
54. I.A. Doronchenkov and M.Iu. Liubimova, "Pis'ma B.D. i E.G. Grigor'evykh k E.I. i L.N. Zamiatinym," *Russ. Stud.* II, 3, 354.
55. Terekhina, 164.
56. Russell (a), 228–248.
57. Zamiatin's 1920 autobiographical notes state that it was written and accepted for publication and performance during 1920—RGALI, F. 1776, op. 2, ed. khr. 3.
58. BAR, Ms Coll. Zamiatin, Box 2, item 17, "Ogni sv. Dominika" (193?), ms 6pp.
59. A.Iu. Galushkin, "E.I. Zamiatin i K.I. Chukovsky—perepiska (1918–28)," in *EZ*, 194.
60. See D.I. Zolotnitsky, "Evgeny Zamiatin i 'Instsenirovka istorii kul'tury,'" *Russ. Stud.* II, 2, 350–60; and his "'Izmena literature': E.I. Zamiatin—dramaturg," in *EZ*, 71–76.
61. "Izmena literature," in *EZ*, 66.
62. "Aleksandr Blok," in Zamiatin, (Munich), vol. 3, 146.
63. Graffy and Ustinov, 351–353, 359–362.
64. Quoted from Evgeny Shvarts, *Memuary*, in ibid., 363, note 2.
65. In Zamiatin, (Munich), vol. 3, 467–472, 473–476.
66. IMLI, F. 47, op. 1, ed. khr. 167.
67. Annenkov, vol. 1, 30–32.
68. IMLI, F. 47, op. 1, ed. khr. 168–169; he dedicated a copy of "Herbert Wells" (published by "Epokha") to Liudmila "on a snowy Twelfth Night," 6 January 1921: see *RNZ*, vol. 2, 523.
69. T.A. Kukushkina, "E.I. Zamiatin v pravlenii Vserossiiskogo Soiuza Pisatelei (Leningradskoe otdelenie)," in *EZ*, 108–125.

70. See notes to letter to Liudmila, 13 May 1921, *RNZ*, 228–229.
71. Letter to Liudmila, summer 1920, *RNZ*, 226–228, note 4.
72. IMLI, F. 47, op. 1, ed. khr. 70.
73. IMLI, F. 47, op. 1, ed. khr. 74–75.
74. 12 October 1920, revised 18 January 1921; IMLI, F. 47, op. 1, ed.khr. 72–73.
75. Letter to Miroliubov, 24 February 1921, "Perepiska E.I. Zamiatina s V.S. Miroliubovym," N.Iu. Griakalova and E.Iu. Litvin (eds), *Russ. Stud.* II, 2, 434–435.
76. "Ia boius'," written not earlier than August 1920, and published not later than 18 January 1921, in *Ia boius'*, 52–53.
77. Malmstad and Fleyshman, 104–108. Although Zamiatin drafted a vigorous retort to Fedin, he didn't publish it—see "O zerkalakh," in *Ia boius'*, 238–239 and 329–330; on Voronsky see Galushkin (b), 367.
78. *RNZ*, vol. 2, 529–530.
79. IMLI, F. 47, op. 3, ed. khr. 156.
80. "Ray," in *Ia boius'*, 58–59.
81. "Zapiski mechtatelei," in *Ia boius'*, 240–241.
82. T.A. Kukushkina, "Materialy E.I. i L.N. Zamiatinykh v sobraniiakh Pushkinskogo Doma. Annotirovannyi katalog," in *EZ*, 440–441.
83. Chukovsky, 180.
84. E.Iu. Litvin, "A.A. Akhmatova i E.I. Zamiatin—Perepiska (1922–1924)," in *EZ*, 240.
85. "Perepiska E.I. Zamiatina s V.S. Miroliubovym," N.Iu. Griakalova and E.Iu. Litvin (eds.), *Russ. Stud.* II, 2, 434–435.
86. Quoted by T. Kukushkina in "Strannoe chuvstvo sytosti," www.taleon.ru/taleonclub_ru/ProjectImages/2021/26_350.pdf (accessed 1 April 2010).
87. Frezinsky (a), 13–24.
88. F. Lefèvre interview: "Odin chas s Zamiatinym, korablestroitelem, prozaikom i dramaturgom," (1932), in *Ia boius'*, 261–262.
89. Letter of 30 September 1920, IMLI, F. 47 op. 3, ed. khr. 148.
90. Strizhev, 110–11, 118; Frezinsky (a), 8.
91. Article of 1923, cited in *Ia boius'*, 303.
92. Levinson article of 2 April 1923 in *Zveno* (Paris), cited in *EZ*, 355–358.
93. *RNZ*, vol. 2, 480–81.
94. Chukovsky, 183.

95. Letters to Liudmila, 13 and 18 May 1921, *RNZ*, 228–230.
96. Briukhanova, 34.
97. Letter to Chukovsky, 2 July 1921, in A. Iu. Galushkin, "E.I. Zamiatin i K.I. Chukovsky—perepiska (1918–28)," in *EZ*, 202–203; for an account of this event see the report by E. Mindlin for *Novyi mir*, (Berlin), cited in *Ia boius'*, 250–251; *Lovets chelovekov* was published towards the end of that year in the 2nd number of the *Dom iskusstv* journal.
98. Letter to Liudmila, 12 June 1921, *RNZ*, 230–233; A. Iu. Galushkin, "E.I. Zamiatin i K.I. Chukovsky—perepiska (1918–28)," in *EZ*, 202–203; the play was reviewed [in its book form] by Avgusta Damanskaia in *Volia Rossii* on 19 Aug. 1921—see *Russ. Stud.* II, 2, 513.
99. Letters to Liudmila, 17, 20 and 25 June 1921, *RNZ*, 233–238.
100. Letter from Pil'niak to Miroliubov, 26 July 1921, in Andronikashvili-Pil'niak, 124.
101. Letters from Chukovsky, early July and 19 July 1921, in A. Iu. Galushkin, "E.I. Zamiatin i K.I. Chukovsky—perepiska (1918–28)," in *EZ*, 205, and see note 6, 208–209.
102. Letters to Chukovsky, 2 and 6/19 July 1921, ibid., 202–203.
103. Letter to Chukovsky, 4 August 1921, ibid., 209–210.
104. T.A. Kukushkina, "Materialy E.I. i L.N. Zamiatinykh v sobraniiakh Pushkinskogo Doma. Annotirovanny katalog," in *EZ*, 420–421.
105. Primochkina (c), 165–166; Gracheva, 21.
106. E. Iu. Litvin, "A.A. Akhmatova i E.I. Zamiatin—Perepiska (1922–1924)," in *EZ*, 241.
107. "Aleksandr Blok," in Zamiatin, (Munich), vol. 3, 147.
108. Letter to Chukovsky, 8 August 1921, A. Iu. Galushkin, "E.I. Zamiatin i K.I. Chukovsky—perepiska (1918–28)," in *EZ*, 210–211. Zamiatin re-used the phrase about Blok being killed by the "cave-like" life of the present in the draft of his piece about the poet, also written that August, for *Zapiski mechtatelei* (in *Ia boius'*, 302, note 2).
109. Annenkov, 1, 85; "A.A. Blok" and "Vospominaniia o Bloke," in *Ia boius'*, 67–68, 122–123; Gor'ky took offence at Zamiatin's hint that he had not acted swiftly enough to save Blok.
110. "M. Gor'ky," (1936).
111. A. Iu. Galushkin, "E.I. Zamiatin i K.I. Chukovsky—perepiska (1918–28)," in *EZ*, 210–211, note 3.

112. Letter from Chukovsky, August 1921, A.Iu. Galushkin, "E.I. Zamiatin i K.I. Chukovsky—perepiska (1918–28)," in *EZ*, 211–213.
113. Strizhev, 106; letter from Chukovsky, mid-August/early September 1921, A.Iu. Galushkin, "E.I. Zamiatin i K.I. Chukovsky—perepiska (1918–28)," in *EZ*, 211–213; T. Kukushkina, in "Strannoe chuvstvo sytosti," at www.taleon.ru/taleonclub_ru/ProjectImages/2021/26_350.pdf (accessed 1 April 2010).
114. Strizhev, 107.
115. Letters of 27 August 1921 and 5 September 1921 to V.G. Lidin and A.I. Khodasevich, quoted at http://khodasevich.ouc.ru/izbrannuye-pisma.html (accessed on 1 November 2010).
116. *Katalog vystavki*, 18; illustrated in *EZ*, 231–232. This proved to be a good year for portraits of Zamiatin, including some seated portraits in pencil by M.D. [Mstislav Dobuzhinsky] (BDIC, dossiers 181a and 175); as well as the ones by V. Milashevsky (probably 1921, Ivanova, 128) and by Nikolai Radlov at Kholomki; and the one by Annenkov.
117. See the letter from Pil'niak to Liudmila (he clearly thought that she was alone at this point), 4 September 1921, Andronikashvili-Pil'niak, 126–127.
118. Letters to Liudmila, 23, 24 and 25 September 1921, *RNZ*, 238–240.
119. Annenkov, 1, 237–238.
120. 1928 autobiography, in *Ia boius'*, 12.
121. Ibid., 247–249.
122. *EZ*, 390; Malmstad and Fleyshman, 108–113.
123. Galushkin (b), 366; Malmstad-Fleyshman 108–113; in *Ia boius'*, 239–240, 330.
124. Galushkin (b), 366–367; letter to Miroliubov, 24 February 1921, *Russ. Stud.*, II, 2, 434–435, note 3.
125. Letter to A. Damanskaia, late 1921, Malmstad-Fleyshman 112, note 33.
126. Malmstad-Fleyshman, 113, note 36; Galushkin (b), 368.
127. Iu. Annenkov, *Portrety*, (St Petersburg: Petropolis, 1922), 19–20.

Chapter 5

1. Graffy and Ustinov, 363–364.
2. *RNZ*, 2, 523.
3. 1922 autobiography, in *Ia boius'*, 3.
4. Galushkin (b), 367.

5. Galushkin (a), 12–14 and 21, note 29; Slonim on 4 March 1922, quoted by R.M. Iangirov in "'Zavetnyi drug' Evgeniia Zamiatina. Novye materialy k tvorcheskoi biografii pisatelia," *Russ. Stud.*, II, 2, 497–498, note 15.
6. Graffy and Ustinov, 350.
7. Letter from Zamiatin and Liudmila to Pil'niak, 22 February 1922, AMHERST.
8. 1922 autobiography, in *Ia boius'*, 3.
9. R.M. Iangirov in "'Zavetnyi drug' Evgeniia Zamiatina. Novye materialy k tvorcheskoi biografii pisatelia," *Russ. Stud.*, II, 2, 482–483.
10. Undated letter to Damanskaia (1922), BAR, Ms Coll Damanskaia.
11. IMLI, F. 47, op. 3, ed. khr. 97; letter from G. Zilboorg of 9 August 1922, IMLI, F. 47, op. 3, ed. khr. 84.
12. R.M. Iangirov in "'Zavetnyi drug' Evgeniia Zamiatina. Novye materialy k tvorcheskoi biografii pisatelia," *Russ. Stud.*, II, 2, 484.
13. Chukovsky, 221, 227, 232; A.Iu. Galushkin, "E.I. Zamiatin i K.I. Chukovsky—perepiska (1918–28)," in *EZ*, 214, note 2; 214–215.
14. Chudakova, 505.
15. A.Iu. Galushkin, "E.I. Zamiatin i K.I. Chukovsky—perepiska (1918–28)," in *EZ*, 195, 197–198, and letters of 19–20 and 30 June 1922, 215–216 and 216–217, 238–239; Chukovsky, 580, 582.
16. Letter of 30 June 1922, IMLI, F. 47, op. 3, ed. khr. 148.
17. Article of 22 February 1922, Frezinsky (a), 247.
18. Chukovsky, 244.
19. "Serapionovy brat'ia," in *Ia boius'*, 71–74; the young authors wrote affectionate inscriptions to Liudmila and to Zamiatin on two copies of this article, *Katalog vystavki*, 19–20.
20. Letter of 29 December 1922, Primochkina (a), 155; Frezinsky (a), 215.
21. Terekhina, 163–166.
22. R.M. Iangirov in "'Zavetnyi drug' Evgeniia Zamiatina. Novye materialy k tvorcheskoi biografii pisatelia," *Russ. Stud.*, II, 2, 494–498; Grzhebin's publishing house in Berlin folded in May 1923; Andronikashvili-Pil'niak, 127, 128.
23. A.Iu. Galushkin, "E.I. Zamiatin—Pis'mo A.K. Voronskomu. K istorii aresta i nesostoiavsheisia vysylki E.I. Zamiatina v 1922–1923 gg.," *de visu*, 0 (1992), 12; I have drawn on this article extensively in the following pages.
24. Sarnov, 518.

25. R.M. Iangirov in "'Zavetnyi drug' Evgeniia Zamiatina. Novye materialy k tvorcheskoi biografii pisatelia," *Russ. Stud.*, II, 2, 483–485.
26. Lahusen, 105.
27. Article in *Segodnia*, 19 March 1937, BDIC, dossier 211.
28. See Clark and Dobrenko, *passim*.
29. T.A. Kukushkina, "E.I. Zamiatin v pravlenii Vserossiiskogo Soiuza Pisatelei (Leningradskoe otdelenie)," in *EZ*, 123–124, note 42; Sarnov, 570–571.
30. Letter to Liudmila, 31 July 1923, *RNZ*, 243, note 1; see the undated letter sent by Marietta Shaginian to Slonimsky during Zamiatin's imprisonment, asking him to let Liudmila know about Voronsky's intervention (Frezinsky (b), 186–87); during 1924 Shaginian published her novel *Mess-Mend*, in which Zamiatin figures in the guise of the engineer Rebrov.
31. Galushkin (a), 14 says it was after 9 September; others say it was on the 9th or 10th (Lahusen, 107).
32. Galushkin (a), 14–16.
33. Grigory Faiman, "'I vsadili ego v temnitsu…'—Zamiatin v 1919, v 1922–24 gg.," in *Novoe o Zamiatine*, 85.
34. Annenkov, 1, 256.
35. Galushkin (a), 22, note 61.
36. Article in *Poslednie novosti*, 11 March 1937, in BDIC, dossier 211.
37. Annenkov, 1, 256; Akhmatova dedicated her short poem "Zdravstvuy Piter!.." to Liudmila on the day the steamship left, see E.Iu. Litvin, "A.A. Akhmatova i E.I. Zamiatin—Perepiska (1922–1924)," in *EZ*, 241, 248.
38. Chukovsky, 252.
39. Galushkin (a), 16–17; Voronsky's article is "Literaturnye siluety III. Evg. Zamiatin"; Annenkov, 1, 251–52, 56; Lahusen, 104–107; Grigory Faiman, "'I vsadili ego v temnitsu…'—Zamiatin v 1919, v 1922–24 gg.," in *Novoe o Zamiatine*, 78–88.
40. IMLI, F. 47, op. 3, ed. khr. 26.
41. I.V. Datsiuk, "E.I. Zamiatin v dnevnikakh izdatelia A.A. Krolenko (1923–31)," in *EZ*, 273.
42. *EZ*, 385.
43. Letter from Pil'niak, 20 November 1922, IMLI, F. 47, op. 3, ed. khr. 101; Frezinsky (b), 186.
44. Sarnov, 524, 604–606.
45. Graffy and Ustinov, 349, 364. Zamiatin had begun work on this project by 22 November 1922.

46. 4 December 1922, IMLI, F. 47, op. 3, ed. khr. 84.
47. R.M. Iangirov, "K istorii izdaniia romana 'My,'" in *EZ*, 174–175.
48. T.A. Kukushkina, "E.I. Zamiatin v pravlenii Vserossiiskogo Soiuza Pisatelei (Leningradskoe otdelenie)," in *EZ*, 112–115.
49. Grigory Faiman, "'I vsadili ego v temnitsu...'—Zamiatin v 1919, v 1922–24 gg.," in *Novoe o Zamiatine*, 85–88; Galushkin (a), 18 and 22, note 62; Sarnov, 607–609.
50. Galushkin (a), 22, note 65.
51. Letter of 3 April 1923, Andronikashvili-Pil'niak, 130; Galushkin (a), 18.
52. Chukovsky, 24 April 1923, 280.
53. RGALI, F. 2853, op. 1, ed. khr. 13.
54. IMLI, F. 47, op. 3, ed. khr. 148.
55. Andronikashvili-Pil'niak, 132–133.
56. It seems more likely that the reading was of the novel, rather than *The Bellringers* as suggested by Rainer Goldt, "Poslednee ubezhishche lichnosti. Zapiski D-503 i psikhologiia lichnosti v podlinnykh dnevnikakh mezhvoennogo perioda," in *EZ*, 47, and reiterated in *EZ*, 196.
57. Chukovsky, 266–267.
58. Letter from V. Kliucharev, 27 February 1923, IMLI, F. 47, op. 3, ed. khr. 100.
59. Letter to S.D. Mstislavsky, 1 March 1923, in R.M. Iangirov, "K istorii izdaniia romana 'My,'" in *EZ*, 173–74; he also mentioned that he had sent an extract for publication in a new Moscow journal called *Utopiia*—this publication didn't take place, although a related publication was still being announced in print in mid-June 1923, (see Galushkin (b), 371 and 375, note 50).
60. Letters to V.P. Polonsky, 15 February and 22 March 1923, RGALI, F. 1328, op. 1, ed. khr. 147; letter to V.P. Polonsky, 2 March 1923, IMLI, F. 47, op. 3, 166.
61. Graffy and Ustinov, 349–350.
62. E.Iu. Litvin, "A.A. Akhmatova i E.I. Zamiatin—Perepiska (1922–1924)," in *EZ*, 242, 243–244, 247–248; BDIC, dossier 166.
63. Letter to M.Ia. Kozyrev, 20 February 1922, RGALI, F. 1776, op. 1, ed. khr. 4.
64. "Novaia russkaia proza," in *Ia boius'*, 82–95.
65. Letter from Erenburg, 31 May 1922, Popov and Frezinsky, 1, 257; letter from Erenburg, 16 May 1923, Frezinsky (c), 171.
66. Galushkin (b), 368–369.

67. Letter to Liudmila, 15 September 1924, *RNZ*, 270, note 9.
68. In February 1928 Zamiatin was also trying to place a translation of Wilkie Collins's *A Woman in White*. The story was published in 1926; Davydova and Tiurin, 142–43; A. Iu. Galushkin, "E. I. Zamiatin i K. I. Chukovsky—perepiska (1918–28)," in *EZ*, 219–220.
69. The summer of 1923 is reflected in his letters to Liudmila of 26 and 31 July; 12–16 August 1923, *RNZ*, 242–245, 249–253. Relevant dates are given after quotations in the text.
70. IMLI, F. 47, op. 3, ed. khr. 91.
71. Kupchenko, 121.
72. Letters to Liudmila, 21 and 26–28 August 1923, *RNZ*, 253–254, 255–256.
73. See Curtis (a) 149–150, 180–181, 226 (footnote 34).
74. Chukovsky, 286–289; letter to Liudmila, 7 September 1923, *RNZ*, 256–257.
75. His visit to Koktebel' is reflected in his letters to Liudmila of 10 September, 28 September-3 October 1923, *RNZ*, 257–260. Relevant dates are given after quotations in the text.
76. Letter to Liudmila, 8–9 October 1923, *RNZ*, 260–262.
77. "O literature, revoliutsii, entropii i o prochem," in *Ia boius'*, 95–101.
78. Kupchenko, 121–122.
79. *RNZ*, 523.
80. Kern, 266–267, 267–268, 268–271; Frezinsky (a), 41, 247; Malmstad and Fleyshman, 120; Lunts, passim.
81. Letter to Liudmila, 5 August 1923, *RNZ*, 245–248; Braun, 204–220; the following summer Braun told Zamiatin that his article had been badly mauled by the censors, but that he was hoping to publish the original version, with some additional comments, in a book (letter from Braun, 1 June 1924, IMLI, F. 47, op. 3, ed. khr. 41).
82. From "Vstrechi s Kustodievym" (1927). Zamiatin may have misremembered these sittings as taking place "early in the winter of 1923." It has been suggested that they took place during the first half of 1923 instead (*EZ*, 218, note 3).
83. Vivian Endicott Barnett, "The Russian Presence in the 1924 Venice Biennale," in *The Great Utopia—The Russian and Soviet Avant-Garde, 1915–1932* (New York: Harry N. Abrams, Inc., 1992), 467–473; Annenkov, 1, 34–35.
84. *EZ*, 250, note 1.

85. 7 April 1924, R.M. Iangirov, "'Zavetnyi drug' Evgeniia Zamiatina. Novye materialy k tvorcheskoi biografii pisatelia," *Russ. Stud.*, II, 2, 492, note 25.
86. IMLI, F. 47, op. 2, 17; Barabanov, 527; Galushkin (b), 369.
87. Letter, probably from A. Efros to A. Tikhonov, quoted in Galushkin (b), 372.
88. See comments on it by V. Iretsky (*EZ*, 169) and Dm. Petrovsky (Galushkin (b), 370); letter from V. Rozhdestvensky, 19 January 1925, IMLI, F. 47, op. 3, ed. khr. 173.
89. Popov and Frezinsky, 2, 9; Frezinsky (c), 162–164, 171, 172–173.
90. IMLI, F. 47, op. 3, ed. khr. 65.
91. Letter of 5 October 1924, IMLI, F. 47, op. 3, ed. khr. 16; letters of 10 August and 4 December 1924, IMLI, F. 47, op. 3, ed. khr. 51.
92. Letter of 1 January 1925, IMLI, F. 47, op. 3, ed. khr. 19.
93. In *Die Neue Rundschau*; see BDIC, dossier 218.
94. Letter of 21 March 1924, Fedina and Starkov, 82.
95. IMLI, F. 47 op. 3, ed. khr. 84.
96. Malmstad and Fleyshman, 119; I.E. Erykalova, "E.I. Zamiatin — redaktor 'Russkogo sovremennika': Diskurs 1924-go goda," in *Literaturovedenie*, 465–475.
97. Kupchenko, 122–123.
98. Chukovsky, 313.
99. Liubimova (b), 100; letter to Liudmila, 20 April 1924, *RNZ*, 263–266.
100. Letter to Liudmila, 23 April 1924, *RNZ*, 266.
101. Letter of 28 May 1924, Andronikashvili-Pil'niak, 140.
102. Letter from Khodasevich, 27 June 1924; reply from Gor'ky, 1 July 1924, Primochkina (b), 184–185; letter from Fedin to Gor'ky, 16 July 1924, (Chudakova, 512).
103. "O segodniashnem i o sovremennom," in *Ia boius'*, 101–112.
104. Letter to Liudmila, 27–28 November 1924, *RNZ*, 278–279.
105. Terekhina, 166–171; letter to Liudmila, 31 July 1923, *RNZ*, 244, note 1.
106. Letter of 10 August 1924, Kupchenko, 123.
107. *Katalog vystavki*, 12.
108. Letters to Liudmila, 8, 15 and 28 September 1924, *RNZ*, 266–268, 268–271, 271–275; Chukovsky, 332–335.
109. A.Iu. Galushkin, "E.I. Zamiatin i K.I. Chukovsky–perepiska (1918–28)," in *EZ*, 231, note 2; Primochkina (a), 151–152; "Vospominaniia o Bloke," in *Ia boius'*, 114–123.
110. Chudakova, 518.
111. Letter from Gor'ky to Slonimsky, Primochkina (b), 185.

112. IMLI, F. 47, op. 3, ed. khr. 95; and see Davies and Keldysh, 707, 710.
113. Letter to K. Trenev, RGALI, F. 1398, op. 2, ed. khr. 325.
114. Letter to Liudmila, 24 November 1924, *RNZ*, 276–278.
115. A.Iu. Galushkin, "E.I. Zamiatin i K.I. Chukovsky–perepiska (1918–28)," in *EZ*, 232, note 2; Chukovsky, 336, 338–339.
116. "Peregudam ot redaktsii 'Russkogo sovremennika,'" in *Ia boius'*, 123–131.
117. Chukovsky, 340–341, 345–349; *Dni*, (Berlin), 7 December 1924, cited in Chudakova, 509–510.
118. Letter to Liudmila, 8–9 October 1923, *RNZ*, 261, note 4; Malmstad and Fleyshman, 120, note 5.
119. *Chukokkala*, 231–238.
120. Chukovsky, 345–352 and 588, notes 1 and 4; Chudakova, 509–510.
121. Letter of 17 September 1925, Primochkina (a), 152.
122. Chudakova, 512.
123. Letter to Liudmila, 20 April 1924, *RNZ*, 264, notes 3 and 5; IMLI, F. 47, op. 3, ed. khr. 100.
124. IMLI, F. 47, op. 1, ed. khr. 129.
125. Contract of 9 January 1925, IMLI, F. 47, op. 2, ed. khr. 86; letters to Liudmila, 15, 28 and 29 September 1924, *RNZ*, 268–271, 271–275, 275; D.I. Zolotnitsky, "'Izmena literature.' E.I. Zamiatin—dramaturg," in *EZ*, 88.
126. Letter from A. Aksarin, IMLI, F. 47, op. 3, ed. khr. 24.
127. Letters to Liudmila, 26, 27 and 31 July; 5, 18, 25 and 30 August; 2, 10, 21 and 28 September 1925, *RNZ*, 283–294.
128. See T.D. Ismagulova, "Evgeny Zamiatin na stsene teatra russkoi emigratsii ('Obshchestvo Pochetnykh Zvonarei' i 'Blokha' v Teatre Russkoi Dramy g. Rigi)," *Russ. Stud.*, II, 2, 361–375.
129. D.I. Zolotnitsky, "'Izmena literature.' E.I. Zamiatin—dramaturg," in *EZ*, 88–90.
130. *RNZ*, 274 (note 12), 524.
131. Quoted in *RNZ*, 264, note 3.
132. M.Iu. Liubimova, "Ya.P. Grebenshchikov i E.I. Zamiatin. Perepiska (1916–28)," in *EZ*, 255.
133. Letter to Liudmila, 20 April 1924, *RNZ*, 263–266.
134. D.I. Zolotnitsky, "'Izmena literature.' E.I. Zamiatin—dramaturg," in *EZ*, 76–77.
135. Letter to Liudmila, 22 November 1924, *RNZ*, 275–276; Turkov, 230.
136. "Vstrechi s B.M. Kustodievym," in *Ia boius'*, 153–155; Turkov, 230–231; letter to Diky, 7 December 1924, RGALI. F. 2376, op. 1, ed. khr. 157.

137. RGALI, F. 2376, op. 1, ed. khr. 157; for the text of the poster and an account of the play see D.I. Zolotnitsky, "'Izmena literature.' E.I. Zamiatin—dramaturg," in *EZ*, 76–81.
138. IMLI, F. 47, op. 3, ed. khr. 40.
139. IMLI, F. 47, op. 1, ed. khr. 198; BDIC, dossier 24.
140. Letter to Liudmila, 6 February 1925, *RNZ*, 28.
141. "Vstrechi s B.M. Kustodievym," in *Ia boius'*, 154.
142. *Katalog vystavki*, 30; illustrated in *RNZ*, 281.
143. Chukovsky, 379, 387.
144. A.Iu. Galushkin, "E.I. Zamiatin i K.I. Chukovsky—perepiska (1918–28)," in *EZ*, 222–226.
145. Review of 18 March 1925, Malmstad and Fleyshman, 117–121, 123.
146. IMLI, F. 47, op. 3, ed. khr. 71.
147. Letters of 4 April, 28 June and 16 November 1925, Frezinsky (c), 173–176.
148. IMLI, F. 47, op. 3, ed. khr. 8; letters of 2 and 10 September and 17 December 1925, IMLI, F. 47, op. 3, ed. khr. 122.
149. R. Goldt, "Mnimaia i istinnaia kritika zapadnoi tsivilizatsii v tvorchestve E.I. Zamiatina. Nabliudeniia nad tsenzurnymi iskazheniiami p'esy 'Atilla,'" *Russ. Stud.*, II, 2, 322–350; Primochkina, (b), 189.
150. Letters from V. Dobrovol'sky, 23 March and 11 July 1925, IMLI, F. 47, op. 3, ed. khr. 73. Another example would be the extensive help Zamiatin offered Georgy Kuklin in 1927–29 with his novel *Kratkosrochniki* (see IMLI, F. 47, op. 3, ed. khr. 111; *RNZ*, 508–509).
151. Kupchenko, 124.
152. Chukovsky, 392.
153. Letter to Liudmila, 20 May 1925, *RNZ*, 282.
154. Letter of 1 September 1925, IMLI, F. 47 op. 3, ed. khr. 84.
155. Letter of 5 July 1925, Malmstad and Fleyshman, 122–123.
156. Zamiatin's trip to the south is reflected in his letters to Liudmila of 26, 27, and 31 July; 5, 18, 25 and 30 August; and 2 and 10 September 1925, *RNZ*, 283–292. Relevant dates will be given after quotations in the text.
157. Letters to Liudmila, 19, 20–21, 24 December 1925, *RNZ*, 294–297.

Chapter 6

1. Letter of 12 January 1926, Frezinsky (c), 176–177.
2. Malmstad and Fleyshman, 126–127, 128–129.
3. Letter of 3 February 1926, IMLI, F. 47, op. 3, ed. khr. 113.
4. Letter of 23 February 1926, IMLI, F. 47, op. 3, ed. khr. 122.
5. Letters of 14 January, March and 3 May 1926, Terekhina, 171–173; for an account of the portrait painting see Davies and Keldysh, 588–591.
6. Letter of 17 January 1926, IMLI, F. 47, op. 3, ed. khr. 81; *Zamiatinskaia entsiklopediia*, 168–169.
7. *RNZ*, 427–428.
8. T.A. Kukushkina, "E.I. Zamiatin v pravlenii Vserossiiskogo Soiuza Pisatelei (Leningradskoe otdelenie)," in *EZ*, 116.
9. "O sovremennoi kritike," in *Ia boius'*, 243–245.
10. Liubimova (b), 101.
11. Article of 22 June 1926 in *Zhizn' iskusstva*—see Popov and Frezinsky, vol. 2, 153.
12. Davydova and Tiurin, 148–149.
13. Letter of 3 June 1926, IMLI, F. 47, op. 3, ed. khr. 93.
14. Letter of 1 July 1926, M.Iu. Liubimova, "Ia.P. Grebenshchikov i E.I. Zamiatin. Perepiska (1916–28)," in *EZ*, 259–262.
15. Contracts of 6 May and 7 June 1926, IMLI, F. 47, op. 2, ed. khr. 89; D.I. Zolotnitsky, "'Izmena literature'. E.I. Zamiatin—dramaturg," in *EZ*, 99; *RNZ*, 299, note 7.
16. BDIC, dossier 11.
17. RGALI, F. 1776, op. 2, ed. khr. 1.
18. M.Iu. Liubimova, "Ia.P. Grebenshchikov i E.I. Zamiatin. Perepiska (1916–28)," in *EZ*, 261 and 262, note 7.
19. Telegram of 26 August 1926, in *RNZ*, 309, note 1.
20. Letter to Vasily Kamensky, 14 June 1926, RGALI, F. 1497, op. 2, ed. khr. 41.
21. A.Iu. Galushkin, "E.I. Zamiatin i K.I. Chukovsky—perepiska (1918–28)," in *EZ*, 234–235.
22. BDIC, dossier 153.
23. Letter of 13 July 1926, A.Iu. Galushkin, "E.I. Zamiatin i K.I. Chukovsky—perepiska (1918–28)," in *EZ*, 236–237.
24. "Vstrechi s B.M. Kustodievym," in *Ia boius'*, 155–156.
25. Graffy and Ustinov, 350–351.

26. Letter of 28 July 1926, IMLI, F. 47, op. 3, ed. khr. 17.
27. Zamiatin's trip to the south is reflected in his letters to Liudmila of 17, 18 and 23 September; and 7 October 1926, *RNZ*, 299–310. Relevant dates will be given after quotations in the text.
28. Letter from Pavel Antokol'sky, IMLI, F. 47, op. 3, ed. khr. 29.
29. IMLI, F. 47, op. 3, ed. khr. 122.
30. Letter from O. Poddiachaia, 30 July 1926, IMLI, F. 47, op. 3, ed. khr. 163.
31. Kaznina, 218–219; Smith, 127, 134.
32. Letter of 16 August 1926, IMLI, F. 47, op. 3, ed. khr. 218.
33. "Rech' na vechere pamiati A. A. Bloka," in *Ia boius'*, 145–146.
34. M. Iu. Liubimova, "Ia.P. Grebenshchikov i E.I. Zamiatin. Perepiska (1916–28)," in *EZ*, 256; IMLI, F. 47, op. 2, ed. khr. 90.
35. D.I. Zolotnitsky, "'Izmena literature'. E.I. Zamiatin—dramaturg," in *EZ*, 82–83; Graffy and Ustinov, 353–354, 357–358.
36. T.A. Kukushkina, "Materialy E.I. i L.N. Zamiatinykh v sobraniiakh Pushkinskogo Doma. Annotirovannyi katalog," in *EZ*, 416.
37. I.V. Datsiuk, "E.I. Zamiatin v dnevnikakh izdatelia A.A. Krolenko (1923–31)," in *EZ*, 281, 289; *RNZ*, 524; see Zamiatin's article "Narodnyi teatr."
38. IMLI, F. 47, op. 1, ed. khr. 201, 202. He later drafted two further pieces about the text, one a comparison of his play with Leskov, and another entitled "My work on *The Flea*."
39. D.I. Zolotnitsky, "'Izmena literature'. E.I. Zamiatin—dramaturg," in *EZ*, 77–85.
40. E.I. Zamiatin, *Sobranie sochinenii*, vol. 3, 356–357.
41. Ibid., 88.
42. Letters of 28 December 1926, 22 July 1927 and January 1928, IMLI, F. 47, op. 3, ed. khr. 54.
43. Letter to Liudmila, 22 January 1927, *RNZ*, 310–312.
44. M. Iu. Liubimova, "Ia.P. Grebenshchikov i E.I. Zamiatin. Perepiska (1916–28)," in *EZ*, 265–266.
45. "Tsel'," in *Ia boius'*, 142–145.
46. IMLI, F. 47, op. 1, ed. khr. 90–92.
47. Primochkina (a), 156, and (b), 188.
48. V. Friche, article of 8 August 1927, quoted in Barabanov, 525.
49. Letter to Liudmila, 6 March 1927, *RNZ*, 313–314.
50. Contract of 22 February 1927, IMLI, F. 47, op. 2, ed. khr. 68.
51. *RNZ*, 524.
52. Letters to Liudmila, 10 and 14 March 1927, *RNZ*, 314–317.

53. Draft in IMLI, F. 47, op. 1, ed. khr. 147; D.I. Zolotnitsky, "'Izmena literature'. E.I. Zamiatin—dramaturg," in *EZ*, 90–94; the text is published in *RNZ*, 495–506.
54. See letter from Ivanov-Razumnik, 4 March 1927, IMLI, F. 47, op. 3, ed. khr. 91; IMLI, F. 47, op. 1, ed. khr. 148–49.
55. IMLI, F. 47, op. 3, ed. khr. 110; IMLI, F. 210, ed. khr. 44.
56. Letter from Iarmolinsky of 19 January 1927, IMLI, F. 47, op. 3, ed. khr. 85.
57. R.M. Iangirov, "'Zavetnyi drug' Evgeniia Zamiatina. Novye materialy k tvorcheskoi biografii pisatelia," *Russ. Stud.*, II, 2, 485–487, 503–504; Guerra (b), 162–67, 300; Perkhin, 15; Barabanov, 527.
58. Letter of 31 January 1928, IMLI, F. 47, op. 3, ed. khr. 140.
59. Primochkina (a), 156, and (b), 188.
60. Aikhenval'd review of 6 April 1927, in R.M. Iangirov, "K istorii izdaniia romana 'My,'" in *EZ*, 172; *EZ*, 358–364.
61. IMLI, F. 47, op. 3, ed. khr. 168.
62. Perkhin, 18.
63. Letter of 11 May 1927, Frezinsky (c), 177.
64. IMLI, F. 47. op. 3, ed. khr. 224.
65. Letter of 16 November 1927, IMLI, F. 47, op. 3, ed. khr. 89.
66. Turkov, 252.
67. IMLI, F. 47. op. 2, ed. khr. 25; *Ia boius'*, 318.
68. IMLI, F. 47, op. 3, ed. khr. 88; *RNZ*, 304–305, note 11; the two versions of the film script are called *North* and *Northern Love*—see IMLI, F. 47, op. 1, ed. khr. 145–146.
69. Letters to Liudmila, 3, 6, 11 and 17 July 1927, *RNZ*, 317–321.
70. IMLI, F. 47, op. 1, ed. khr. 93–95.
71. Letters to Liudmila, 21, 25 and 31 August, 12–13 and 23 September, and 7 and 11 October 1927, *RNZ*, 321–330.
72. Chukovsky 490–491, 493–494; see Shklovsky's rather condescending article about Zamiatin, "Potolok Evgeniia Zamiatina," published in 1927 in his *Piat' chelovek znakomykh*.
73. Article by I. Mashbits-Verov, Liubimova (b), 101.
74. Frezinsky (a), 207.
75. In fact the BDT confirmed its plans for the 1927–28 season at a meeting on 18 July—see IMLI, F. 47, op. 2, ed. khr. 107; D.I. Zolotnitsky, "'Izmena literature'. E.I. Zamiatin—dramaturg," in *EZ*, 95–103; IMLI, F. 47, op. 2, ed. khr. 92; IMLI, F. 47, op. 3, ed. khr. 110.
76. For the correspondence between Zamiatin and Kunina-Aleksander see E.Iu. Litvin, "Dva pis'ma I.E. Kuninoi-Aleksander

k E.I. Zamiatinu," in *EZ*, 294–300; J.A.E. Curtis, "Neizvestnye pis'ma Evgeniia Zamiatina iz amerikanskogo arkhiva," in *EZ*, 301–351. The copy of the typescript of *We* which Kunina-Aleksander eventually obtained from Zamiatin has survived, and is now held in the archives of the State University of New York at Albany. At the time of writing it is the only extant original source material for the text of the novel in Russian anywhere in the world, and has been published in *My* (2011).
77. Letter of 20 May 1927, IMLI, F. 47, op. 3, ed. khr. 146.
78. Contract of 28 January 1928, IMLI, F. 47, op. 2, ed. khr. 71.
79. *RNZ*, 337, note 3.
80. Chukovsky, 509–510; A.Iu. Galushkin, "E.I. Zamiatin i K.I. Chukovsky—perepiska (1918–28)," in *EZ*, 237–238.
81. D.I. Zolotnitsky, "'Izmena literature.' E.I. Zamiatin—dramaturg," in *EZ*, 94–95; Rainer Goldt, "'Podzemel'e Guntona': neizvestnyi stsenarii E. Zamiatina," in *Novoe o Zamiatine*, 150–152.
82. Buznik (c), 179; Curtis (b), 88.
83. T.A. Kukushkina, "Materialy E.I. i L.N. Zamiatinykh v sobraniiakh Pushkinskogo Doma. Annotirovannyi katalog," in *EZ*, 444. A 1927 portrait by Georgy Vereisky, of Zamiatin smoking a cigarette in a stylish jacket, lays similar emphasis on his Western elegance: see *RNZ*, 4.
84. 1928 autobiography, in *Ia boius'*, 6–12.
85. "O svoei rabote," in *Ia boius'*, 253–254.
86. I.V. Datsiuk, "E.I. Zamiatin v dnevnikakh izdatelia A.A. Krolenko (1923–31)," in *EZ*, 274–276; *RNZ*, 515–516.
87. Letters of 26 February, 21 March, 6 May, and 1 June 1928, Frezinsky (c), 178–180; Popov and Frezinsky, vol. 2, 265.
88. Frezinsky (c), 180.
89. Letter of 16 February 1928, RGALI, F. 1776, op. 1, ed. khr. 7.
90. IMLI, F. 47, op. 2, ed. khr. 110; Primochkina (b), 188–189; R. Goldt, "Mnimaia i istinnaia kritika zapadnoi tsivilizatsii v tvorchestve E.I. Zamiatina. Nabliudeniia nad tsenzurnymi iskazheniiami p'esy 'Atilla,'" *Russ. Stud.*, II, 2, 345; *RNZ*, 330–331, note 4.
91. In another example of their shared difficulties, a certain Zakhar Kagansky from Berlin tried to persuade Zamiatin during the summer of 1928 to give him permission to translate and stage a number of his works in Germany and England. Zamiatin wisely referred him to Liberman, since this was the same Kagansky who over the previous year or two had caused Bulgakov a great deal

of irritation by claiming to be his representative abroad, and then pocketing the profits (IMLI, F. 47, op. 3, ed. khr. 6 and 92; Curtis (b), 87, 91).
92. Zamiatin's trip to Moscow is reflected in his letters to Liudmila of 5, 6, 8, 11, 14, 17, 18, 22, 23, 26 and 27 June 1928, *RNZ*, 330–346. Relevant dates are given after quotations in the text.
93. This was signed on 19 June 1928 by Zamiatin and Tikhonov; the provisional fifth volume of articles was given the title *Litsa*—see *Ia boius'*, 282.
94. *Ia boius'*, 288; letter of 4 January 1929, IMLI, F. 47, op. 3, ed. khr. 15.
95. Letter to P.E. Shchegolev, 12 July 1928, IMLI, F. 47, op. 3, ed. khr. 17.
96. Letter from Fedor Raskol'nikov of 26 July 1928, *RNZ*, 344, note 1.
97. Buznik (c), 180–81.
98. Letter of 27 September 1928, Buznik (c), 180–181, note 4; Curtis (b), 90–91.
99. D.I. Zolotnitsky, "'Izmena literature.' E.I. Zamiatin—dramaturg," in *EZ*, 101; Malmstad and Fleyshman, 129.
100. *RNZ*, 342, note 5.
101. IMLI, F. 47, op. 2, ed. khr. 111.
102. Primochkina (a), 157–158; Primochkina (b), 190–191.
103. Primochkina (b), 190; "Dlia sbornika o knige," in *Ia boius'*, 254.
104. BDIC, dossier 16.
105. IMLI, F. 47, op. 1, ed. khr. 96–99.
106. Letter of 15 January 1929, Davydova and Tiurin, 150.
107. M.Iu. Liubimova, "Ia.P. Grebenshchikov i E.I. Zamiatin. Perepiska (1916–28)," in *EZ*, 267–268.
108. RNB, F. 292, ed. khr. 56.
109. November and December 1928, IMLI, F. 47, op. 1, ed. khr. 100–101.
110. Frezinsky (a), 61; *RNZ*, 510–511.
111. *Anthologie de la prose russe contemporaine* and *Panorama de la littérature russe contemporaine*; see *RNZ*, 534–535.
112. Letter of 3 March 1929, Frezinsky (c), 180; for an account of the background to "NRF"'s interest in the novel, see: http://www.gallimard.fr/catalog/Html/actu/lettres-russes01.htm (accessed 17 August 2008); for a description of the fairly muted reaction to the publication in France see Annenkov, 267.
113. *RNZ*, 426; letter of 14 September 1928 from Boris Rozov, in N.Iu. Griakalova and E. Iu. Litvin (eds.), "Perepiska E.I. Zamiatina s V.S. Miroliubovym," *Russ. Stud.*, II, 2, 419.

114. I.V. Datsiuk, "E.I. Zamiatin v dnevnikakh izdatelia A.A. Krolenko (1923–31)," in *EZ*, 282–283; letter of 22 February 1929, in N.Iu. Griakalova and E. Iu. Litvin (eds.), "Perepiska E.I. Za-miatina s V.S. Miroliubovym," *Russ. Stud.*, II, 2, 436–437; *RNZ*, 429–430.
115. Letter of 27 April 1929, IMLI, F. 47, op. 3, ed. khr. 190; *Ia boius'*, 282.
116. Letter of 12 April 1929, Malmstad and Fleyshman, 129–130.
117. Liubimova (b), 102.
118. In analysing this entire episode I have drawn on T.A. Kukushkina, "E.I. Zamiatin v pravlenii Vserossiiskogo Soiuza Pisatelei (Leningradskoe otdelenie)," in *EZ*, 116–119.
119. IMLI, F. 47, op. 3, ed. khr. 3; the drafts of their collaborative work on *The Front Page* are in IMLI, F. 47, op. 1, ed. khr. 150–155.
120. IMLI, F. 47, op. 3, ed. khr. 54.
121. IMLI, F. 47, op. 1, ed. khr. 204–205 dates these as 1926, but they may relate to 1929–30.
122. "Zakulisy," in *Ia boius'*, 158–169.
123. Primochkina (b), 190–191; for a full account of these events see Goldt, 244–257.
124. Curtis (b), 93–95.
125. Buznik (c), 180–182 (mistakenly dated 1928).
126. Letter to Liudmila, 8 August 1929, *RNZ*, 346–347.
127. Letter of 1 August 1929, Primochkina (a), 158.
128. Letter of 9 August 1929, IMLI, F. 47, op. 3, ed. khr. 154.
129. Letters to Liudmila, 11, 13, 18, 23 and 27 August 1929, *RNZ*, 347–353.
130. Kupchenko, 124, 125.

Chapter 7

1. Letter to Liudmila, 29 August 1929, *RNZ*, 353–355.
2. This campaign has been extensively covered in a number of publications, such as Aleksandr Galushkin, "Iz istorii literaturnoi 'kollektivizatsii,'" *Russ. Stud.*, II, 2, 437–478; and the same author's "'Delo Pil'niaka i Zamiatina.' Predvaritel'nye itogi rassledovaniia," in *Novoe o Zamiatine*, 89–146. I have drawn closely on these two very thorough analyses for my account of the entire episode in the following pages. See also T.A. Kukushkina, "Materialy E.I. i L.N. Zamiatinykh v sobraniiakh Pushkinskogo Doma. Annotirovannyi katalog," in *EZ*, 428–434; Andronikashvili-Pil'niak, 143–152; Liubimova (b), 102–106; Barabanov, 529–537.

3. Letter to Liudmila, 29 August 1929, *RNZ*, 353–355.
4. I. Basalaev, quoted in Kupchenko, 125.
5. Telegram to Liudmila, 5 September 1929, *RNZ*, 356; Kupchenko, 125.
6. Aleksandr Galushkin, "Iz istorii literaturnoi 'kollektivizatsii,'" *Russ. Stud.*, II, 2, 450.
7. Letter to VSP, 12 September 1929, Aleksandr Galushkin, "Iz istorii literaturnoi 'kollektivizatsii,'" *Russ. Stud.*, II, 2, 451.
8. Frezinsky (a), 25.
9. Aleksandr Galushkin, "Iz istorii literaturnoi 'kollektivizatsii,'" *Russ. Stud.*, II, 2, 442.
10. Letter to Fedin, 21 September 1929, Fedina and Starkov, 82–83.
11. Letter from Fedin, 23 September 1929, Fedina and Starkov, 83.
12. Barabanov, 534–35.
13. Aleksandr Galushkin, "Iz istorii literaturnoi 'kollektivizatsii,'" *Russ. Stud.*, II, 2, 444.
14. Aleksandr Galushkin, "'Delo Pil'niaka i Zamiatina.' Predvaritel'nye itogi rassledovaniia," in *Novoe o Zamiatine*, 124–25.
15. Letter to Liudmila, 24 September 1929, *RNZ*, 356–358.
16. Letter to Liudmila, 28 September 1929, *RNZ*, 358.
17. Curtis (b), 95, 98; Chudakova, 500.
18. *RNZ*, 434–435.
19. Barabanov, 537; *Katalog vystavki*, 26.
20. Primochkina (a), 159.
21. Barabanov, 528.
22. Article of 18 September 1929, R.M. Iangirov, "'Zavetnyi drug' Evgeniia Zamiatina. Novye materialy k tvorcheskoi biografii pisatelia," *Russ. Stud.*, II, 2, 492–493, note 29.
23. Article of 19 September 1929, R.M. Iangirov, "Sovremenniki o E.I. Zamiatine. Po materialam russkoi zarubezhnoi pechati 1920-kh−1930-kh godov," in *EZ*, 364–366.
24. Letter of 23 September 1929, R.M. Iangirov, "'Zavetnyi drug' Evgeniia Zamiatina. Novye materialy k tvorcheskoi biografii pisatelia," *Russ. Stud.*, II, 2, 507–508, note 1.
25. Article of 17 October 1929, R.M. Iangirov, "Sovremenniki o E.I. Zamiatine. Po materialam russkoi zarubezhnoi pechati 1920-kh−1930-kh godov," in *EZ*, 368–369.
26. Letters to Liudmila, 21 and 24 October 1929, *RNZ*, 359–361.
27. Letter of 14 October 1929, IMLI, F. 47, op. 3, ed. khr. 54.
28. Letters to Liudmila, 24, 25 and 29 October 1929, *RNZ*, 360–362.

29. Liubimova (b), 106.
30. Letter to Liudmila, 31 October-1 November 1929, *RNZ*, 362–363.
31. Frezinsky (a), 252–253.
32. *RNZ*, 517.
33. Letter of 4 December 1929, IMLI, F. 47, op. 3, ed. khr. 110; IMLI, F. 47, op. 2, ed. khr. 101. The contract was signed on 20 December 1929.
34. Letters of 7 and 12 January 1930, IMLI, F. 47, op. 3, ed. khr. 54.
35. Primochkina (b), 192; Liubimova (b), 106. For other examples of the extensive discussions and disagreements that went on within the Politbiuro about individual authors and their works, see Clark and Dobrenko, chapter 6, 88–136.
36. See letter to L.P. Grossman, 30–31 December 1929, RGALI, F. 1386, op. 1, ed. khr. 83.
37. IMLI, F. 47, op. 3, ed. khr. 36.
38. Letter to Liudmila, 19 January 1930, *RNZ*, 363–364; contracts dated 9 and 25 January 1930, IMLI, F. 47, op. 2, ed. khr. 86.
39. Letters to Liudmila, 25–26 and 29–30 January, 1–3, 6 and 11 February 1930, *RNZ*, 364–372.
40. D.I. Zolotnitsky, "'Izmena literature.' E.I. Zamiatin—dramaturg," in *EZ*, 95. The three drafts of *The African Visitor* were completed between February and 17 May 1930, IMLI, F. 47, op. 1, ed. khr. 156–159.
41. R.M. Iangirov, "Sovremenniki o E.I. Zamiatine. Po materialam russkoi zarubezhnoi pechati 1920-kh—1930-kh godov," in *EZ*, 368–370; D.I. Zolotnitsky, "'Izmena literature.' E.I. Zamiatin—dramaturg," in *EZ*, 75–76; Barabanov 528, 535–536.
42. Letters to Liudmila, 26–27 February and 1, 9, 10, 14, 18 and 20 March 1930, *RNZ*, 372–383.
43. IMLI, F. 47, op. 3, ed. khr. 177.
44. Letter to Liudmila, 10 June 1930, *RNZ*, 384–385.
45. I.V. Datsiuk, "E.I. Zamiatin v dnevnikakh izdatelia A.A. Krolenko (1923–31)," in *EZ*, 283.
46. Letters to Liudmila, 7 and 8 July 1930, *RNZ*, 385–386, 386–387, note 2.
47. Photos by Krolenko have survived of Zamiatin on the Kreshchatik in Kiev, and at Olefirovka; see *RNZ*, 539.
48. Letter to Liudmila, 12 July 1930, *RNZ*, 387–389; Nikitina (1902–73) was the first wife of N. Nikitin—see *RNZ*, 529; in fact she went to Gagry—see her affectionate letter to Liudmila of 8 September

1930, asking whether Zamiatin had returned yet, RNB, F. 292, ed. khr. 20.
49. Letter to Liudmila, 14 July 1930, *RNZ*, 389–391.
50. I. V. Datsiuk, "E. I. Zamiatin v dnevnikakh izdatelia A. A. Krolenko (1923–31)," in *EZ*, 283–284.
51. Letters to Liudmila, 21–22, and 29 July, 6 August 1930, *RNZ*, 392–399.
52. Letters and telegram to Liudmila, 21–22, 27–28 July, 6, 17, 23 August, 9 and 16 September 1930, *RNZ*, 392–407; I. V. Datsiuk, "E. I. Zamiatin v dnevnikakh izdatelia A. A. Krolenko (1923–31)," in *EZ*, 284.
53. IMLI, F. 47, op. 3, ed. khr. 71.
54. Letters from Mechislav Volk, 21 August and 23 December 1930, IMLI, F. 47, op. 3, ed. khr. 56.
55. Letters of 11 December 1929 and 13 October 1930, IMLI, F. 47, op. 3, ed. khr. 162.
56. Buznik (c), 182.
57. Golikova, 4.
58. IMLI, F. 47, op. 1, ed. khr. 208; and op. 2, ed. khr. 79.
59. Letter of 16 November 1930, Andronikashvili-Pil'niak, 148–53; see Pil'niak's piece "Slushaite postup istorii" in *Izvestiia* on 14 December 1930, and his conciliatory letter that month to Stalin. He made trips to the USA (via Paris, where he saw Annenkov, who accompanied him to Le Havre) and Japan, in 1931 and 1932.
60. Letters of 12 and 14 January, 9 March, 1 June, 23 October 1930 and 2 August 1932, IMLI, F. 47, op. 3, ed. khr. 169.
61. Letter of 17 December 1930, IMLI, F. 47. op. 3, ed. khr. 130; Zamiatin had evidently met Ray Long earlier that year.
62. Letter of 20 January 1931, IMLI, F. 47, op. 3, ed. khr. 115.
63. I. V. Datsiuk, "E. I. Zamiatin v dnevnikakh izdatelia A. A. Krolenko (1923–31)," in *EZ*, 284–285.
64. RGALI, F. 341, op. 1, ed. khr. 90.
65. Letter of 27 April 1931, in *Ia boius'*, 282–283.
66. Letter of 11 May 1931, RGALI, F. 341, op. 1, ed. khr. 90.
67. IMLI, F. 47, op. 1, ed. khr. 160.
68. IMLI, F. 47, op. 3, ed. khr. 162.
69. IMLI, F. 47, op. 1, ed. khr. 161.
70. IMLI, F. 47, op. 1, ed. khr. 162; for this text and a commentary see Rainer Goldt, "'Podzemel'e Guntona': neizvestnyi stsenarii E. Zamiatina," in *Novoe o Zamiatine*, 147–175.

71. Myers, "Zamyatin in Newcastle," http://www/seaham.i12.com/myers/zamyatin.html (accessed 24 February 2008).
72. IMLI, F. 47, op. 3, ed. khr. 33.
73. IMLI, F. 47. op. 2, ed. khr. 3 and 4.
74. Malmstad and Fleyshman, 132; Primochkina (b), 192.
75. "Pis'mo I.V. Stalinu," in *Ia boius'*, 169–173; see Malmstad and Fleyshman, 132.
76. IMLI, F. 47, op. 3, ed. khr. 77; letter to Liudmila, 3 June 1931, *RNZ*, 408–409; this dating may be inaccurate: it is more likely to be 13 June.
77. Letter to Liudmila, 16 June 1931, *RNZ*, 409–411.
78. Quoted in Liubimova (b), 106–107.
79. Letters to Liudmila, 22 and 25 June 1931, *RNZ*, 411–413, 413–414.
80. He received 1,000 roubles, with the text of *The Yawl* film script due to be submitted by 8 August 1931; see IMLI, F. 47, op. 2, ed. khr. 104.
81. Letter to Liudmila, 29 June 1931, *RNZ*, 414–416.
82. He submitted this but it was not accepted—see letter from studio of 23 July 1931; IMLI, F. 47. op. 1, ed. khr. 163 and 164, and op. 2, ed. khr. 105 and 106.
83. Letter to Liudmila, 9–10 July 1931, *RNZ*, 416–17.
84. "M. Gor'ky" in *Ia boius'*, 230–231; the piece was written within weeks of Gor'ky's death in 1936. Gor'ky left for Sorrento again that October.
85. Sarnov, 702.
86. From the last surviving letter to Liudmila, 10 August 1931, *RNZ*, 417–419.
87. Curtis (b), 129–132.
88. POZNER, copy of unpublished letter of 26 August 1931; I am grateful to M. André Pozner, and to Mme Valérie Pozner, for permission to quote from this and copies of other letters to Vladimir Pozner held in the Pozner Family Archive in Paris.
89. IMLI, F. 47, op. 3, ed. khr. 164 (letter incorrectly dated 3 September 1930, instead of 1931).
90. POZNER, copy of unpublished letter of 2 October 1931.
91. IMLI, F. 47, op. 3, ed. khr. 164, (incorrectly dated 9 October 1930, instead of 1931).
92. Letter of 13 October 1931, Frezinsky (c), 181.
93. Terekhina, 173; on his departure Zamiatin presented an album of Grigor'ev's drawings to Akhmatova.

94. BDIC, dossier 131.
95. I.V. Datsiuk, "E.I. Zamiatin v dnevnikakh izdatelia A.A. Krolenko (1923–31)," in *EZ*, 286.
96. *RNZ*, 524–525; see D.I. Zolotnitsky, "'Izmena literature.' E.I. Zamiatin—dramaturg," in *EZ*, 88.
97. BDIC, dossier 117.
98. IMLI, F. 47, op. 3, ed. khr. 162.
99. Undated letter to Varvara Aleksandrovna Platonova, Zamiatin Museum (uncatalogued).
100. Curtis (b), 134.
101. Buznik (c), 182–183; and see Primochkina (b), 220–221.
102. I.V. Datsiuk, "E.I. Zamiatin v dnevnikakh izdatelia A.A. Krolenko (1923–31)," in *EZ*, 286.

Chapter 8

1. Fedina and Konovalova, 106, 101. The abbreviation "EI" had by now become the usual way Liudmila and some of his friends referred to him. Zamiatin's letter is mistakenly dated here 11 November, and was probably written on 17 November 1931.
2. Shane, 83; B.S. Orechkin article, in *Ia boius'*, 254–255; a different version of the same interview was published in *Poslednie novosti* (Paris) on 21 November 1931.
3. POZNER, letter to Pozner, 22 November 1931; Shane, 88.
4. RGALI, F. 2533, op. 1, ed. khr. 188.
5. Fedina and Konovalova, 102; Shane, 84.
6. A. Shteinberg, quoted by R. Goldt in "Mnimaia i istinnaia kritika zapadnoi tsivilizatsii v tvorchestve E.I. Zamiatina. Nabliudeniia nad tsenzurnymi iskazheniiami p'esy 'Atilla,'" *Russ. Stud.*, II, 2, 346, note 4.
7. BAR, Box 2.
8. Strizhev, 105; Komlik and Uriupin, 97–102.
9. Letter of 1 December 1931, R.M. Iangirov, "'Zavetnyi drug' Evgeniia Zamiatina. Novye materialy k tvorcheskoi biografii pisatelia," *Russ. Stud.*, II, 2, 487.
10. Malmstad and Fleyshman, 134–135; for more on Ray Long see Gor'ky's letters to Stalin, 1 December 1931 and February 1932 in Dubinskaia-Dzhalilova and Chernev, (1997), 192, and (1998), 164–169; on de Mille see Lyons, 501–502.

11. Shane, 84.
12. R.M. Iangirov, "'Zavetnyi drug' Evgeniia Zamiatina. Novye materialy k tvorcheskoi biografii pisatelia," *Russ. Stud.*, II, 2, 488.
13. Letter of 20 December 1931, J. Curtis, "Neizvestnye pis'ma Evgeniia Zamiatina iz amerikanskogo arkhiva," in *EZ*, 308–309.
14. Fedina and Konovalova, 102.
15. R.M. Iangirov, "'Zavetnyi drug' Evgeniia Zamiatina. Novye materialy k tvorcheskoi biografii pisatelia," *Russ. Stud.*, II, 2, 499, note 1.
16. BDIC, dossiers 188 and 189.
17. Baran and Gindin (no page number) has a photo of the Erenburgs and Jakobsons in Slovakia in the summer of 1932.
18. R.M. Iangirov, "'Zavetnyi drug' Evgeniia Zamiatina. Novye materialy k tvorcheskoi biografii pisatelia," *Russ. Stud.*, II, 2, 499, note 1.
19. Letter from Gor'ky to Stalin, 25 January 1932, Dubinskaia-Dzhalilova and Chernev, 157; Ermolaev and Shane, 192.
20. Article of 3 January 1932, in *Ia boius'*, 255–256; Malmstad and Fleyshman, 136–137.
21. Galushkin (c).
22. Malmstad and Fleyshman, 135–36. Photograph in AMHERST.
23. POZNER, letters to Pozner of 30 January and 4 and 5 February 1932.
24. Shane mistakenly dates the Zamiatins' arrival in Paris to "late" February 1932 (Shane, 88).
25. Dubinskaia-Dzhalilova and Chernev, letters from Gor'ky to Stalin of early and late February 1932, 163–168.
26. Letter from Pozner to Lily Brik and V. Katanian, 12 August 1956, in *Dialog pisatelei*, 575–576.
27. Popov and Frezinsky, vol. 3, 9; Savich, 69–88; letter to Fedin, 22 February 1932, quoted in Savich, 96, note 36; postcard of 14 February 1932 from Zamiatin and Liudmila to Z.A. Nikitina, RGALI, F. 2533, op. 1, ed. khr. 187.
28. Undated letter, late 1931/early 1932, Terekhina, 173–174.
29. I.A. Doronchenkov and M.Iu. Liubimova, "Pis'ma B.D. i E.G. Grigor'evykh k E.I. i L.N. Zamiatinym," *Russ. Stud.*, II, 3, 358–359.
30. Fedina and Konovalova, 104.
31. J. Curtis, "Neizvestnye pis'ma Evgeniia Zamiatina iz amerikanskogo arkhiva," in *EZ*, 313.
32. Jean-Claude Ambroise, "Ecrivain prolétarien: une identité paradoxale," *Sociétés contemporaines*, 44, (2001/4), 41–55. Barbusse's

Monde should not be confused with the newspaper *Le Monde*, founded in 1944.
33. Princeton, Folder 9, letter to Reavey, 30 March 1932.
34. "Avtointerv'iu" (April 1932), in *Ia boius'*, 247–250.
35. POZNER, letter to Pozner, 21 April 1932.
36. Publication of 4 May 1932, BDIC, dossier 212.
37. Publication of 1 July 1932; see *Russ. Stud.*, II, 2, 506.
38. Lyons, 501.
39. BAR, letter to de Mille, 12 February 1932; Kaznina, 216.
40. Letter to Fedin of 27 March 1932, Fedina and Konovalova, 104–105.
41. Dullin, 70–79.
42. Letter of 27 March 1932, Fedina and Konovalova, 104–105; *Zapisnye knizhki*, 232–233, 240–243; letter from Liudmila to Nikitina, 24 April 1932, RGALI, F. 2533, op. 1, ed. khr. 188; Annenkov, vol. 1, 235; Guerra (b).
43. Savich, 88.
44. I.V. Obukhova-Zelin'skaia, "'Kursirovali iz Moskvy v Parizh…' Iz perepiski Iu. Annenkova i L'va Nikulina," *Diaspora*, 4 (2002), 620–621.
45. BOSTON, M. Slonim, "E.I. Zamiatin—Iz vospominanii" (draft).
46. Menegaldo, 97; Livak, 10.
47. V.A. Tunimanov, "Poslednee zagranichnoe stranstvie i pokhorony Evgeniia Ivanovicha Zamiatina (evropeiskaia sud'ba 'skifa' i 'eretika')," *Russ. Stud.*, II, 2, 400–401, note 4.
48. Letter from E. Grigor'eva to Liudmila, 10 December 1931, in I.A. Doronchenkov and M.Iu. Liubimova, "Pis'ma B.D. i E.G. Grigor'evykh k E.I. i L.N. Zamiatinym," *Russ. Stud.*, II, 3, 362–363.
49. Article of 4 February 1932; letters to Fedin, 22 February and 27 March 1932, Fedina and Konovalova, 104–105.
50. Letter to Fedin, 14 April 1932, Fedina and Starkov, 83, 94 note 15.
51. Letter from Zamiatin and Liudmila, 18–19 April 1932, RGALI, F. 2533, op. 1, ed. khr. 187 and 188.
52. Frezinsky (b), 188–189.
53. *Comoedia*, 12 April 1932; *Carnet de la Semaine*, 17 April 1932; see R.M. Iangirov, "'Zavetnyi drug' Evgeniia Zamiatina. Novye materialy k tvorcheskoi biografii pisatelia," *Russ. Stud.*, II, 2, 501, note 2.
54. Galushkin (c).
55. *Ia boius'*, 337.

56. "Une heure avec Zamiatine, constructeur de navires, romancier et dramaturge," Russian version in *Ia boius'*, 257–258.
57. Aldous Huxley, "New World Drama," *Hearst*, 23 July 1932, cited in his *Complete Essays*, vol. 3, 1930–1935, (2001), 336–337.
58. "Une heure avec Zamiatine, constructeur de navires, romancier et dramaturge," Russian version in *Ia boius'*, 258–259.
59. POZNER, letter to Pozner, 24 April 1932; "Avtointerv'iu," in *Ia boius'*, 247–250.
60. Dullin, 75.
61. "Avtointerv'iu," in *Ia boius'*, 247–250.
62. POZNER, letter to Pozner, 24 April 1932.
63. Tejerizo, 80–83; the interview was published on 9 August 1932.
64. Letter of 4 April 1932, in I.A. Doronchenkov and M.Iu. Liubimova, "Pis'ma B.D. i E.G. Grigor'evykh k E.I. i L.N. Zamiatinym," *Russ. Stud.*, II, 3, 364–365.
65. RGALI, F. 2533, op. 1, ed. khr. 188, letters of 6 and 19 April 1932.
66. Letter of 14 April 1932, Fedina and Starkov, 83.
67. Letter of 18 April 1932, RGALI, F. 2533, op. 1, ed. khr. 187.
68. Letter to Fedin, 12 May 1932, Fedina and Konovalova, 103.
69. Letter of 24 March 1932, Dubinskaia-Dzhalilova and Chernev, 168.
70. "En URSS," in *Ia boius'*, 246–247.
71. Postcard of 12 May 1932, Fedina and Konovalova, 103.
72. Tejerizo, 80–83.
73. Letter of 26 April 1932, R.M. Iangirov, "'Zavetnyi drug' Evgeniia Zamiatina. Novye materialy k tvorcheskoi biografii pisatelia," *Russ. Stud.*, II, 2, 500–501.
74. AMHERST, letter to the Remizovs, 29 April 1932.
75. POZNER, letters to Pozner, 14 and 21 April 1932.
76. "O moikh zhenakh, o ledokolakh i o Rossii," in *Ia boius'*, 178, 181.
77. POZNER, letter to Pozner, 6 May 1932.
78. BDIC, dossier 190. "an ambush; to advocate; to filch / to spirit away [...] buttocks; tits; hooker; a dumb appearance; a bit tipsy; a swindler; to become infatuated; beddable; she'd be a good lay, but..."
79. Buznik (c), 182–183.
80. Tiurin (1987), 147–153, 156–159.
81. Letter of 11 May 1932, Malmstad and Fleyshman, 137–141.
82. Letter of 31 May 1932, Buznik (c), 183.
83. J. Curtis, "Neizvestnye pis'ma Evgeniia Zamiatina iz amerikanskogo arkhiva," in *EZ*, 313–314.

84. BAR, Ms Collection Zamiatin, Box 1, 38.
85. Shane, 91.
86. PRINCETON, letters of 4 June 1932 and one dated 2 June, although the postmark indicates, more plausibly, July 1932.
87. BAR, Ms Collection Charles Malamuth, catalogued correspondence (note on the career of E.I. Zamiatin).
88. PRINCETON.
89. Kemp-Welch, 117.
90. Letter of 21 June 1932, Ermolaev and Shane, 188–193; Fedina and Starkov, 83–84.
91. Annenkov, vol. 1, 267, 269.
92. PRINCETON and AMHERST.
93. V.A. Tunimanov, "Poslednee zagranichnoe stranstvie i pokhorony Evgeniia Ivanovicha Zamiatina (evropeiskaia sud'ba 'skifa' i 'eretika')," *Russ. Stud.*, II, 2, 389, 397.
94. Quoted in Frezinsky, (c), 167.
95. *Khudozhniki russkogo zarubezh'ia*; exhibition of 2–15 June 1932.
96. Letter of 1 August 1932, Davydova and Tiurin, 155–157.
97. Letter of 4 August 1932, PRINCETON.
98. Letters to Leonid Miasin, 22 July, 8 September and 1 October 1932, BAR, Box 5.
99. Letter of 19 September 1932, R.M. Iangirov, "'Zavetnyi drug' Evgeniia Zamiatina. Novye materialy k tvorcheskoi biografii pisatelia," *Russ. Stud.*, II, 2, 502.
100. Letter from Grigor'ev to František Kubka, 2 September 1932, I.A. Doronchenkov and M.Iu. Liubimova, "Pis'ma B.D. i E.G. Grigor'evykh k E.I. i L.N. Zamiatinym," *Russ. Stud.*, II, 3, 358.
101. Fedina and Starkov, 84–85.
102. Letter to S.V. Pozner, 30 September 1932, RGALI, F. 2535, op. 1, ed. khr. 67. I am grateful to M. André Pozner and Mme Valérie Pozner for permission to consult these letters.
103. Letter of 14 August 1932, RGALI, F. 2533, op. 1, ed. khr. 187.
104. Letter to Postnikov, R.M. Iangirov, "'Zavetnyi drug' Evgeniia Zamiatina. Novye materialy k tvorcheskoi biografii pisatelia," *Russ. Stud.*, II, 2, 502–504.
105. Postcard to Fedin, Fedina and Konovalova, 103; Letter to I.E. Kunina-Aleksander, 27 September 1932, J. Curtis, "Neizvestnye pis'ma Evgeniia Zamiatina iz amerikanskogo arkhiva," in *EZ*, 315.
106. Lyons, 499.

107. Fedina and Starkov, 85–86.
108. Galushkin (c).
109. Letters of 30 September and 14 and 24 October, Annenkov, vol. 1, 269–272.
110. Letter of 19 October 1932, PRINCETON.
111. Fedina and Starkov, 86.
112. Menegaldo, 182.
113. J. Curtis, "Neizvestnye pis'ma Evgeniia Zamiatina iz amerikanskogo arkhiva," in *EZ*, 314–315, 320.
114. BDIC, dossier 229.
115. "Sovetskie deti," in *Ia boius'*, 173–177.
116. Tejerizo, 83–89.
117. Fedina and Konovalova, 105–106.
118. J. Curtis, "Neizvestnye pis'ma Evgeniia Zamiatina iz amerikanskogo arkhiva," in *EZ*, 315.
119. R.M. Iangirov, "'Zavetnyi drug' Evgeniia Zamiatina. Novye materialy k tvorcheskoi biografii pisatelia," *Russ. Stud.*, II, 2, 504.
120. Buznik (c), 184–185.
121. Letter of 29 December 1932, R.M. Iangirov, "'Zavetnyi drug' Evgeniia Zamiatina. Novye materialy k tvorcheskoi biografii pisatelia," *Russ. Stud.*, II, 2, 505–506.
122. Tejerizo, 69–74.
123. BDIC, dossier 123.

Chapter 9

1. Letter of 5 January 1933, Davydova and Tiurin, 157–158; *Zapisnye knizhki*, 232–233.
2. Letter of 12 February 1933, Buznik (c), 185–186.
3. Buznik (c), 186.
4. Letter to Pavel Popov, 19 May 1933, Curtis (b), 159.
5. Letter of 17 March 1933, Davydova and Tiurin, 158–159; the *Anna Karenina* typescript is in BDIC, dossiers 6 and 7.
6. Harvey, at http://www.kinozapiski.ru/article/739 (accessed 9 January 2011).
7. Savina and Nechiporenko, 91.
8. *Ia boius'*, 322; and see *Russ. Stud.*, II, 2, 501.

9. Letters of 14 August and 2 September 1933, J. Curtis, "Neizvestnye pis'ma Evgeniia Zamiatina iz amerikanskogo arkhiva," in *EZ*, 316–318.
10. Letter of 2 September 1933, Malmstad and Fleyshman, 141–142.
11. Interview with Oettly in *Comoedia*, 10 October 1933, in L. Geller, "O neudobstve byt' russkim (emigrantom). Po povodu pisem Zamiatina iz parizhskogo arkhiva V. Krymova," in *Novoe o Zamiatine*, 187–189.
12. Letter to I. Kunina-Aleksander of 10 October 1933, J. Curtis, "Neizvestnye pis'ma Evgeniia Zamiatina iz amerikanskogo arkhiva," in *EZ*, 319.
13. Letter of 3 November 1933, Buznik (c), 186–187.
14. L. Geller, "O neudobstve byt' russkim (emigrantom). Po povodu pisem Zamiatina iz parizhskogo arkhiva V. Krymova," in *Novoe o Zamiatine*, 192; Annenkov, 1, 272–733, 279–280; *Khudozhniki russkogo zarubezh'ia*, 191.
15. Letter to I. Kunina-Aleksander of 27 November 1933, J. Curtis, "Neizvestnye pis'ma Evgeniia Zamiatina iz amerikanskogo arkhiva," in *EZ*, 320–321.
16. BAR, letter from D.S. Watt.
17. ALBANY, inscription dated 29 September 1933.
18. Letters of 10, 19 and 27 October 1933, J. Curtis, "Neizvestnye pis'ma Evgeniia Zamiatina iz amerikanskogo arkhiva," in *EZ*, 318–320; "Moskou en Petersburg," in *Haagsch Maandblad*, BDIC, dossier 226; her translation appeared in *Nova Evropa*.
19. Letter of 3 November 1933, Buznik (c), 186–187.
20. Letters of [?] October and 13 November 1933, Fedina and Starkov, 86–88.
21. Letter of 18 November 1933, Fedina and Konovalova, 107.
22. BAR, Box 1, 18, 19, letter of 29 December [probably 1933]: "I read the first two acts this morning, and like them very much."
23. Letters of 19 and 21 November, 3 December 1933, Fedina and Starkov, 88–89. Vladimir Pozner attended the 1934 Congress of the Writers' Union in Moscow but was then, to his baffled dismay, unaccountably expelled from the French Communist Party. He gradually drifted away from Russian circles in France thereafter.
24. RGALI, F. 2535, op. 1, ed. khr. 67, (19 letters to S.V. Pozner, 29 February 1932–30 December 1933).

25. Letter of 27 November 1933, J. Curtis, "Neizvestnye pis'ma Evgeniia Zamiatina iz amerikanskogo arkhiva," in *EZ*, 320–321.
26. V.A. Tunimanov, "Poslednee zagranichnoe stranstvie i pokhorony Evgeniia Ivanovicha Zamiatina (evropeiskaia sud'ba 'skifa' i 'eretika')," *Russ. Stud.*, II, 2, 391–392.
27. Shakhovskaia, 176–178.
28. In *Nation belge* and *L'Eventail*, quoted in L. Geller, "O neudobstve byt' russkim (emigrantom). Po povodu pisem Zamiatina iz parizhskogo arkhiva V. Krymova," in *Novoe o Zamiatine*, 193–196.
29. Letter of 11 December 1933, J. Curtis, "Neizvestnye pis'ma Evgeniia Zamiatina iz amerikanskogo arkhiva," in *EZ*, 321–322.
30. Shakhovskaia, 179.
31. Letter of 12 December 1933, Fedina and Starkov, 90.
32. *Ia boius'*, 183–205.
33. Letter of 22 December 1933, Fedina and Starkov, 90.
34. Letter of 26 December 1933, J. Curtis, "Neizvestnye pis'ma Evgeniia Zamiatina iz amerikanskogo arkhiva," in *EZ*, 322–323.
35. BDIC, dossier 228.
36. BDIC, dossier 227.
37. Tejerizo, 74–77.
38. BAR; Annenkov, I, 199, 213.
39. AMHERST, letter from A. Remizov, 18 January 1934.
40. POZNER, letter from K. Fedin to V. Pozner, 4 January 1934.
41. Letter of 31 January 1934, J. Curtis, "Neizvestnye pis'ma Evgeniia Zamiatina iz amerikanskogo arkhiva," in *EZ*, 323–324.
42. "Andrei Bely," in *Ia boius'*, 208–212, 269.
43. Dated 4 February 1934, illustrated in Evgeny Zamiatin, *Sochineniia*, (Moscow: Kniga, 1988), 496–497.
44. Pozner, 33–36.
45. Letter of 22 February 1934, Fedina and Starkov, 90–91.
46. Letter of 16 April 1934, Fedina and Starkov, 91–92.
47. BAR.
48. PRINCETON, letter of 17 February 1934.
49. Letter of 14 March 1934, J. Curtis, "Neizvestnye pis'ma Evgeniia Zamiatina iz amerikanskogo arkhiva," in *EZ*, 325–327.
50. Livak, 30.
51. Letter of 13 March 1934, J. Curtis, "Neizvestnye pis'ma Evgeniia Zamiatina iz amerikanskogo arkhiva," in *EZ*, 325–327; BDIC, dossier 51.

52. *Ia boius'*, 205–208.
53. Letters of 7 and 23 May 1934, J. Curtis, "Neizvestnye pis'ma Evgeniia Zamiatina iz amerikanskogo arkhiva," in *EZ*, 329–331.
54. Shakhovskaia, 180–181.
55. Galushkin, (c).
56. Fedina and Starkov, 92.
57. Fleishman, 178–183.
58. J. Curtis, "Neizvestnye pis'ma Evgeniia Zamiatina iz amerikanskogo arkhiva," in *EZ*, 331.
59. BAR, Box 5.
60. Fedina and Konovalova, 107.
61. Letter of 26 July 1934, J. Curtis, "Neizvestnye pis'ma Evgeniia Zamiatina iz amerikanskogo arkhiva," in *EZ*, 332.
62. Kaznina, 216–217.
63. BAR, Box 5, letter of 3 June 1934.
64. Letters of late July 1934, Malmstad and Fleyshman, 146, note 11.
65. J. Curtis, "Neizvestnye pis'ma Evgeniia Zamiatina iz amerikanskogo arkhiva," in *EZ*, 334, note 3; Dr Rubakin returned to the USSR during the Second World War.
66. Fedina and Starkov, 92
67. Nice, 317, 336.
68. *Ia boius'*, 268–269.
69. Letter of 4 September 1934, Fedina and Starkov, 92–93.
70. RGALI, F. 2618, op. 1, ed. khr. 71.
71. Kunina, 96.
72. Letter from D.S. Watt, 13 November 1934, Tejerizo, 77–79.
73. Letter of 23 November 1934, J. Curtis, "Neizvestnye pis'ma Evgeniia Zamiatina iz amerikanskogo arkhiva," in *EZ*, 332–335.
74. Letter of 28 December 1934, J. Curtis, "Neizvestnye pis'ma Evgeniia Zamiatina iz amerikanskogo arkhiva," in *EZ*, 335–336.
75. Fleishman, 189; Barnes, 102.
76. Fedina and Konovalova, 108.
77. Letter of 26 (28) –29 January 1935, J. Curtis, "Neizvestnye pis'ma Evgeniia Zamiatina iz amerikanskogo arkhiva," in *EZ*, 336–337.
78. In May, it would be published in the USA in *Fiction Parade* (Malmstad and Fleyshman, 148).
79. BDIC, dossiers 20, 188 and 189.
80. Letter of 14 March 1935, J. Curtis, "Neizvestnye pis'ma Evgeniia Zamiatina iz amerikanskogo arkhiva," in *EZ*, 338–339; Remizov

recalled that Zamiatin sold his "smoking jacket" for 150 francs in 1937 (AMHERST).
81. Shakhovskaia, 181–182.
82. *Ia boius'*, 212–216.
83. Letter of 19 April 1935, J. Curtis, "Neizvestnye pis'ma Evgeniia Zamiatina iz amerikanskogo arkhiva," in *EZ*, 340–341; this portrait of Zamiatin by Tabaković was frequently reproduced in Yugoslavia; in return, Zamiatin made a preliminary draft of a literary portrait of Tabaković, which was preserved in Kunina-Aleksander's archive.
84. On Grigor'ev see *Khudozhniki russkogo zarubezh'ia*, 241; letter of 14 May 1935, Malmstad and Fleyshman, 143–46; Malamuth owned a copy of Eastman's book with an admiring dedication from the author in 1934; on the impact of this book see Fleishman, 184. Zamiatin here underestimated the helpfulness of Eugene Lyons, who had in fact arranged early in April 1934 to take a copy of the Attila proposal with him to de Mille in Hollywood (Harvey).
85. BDIC, dossier 88.
86. *Zapisnye knizhki*, 244.
87. BDIC, dossier 69; Columbia Box 2, 23 and 36; and see Shane, 91.
88. Menegaldo, 183.
89. Saakiants, 648.
90. Tikhonov, 175. Savina and Nechiporenko even claim that Zamiatin made a speech, apparently consisting in extracts from his article about icebreakers.
91. Frezinsky, (c), 166–168 and (d), 197.
92. Fleishman, 193–194.
93. Frezinsky (a), 70–71; the Saviches lived in the same house in Paris as the artist Natan Al'tman, who also returned to the USSR in 1935.
94. Letter from Franz Hellens of 2 July 1935, BAR, Box 1, 15.
95. Annenkov, 1, 273–275.
96. Letter of 27 August 1935, J. Curtis, "Neizvestnye pis'ma Evgeniia Zamiatina iz amerikanskogo arkhiva," in *EZ*, 341.
97. Letter of 30 September 1935, Shakhovskaia, 183.
98. Slonim, xxiii.
99. BDIC, dossiers 54, 110 and 111.
100. On Otsep and Strizhevsky see Malmstad and Fleyshman, 148; see also Annenkov, 1, 280–281 and Shane, 92 and 224.
101. *Zapisnye knizhki*, 254.

102. J. Curtis, "Neizvestnye pis'ma Evgeniia Zamiatina iz amerikanskogo arkhiva," in *EZ*, 342.
103. See M.Iu. Liubimova, "O zakone khudozhestvennoi ekonomii, fabule i novykh kontsakh... E. Zamiatin—stsenarist frantsuzskogo fil'ma *Na dne*," *Russ Stud.*, II, 2, 375–385.
104. BAR, Box 2, 6; BDIC, dossier 58.
105. Tolstoy, 250–251.
106. *Ia boius'*, 216–219.
107. Fleishman, 196–203.
108. *Ia boius'*, 327.
109. *Ia boius'*, 219–221.
110. *Ia boius'*, 329; Andronikashvili-Pil'niak, 152.
111. Annenkov, 1, 275–276.
112. *Russ. Stud.*, II, 2, 508–514.
113. Buznik (c), 187–188.
114. M. Gor'ky died on 18 June 1936.
115. Annenkov, 1, 268; for "Une manifestation littéraire à la mémoire de Maxime Gorki," see *Ia boius'*, 328.
116. BDIC dossiers 59 and 222; *Ia boius'*, 221–232.
117. See G. Adamovich, 4 December 1936, in *Poslednie novosti*.
118. M.Iu. Liubimova, "O zakone khudozhestvennoi ekonomii, fabule i novykh kontsakh... E. Zamiatin—stsenarist frantsuzskogo fil'ma *Na dne*," *Russ Stud.*, II, 2, 375–385; Shane, 93.
119. Slonim, xxv.
120. J. Curtis, "Neizvestnye pis'ma Evgeniia Zamiatina iz amerikanskogo arkhiva," in *EZ*, 342–343. In fact *The Islanders* did not appear in French until 1939, and it is not clear whether *The North* came out in French at that time.
121. Letters of 24 June and 1 August 1934; 8 April 1935; 9 December 1936, Curtis (b), 176, 181, 194, 244.
122. Malmstad and Fleyshman, 148–49; Frezinsky (d), 238.
123. Malmstad and Fleyshman, 149–51; the book by Eugene Lyons, *Assignment in Utopia*, was published in 1937.
124. J. Curtis, "Neizvestnye pis'ma Evgeniia Zamiatina iz amerikanskogo arkhiva," in *EZ*, 342–346.
125. *Ia boius'*, 232–236.
126. Andronikashvili-Pil'niak, 152–153.
127. Letters of 4 and 19 February 1937, J. Curtis, "Neizvestnye pis'ma Evgeniia Zamiatina iz amerikanskogo arkhiva," in *EZ*, 346–351.
128. Annenkov, 1, 278.

129. Slonim, xxv.
130. Letter of 11 March 1937 to Vera Bunina, Tsvetaeva, 1, 298.
131. A. Damanskaia, "Smert' E.I. Zamiatina (Pis'mo iz Parizha)," *Segodnia* (Riga), in *EZ*, 377–79.
132. Annenkov 1, 278; BDIC, dossier 211 contains a report on the day from *Poslednie novosti* (13 March 1937).
133. ALBANY, copy of an article by Tat'iana Ivanovna Manukhina (pseudonym T. Tamanin), wife of Dr Manukhin (friends of Zamiatin's), from *Russkie zapiski*, 16 (1939), 98.
134. Letter of 11 March 1937 to Vera Bunina, Tsvetaeva, 1, 298.
135. Letter to Vladislav and Ol'ga Khodasevich of Saturday 13 March 1937, Tsvetaeva, 2, 54.
136. Letter of 11 March 1937 to Vera Bunina, Tsvetaeva, 1, 298.

Conclusion

1. Letter of 11 March 1937, *Russ. Stud.*, II, 3, 365.
2. Letter of 13 March 1937, BDIC, dossier 139.
3. Letter of 12 March 1937, BDIC, dossier 136.
4. Letter of 18 March 1937, BDIC, dossier 149.
5. Curtis (b), 247; *Zamiatinskaia entsiklopediia*, 252; Komlik and Uriupin, 145–161.
6. Article of 20 March 1937, BDIC, dossier 211 ("That excellent writer, who had made himself many friends in French literary circles"); letter of 19 April 1937 from B. Cauvet-Duhamel, BDIC, dossier 138 ("I liked Monsieur Zamiatine, whose talent and sincerity were so remarkable, very much.").
7. Letter of 26 April 1937, BDIC, dossier 142.
8. BDIC, dossier 211.
9. A. Damanskaia, "Smert' E.I. Zamiatina (Pis'mo iz Parizha)," in *Segodnia* (Riga), quoted in *EZ*, 377–379.
10. Article of 11 March 1937 in *Poslednie novosti*, BDIC, dossier 211.
11. AMHERST; BDIC, dossier 211. Roman Gul' cast doubt on Berberova's account of the funeral as well, suggesting that she had not been there as she implied (V.A. Tunimanov, "Poslednee zagranichnoe stranstvie i pokhorony Evgeniia Ivanovicha Zamiatina [evropeiskaia sud'ba 'skifa' i 'eretika']," *Russ. Stud.*, II, 2, 390).
12. Article of 11 May 1937 (under the pseudonym "Sizif"), BDIC, dossier 211.

13. For this survey of Zamiatin's archives I have drawn extensively on M.Iu. Liubimova, *Tvorcheskoe nasledie E.I. Zamiatina v istorii kul'tury XX veka (avtoreferat)*, (doctoral dissertation, St Petersburg State University of Culture and the Arts, 2000), 16–19.
14. Annenkov, 1, 279–280.
15. Sheron, 73–74.
16. *Bich Bozhii* (Paris: Dom knigi, 1939). See review by M. Osorgin in BDIC, dossier 211.
17. BAR, correspondence between L.N. Zamiatina and V. Aleksandrova at the Chekhov Press.
18. See BDIC, dossier 147 for 7 letters from Gleb Struve to Liudmila in 1946–48. G. Orwell, *The Collected Essays, Journalism and Letters of George Orwell*, (Harmondsworth: Penguin, 1970), vol. 3, *1943–45*, 95–96, and vol. 4, *1945–50*, 417–418, 485–486; G. Orwell, "We by E.I. Zamyatin" (*Tribune*, 4 January 1946), in ibid., vol. 4, *1945–50*, 72–75; G. Orwell, *The Complete Works* (London: Secker and Warburg, 1998), vol. 18 (1998), 16–17, (note 2), 23, 75, 526, and vol. 19 (1998), 13, 26, 276, 471–473, and vol. 20 (1998), 18, 72, (note 1), 95, 152–153.
19. BAR; 1951–55 letters from LNZ to Vera Aleksandrova.
20. BDIC, dossier 145.
21. M. Glenny, "Introduction" to Yevgeny Zamyatin, *We*, trans. B.G. Guerney (London: Jonathan Cape, 1960), 21–22.
22. Letter from Malamuth, 18 August 1964, Shane, 88.
23. Quoted by Annenkov (1, 278–279) from the 1936 *Malaia sovetskaia entsiklopediia* (vol. 6).
24. EZ, 5–7: M.Iu. Liubimova, *Tvorcheskoe nasledie E.I. Zamiatina v istorii kul'tury XX veka (avtoreferat)*, (doctoral dissertation, St Petersburg State University of Culture and the Arts, 2000).
25. My discovery of a unique typescript of the novel, donated by Irina Kunina-Aleksander to the archives of the State University of New York at Albany—where Alex Shane taught—has enabled the preparation of a new, verified text of the work in Russian. See Evgeny Zamiatin, *My. Tekst i materialy k tvorcheskoi istorii romana*, M. Iu. Liubimova and J.A.E. Curtis (eds.) (St Petersburg: Mir, 2011).
26. BAR.
27. Marc Slonim, writing in 1964 (revised 1977) in *Soviet Russian Literature—Writers and Problems 1917–77*, 84.

Bibliography

1) ARCHIVES and MUSEUMS:

ALBANY — M. E. Grenander Department of Special Collections and Archives, University Libraries, University of Albany, State University of New York. (Evgenii Zamiatin Collection).

AMHERST — Amherst Center for Russian Culture, Archive Collection (Amherst College, Amherst MA). (A. Remizov and S. Dovgello-Remizova Papers, 2.6, Evgenii Ivanovich Zamiatin Scrapbook).

BAR — The Bakhmeteff Archive of Russian and East European History and Culture. Rare Book and Manuscript Library, Columbia University in the City of New York. (Ms Collection Zamiatin).

BDIC — Bibliothèque de Documentation Internationale Contemporaine, Université de Paris (Nanterre) (Collection E. Zamiatine, F DELTA RES 614; this collection has been recatalogued in recent years, so the numbering of individual dossiers may vary).

BOSTON — Special Collections, Mugar Memorial Library, Boston University (Marc Slonim Collection; Box 12, Folder 5/166, Zamiatin, Eugene).

IMLI — Otdel rukopisei Instituta mirovoi literatury im. A.M. Gor'kogo (Moscow). (Zamiatin archive, Fond 47).

POZNER	Pozner Family Archive, Paris.
PRINCETON	Manuscripts Division, Department of Rare Books and Special Collections, Princeton University Library. (Evgenii Ivanovich Zamiatin Collection, C0824).
RGALI	Rossiiskii gosudarstvennyi arkhiv literatury i iskusstva (Moscow). (Zamiatin archive, Fond 1776).
RGB	Rukopisnyi otdel Rossiiskoi gosudarstvennoi biblioteki (Moscow).
RNB	Otdel rukopisei Rossiiskoi natsional'noi biblioteki (St Petersburg). (Zamiatin archive, Fond 292).
TEATRAL'NAIA BIBLIOTEKA	Sankt-Peterburgskaia gosudarstvennaia teatral'naia biblioteka.
TSGIA	Tsentral'nyi gosudarstvennyi istoricheskii arkhiv Sankt-Peterburga.
TYNE and WEAR	Tyne and Wear Archives and Museums (Newcastle-upon-Tyne).
ZAMIATIN MUSEUM	Dom-muzei Zamiatina, 14, ul. Sitnikova (formerly ul. Pokrovskaia), Lebedian' (opened 2009).

2) PRIMARY SOURCES:

All translations are my own.
— Unless otherwise indicated, Zamiatin's fictional works, reviews, essays, and articles are quoted from the 5-volume edition of his work: Evgeny Zamiatin, *Sobranie sochinenii v piati tomakh*. Edited by S.S. Nikonenko and A.N. Tiurin. Moscow: Russkaia Kniga / Respublika / Dmitrii Sechin, 2003–2011.

— References to *We* [*My*] are from Evgeny Zamiatin, *My. Tekst i materialy k tvorcheskoi istorii romana*. Edited by M.Iu. Liubimova and J.A.E. Curtis. St Petersburg: Mir, 2011. Cited in the text as *My* (2011).

— I have also used the following editions where appropriate:
  Evgeny Zamiatin. *Sochineniia*. Munich: Neimanis, vols 1–4, 1970–1988. Cited in the text as Zamiatin (Munich).
  E.I. Zamiatin. *Ia boius'*: *Literaturnaia kritika. Publitsistika. Vospominaniia*. Edited by A.Iu. Galushkin and M.Iu. Liubimova. Moscow: Nasledie, 1999. Cited in the text as *Ia boius'*.

3) SECONDARY SOURCES:

Andronikashvili-Pil'niak	Boris Andronikashvili-Pil'niak. "Dva izgoia, dva muchenika: B. Pil'niak i E. Zamiatin." *Znamia* 9 (1994): 123–153.
Annenkov	Iu. Annenkov. *Dnevnik moikh vstrech. Tsikl tragedii*, vols. 1 and 2. Leningrad: Iskusstvo, 1991.
Barabanov	E. Barabanov. "Kommentarii," in Evgeny Zamiatin, *Sochineniia*, 524–575. Moscow: Kniga, 1988.
Baran and Gindin	H. Baran and S.I. Gindin, eds. *Roman Jakobson: Teksty, dokumenty, issledovaniia*. Moscow: RGGU, 1999.
Barnes	Christopher Barnes. *Boris Pasternak: A Literary Biography*, vol. 2. Cambridge: Cambridge University Press, 2004.
Barratt and Scherr	A. Barratt and Barry P. Scherr, eds. *Maksim Gorky — Selected Letters*. Oxford: Clarendon Press, 1997.
Braun	N.N. Sobolevskai. "Stat'ia Iak. Brauna 'Vzyskuiushchii chelovek (Tvorchestvo Evgeniia

	Zamiatina),'" in L.P. Iakimova, ed., *Kritika i kritiki v literaturnom protsesse Sibiri XIX–XX vv.—sbornik nauchnykh trudov*, Novosibirsk: Nauka, 1990, 202–220.
Briukhanova	I. Briukhanova. "'Vospitannik tochnykh nauk'—E.I. Zamiatin v Sankt-Peterburgskom-Leningradskom Politekhnicheskom Institute." *Avrora* 1 (2008): 23–37.
Buznik (a)	V.V. Buznik. "Pis'ma E.I. Zamiatina A.M. Remizovu." *Russkaia Literatura* 1 (1992): 176–180.
Buznik (b)	V.V. Buznik. "'Avtobiografiia' E.I. Zamiatina." *Russkaia Literatura* 1 (1992): 174–176.
Buznik (c)	V.V. Buznik. "Iz perepiski M.A. Bulgakova s E.I. Zamiatinym i L.N. Zamiatinoi (1928–1936)." *Russkaia Literatura* 4 (1989): 178–188.
Cavendish	Philip Cavendish. *Mining for Jewels—Evgenii Zamiatin and the Literary Stylization of Rus'*. London: Maney Publishing for the MHRA, 2000.
Chudakova	M. Chudakova. "Eretik, ili matros na machte," in Evgeny Zamiatin, *Sochineniia*, 498–523. Moscow: Kniga, 1988.
Chukokkala	*Chukokkala. Rukopisnyi al'manakh Korneia Chukovskogo*. Moscow: Iskusstvo, 1979.
Chukovsky	Korney Chukovsky. *Dnevnik 1901–69*, vol. 1, 1901–1929. Moscow: OLMA-Press, 2003.
Clark and Dobrenko	Katerina Clark and Evgeny Dobrenko, with Andrei Artizov and Oleg Naumov. *Soviet Culture and Power: A History in Documents, 1917–1953*. New Haven and London: Yale University Press, 2007.

Curtis (a)	J. A. E. Curtis. *Bulgakov's Last Decade: The Writer as Hero.* Cambridge: Cambridge University Press, 1987.
Curtis (b)	J. A. E. Curtis. *Manuscripts Don't Burn—Mikhail Bulgakov. A Life in Letters and Diaries.* London: Bloomsbury, 1991.
Davies and Keldysh	Richard Davies and V. A. Keldysh. *S dvukh beregov. Russkaia literatura XX veka v Rossii i za rubezhom.* Moscow: IMLI RAN, 2002.
Davydova and Tiurin	T. T. Davydova and A. N. Tiurin. "'…ia chelovek negnushchiisia i svoevol'nyi. Takim i ostanus'.' Pis'ma E. I. Zamiatina raznym adresatam." *Novyi mir* 10 (1996): 136–159.
Dialog pisatelei	T. V. Balashova et al., eds. *Dialog pisatelei. Iz istorii russko-frantsuzskikh kul'turnykh sviazei XX veka. 1920–1970.* Moscow: IMLI RAN, 2002.
Dougan	David Dougan. *The History of North East Shipbuilding.* London: Allen & Unwin, 1968.
Dubinskaia-Dzhalilova and Chernev	T. Dubinskaia-Dzhalilova and A. Chernev, "'Zhmu Vashu ruku, dorogoi tovarishch.' Perepiska Maksima Gor'kogo i Iosifa Stalina." *Novyi mir* 9 (1997): 167–192, and 9 (1998): 156–178.
Dullin	Sabine Dullin. *Men of Influence—Stalin's Diplomats in Europe 1930–1939.* Edinburgh: Edinburgh University Press, 2008.
Ellis	W. B. Ellis, ed. *The Newcastle-upon-Tyne Official Blue Book 1920—A Compendium of Municipal and Social Information* (1920).
Ermolaev and Shane	H. Ermolaev and A. Shane. "'Pis'ma K. Fedina k E. Zamiatinu." *Novyi zhurnal* 92 (1968): 188–205.

Erykalova	I. E. Erykalova. "K istorii sozdaniia p'esy E. I. Zamiatina 'Atilla.'" *Tvorcheskoe nasledie Evgeniia Zamiatina: Vzgliad iz segodnia. Kniga III*. Tambov: Tambovskii Gosudarstvennyi Pedagogicheskii Institut, 1997, 137–158.
EZ	*Evgeny Zamiatin i kul'tura XX veka: Issledovaniia i publikatsii*. Edited by M. Iu. Liubimova. St Petersburg: RNB, 2002.
Fedina and Konovalova	N. K. Fedina and L. Iu. Konovalova. "'Molchanie— moia osnovnaia literaturnaia professiia.' Pis'ma E. Zamiatina K. Fedinu." *Russkaia literatura* 1 (1998): 94–109.
Fedina and Starkov	N. K. Fedina and A. N. Starkov. "'…Mne seichas khochetsia tebe skazat'…' Iz perepiski Bor. Pil'niaka i Evg. Zamiatina s Konst. Fedinym." *Literaturnaia ucheba* 2 (1990): 79–95.
Fleishman	L. Fleishman. *Boris Pasternak. The Poet and his Politics*. Cambridge, MA and London: Harvard University Press, 1990.
French and Smith	Ron French and Ken Smith. *Lost Shipyards of the Tyne*. Newcastle upon Tyne: Tyne Bridge Publishing, 2004.
Frezinsky (a)	Boris Frezinsky. *Sud'by serapionov (portrety i siuzhety)*. St Petersburg: Akademicheskii Proekt, 2003.
Frezinsky (b)	Boris Frezinsky. "Zamiatin v arkhive M. Slonimskogo." *Novoe literaturnoe obozrenie* 19 (1996): 186–190.
Frezinsky (c)	Boris Frezinsky. "Erenburg i Zamiatin." *Novoe literaturnoe obozrenie* 19 (1996): 162–185.

Frezinsky (d)	Boris Frezinsky. "Velikaia illiuziia—Parizh 1935 (Materialy k istorii Mezhdunarodnogo kongressa pisatelei v zashchitu kul'tury)." *Minuvshee* 24 (1998): 166–239.
Galushkin (a)	A.Iu. Galushkin. "E.I. Zamiatin—Pis'mo A.K. Voronskomu. K istorii aresta i nesostoiavsheisia vysylki E.I. Zamiatina v 1922–1923 gg." *de visu* 0 (1992): 12–23.
Galushkin (b)	A.Iu. Galushkin. "K 'dopechatnoi' istorii romana E.I. Zamiatina 'My' (1921–1924)," in *Stanford Slavic Studies. Vol. 8. Themes and Variations: In Honor of Lazar Fleishman*, 366–375. Stanford: Berkeley Slavic Specialties, 1994.
Galushkin (c)	A.Iu. Galushkin. "Bezrabotnyi eretik. Evgeny Zamiatin—chlen Soiuza sovetskikh pisatelei." *Russkaia mysl'*, no. 4285 (23–29 Septem-ber 1999), 13.
Goldt	Rainer Goldt. *Thermodynamik als Textem. Der Entropiesatz als poetologische Chiffre bei E.I. Zamjatin*. Mainz: Liber Verlag, 1995.
Golikova	N. Golikova. "Evgeny Zamiatin—chelovek-amfibiia." *Za kadry verfiam* 6, no. 2396 (March 2009): 2–3, and 8–9, no. 2398–99 (April 2009): 4.
Gorky	Maxim Gorky. *Untimely Thoughts—Essays on Revolution, Culture and the Bolsheviks 1917–18*. New Haven and London: Yale University Press, 1995.
Gracheva	A.M. Gracheva. "Aleksei Remizov—chitatel' romana E. Zamiatina 'My'," in *Tvorcheskoe nasledie Evgeniia Zamiatina: Vzgliad iz segodnia. Kniga V*, 6–21. Tambov: Tambovskii Gosudarstvennyi Pedagogicheskii Institut, 1997.

Graffy and Ustinov	Julian Graffy and Andrei Ustinov. "'Moi deti—moi knigi': From Evgenii Zamiatin's Letters," in *Stanford Slavic Studies. Vol. 8. Themes and Variations: In Honor of Lazar Fleishman*, 342–365. Stanford: Berkeley Slavic Specialities, 1994.
Guerra (a)	René Guerra. "L'émigration russe des années trente aux années soixante," in E. Etkind and G. Nivat, eds., *Histoire de la littérature russe*, (vol. 6) *Le XXe siècle—Gels et dégels*. Paris: Fayard, 1990, 116–139.
Guerra (b)	René Guerra. *Oni unesli s soboi Rossiiu… Russkie emigranty—pisateli i khudozhniki vo Frantsii (1920–1970)*. 2nd ed. St Petersburg: BLITs, 2004.
Harvey	B. Harvey. "Evgeny Zamiatin—stsenarist." *Kinovedcheskie zapiski* 53 (2001).
Heywood	Anthony Heywood. "The Armstrong Affair and the Making of the Anglo-Soviet Trade Agreement 1920–21." *Revolutionary Russia* 5, 1 (June 1992): 53–91.
Ia boius'	E.I. Zamiatin. *Ia boius': Literaturnaia kritika. Publitsistika. Vospominaniia*. Edited by A.Iu. Galushkin and M.Iu. Liubimova. Moscow: Nasledie, 1999.
Ivanova	E.M. Ivanova. *Shestoe chuvstvo. Kniga dlia chteniia po istorii i kul'ture Petrograda*. St Petersburg: Beloe i Chernoe, 1997.
Katalog vystavki	*Evgeny Zamiatin, 1884–1937: Katalog vystavki*. St Petersburg: RNB, 1997.
Kaznina	O.A. Kaznina. *Russkie v Anglii. Russkaia emigratsiia v kontekste russko-angliiskikh literaturnykh sviazei v pervoi polovine XX veka*. Moscow: Nasledie, 1997.
Kemp-Welch	A. Kemp-Welch. *Stalin and the Literary Intelligentsia—1928–39*. Basingstoke and London: Macmillan, 1991.

Kern	Gary Kern, ed. *Zamyatin's "We": A Collection of Critical Essays*. Ann Arbor: Ardis, 1988.
Keys and Smith (a)	Dick Keys and Ken Smith. *From Walker to the World: Charles Mitchell's Low Walker Shipyard*. Newcastle upon Tyne: Newcastle Libraries & Information Service, 1997.
Keys and Smith (b)	Dick Keys and Ken Smith. *Ferry Tales — Tyne-Norway Voyages 1864–2001*. Newcastle upon Tyne: Tyne Bridge Publishing, 2002.
Khudozhniki russkogo zarubezh'ia	O.L. Leikind, K.V. Makhrov, and D.Ia. Severiukhin, eds. *Khudozhniki russkogo zarubezh'ia. Biograficheskii slovar'*. St Petersburg: Notabene, 2000.
Kitchen	Phil Kitchen, ed. *Voices from Vickers. The Workers' Story*. Newcastle upon Tyne: Tyne Bridge Publishing, 2001.
Komlik	N.N. Komlik. "Lebedianskii kommentarii k khudozhestvennomu tvorchestvu E.I. Zamiatina." In *Tvorcheskoe nasledie Evgeniia Zamiatina: Vzgliad iz segodnia, Kniga VI*, 108–127. Tambov, 1997.
Komlik and Uriupin	N.N. Komlik and I.S. Iriupin. *"…Pishu Vam iz Rossii…" Russkoe podstep'e v tvorcheskoi biografii E.I. Zamiatina i M.A. Bulgakova*. Elets: EGU im. I.A. Bunina, 2007.
Kukushkina	T. Kukushkina. "Strannoe chuvstvo sytosti." www.taleon.ru/taleonclub_ru/ProjectImages/2021/26_350.pdf. Accessed 27 September 2008.
Kunina	I. Kunina[-Aleksander]. "Vstrecha s Blokom." *Literaturnoe obozrenie* 9 (1991): 92–101.
Kupchenko	V. Kupchenko, "'Pishu Vam iz Rossii…' (Pis'ma E.I. Zamiatina M.A. Voloshinu)." *Pod'em* 5 (1988): 121–125.

Lahusen	T. Lahusen, E. Maksimova, and E. Andrews. *O sintetizme, matematike i prochem... Roman "My" E.I. Zamiatina. K 100-letiiu E.I. Zamiatina*. St Petersburg: Sudarynia, 1994.
Literaturovedenie	*Literaturovedenie na sovremennom etape (Materialy mezhdunarodnogo kongressa literaturovedov. K 125-letiiu E.I. Zamiatina)*. Edited by L.V. Poliakova. Tambov: TGU imeni G.R. Derzhavina, 2009.
Liubimova (a)	M.Iu. Liubimova. "E.I. Zamiatin v gody pervoi russkoi revoliutsii. (Iz pisem Zamiatina 1906 g.)." In *Istochnikovedcheskoe izuchenie pamiatnikov pis'mennoi kul'tury v sobraniiakh i arkhivakh GPB. Istoriia Rossii XIX–XX vekov*, edited by V.N. Sazhin and N.A. Efimova, 97–107. Leningrad: GPB im. M.E. Saltykova-Shchedrina, 1991.
Liubimova (b)	M.Iu. Liubimova. "E.I. Zamiatin i B.A. Pil'niak (materialy k biografiiam)." In *Istochnikovedcheskoe izuchenie pamiatnikov pis'mennoy kul'tury*, 98–108. St Petersburg: RNB, 1994.
Livak	Leonid Livak. *How it was Done in Paris — Russian Emigré Literature and French Modernism*. Wisconsin: University of Wisconsin Press, 2003.
Lunts	Lev Lunts. *Literaturnoe nasledie*. Edited by A.L. Evstigneeva. Moscow: Nauchnyi mir, 2007.
Lyons	Eugene Lyons. *Assignment in Utopia*. New York: Harcourt Brace, 1937.
Malmstad and Fleyshman	John Malmstad and Lazar Fleyshman. "Iz biografii Zamiatina (po novym materialam)." In *Stanford Slavic Studies*. Vol. 1, 103–151. Stanford, 1987.
McGuire	D.F. McGuire. *Charles Mitchell 1820–1895. Victorian Shipbuilder*. Newcastle-upon-Tyne: Newcastle upon Tyne City Libraries & Arts, 1988.

Menegaldo	Hélène Menegaldo. *Les Russes à Paris—1919–1939*. Paris: Autrement, 1998.
Myers A. (a)	Alan Myers. "Evgenii Zamiatin in Newcastle." *Slavonic and East European Review* 68, no. 1 (1990): 91–99.
Myers A. (b)	Alan Myers. "Evgenii Zamiatin in Newcastle: A Source for <u>Islanders.</u>" *Slavonic and East European Review* 68, no. 3 (1990): 498–501.
Myers A. (c)	Alan Myers. "Zamiatin in Newcastle: The Green Wall and The Pink Ticket." *Slavonic and East European Review* 71, no. 3 (1993): 417–427.
Myers J.	Jeffrey Myers. *George Orwell: The Critical Heritage*. London: Routledge and Kegan Paul, 1975.
Nechiporenko	V. Nechiporenko. "Novye fakty iz biografii Evgeniia Zamiatina." In *Peterburgskii tekst—iz istorii russkoi literatury 20–30kh godov XX veka*, 69–72. St Petersburg: Izd-vo S.—Peterburgskogo universiteta, 1996.
Neizdannyi Sologub	M.M. Pavlova and A.V. Lavrov, eds. *Neizdannyi Fedor Sologub*. Moscow: Novoe Literaturnoe Obozrenie, 1997.
Nerler	P. Nerler. "O.E. Mandel'shtam—E.I. Zamiatinu." *Literaturnaia ucheba* 1 (1991): 161.
Nice	David Nice. *Prokofiev—From Russia to the West 1891–1935*. New Haven and London: Yale University Press, 2003.
Novoe o Zamiatine	Leonid Geller, ed. *Novoe o Zamiatine*. Moscow: MIK, 1997.
Parish	Charles Parish. *The History of the Lit & Phil*, vol. 2: 1896–1989. Newcastle upon Tyne: Literary and Philosophical Society of Newcastle upon Tyne, 1990.

Peacock	Basil Peacock. *A Newcastle Boyhood 1898–1914*. Sutton: Newcastle upon Tyne City Libraries and London Borough of Sutton Libraries & Arts Services, 1986.
Perkhin	V.V. Perkhin. "E.I. Zamiatin i 'Serapionovy brat'ia' v 1929 godu (po neopublikovannym darstvennym nadpisiam)." *Filologicheskie nauki* 3 (2001): 13–20.
Popov and Frezinsky	V. Popov and B. Frezinsky, eds. *Il'ia Erenburg. Khronika zhizni i tvorchestva*, vols 1–5. St Petersburg: Lina, 1993–2001.
Pozner	V. Pozner. *Souvenirs sur Aragon et Elsa*. Rambouillet: Société des amis de Louis Aragon et Elsa Triolet, 2001.
Primochkina (a)	N.N. Primochkina. "M. Gor'ky i E. Zamiatin (k istorii literaturnykh vzaimootnoshenii." *Russkaia Literatura* 4 (1987): 148–160.
Primochkina (b)	N.N. Primochkina. *Pisatel' i vlast'. M. Gor'ky v literaturnom dvizhenii 20-kh godov*. Moscow: ROSSPEN, 1996.
Primochkina (c)	N.N. Primochkina. *Gor'ky i pisateli russkogo zarubezh'ia*, (Moscow: IMLI RAN, 2003).
Pyman	Avril Pyman. *The Life of Aleksandr Blok, (Vol. II, The Release of Harmony — 1908–1921)*. Oxford, London and New York: Oxford University Press, 1980.
RNZ	*Rukopisnoe nasledie Evgeniia Ivanovicha Zamiatina*. Edited by L.I. Buchina and M.Iu. Liubimova. Rossiiskaia Natsional'naia Biblioteka, *Rukopisnye pamiatniki*, Vypusk 3, 1–2. St Petersburg: RNB, 1997.
Russell	R. Russell. "The Drama of Evgenii Zamiatin." *Slavonic and East European Review* 70, 2 (1992): 228–248.

Russ. Stud.	*Russian Studies (Ezhekvartal'nik russkoy filologii i kul'tury)*, vol. II, 2 and 3. St Petersburg, 1996.
Saakiants	Anna Saakiants. *Marina Tsvetaeva. Zhizn' i tvorchestvo*. Moscow: Ellis Lak, 1997.
Sarnov	Benedikt Sarnov. *Stalin i pisateli*, vol. 3. Moscow: Eksmo, 2010.
Savich	A.Ia. Savich. "'Minuvshee prokhodit predo mnoiu...' Iz vospominanii." Edited by B.Ia. Frezinsky. *Diaspora* 5 (2003): 68–98.
Savina and Nechiporenko	V. Savina and V. Nechiporenko. "Dotsent LKI Evgeny Zamiatin." *Vestnik vysshei shkoly* 7 (1989): 88–92.
Seton-Watson	H. Seton-Watson. *The Russian Empire 1801–1917*. Oxford: Clarendon Press, 1967.
Shakhovskaia	Z.A. Shakhovskaia. *Otrazheniia*. Paris: YMCA Press, 1975.
Shane	Alex M. Shane. *The Life and Works of Evgenij Zamjatin*. Berkeley and Los Angeles: University of California Press, 1968.
Sheron	Zh. Sheron. "K sud'be zarubezhnogo arkhiva E.I. Zamiatina." *de visu* 3/4 (1994): 73–74.
Slonim	Marc Slonim. "Preface" to the 1959 Dutton reprint of *We*, xxi-xxv.
Smith	G.S. Smith. *D.S. Mirsky—A Russian-English Life, 1890–1939*. Oxford: Oxford University Press, 2000.
Strizhev	A. Strizhev. "Zamiatin na fone epokhi." *Literaturnaia ucheba* 3 (1994): 101–121.
Struve	G.P. Struve. *Russkaia literatura v izgnanii*, 3rd edition. Paris and Moscow: YMCA Press and Russkii Put', 1996.

Tejerizo	M. Tejerizo. "Evgeny Zamyatin in the British Press. Three Articles and Three Interviews (1932–34)." *Scottish Slavonic Review* 11 (1988): 65–89.
Terekhina	V.N. Terekhina. "'Vse tot zhe, russkii i nichei...' — Pis'ma Borisa Grigor'eva k Evgeniiu Zamiatinu." *Znamia* 8 (1988): 163–176.
Tikhonov	N. Tikhonov. "Ustnaia kniga. Kongress v zashchitu kul'tury." *Voprosy literatury* 8 (1980): 163–178.
Tiurin	A. Tiurin. "Evgeny Zamiatin. Iz bloknota 1931–1936 godov / Iz bloknotov 1914–1928 godov." *Novyi zhurnal* 168-169 (1987), 141-174; 172-173 (1988), 89-127; 175 (1989), 103-134.
Tolstoy	*Perepiska A.N. Tolstogo v dvukh tomakh*, vol. 2. Moscow: Khudozhestvennaia Literatura, 1989.
Tsvetaeva	M. Tsvetaeva. *Sobranie sochinenii v semi tomakh*, vol. 7, books 1 and 2. Moscow: Terra, 1998.
Turkov	A.M. Turkov. *Boris Mikhailovich Kustodiev*. Moscow: Terra, 1998.
Veidle	V. Veidle. "Vospominaniia." *Diaspora* 3 (2002): 7–159.
Victory Meeting	*Victory Meeting. North East Coast Institution of Engineers and Shipbuilders, Newcastle-upon-Tyne. July 8, 9, 10 and 11, 1919* (record of proceedings).
Zamiatinskaia entsiklopediia	*Zamiatinskaia entsiklopediia. Lebedianskii kontekst.* Edited by L.V. Poliakova and N.N. Komlik. Tambov and Elets: TGU imeni G.R. Derzhavina and EGU im. I.A. Bunina, 2007, 2004.
Zapisnye knizhki	E.I. Zamiatin. *Zapisnye knizhki*. Edited by S. Nikonenko and A. Tiurin. Moscow: Vagrius, 2001.

Acknowledgements

This book has been many years in the making, and I have accumulated countless debts of gratitude for the support and help I have been afforded by friends and colleagues, as well as academic institutions.

I have been particularly privileged to draw upon the wide scholarship, personal generosity and friendship of other Zamiatin specialists, especially Marina Liubimova and Aleksandr Galushkin, as well as the late Rashid Iangirov and the late Alan Myers. Professor L.V. Poliakova and Professor N.N. Komlik, together with many other contributors to the 2009 Zamiatin Conference in Tambov and Elets, have been unstinting in their helpfulness. And naturally, any biographer of Zamiatin must pay warm tribute to the groundbreaking scholarly work of Professor Alex Shane in the 1960s.

I was exceptionally fortunate to be able to rely on Jon Stallworthy and David Bethea, as well as Ray Ockenden and Philip Bullock, for their eagle-eyed attention to detail and the warm encouragement they offered in their close readings of this book as it took shape. I am also grateful for the suggestions made by the anonymous reviewers of this manuscript. Others who generously helped me, in a wide variety of ways, with this project include David Bradshaw, Catherine Ciepiela, Henrietta Curtis, Miranda Curtis, Richard Davies, Hugues Delaunay, Julian Graffy, René Guerra, Brian Harvey, Edward Higginbottom, Deva Jasheway, Sergei Kazakov, Catriona Kelly, Jeremy and Janey Knowles, Larisa Konovalova, Sergei Krolenko, Jim Naughton, Igor Nemirovsky, Kira Nemirovsky, Janice Pilcher, André and Valérie Pozner, Stanley Rabinowitz, Donald Rayfield, David Saunders, Gerry Smith, Igor Uriupin, Sharona Vedol, Azélie, Guy and Suzanne Williams, Nina Zamiatina, and Andrei Zorin.

The staff of many libraries and archives went out of their way to be helpful. In Britain, these included the Taylor Bodleian Slavonic Library in Oxford, the British Library in London, and the Tyne and Wear Archives in Newcastle; in France, they were the Bibliothèque de Documentation Internationale Contemporaine at Nanterre and the Institut d'Etudes Slaves in Paris; in Italy, the National Library in Rome; in the USA, the archives and libraries at the University of Albany (SUNY), the Amherst Center for Russian Culture, Boston University, the Bakhmeteff Archive at the University of Columbia, Harvard University, Pennsylvania State University, Princeton University, and Stanford University. In Russia, I was given wonderful help by the staff at RGALI, RGB and IMLI in Moscow; the Manuscripts Department of the Russian National Library, Pushkinsky Dom and the Theatre Library in St Petersburg; as well as the Zamiatin Museum and the Town Museum in Lebedian'.

I was fortunate to be supported by several grants for research and travel awarded to me by the AHRC, the British Academy, the Faculty of Modern and Medieval Languages and Wolfson College, University of Oxford.

I am ever grateful for the loving encouragement and great patience of my family, and especially of Ray, Sasha and Jessica.

Index

Adamovich, Georgy V. 249, 308
Adrianov, Sergei A. 198
Agranov, Iakov S. 130
Aikhenval'd, Iuly I. 49, 165
Akhmatov, doctor 167
Akhmatova, Anna A. 92, 104, 106, 107, 111, 112, 116, 124, 127, 131, 133, 136, 143, 154, 157, 166, 204, 207, 209, 214, 224, 268–270, 292, 297, 330n37, 345n93; *Anno Domini* 106; *The White Flock* 124; "Zdravstvuy Piter!.." 330n37
Al'tman, Natan I. 355n93
Aldanov, Mark A. 307
Aleksander, Bozhidar 263–264, 285, 303, 304, 308
Aleksandrinsky Theatre 148, 161, 209
Aleksandrova, Vera 312
Alexander II, Tsar 52, 289
Aliansky, Samuil [later Mikhail] M. 127, 224, 225, 254
American Theater [Paris] 233
Amfiteatrov, Aleksandr V. 104
Andreev, Leonid N. 23, 101, 143, 169

Angarsky, Nikolai S. 41
Annenkov [pen name B. Temiriazev], Iury P. 1, 81–85, 98, 99, 102, 104, 112–118, 124–126, 135, 140–141, 230, 234–236, 246, 249, 254, 260, 263, 267, 270, 274, 279, 285, 286, 291–293, 297–299, 304–306, 328n116, 344n59; *Story about Trifles, A* 274
Annenkova, Elena B. 141, 258–259, 282
Annenkova, Valentina 141
Annenkovs, family 105
Antonov, Aleksandr S. 110
Aragon, Louis 272, 280, 305
Armstrong, William 51, 52, 54, 64, 66
Arosev, Aleksandr Ia. 228, 229, 234
Attila the Hun 149, 150, 157, 184, 229, 293–294
Avdieva, Irina D. 211
Averbakh, Leopol'd L. 156, 162, 204, 248–249, 252
Babel', Isaak E. 143, 145, 163, 254, 257, 259, 280, 281, 291, 292,

301, 302; *The Red Army Cavalry* 143
Bal'mont, Konstantin D. 92
Balderston, John L. 162
Balzac, Honoré de 280
Barbusse, Henri 233, 238, 240, 267, 347n32
Barkov, Vladimir N. 231, 239
Basalaev, Innokenty M. 184
Baudelaire, Charles 63; *Les Fleurs du Mal* 63
BDT (Bol'shoi Dramatichesky Theatre) 103, 111, 157, 159–161, 168, 173–177
Bebel, August 19
Beethoven, Ludwig van 8, 17
Beliaev, Sergei M. 297; *Meat* [co-authored with Pil'niak] 297
Bellini, Giovanni 155
Bely, Andrei [Boris N. Bugaev] 92, 97, 98, 111, 208, 218, 255, 270–272
Bem, Al'fred L. 228, 229
Bennett, Arnold 134; *The Card* 134
Benois, Aleksandr N. 103, 116, 166, 250
Berberova, Nina N. 209, 249, 306, 308, 357n11; *The Italics are Mine* 249
Bezymensky, Aleksandr I. 180, 181
Birzhevye vedomosti (Stock-Exchange Gazette), newspaper 49, 62
Blium, Vladimir I. 103, 148
Bloch, Jean-Richard 280, 281, 287, 291, 297
Blok, Aleksandr A. 57, 85, 91, 92, 97–100, 103, 111–113, 116–118, 145, 146, 160, 169, 173, 267, 314, 327n107–109; *The Twelve* 91, 118, 267
Blokh, Iakov N. 131
Boklevsky, Konstantin P. 22, 24, 26, 27, 39, 124
Bolshoy Theater 253
Borodin, Aleksandr P. 251
Botticelli, Sandro 116, 155
Boudberg, Moura I. 248
Brahms, Johannes 8
Braun, Iakov V. 140, 332n81; "An Exacting Man" 140
Brecht, Bertolt 290
Brodsky, Iosif A. 79, 320–321n11
Bryant, Louise 323n5; *Six Red Months in Russia* 323n5
Buchina, Liudmila I. 317n35
Budenny, Semen M. 143
Bukharin, Nikolai I. 205, 265, 277, 281, 285
Bulgakov Nikolai A. 203, 299
Bulgakov, Mikhail A. 2, 3, 4, 94, 137, 143, 152, 156, 163, 168, 171, 174, 176, 182, 198, 203, 204, 206, 209, 211, 213, 218, 221, 224, 226, 246, 247, 256, 259, 260, 263, 264, 270, 276, 277, 296, 298, 299, 307, 309, 339–340n91; *Cabal of Hypocrites, The (Molière)* 209, 224, 246, 247, 298; *Crimson Island, The* 168, 171, 176; *Days of the Turbins, The* 152, 163, 168, 171, 211, 226, 246, 298; *Diaboliada* 143; "The Dramatist and the Critics" [not completed] 171, 176; *Flight* 174, 176; *Master and Margarita, The* 4, 137, 259, 276; *White Guard,*

The 94, 152, 211, 226; *Zoika's Apartment* 168
Bulgakova (Shilovskaia), Elena S. 182, 259, 264, 298, 307, 309
Bulgakova, Liubov' E. 182, 203, 259
Bunin, Ivan A. 236, 237, 265, 304, 305, 307, 308
Bystrova, censor 145–146
Cauvet-Duhamel, B. 179, 307
Chagall, Marc Z. 292
Chaliapin, Fedor I. 250, 257
Chaliapins, family 105
"Chaotic Din instead of Music", article in *Pravda* 296
Charol, translator 150, 154
Cheka (Committee for Suppressing Counter-revolution and Speculation; later GPU, OGPU) 3, 99, 112, 150, 246
Chekhov, Anton P. 2, 21, 29, 44, 46, 62, 97, 148, 183, 245, 253; *The Cherry Orchard* 21, 60, 183; *Uncle Vania* 21
Chirikov, Evgeny N. 14; *The Jews* 14
Chopin, Frédéric 8, 17
Chukovsky, Kornei I. 84, 97, 98, 102, 107, 109–113, 116, 117, 119, 120, 126, 131, 132, 134, 137, 138, 142–146, 149, 151, 158, 164, 168, 170; *Chukokkala* 146; *Crocodile, The* 170
Chukovsky, Nikolai K. 149
Chukovskys, family 105
Collins, Wilkie 332n68; *Woman in White, A* 332n68
Comédie Française 232, 272
Companeez, Jacques 298

Conan Doyle, Arthur 135
Conrad, Joseph 134
Constantine, Grand Duke 52
Copernicus 90
Cosmopolitan, magazine 214
Crémieux, Benjamin 222, 266
Critical and Biographical Dictionary of Russian Writers and Scientists 46, 62
Damanskaia, Avgusta F. 86, 102, 121, 205, 304, 306, 308, 327n98
Danilevsky, Grigory P. 9; *Freedom* 9
Dante 139
Delo naroda (*The People's Cause*) 89, 92, 99
Despotuli, Vladimir M. 230
Deutsch, Babette 149, 150, 212–213
Diaghilev, Sergei P. 141
Dickens, Charles 97, 120; *Hard Times* 120
Dictionary of Dramatists [which never appeared] 216
Diky, Aleksei D. 147, 148, 149, 151, 159
Dobrovol'sky, Viktor 151
Dobuzhinsky, Mstislav V. 103, 109, 113, 166, 236, 305, 306, 328n116
Dobuzhinskys, family 113
Dom iskusstv (*House of Arts*), journal 106, 110, 172, 327n97
Don-Aminado 268
Donskoi, Dmitry 105
Dostoevsky, Fedor M. 11, 111, 115, 129, 137, 140, 177, 274 *Idiot* 274; *Gambler* 274
Drieu la Rochelle, Pierre 226, 239, 266, 308

Dumas, Alexandre 113;
    Ange-Pitou 113
Dzerzhinsky, Feliks E. 122, 124
Eastman, Max 289, 300, 355n84;
    Artists in Uniform 289
Efron, Ariadna S. 291, 294, 306
Efron, Georgii (Mur) S. 294
Efron, Sergei Ia. 291, 292, 294
Efros, Abram M. 141, 142, 333n87
Eikhenbaum, Boris M. 41, 98, 117,
    143, 160, 296
Einstein, Albert 137, 139, 145
Erdman, Boris R. 147
Erdman, Nikolai R. 147, 163, 226;
    The Mandate 163
Erenburg, Il'ia G. 133, 134, 141,
    150, 154, 156, 160, 164–166,
    173, 179, 200, 222, 229, 231,
    233, 234, 235, 254, 257, 267,
    272, 277, 281–282, 290–291,
    292, 313; *Julio Jurenito* 134,
    231
Erenburgs, family 229, 231, 233,
    260, 292, 347n17
Ermler, Fridrikh M. 164
Eroshin, Ivan E. 156
Esenin, Sergei A. 49, 62;
    Radunitsa (All Souls' Day)
    49; *The Ravine* 62
Esenina-Tolstaia, Sof'ia A. 309
Euclid 139
Evreinov, Nikolai N. 270, 273
*Ezhemesiachnyi zhurnal dlia vsekh
    (Monthly Journal for All)* 41,
    46
Fadeev, Aleksandr A. 175, 180,
    202, 204; *The Rout* 175, 180
Fedin, Konstantin A. 4, 106, 107,
    121, 142, 143, 145, 146, 166,
    169, 179, 187, 196, 199–202,
    207, 210, 211, 225, 226, 229,
    230, 232–234, 237, 238,
    243, 244, 248, 249, 252–255,
    264–266, 269–274, 276–282,
    286, 289, 294, 300, 302, 313,
    326n77; *The Rape of Europe*
    271, 300, 301
Fedina, Dora S. 225, 248, 252, 300
Fedins, family 117, 307
Feuchtwanger, Lion 290
Florensky, Pavel A. 137, 139;
    *Concepts of the Imaginary in
    Geometry* 137
Fonvizin, Denis I. 98
Ford, Henry 201, 239
Forsh, Ol'ga D. 98, 287, 324n38;
    Sumasshedshii korabl'
    324n38
Forster, E. M. 290
FOSP — see Writers' Federation.
Franz Ferdinand, Archduke 44
Freud, Sigmund 178, 275
Frezinsky, Boris Ia. 207
Gabin, Jean 298, 308
Gagarin, Andrei G., 16, 24, 25,
    109, 111
Gagarina, Maria D. 109
Gagarina, Sof'ia A. 109, 111, 113
Galsworthy, John 132, 211; *The
    Forsyte Saga* 132
Galushkin, Aleksandr Iu. 122,
    204, 206, 230, 276, 323n6
Gapon, Georgy A. 12
Garbo, Greta 260
Gauguin, Paul 116
Gazdanov, Gaito I. 305
Gedroyts, Vera I. 211
George V, King 64, 65
German, Iury P. 301; *Our Friends*
    301

Gide, André 260, 291, 298, 299–300, 302; *Le retour de l'URSS* 299–300, 302
Gingerbread for Orphaned Children, collection 48
Gippius, Zinaida N. 249, 305
Glasgow Herald, The, newspaper 257, 263, 270, 284
Glaviskusstvo [Chief Directorate of the Arts] 213
Glavrepertkom [the Chief Repertory Committee] 174–177, 208, 209, 213. See also "Repertkom".
Glebova-Sudeikina, Ol'ga A. 297
Glenny, Michael 312
Gogol', Nikolai V. 9, 35, 63, 64, 143, 161, 178, 261, 288, 298; *Dead Souls* 9, 298; *Government Inspector* 161, 163; *Nose, The* 178; *Taras Bul'ba* 279, 288–289
Golos Rossii (*Voice of Russia*), journal 118, 119
Goncharova, Natal'ia S. 292
Gor'ky, Maksim [Aleksei Maksimovich Peshkov] 3, 35, 62, 87–88, 89, 91, 92, 93, 94, 97–100, 102, 104, 106–108, 110–112, 116, 117, 121, 140, 142, 143, 145, 146, 151, 155, 163, 165, 166, 168–169, 170, 172–174, 176, 177, 179, 182, 183, 196, 200, 202–206, 208, 209, 216–220, 224, 230, 231, 243, 244, 248, 253, 259, 265, 276, 281, 286, 291, 292, 294–296, 298, 302, 305, 327n109, 345n84, 356n114; *Lower Depths, The* 87, 168, 294, 298; *Mother* 87; "Waste of Energy" 205
Gorbachev, Georgy E. 156
Gornfel'd, Arkady G. 46
Gorodetsky, Sergei M. 121
GPU (formerly Cheka, later OGPU) 3, 123, 124, 129–132, 134, 135, 138, 292, 301
Granovsky, Aleksei M. 279, 288, 293
Grebenshchikov, Iakov P. 14, 37–38, 49, 54, 59, 63, 105, 147, 156, 160, 162, 178, 224, 316n23, 325n52
Griboedov, Aleksandr. S. 180
Grigor'ev, Boris D. 102, 121, 144, 155, 192, 222, 230, 232, 242, 245, 250, 251–252, 289, 345n93, 355n84
Grigor'eva, Elizaveta G. 232, 237, 242
Grigor'evs, family 102, 155, 233, 242, 307
Groeger, Wolfgang 142
Gronsky, Ivan M. 230, 253
Grossman, Leonid P. 208
Grozdova, Agrafena P. 39, 96, 135–136, 210, 226, 250, 265, 269, 273, 282, 295, 310
Gruzdev, Il'ia A. 146, 179
Grzhebin, Zinovy I. 98, 110, 115, 116, 118, 121, 122, 172, 329n22
Grzhebins, family 105
Guerney, B. G. 312
Guild Theatre, (New York) 213
Gul', Roman B. 306, 357n11
Gumilev, Nikolai S. 98, 112, 117, 146, 324n37
Hardy, Thomas 134; *Far from the Madding Crowd* 134

Hecht, Ben 181, 182; *Front Page, The* (coauthored with Charles MacArthur) 181, 182, 206, 208, 210–211
Heilbronner, Renée 288, 303, 304
Hemingway, Ernest 290
Heslop, Harold 215, 216; *Goaf* 215
Hitler, Adolf 226, 262, 285, 291
Hoffmann, E. T. A. 91, 107; *Serapion Brothers, The* 107
Honegger, Arthur 165; *Judith* 165
Hoover, Herbert 231
Humanité, L', newspaper 267, 272
Huxley, Aldous 4, 238–239, 290, 292, 311, 312; *Brave New World* 4, 238–239, 311
Iagoda, Genrikh G. 124–125, 206, 208, 209
Iakovlev, Boris 236
Iangirov, Rashit M. 123
Ianovsky Iury I. 295–296
Iarmolinsky, Avraam Ts. (Avrahm Yarmolinsky) 149–150, 151, 154, 179–180, 228, 246
Il'f, Il'ia A. 259
Inkizhinov, Valery I. 279
Ionin, Georgy 178
Ionov, Il'ia I. 146
Iretsky, V. Ia. 333n88
Iudin, Pavel F. 276
Iudina, Maria V. 210
Iur'evskaia, Ekaterina M. 289
Iurkevich, Vladimir I. 236
Ivanov, Vsevolod V. 121, 221–222, 276
Ivanov-Razumnik, R. V. 35, 39, 46, 63, 92, 99, 129, 136
Izmailov, Aleksandr A. 49
Izvestiia (*The News*), newspaper 121, 230, 235, 253

Jakobson, Roman O. 160, 173, 229, 244, 261
Jakobsons, family 347n17
Jouvet, Louis 298
Joyce, James 233, 272
Kadet [Constitutional-Democratic] Party 14, 19, 44, 89
Kagan, Abram S. 227
Kaganovich, Lazar' M. 265
Kagansky, Zakhar L. 339n91
Kaleidoscope, magazine 9
Kamenev, Lev B. 125, 135, 286
Kapitsa, Petr L. 166
Kaplan, Fanny E. 94
Kataev, Valentin P. 222
Katia, family relative 7
Kautsky, Karl 19
Kazarnovsky, Iury A. 156, 158
Kennaday, Paul 118–119, 136
Khodasevich, Vladislav F. 113, 116, 121, 143, 154, 209, 294, 306, 308
Khodaseviches, family 117
Kiki [Alice Prin], 235, 258–259
Kiodzi Isida 166
Kirillov, Vladimir T. 89, 100; *We* 89, 100
Kirov, Sergei M. 285
Kizevetter, Aleksandr A. 228
Kliucharev, Viktor P. 132, 147, 151
Kliuev, Nikolai A. 48
Kniga i revoliutsiia (*Books and the Revolution*), journal 106
Kock, Johan 23
Koenig, Václav 160, 164
Kommissarzhevsky, Fedor F. 273
Komsomol'skaia pravda (*Komsomol Truth*), newspaper 198, 235
Korchagina-Aleksandrovskaia, Ekaterina P. 224

Korsh Theatre 147
Kosykh, school director 42
Krandievskaia-Tolstaia, Natalia V. 183, 200
Krasin, Leonid B. 131
Krasnaia gazeta, newspaper 199, 204
Krasnaia nov' (*Red Virgin Soil*), journal 117, 126, 131, 144, 209
Kriuchkov, Petr P. 218, 220, 221
Krolenko, Aleksandr A. 172–173, 179, 191, 211–212, 214–215, 223, 224, 343n47
Krupskaia, Nadezhda K. 170
Krylenko, Nikolai V. 182
Krylov, Boris 14, 16, 43, 259
Krymov, Nikolai P. 148
Krymov, Vladimir P. 262
Kuklin, Georgy O. 335n150
Kukushkina, Tat'iana A. 326n86
Kunina-Aleksander, Irina E. 169, 195, 228, 247, 255, 261, 263–264, 267–271, 274, 275, 278–279, 283–288, 293, 294, 299, 300–301, 302–304, 307–308, 339n76, 355n83, 358n25; *Red Fez* 275
Kuroda, Otokichi 154, 166
Kustodiev, Boris M. 118, 127–128, 132, 140, 148–150, 157–161, 166, 169, 170, 185, 186
Kustodiev, Kirill B. 158
Kutkin, engineer 37
Kuz'min, N. M., editor 42
Kuz'min, Mikhail A. 116
Lane, Allen 273
Larionov, Mikhail F. 233, 292
Lawrence, D. H. 134; *Sons and Lovers* 134
Lazarevsky, Boris A. 48

Lefèvre, Frédéric 238, 239, 240
Lenin, Vladimir I. 2, 88, 89, 94, 101, 107, 117–118, 122–123, 127, 141, 170
Leningradskaia pravda, newspaper 172
Leonidov, Boris L. 164
Leonov, Leonid M. 143, 145, 169, 301, 302; *Road to the Ocean* 301; *Thief* 169
Leskov, Nikolai S. 109, 145, 147–149, 160, 267, 337n38; *Leftie* 147
Letopis' (*The Chronicle*), journal 62, 87
Levinson, Andrei Ia. 108–109, 121
Lewis, Sinclair 134
Liberman, Semen P. 150, 154, 159–160, 339n91
Lidin, Vladimir G. 302
Lidové noviny, newspaper 160, 164
Likhachev, Nikolai P. 209
Literaturnaia gazeta (*The Literary Gazette*), journal [banned] 109, 110
Literaturnaia gazeta (*The Literary Gazette*), newspaper 180–181, 198–199, 201–204, 208, 237–238, 242, 248, 253, 254, 259, 276, 289
Liubimova, Marina Iu. 316n23, 317n35n36
Lloyd George, David 68
Lo Gatto, Ettore 214, 247
Locke, William J. 62; *Derelicts* 62
London, Jack 46, 62, 97; *The Iron Heel* 62
Long, Ray 214, 228, 231, 247, 346n10
Lu, journal 233

Luknitsky, Pavel N. 133
Lunacharsky, Anatoly V. 110, 135, 205–206
Lundberg, Evgeny G. 46
Lunts, Lev N. 102, 107–108, 113, 121, 139–140; *Outside the Law* 102
Lyons, Eugene 207, 214, 234, 253, 288–289, 300, 355n84; *Autobiography* 300
MacArthur, Charles 181, 182; *The Front Page* (coauthored with Ben Hecht) 181, 182, 206, 208, 210–211
Maclay, Joseph 65
Magaram, Nikolai I. 142–143, 145
Magerovsky, Lev F. 310
Maiakovsky, Vladimir V. 60, 97, 106, 206, 211; *Mystery-Bouffe* 106
Maksimov, Sergei V. 49, 320n59; *Nechistaia sila* 320n59
Malamuth, Charles 214, 248, 288–290, 299–300, 313–314, 355n84
Malraux, André 277, 291
Malyi Opernyi (formerly Mikhailovsky) Theatre 147
Malyi Theatre 163
Mamai 38
Man Ray 258
Manchester Guardian, newspaper 241, 255
Mandel'shtam, Nadezhda Ia. 309
Mandel'shtam, Osip E. 98, 113, 277, 309
Mann, Heinrich 290
Manukhin, Ivan I. 357n133
Manukhina, Tat'iana I. 306, 357n133

Marakuev, Nikolai N. 325n52
Marianne, magazine 245, 255, 271, 275, 287, 293, 295, 301
Marr, Nikolai Ia. 209
Marshak, Samuil Ia. 103, 161, 169
Marx, Karl 19, 63, 163
Matisse, Henri 242
Maurois, André 238, 256, 266, 271
Mayer, Julius Robert 102, 325n52
Meierkhol'd, Vsevolod E. 161, 163, 255, 261, 296
Mel'nikova-Papoushkova, Nadezhda F. 164–165, 229
Mendeleeva, Liubov' D. 173
Mercure de France, journal 251
Merezhkovsky, Dmitry S. 305
Miasin [Massine], Leonid F. 251
Milashevsky, Vladimir A. 328n116
Mille, Cecil B. de 226, 228, 234, 289, 346n10, 355n84
Mindlin, Emilii L. 327n97
Mir prikliuchenii (World of Adventures), magazine 45, 135
Miroliubov, Viktor S. 35, 37–38, 41, 46, 61–62, 99, 106, 179
Mirsky, D. S. [D.P. Sviatopolk-Mirsky] 142, 160
Mitchell, Charles 51, 52
Mitrokhin, Dmitry I. 49
MKhAT [the Moscow Arts Theatre] 132, 146–149, 152, 157, 158, 161, 163, 174, 209, 210, 213, 215, 219, 223, 224, 253
MKhAT Studio 138, 147
Mogila, P. S. 320n59
Mogilianskaia, Maria 56
Mogiliansky, Aleksandr P. 310
Mois, Le, journal 239, 243–244, 251
Mokul'sky, Stefan S. 161, 214

Mokul'skys, family 215
Molière, Jean-Baptiste P. de 209, 224, 246, 247, 259, 264, 280
Monakhov, Nikolai F. 157, 160, 161
Monde, newspaper 233, 238, 240–241, 347n32
Monde, Le, newspaper 347n32
Mozart, Wolfgang Amadeus 17
Mstislavsky, Sergei D. 129, 132, 136
Mukařovský, Jan 229
Musil, Robert 290
Musorgski, Modest P. 304; *Boris Godunov* 304
Mussolini, Benito 155
Myers, Alan 320–321n11, 322n48n53
Na literaturnom postu (On Literary Guard), journal 156, 168
Nabokov, Vladimir V. (Sirin) 268, 308
Nakanune (On the Eve), newspaper 120, 121
Nappel'baum, Moisei S. 146
Narbut, Vladimir I. 169
Nechiporenko, V. 355n90
New Republic, The, magazine 150
Nicholas II, Tsar 11–13, 14, 23–25, 39, 51, 64, 68, 88, 109
Nietzsche, F. 18, 19, 63, 116, 317n36; *Beyond Good and Evil* 317n36
Nijinsky, Vatslav F. 286
Nikitin, Nikolai 107, 108, 120, 121, 131, 132, 159, 166, 173, 179, 292, 343n48
Nikitina, Evdoksiia F. 215
Nikitina, Zoia A. 211, 224, 226, 238, 243, 248–250, 252, 260, 265, 343n48

Nikolaevsky, Boris I. 309–310
Nikon, Father 305
Noble, Andrew 64, 322n48
Noble, Margery Durham 64
Nordau, Max 16; *In Search of the Truth (Paradoxes)* 16
Nouvelles Littéraires, Les, journal 238, 270, 286, 307
Novaia zhizn' (New Life), journal 88, 89
Novitsky, Pavel I. 176
Novy mir (New World) 301
Novy mir (New World), Berlin 327n97
Novye mysli (New Thoughts), journal 29
O. Henry 97
O'Casey, Sean 208; *Silver Tassie* 208
"Obezvelvolpal" ("The Great and Free Monkey Chamber"), literary group 91–92, 111
Obradovich, Sergei A. 177, 178
Obrazovanie (Education), journal 28
Oettly, Paul 262, 268, 272, 308
Offenbach, Jacques 232; *Tales of Hoffmann* 232
OGPU (formerly Cheka; GPU) 144, 208, 209
Okhrana 27
Olesha, Iury K. 211, 301, 302
Orechkin, Boris S. 225–226
Orwell, George 4, 101, 310–313; *1984* 4, 101, 311, 312
Osnovy (Foundations), journal 129, 132, 136
Osorgin, Mikhail A. 126, 236, 308, 358n16
Ost-Europa, journal 244

Ostrovsky, Nikolai A. 301, 302; *How the Steel was Tempered* 301
Otsep, Fedor A. 259, 260, 285, 293, 355n100
Pares, Bernard 160
Paris-Soir, newspaper 270, 293
Pasternak, Boris L. 109, 116, 133, 154, 159, 183, 200, 255, 276, 277, 281, 291–292, 297; *Safe Conduct* 183
Perr'e, Konrad 214
Peshkova, Ekaterina P. 151, 209
Peter I, Tsar 51
Petrov, Evgeny [Evgeny Petrovich Kataev] 259
Petrovsky, Dmitry V. 333n88
Petrov-Vodkin, Kuz'ma S. 99
Picasso, Pablo 116
Pierre, André 307
Pil'niak, Boris A. 106, 109, 110, 118, 121, 122, 124–127, 130–133, 138, 141, 143, 145, 154, 156, 159, 163, 183, 198–202, 204, 205, 206, 207, 209, 214, 217, 265, 275, 277, 297, 301, 302, 344n59; *Mahogany* 198, 199, 207; *Meat*, coauthored with S. Beliaev 297; *Volga Flows into the Caspian Sea, The* 207, 214
Pitirim, bishop 45
Platonova, Anastasia Vasil'evna, grandmother 8, 63
Platonova, Varvara Aleksandrovna (Varia), aunt 8, 153, 162, 210, 223, 227
Podgorny, Vladimir A. 213, 215, 223
Poggioli, Renato 214, 247
Polonskaia, Elizaveta G. 107, 108, 179
Polonsky, Viacheslav P. 62, 93
Poslednie novosti (*Latest News*), newspaper 205, 230, 308, 346n2, 356n132, 357n10
Posnikov, Aleksandr S. 24
Postnikov, Sergei P. 35–36, 39, 92, 118, 121, 122, 164, 205, 227, 229, 245, 251, 256, 297
Postnikovs, family 257
Pottecher, F. 280; "Three Hours at Bellevue with the Russian Writer Evgeny Zamiatin" 280
Povolotsky, Leonid S. 211
Pozdiunin, Valentin L. 213
Pozner, André 345n88
Pozner, Solomon V. 252, 267
Pozner, Valérie 345n88
Pozner, Vladimir S. 101, 107, 121, 179, 221–222, 226, 230–231, 233, 234, 238–241, 245, 246, 252, 264, 266–267, 272, 291, 345n88, 352n23
Pravda (*The Truth*), newspaper 89, 112, 123, 125, 145, 163, 170, 296, 297, 300
Preis, Aleksandr G. 178
Prévost, Marcel 256, 270, 278; *Les Demi-vierges* 256
Prim, Suzy 298, 308
Priscus 157, 293
Prishvin, Mikhail M. 36, 92, 295–296
Prokof'ev, Sergei S. 165, 280, 282, 289, 294
Proletkul't [Proletarian Culture] movement 89, 100, 123

Pudovkin, Vsevolod I. 206, 279; *Storm over Asia* 279
Punin, Nikolai N. 166
Pushkin, Aleksandr S. 10, 112, 302–304
Rabinovich, Iosif Ia. 224
Racine, Jean 280
Radishchev, Aleksandr N. 287
Radlov, Nikolai E. 171, 187, 188, 328n116
Radlova, Nadezhda K. 224
Radlovs, family 215
Raphael 89
RAPP (proletarian writers' organization) 3, 155, 180–181, 198, 202, 204, 217, 244, 248, 269, 276, 281, 289
Rasputin, Grigory E. 44, 163
Reavey, George 233, 248, 249, 251, 254, 273
Rech' (*Speech*), newspaper 44–46, 49, 68
Reed, John 323n5
Reinhardt, Maria 308
Reinhardt, Max 226, 232
Remarque, Erich Maria, 275; *All Quiet on the Western Front* 275
Remizov, Aleksei M. 36, 40–41, 48, 49, 54, 61, 62–63, 83, 91–92, 99, 102, 111, 116, 121, 122, 205, 230, 233, 236, 237, 270, 305, 306, 308, 311, 312, 319n41, 320n64, 354n80; *Ukrepa: Slovo k russkoi zemle, o zemle rodnoi, tainostiakh zemnykh i sud'be* 320n64
Remizovs, family 105, 111, 245, 249, 260

Renoir, Jean 294, 298, 308
Renoir, Pierre-Auguste 242
Repertkom [the Repertory Committee] 174, 175, 176, 210, 224. See also Glavrepertkom.
Repin, Il'ia E. 116
Revue de France, La 255, 256, 270, 278, 298
Riabushinsky, Stepan P. 219
Rice, Elmer 181; *Street Scene* 181
Riga Theatre of Russian Drama 161, 164
Rimsky-Korsakov, Andrei N., musicologist 211
Rivera, Diego 300
Rodin, Auguste 98
Rolland, Romain 97
Romanov, dynasty 35
Romanov, E. A., engineer 43
Rothschild (family) 243; Edouard de 250
Rouge et le Noir, Le newspaper 267
Rousseau, Jean-Jacques 295
Rozanov, Vasily V. 92
Rozhdestvensky, Vsevolod A. 141
RSDWP (b) [Bolshevik wing of Russian Social-Democratic Workers' Party] 13–16, 18, 99, 217
Rubakin, Aleksandr N. 279, 293, 354n65
Rubakin, Nikolai A. 279
Rubens, Peter Paul 116
Rudé právo, newspaper 237–238
Rul' (*The Helm*), journal 165
Ruski arkhiv, journal 255
Russian Soviet Writers, encyclopaedia 313

Russische Rundschau, journal 150
Russkaia mysl' (*Russian Thought*), journal 319n51
Russkie zapiski (*Russian Notes*), journal 46
Russkoe sudokhodstvo (*Russian Shipping*), journal 27
Russky sovremennik (*The Russian Contemporary*), journal 134, 142–146, 149, 150, 156, 165, 172, 183
Rutherford, Ernest 166
Rykov, Aleksei I. 177, 203, 206, 208
Saltykov-Shchedrin, Mikhail E. 164, 168; *History of a Town* 164
Savich, Alia Ia. 229, 231, 235, 292
Savich, Ovady G. 173, 229, 231, 233, 235, 254, 291, 292
Saviches, family 231, 232, 235, 267, 272, 292, 355n93
Savina, V. 355n90
Savitsky, Petr N. 229
Schopenhauer, Arthur 116
Schumann, Robert 8
Scriabin, Aleksandr N. 80, 87, 115
Seghers, Anna 290
Segodnia (*Today*), newspaper 225
Serapion Brotherhood (Serapion Brothers; Serapions), literary group 92, 98, 105, 107–108, 120, 121, 125, 126, 133, 139, 146, 162, 179, 221, 242, 302
Sergeev, Mikhail A. 224, 225
Seurat, Georges 116
Severnye zapiski (*Northern Notes*), journal 62
Shaginian, Marietta S. 162, 330n30; *Mess-Mend* 330n30

Shakespeare, William 103, 115, 217, 280; *King Lear* 103; *Merchant of Venice, The* 103; *Othello* 103
Shakhovskaia, Zinaida A. 267–269, 275–276, 287, 290, 293
Shakhovskoi, Vsevolod N. 51
Shane, Alex 100, 313, 358n25; *The Life and Works of Evgenij Zamjatin* 313
Shapiro, Ruvim A. 168
Shaporin, Iury A. 178
Shaw, George Bernard 97
Shchegolev, Pavel E. 10, 48, 92, 116, 124, 151, 157, 159, 209, 215
Shchurovsky, Vladimir A. 33
Sheridan, Richard Brinsley 214, 217; *School for Scandal* 214, 217, 223
Sherriff, R. C. 206; *Journey's End* 206
Shishkov, Viacheslav Ia. 42; *A Rapid Trial* 42
Shklovsky, Viktor B. 98, 104, 106, 116, 145, 168, 296, 338n72; "*Siuzhet*" as an Aspect of Style 106
Shmidt, Vasily V. 209
Sholokhov, Mikhail A. 199, 295 *Virgin Soil Upturned* 295
Shostakovich, Dmitry D. 178, 296
Shteinberg, A. Z. 346n6
Shul'man, Konstantin von 15
Sibirskie ogni (*Siberian Lights*), journal 140
Sicault, Paul 279
Sienkiewicz, Henryk 16
Simonov, Ruben N. 208, 210
Sinclair, Upton 97

Slavische Rundschau, journal 244, 261
Slonim, Marc L. 118, 164, 165, 198, 205, 235–237, 255, 268, 287, 293, 294, 299, 301, 304, 306, 308, 310, 311, 313, 314; *Portraits of Soviet Writers* 255
Slonimsky, Mikhail L. 98, 107, 113, 121, 145, 179, 200, 207, 222, 225, 229–230, 238, 276, 330n30
Socialist-Revolutionary Party 15, 19, 24, 44, 89, 92, 94, 99, 110, 122, 267
Society for Assistance to Needy Writers and Scientists 46
Sologub, Fedor K. 92, 116, 143
Sovremennik (*The Contemporary*), journal 46
Sovremennye zapiski (*Contemporary Notes*), journal 118, 122
Sovremennyi zapad (*The West Today*), journal 119–120, 172
Spendiarov, Aleksandr A. 183
Stalin, Iosif V. 3, 4, 101, 123, 127, 175, 182, 205, 206, 213, 216–221, 223, 230, 231, 244, 246, 249, 253–254, 259, 265, 276–278, 286, 288, 290, 291, 297, 298, 300–302, 307, 312, 344n59
Stanislavsky, Konstantin S. 255, 261
Stavi[t]sky, Alexandre 271, 272
Sterne, Laurence: *Tristram Shandy* 104
Strizhevsky, Vladimir F. 293, 355n100
Struve, Gleb P. 4, 310–313; *25 Years of Soviet Russian Literature* 311
Swan, Henry 51, 52
Tabaković, Ivan 284, 287, 288, 354–355n83
Tarasov-Rodionov, Aleksandr I. 222
Tarle, Evgeny V. 209
Tchaikovsky, Petr I. 17
Teatral'naia zhizn' (*Theatrical Life*), journal 119
Teffi [Nadezhda A. Lokhvitskaia] 268
Tesková, Anna 229
Thackeray, William Makepeace 114
Tikhanov, Pavel N. 320n59; *Kriptoglossariy* 320n59
Tikhonov, Aleksandr N. 219, 333n87
Tikhonov, Nikolai S. 92, 97–99, 107, 109, 117, 119, 142, 144–145, 151, 163, 168, 169, 175, 179, 180, 218, 276, 292, 340n93
Tikhonovs, family 215
Tolstaia-Krandievskaia — see Krandievskaia-Tolstaia
Tolstoy, Aleksei N. 41, 92, 120, 133, 156, 168, 169, 183, 188, 199, 210, 214, 265, 275, 276, 279, 287, 292, 294–295, 300–301; *Aelita* 133; *Defence of Tsaritsyn, The* 300–301; *Peter I* 279, 287, 295, 300
Tolstoy, Lev N. 90, 116, 129, 161, 259, 260; *Anna Karenina* 259, 260; *Power of Darkness* 161; *War and Peace* 259

Tomorrow, almanac 97
Tribune, newspaper 311, 312
Triolet, Elsa 272
Trotsky, Lev D. 15, 19, 125–127, 130, 140, 156, 205, 300–302; *One or Two Chambers?* 19
Tsvetaeva, Marina I. 154, 229, 268, 291–292, 294, 304, 306
Turgenev, Ivan S. 7, 161, 274; *Lebedian'* 7, *Hunter's Notebook* 7; *Month in the Country* 161; *Spring Torrents* 274
Tynianov, Iury N. 98, 117, 143, 168, 180, 296; *The Death of Vazir-Mukhtar* 180
Umansky, Dmitry A. 142, 150, 154
Unbegaun, Boris O. 294
Unshlikht, Iosif S. 124, 135
UPI (United Press International) 207, 214, 234, 288
Uritsky, Moisei S. 94
Usova, Elizaveta I. 14, 16
Usova, Maria N., sister-in-law 16, 20, 210, 218, 221
Usovs, family, 15
Utopiia, journal 331n59
V., Nikolai 15, 18
Vaginov, Konstantin K. 161
Vaillant-Couturier, Paul 267, 305
Vakhtangov Theatre 159, 164, 168, 206, 208–211, 159
VAPP (the All-Union Association of Proletarian Writers, renamed RAPP in 1928) 155, 156, 162
Varia, family relative 61
Vasil'eva, Klavdia N. 218
Vecherniaia krasnaia (*The Red Evening Paper*) 198

Vendredi, magazine 296
Vengerov, Semen A. 46, 62–63, 319n55
Vengerova, Zinaida A. 53, 161, 181, 203, 206, 208, 216
Vereisky, Georgy S. 339n83
Veresaev, Vikenty V.183, 198, 204, 221
Verlaine, Paul 116
Vildrac, Charles 221, 232, 294
Vinogradov, Viktor V. 161
"Vol'fil" [The Free Philosophical Association] 136
Volia Rossii (*Freedom of Russia*), journal 118, 164–165, 198–200, 235–236, 327n98
Volkovysky, Nikolai M. 123, 127
Volkov, Evgeny V., nephew 153
Volkov, Vladimir V., brother-in-law 21, 32, 42, 227
Voloshin, Maksimilian A. 136–137, 144, 151, 182–183, 198, 199
Volynsky, Akim L. 104, 109, 198, 116, 124
Voronsky, Aleksandr K. 106, 117–118, 121, 124–126, 129, 131, 135, 138, 139, 144, 156, 209, 230, 302, 326n77, 330n30
Vozrozhdenie (*Rebirth*), newspaper 209, 308
Vrubel', Mikhail A. 116
VSP [All-Russian Union of Writers, re-named VSSP in 1929] 104, 107, 124, 129, 134, 150, 155, 160, 168, 172, 179–181, 198–202, 204, 205, 207
VSSP (The All-Russian Union of Soviet Writers) 204

Vul'f, family relative 61
Wagner, Richard 17
Walter, Roman 142
Warburg, Fredric 312, 358n18
Watt, D. S. 284
Wells, H. G. 97, 103–104, 111, 114, 116, 117, 132, 138, 142, 273, 290, 292; *Time Machine, The* 103; *War of the Worlds, The* 103
Werth, Alexander 241, 244, 255, 263
West, Rebecca 132
Whitman, Walt 116
Wilde, Oscar 60
Witte, Sergei Iu. 10
"World Literature", publishing program 87, 91, 97–100, 103, 105, 107, 117, 120, 123, 124, 128, 130, 132, 134, 146, 170, 172, 249
"World of Art", art association 49, 128, 250, 292
Wrangel', Petr N. 107
Writers' Federation (FOSP) 180–181, 199
Writers' Union 4, 159, 163, 175, 206, 244, 248, 254–255, 276–278, 280–282, 285, 287, 291, 292, 297, 352n23
Young Workers' Theatre (TRAM) 213
Zaitsev, Boris K. 307, 310
Zaitseva, Natal'ia B. 310
Zamiatin, Andrei Dmitrievich, uncle 155

Zamiatin, Evgenii Ivanovich:
"About Lackeys" ("O lakeiakh") 89; "About my Work" ("O svoei rabote") 172; "Actualités soviétiques" 296; *Africa (Afrika)* 48, 62, 63; *African Visitor, The (Afrikanskii gost')* 209, 210–211, 215, 223; *Alone (Odin)*, 24, 28–29; *Anna Karenina*, filmscript 259, 285, 293; *April (Aprel')* 46, 308; *At the Back of Beyond (Na kulichkakh)* 2, 35, 39, 41–42, 62, 118, 139, 169, 227, 233, 284; *Attila*, filmscript 273–274, 279, 289, 355n84; *Attila*, play 150, 151, 152, 157, 159, 163, 165, 166, 167, 168, 172–178, 182, 203, 217, 218, 229, 273;
"*Ballet et la révolution, Le*" 286; "Behind the Scenes" ("Zakulisy") 181, 255; *Biography of the Flea, The (Zhitie blokhi)* 161, 170, 186; *Birth of Ivan, The (Rozhdenie Ivana)* 215, 223; *Brief History of "World Literature" from its Foundation to the Present Day (Kratkaia istoriia "Vsemirnoi literatury" ot osnovaniia i do sego dnia)* 128, 146;
Campbell — A Tale (Kembl — Povest') 64; *Captured Tsar, The (Tsar' v plenu)* 289; *Cave, The (Peshchera)* 105, 109, 118, 137, 142, 154, 160, 163–164, 166, 170, 233, 248, 251, 293, 308; *Cherubim, The (Kheruvimy)* 89, 323n9; *Church of God, The (Tserkov'*

bozhiia) 101, 117; *Collected Works* (*Sobranie sochinenii*) 115; 118; *Comrade Churygin Takes the Floor* (*Slovo predostavliaetsia tovarishchu Churyginu*) 162–163, 209, 270, 273; *Condemned Men, The* [uncompleted filmscript] 279;

D-503, filmscript of *We* 247, 243; *Desire* (*Zhelanie*) 29; *Dieu de la Danse, Le* (*The God of the Dance*) 286; *Dragon, The* (*Drakon*) 89, 118, 126, 139, 248, 308;

"Elizabeth of England" ("Elizaveta angliiskaia") 323n6; "Enfants Soviétiques" ("Soviet Children") 255; "En URSS" ("In the USSR") 244; *Eyes, The* (*Glaza*) 87, 154;

Fairytales about Fita (*Pervaia, vtoraia, tret'ia i posledniaia skazki pro Fitu*) 88; *Fires of Santo Domingo, The* (*Ogni Sv. Dominika*) 102, 110, 127, 129, 140, 157, 159, 168, 209; *Fisher of Men, The* (*Lovets chelovekov*) 64, 82, 92, 109, 327n97; *Flea, The* (*Blokha*) 147–149, 152, 154, 157–158, 160–162, 165, 170, 178, 181, 203, 206, 207, 213, 215, 217, 219, 223–227, 233, 246, 249, 250, 251, 262–263, 266–268, 269–270, 271, 273–276, 283, 295, 308; *Flood, The* (*Navodnenie*) 177–178, 208, 249, 255, 256, 270; *Flowers Speak to Me at Twilight, The — Mirror of Flowers, A* (*Tsvety govoriat mne v sumerkakh — Zerkalo tsvetov*) 317–318n9; "Folk Theatre" ("Narodnyi teatr") 161, 337n37; "For a Volume about Books" ("Dlia sbornika o knige") 177; *Front Page, The,* (*Sensatsiia*) adaptation 206, 208, 210–211, 341n119; "Future of maritime shipbuilding and of dredging projects in sea canals and ports, The" ("Budushchee morskogo sudostroeniia i dnouglubitel'nye raboty v morskikh kanalakh i portakh") 27; "Future of the Theatre, The" ("Budushchee teatra") 227, 239, 243–244, 248, 251;

Girl, A (*Devushka*) 28, 41; *God — A Story* (*Bog*) 49, 62, 63; *Goya's Great Love* (*Velikaia liubov' Goyi*) 279, 289; *Great Sewage Disposal Man, The* (*Velikii assenizator*) 88;

"Higher Production at any Price — Watershed of the Two Five-year Plans — The Search for Higher Productivity — Intolerable Delay — The Cost of Production — Not According to Plan — the 1933 Programme — Recent Products of the Soviet Shipyards" 270; *History*

of the Flea, The — see
Biography of the Flea, The
170; *Honest Truth, The*
(*Pravda istinnaia*) 63; *How
the Monk Erasmus was
Healed* (*O tom, kak ist-
selen byl inok Erazm*) 105,
118, 139; *How We Write*
(*Kak my pishem*), edited
collection 181–183, 208;
Hunton Colliery (*Podzemel'e
Guntona*), 215, 219;
"I am Afraid" ("Ia boius' ")
5, 106; *Impious Tales*
(*Nechestivye rasskazy*), col-
lection 163, 169; *Impractical
Chap, An* (*Neputevyi*)
37–39, 41; *In the Crowd*
(*V tolpe*) 317n9; *In Writing*
(*Pis'menno*) 62; *Islanders,
The* (*Ostrovitiane*) 54, 60,
64–65, 92, 96, 117–119, 122,
125, 132, 136, 138, 140, 147,
150, 159, 165, 169, 285, 299;
"Lettres russes" 271, 275, 285, 287,
295, 296, 301; *Lion, The* (*Lev*)
286, 293; *Little Deacon, The*
(*D'iachok*) 48, 62, 63; *Little
Pictures, The* (*Kartinki*) 48;
Lower Depths (*Na dne*; *Les
Bas-fonds*), film script 294,
298–299, 308;
Mamai (originally entitled
Mamai in 1917) 38, 105,
150, 233, 248; *Martyrs to
Learning, The* (*Mucheniki
nauki*) 178, 214, 223, 233;
Marusia. Siberia, filmscript
based on *At the Back of
Beyond*, 227, 273; "Maxime

Gorki" 298; *Mazepa* 294;
Meeting, The (*Vstrecha*)
285, 286; "Meetings with
B.M. Kustodiev" ("Vstrechi
s B.M. Kustodievym") 166;
*Miracle of Ash Wednesday,
The* (*O chude, proisshedshem
v Pepel'nuiu Sredu*) 134, 139,
161; *Morning and Evening*
(*Utrom i vecherom*) 317n9;
"Moscow–Petersburg" 261,
263–264, 269; "My work
on *The Flea*" ("Moia rabota
nad *Blokhoi*") 337n38;
Natives, The (*Arapy*) 101, 117, 125;
"New Russian Prose,
The" ("Novaia russkaia
proza"), 133; *Ngabami the
Wise* (*Premudryi Ngabami.
Pritcha*) 317–318n9; *North,
The* (*Sever*) 48, 93, 96,
97, 166, 170, 299, 338n68;
Northern Love, film-
script based on *The
North*, 166, 170, 338n68;
Notebooks 235, 285, 290,
294; "Notes of a Dreamer"
("Zapiski mechtatelei")
106; "Notes on the Works
of H.G. Wells" ("Gerbert
Uells") 104, 325n68;
Oaks, The (*Duby*) 109; "On
Language" ("O iazyke")
98; "On Literature,
Revolution, Entropy and
Other Matters" ("O litera-
ture, revoliutsii, entropii i
o prochem") 129, 139; "On
my Wives, on Icebreakers
and on Russia" ("O moikh

zhenakh, o ledokolakh i o Rossii") 245–246, 248; "On *siuzhet* and *fabula*" ("O siuzhete i fabule") 98; "On Synthetism" ("O sintetizme") 1, 115; "On the Contemporary and the Modern" ("O segodniashnem i o sovremennom") 143;

"Paradise" ("Ray") 106, 118; *People* (*Litsa*), collection 215, 312; *Peter I*, filmscript 279; *Pet'ka — A Bad Lad* (*Pet'ka — Drian'-mal'chishka*) 48, 62, 63; *Protectress of Sinners, The* (*Spodruchnitsa greshnykh*) 93, 96, 139, 270; *Provincial Life* (*Uezdnoe*), collection 48, 49, 59, 62, 132, 169, 319n42; *Provincial Tale, A* (*Uezdnoe*) 2, 34–36, 40–41, 62, 117, 126, 128, 143, 169, 319n42; "Psychology of Creativity, The" ("Psikhologiia tvorchestva") 98; "Purpose, The" ("Tsel'") 162;

Queen of Spades, The (*Pikovaia dama*), filmscript 289;

"Rebellion of the Capitalists, The" ("Bunt kapitalistov") 89; "Recollections of Blok" ("Vospominaniia o Bloke") 323n15; "Robert Mayer" 215; *Rus'* 128, 132–133; "Russian Shipbuilding: Problems Following the Revolution. Recovery from Industrial Paralysis. Second Five-Year Plan" 320n1; "Russian Theatre Today, The" 228, 237, 255, 257, 263, 290;

Salted Beef (*Solonina*) 46; *Scourge of God, The* (*Bich Bozhii*) 96, 149, 167, 177, 179, 207, 223, 235, 252, 271, 279, 285, 286, 293–294, 297, 310; *Sergeant-Major, The* (*Starshina*) 45, 46; "Shipbuilding in Soviet Russia. Efforts Towards Better Production. Turning Point in Industry. Projected Ice-breaking Flotilla" 284; *Siberia* 227, 273 [see *Marusia. Siberia*]; *Sign, The* (*Znamenie*) 64; *Smiles* (*Ulybki*) [not completed] 317–318n9; *Snowy Window, A* (*Snezhnoe okno*) 317–318n9; *Society of Honourable Bellringers, The* (*Obshchestvo pochetnykh zvonarei*), stage adaptation of *The Islanders* 147, 149, 159, 161, 165, 213, 225, 233, 251, 273, 299, 331n56; "Speech at a Memorial Evening for A. A. Blok" ("Rech' na vechere pamiati A. A. Bloka) 323n15; *Sten'ka Razin* 257, 274, 289–290; *Story about the Most Important Thing, A* (*Rasskaz o samom glavnom*) 134, 137, 143, 145; *Stubborn Folk — Ivan and Maria*

(*Kriazhi — Ivan da Mar'ia*)
48, 62; [*Stupid*] *Angel
Dormidon* ([*Glupyi*] *angel
Dormidon*) 48; *Surprise, The*
(*Siurpriz*) 215;
Tale of a Sweet Young Lady, The
(*Skazka o miloi baryshne*)
[not completed] 317–318n9;
Tales for Grown-up Children
(*Bol'shim detiam skazki*), collection 248; *Taras Bul'ba*,
filmscript 279, 288–289;
Tea Rose, The (*O chainoi
roze*) 29; *Ten-minute Drama*
(*Desiatiminutnaia drama*)
270; "Theatrical Parallels"
("Teatral'nye paralleli")
290; *Three Days (From
the Past)* (*Tri dnia*) 13, 38,
41; *Thursday* (*Chetverg*)
88, 323n5; "Tomorrow"
("Zavtra") 90, 97; "To the
Pereguds from the editorial board of *Russky
sovremennik*" ("Peregudam.
Ot redaktsii *Russkogo sovremennika*") 145; *Town of
Alatyr', The* (*Alatyr'*) 44,
49, 97, 137, 319n51; *Town
of Glupov, The* (*Gorod
Glupov*), stage adaptation
of Saltykov-Shchedrin's
Istoriia odnogo goroda 164;
Vision, The (*Videnie*) 286;
Watch, The (*Chasy*) 278, 285, 286;
We (*My*; *Nous autres*) 4,
5, 15, 29, 65, 88, 91, 92, 96,
100–102, 104, 111, 113–115, 118,
119, 121–122, 123, 126–129,
132–134, 136, 137, 139–142,
149–151, 154, 160, 164–166,
168–170, 172, 173, 179,
198–202, 204, 205, 209, 221,
227, 228, 235–236, 238, 239,
247, 255, 273, 275, 304, 307,
309–313, 339n76; *Widow
Polivanova — A Safe Place
[The Pilgrimage to Zadonsk]*
(*Vdova Polivanova —
Nadezhnoe mesto [V Zadonsk
na bogomol'e]* 324n25;
Womb, The (*Chrevo*) 39;
X (*L'aventure du diacre
Indikoplev*) 150, 169, 233;
Yawl, The (*Ela*) 167, 172, 219, 255,
345n80

Zamiatin, Ivan Dmitrievich,
father 7, 8, 9, 15, 21–22,
32, 36, 42, 50, 74, 105, 135,
152–153
Zamiatin, Mitrofan Andreevich,
cousin 155
Zamiatina (née Platonova) Maria
Aleksandrovna, mother
7–8, 15–17, 21, 29, 32, 33,
38–39, 50, 74, 95, 99, 124,
149, 152–153, 162
Zamiatina (née Usova), Liudmila
Nikolaevna, wife 2, 3, 6,
14, 16–20, 22–23, 24, 27–40,
43–48, 52–64, 66, 68–69,
86, 93–96, 104–105, 110–111,
113–114, 117, 124, 130, 133,
135–139, 143, 144, 147, 149,
152–153, 155, 158, 159,
162, 163, 167–168, 170, 171,
174–176, 182–183, 197, 199,
202, 204, 206, 208, 210–212,
214–215, 217, 218, 221, 223,

225–226, 229, 231–235,
241–243, 247, 249–252, 254,
256–257, 259, 260, 264, 266,
269–272, 278, 282–284, 287,
293, 294, 298, 299, 305–313,
315n1, 316n23n24n34,
317n35, 330n37, 346n1
Zamiatina (Volkova), Aleksandra
Ivanovna, sister 7–10, 21,
29, 42, 71, 73, 74, 221, 223,
227, 315n3
Zapiski mechtatelei (*Notes by Dreamers*), almanac 112, 115, 118, 127
Zavety (*Precepts*), journal 35–37, 39, 41, 62, 91, 92, 129
Zelenin, Dmitry K. 320n59; *Velikorusskie skazki permskoi gubernii; Kurioznoe i kratkoe iz'iasnenie liubopytstva dostoinykh nauk fiziognomii i khiromantii* 320n59
Zemlia i Fabrika [*ZiF*], almanac 177, 178
Zhirmunsky, Viktor M. 98, 161
Zhizn' iskusstva (*Life of Art*), newspaper (before 1923), later journal 115, 170
Zilboorg, Gregory [Grigory Zilburg] 119, 128–129, 136, 142, 149–151, 154, 164, 248, 312
Zinoviev, Grigory E. 285
Znamia (*The Banner*), journal 313
Zola, Emile 16, 116
Zoshchenko, Mikhail M. 98, 107, 113, 121, 161, 163, 168, 179, 198, 200, 210, 238
Zuckmayer, Carl 227
Zweig, Stefan 238

www.ingramcontent.com/pod-product-compliance
Lightning Source LLC
Chambersburg PA
CBHW071810230426
43670CB00013B/2411